The Spiritual Conflict and Conquest

BY

DOM J. CASTANIZA, O.S.B.

EDITED, WITH PREFACE AND NOTES

BY

THE VERY REV. JEROME VAUGHAN, O.S.B.

Reprinted from the old English Translation of 1652.

THIRD EDITION

LONDON: BURNS & OATES, LIMITED
NEW YORK, CINCINNATI, CHICAGO: BENZIGER BROTHERS

—

1903

ISBN: 978-0-9819901-9-4

Published by:

St Athanasius Press
133 Slazing Rd
Potosi, WI 53820
melwaller@gmail.com
www.stathanasiuspress.com

Specializing in reprinting Catholic Classics!

TO

THE COMMUNITIES

OF

ST. SCHOLASTICA'S ABBEY, TEIGNMOUTH;

ST. BENEDICT'S PRIORY, COLWICH;

AND

ST. SCHOLASTICA'S PRIORY, ATHERSTONE,

LIVING A

BENEDICTINE LIFE OF PEACE, SILENCE, RECOLLECTION, AND PRAYER,

AND

NEVER CEASING TO WATCH DAY AND NIGHT

BEFORE OUR DIVINE LORD IN THE SACRAMENT OF HIS LOVE,

This Book

IS REVERENTLY AND AFFECTIONATELY INSCRIBED

BY THEIR UNWORTHY BROTHER,

THE EDITOR.

PREFACE TO THE SECOND EDITION.

The demand for a second edition proves how highly this work, prized so much by our persecuted forefathers, is appreciated by English Catholics of the present day. Its sturdy, masculine, and practical teaching, informed with a sweet, gentle, and loving spirit, seems to be the reason of its popularity, and the secret of its power in awakening souls, and creating in them a hunger and thirst after God. It is God that the spiritual man yearns after, and God alone, and to increase and strengthen this yearning is the object of this volume. The human heart, which is influenced so much more by things which have shape and size and colour than by things which are unseen and untangible, is apt oftentimes to fix its love too eagerly and intensely upon sensible objects, allowing them to rule and master it, and interpose between the soul and God. The due and right controlling, regulating, and directing of the affections, which, while they are the most perfect means of union with God, may also be the greatest obstacle thereto, is one of the most difficult tasks in the supernatural life, and with the large majority of men is absolutely altogether the most difficult. The methods and maxims, however, which the *Spiritual Conflict and Conquest* prescribes for the accomplishing this arduous work are neither harsh nor violent. Whilst recognising love to be a gift from the hand of the Creator and an essential constituent of human nature, it would have the erring soul overcome and destroy its inordinate affections by purifying and supernaturalising the heart, and by gradually making it feel and realise by a blessed experience how poor and insipid are all earthly pleasures when compared with the divine and ineffable delights which spring from the total love of Jesus Christ. In harmony with this same spirit, this volume lays special stress on the exercise of the will in prayer and meditation, silently and unconsciously leading souls on to the practice of that higher exercise of pure affective prayer, wherein the 'material objects, images, and conceptions of the understanding' give place to the 'secret motions of the will, and a harmonious correspondence with the divine operations and inward impulses of the Holy Spirit.' It has in this respect, I may venture to hope, if in no other, supplied (I refer more particularly to the five treatises of the *Conquest*) what has long been a felt want amongst us. For whilst there are a number of excellent works which set forth the manifold rules and elaborate methods prescribed for meditation by more modern writers, suitable indeed, and admirably adapted for certain dispositions, and more especially, as F. Baker remarks (*Sancta Sophia*, vol. ii. tr. iii. sect. 2, ch. ii. § 7: Douay, 1657), for those engaged in active lives, we have comparatively but few books written for the wants of that other large class of souls, who, either owing to weakness of health, natural character, habit of mind, or progress in spirituality and divine love, experience difficulty, disinclination, or even repugnance in making much use of their understanding in prayer, and feel drawn more strongly to that ancient and patristic method, which, without depreciating the due use of the understanding, insists chiefly on the exercise of the will, on fervent and frequent devout acts, aspirations, and supplications. That the end of all meditation is to excite the will and secure good resolutions, one system differing from another only in its method of attaining this common end, is acknowledged by all ascetical writers. And yet there is a certain class of persons who, not knowing what meditation really is, and imagining it to be, as it were, some philosophical or intellectual speculation in which the brain alone is employed, have long since abandoned the practice of it as a work of supererogation to which they have no calling. It is not that these persons are callous or indifferent about their souls or the next life. Oftentimes they are good and devout Catholics, penetrated with a lively faith in the mysteries of religion, and anxious about their salvation and sanctification; and it is only after they have found themselves unable to elicit a continuous stream of thoughts, motives, and arguments from the points of their meditation, and follow out all the rules laid down in books for the performance of such exercises, that they have grown weary and disheartened, and have ended by giving up meditation altogether, as something beyond them, and for which they are unfit. O, if these souls would bear in mind that golden maxim of S. Teresa, 'The essential point is not to think much, but to love much,' they would indeed act in a very different manner; the time spent in meditation would no longer be burdensome to them, but sweet and delightful; they would hail it with unspeakable eagerness, as the appointed hour wherein to meet and converse with their dear Lord as a friend with a friend, pouring out their affectionate hearts before Him in copious acts of love, and rising from His presence each day with fresh joy, comfort, and spiritual strength. To such souls I commend the careful consideration of the following passages of the glorious and illuminated S. Teresa, quoted by the Very Rev. F. Provincial Coffin, C.SS.R., in his short and valuable Preface to S. Liguori's *Preparation for Death*: 'I have met with some who seem to imagine that the essential point [in prayer] consists in the exercise of the understanding; so that if they can keep their minds for a long time fixed upon God, even by making great efforts, they immediately consider themselves spiritual persons. . . . . I admit that it is a favour of our Lord to be able always to keep our thoughts fixed upon Him, and to be meditating on His works, and it is good to aspire to this state; but we must remember that all minds are not naturally fit for such an exercise, whilst all souls are fit to love. . . . Hence the advancement of the soul consists, not in thinking much, but in loving much' (*Foundations*, ch. v.). 'Again,' says F. Coffin, 'in her *Life*, written by herself, addressing those who are able to *discourse*, as it is called, with the understanding, and who find in every subject abundant matter for thought and consideration, she begs them not to occupy the whole time of their prayer in endeavouring to fathom the subject of the meditation. "Let them place themselves," she says, "in the presence of our Lord, and converse with Him heart to heart, without fatiguing the understanding, and taste the happiness of being in His company. There, in this sweet conversation, will be no painful reasonings, but a simple exposure of the wants of the soul, and of the many motives the Divine Master might have for not suffering her to be at His feet. . . . The soul will occupy herself sweetly in considering that He is looking at her; she will keep Him company, will speak to Him, and will address to Him her petitions; she will humble herself before Him, remembering always that she is unworthy to enjoy His divine presence. If she can arrive at this point, even at the very beginning of her prayer, she will reap great profit from it. Such a method is the source of great blessing; at least, it has been so for my own soul" (*Life*, ch. xiii.).'

If this *omnipotent exercise of the will*, as Seraphinus Firinanus calls it, were better known and more generally practised in the world, it would soon bear rich and precious fruits, and create in souls a more truly internal and contemplative spirit, a wider sympathy for the Church, and a more tender love of God. The reason why there are so many 'pious persons' who make but little advancement in real holiness of life, and seldom arrive at what may be called saintliness, is this:—that they are kept tied down to the earth, and hindered from soaring heavenwards by over-tenderness of affection to some person or thing, or are unwilling to follow the interior voice of God's Spirit when it calls upon them to renounce self, and ascend to some higher and purer degree of divine love, preferring rather to remain in those accustomed and lower discoursive exercises, which, though good for beginners, are intended simply as preparations to true internal affective prayer. Cardinal Bellarmine, in a passage cited by F. Baker, points out the necessity of internal prayer: 'This I believe I may most truly and confidently affirm, that without a diligent pursuit of internal prayer none will ever become truly spiritual, nor attain to any degree of perfection. We see many who oftentimes in the year approach the Sacrament of Penance, and as far as human frailty and infirmity will permit endeavour with sufficient diligence to purge away all the stains and uncleanness of sin; and yet they make no progress, but are just the same as they ever were, and having been to confession, if on the following week they come to the same tribunal, they bring neither fewer nor lesser faults than they formerly confessed. Yea, without offending against truth, I may add what is more strange than all this, that we sometimes see religious persons, and of priests not a few, who by their vocation and habits profess sanctity, and moreover assiduously read divine Scripture and books of piety, who often, if not daily, celebrate the most Holy Sacrifice, who have neither wives nor children, but are free from all cares and solicitudes which may distract them from a continual attendance to divine things, and who yet, after all this, are so void of all devotion and the Spirit of God, so cold in divine love, and so earnest in the love of secular vanities, so replenished with impatience, envy, and all inordinate desires, that they seem not one iota different from secular persons engaged in the world. Now the only cause of these disorders is, that they do not seriously enter into their own hearts by exercises of introversion, but only look to the exterior,' &c.

With a view to stimulate souls to the 'exercises of introversion,' and to a 'diligent pursuit of internal prayer,' the neglect of which, as the learned and pious Cardinal shows, is fraught with so much spiritual loss and peril, it will be well to cite at length the following striking passages from *Sancta Sophia*, portraying the immense profit and advantages derived from internal affective prayer: 'The first and chief excellency of internal affective prayer lies in this, That only by such prayer is our union in spirit with God (in which consists eternal happiness) perfectly obtained. For therein the will, with all the powers and affections of the soul, are applied and fixed to the loving, adoring, and glorifying this only beatifying Object; whereas in vocal prayer there is continually suggested a variety and succession of images, which distract the souls of the imperfect from such an application. And meditation in which discourse is employed is, so far as the discourse is concerned, little more than a philosophical contemplation of God, delaying that fixing of the heart and affections on God which alone are acceptable to Him.

'The second excellency is found in this, That by this prayer of the will the soul, entering far more profoundly into God, the Fountain of lights, partakes of the beams of His divine light far more plentifully, by which it both discovers God's perfections more clearly, and also sees the way wherein it is to walk more perfectly, than by any other prayer; and the reason of this is, that when the soul endeavours to engage all its affections entirely upon God, then only is it that, being profoundly introverted, a world of impurities of intention and inordinate affections which lurk in it discover themselves, and the obscure mists of them are dispelled, the soul then finding by a real perception and feeling how prejudicial they are to its present union in will with God; whereas when the understanding alone or principally is busied in the consideration of God or of the soul itself, the imagination, which is very active and subtle, will not represent to the soul either God or itself so purely and sincerely, but, being blinded and seduced by natural self-love, will invent a hundred excuses and pretexts to deceive the soul, and to make it believe that many things are intended and done purely for God which proceeded principally, if not totally, from the root of concupiscence and self-love.

'A third admirable perfection of internal affective prayer is this, That not only divine light, but also grace and spiritual strength to put in practice all things to which supernatural light directs, is principally obtained by this internal prayer of the heart; and this in two ways. 1. By way of impetration, grounded on the rich and precious promises which God has made to prayer above all other actions. 2. By a direct and proper efficiency; for since all the virtue and merit of our external actions depend upon and flow from the internal disposition and operations of the soul, exercising charity and purity of intention in them, and conquering the resistance of nature; and since the internal exercises of all virtues are truly and in very deed direct prayers of the spirit, hence it follows that as all habits are acquired by frequent repetition, so by the persevering in the exercise of internal prayer the soul is enabled with facility to practise perfectly all virtues.

'To this may be added that such prayer is a universal mortification, and in time a mortification the most profound and perfect that a soul can possibly perform, being entirely destructive of sensual satisfaction. For therein the will forces inferior nature and all the powers of the soul to turn themselves from all other objects pleasing to them, and concur to the internal actuation of God; and this oftentimes in the midst of distractions of vain images, during a torpid dulness of the heart; yea, during a violent contradiction of sensuality, when there is a total disgust in the soul to such an exercise; ay, when the spirit itself is in obscurity, and cannot by any reflexed act reap any consolation from such an exercise. Such an *exilium cordis*, such a desertion and internal desolation, is indeed a mortification to the purpose; yet as it is of extreme bitterness, so is it of inexpressible efficacy to the purifying and universal perfecting of the soul's spirit. Therefore S. Chrysostom had good reason to say, "It is impossible, again I say, it is utterly impossible that a soul, who with a due care and assiduity prays unto God, should ever sin" (*Tract. de Oratione*).

'A fourth excellence of internal affective prayer is, That it is the only action that cannot possibly want purity of intention. Souls may, from an impulse of nature and its satisfaction, exactly observe fasts, perform obediences, keep the choir, approach to sacraments, yea, exercise themselves in curious speculations during meditation; perhaps in the exercise of sensible devotion they comply with self-love; but these actions of theirs are performed with purity of intention only in proportion as they proceed from internal affective prayer, that is to say, from the will fixed by charity on God. If, however, any oblique intention should endeavour to insinuate itself into internal prayer of the will, it would presently be observed, and unless it were contradicted and expelled, there could be no progress in such prayer. Therefore it is not possible to find an exercise either more secure or profitable than this, since it is by virtue of it alone that all other exercises have any concurrence towards the perfecting of the soul.

'Lastly, affective prayer of the will is that alone which makes all other sorts of prayer deserve the name of prayer, for were that excluded, meditation is but an useless speculation and curiosity of the understanding, and vocal prayer but an empty sound of words; for God only desires our hearts and affections, without which our tongues or brains are of no worth. Yea, there is not as much as any profitable attention in any prayer further than the heart concurs. If the attention be only of the mind, that will not constitute prayer, for otherwise study or disputation about divine things might be called prayer. Hence a certain ancient and holy hermit saith: *Nunquam veri orat quisquis etiam flexis genibus evagatione cordis etiam qualicumque distrahitur*; that is, no man does ever truly pray who, though he be upon his knees, is distracted with any wandering or inattention of his heart. And likewise the learned Loto to the same purpose conclusively affirms: *Orationi mentali deesse non potest attentio, cum ipsa attentio*, &c.; that is, attention cannot possibly be wanting to mental prayer of the heart, since the attention itself is the very prayer. Hence it is an evident contradiction to say that one prays mentally and is not attentive, for as soon as ever the mind begins to wander it ceases to pray. Therefore there is no other but vocal prayer which may be performed without attention; and this it is when, the thoughts turning themselves to other subjects, the tongue, without the concurrence of the mind, gives an uncertain sound. We may further add, that the attention of the mind which cannot be separated from discursive prayer is of little value except it be accompanied with or performed in order to the causing an attention, as we may call it, of the heart or affections.

'These inestimable benefits that flow from internal prayer of the will, and to which many more might be added, being duly weighed, a well-minded soul will think no pains too much that may avail to purchase so invaluable a jewel. Religious superiors will consider that there is no part of their duty so essential as to instruct and further their subjects in the practice of it, remembering that counsel of S. Bernard: *Docendus est incipiens spiritualiter orare, et a corporibus vel corporum imaginibus cum Deum cogitat quantum potest recedere*—Whosoever begins a religious course of life must be taught spiritual prayer, and how, in elevating his mind to God, to transcend all bodies and bodily images. And with good reason used the holy Greek Abbot Nilus, a disciple of S. John Chrysostom, say: *Beata mens quæ dum orat*, &c.—Happy is the soul who when it prays empties itself of all images and forms; happy is the soul who prays fervently and without distraction, increasing continually in the desire and love of God; happy is the soul who when it prays does altogether quit the use and exercise of all its senses, and loses the possession and interest in all manner of things but God. And indeed a soul must expect to pass through a world of difficulties before it can attain to such a purity in prayer; for as the same author says: *Universum bellum quod inter nos et dæmones conflatur, non est de alia re quam de oratione;* that is, all the war and controversy that is between us and the devil is about no other thing but prayer, as being most necessary to us and most destructive to all his designs. And hereupon a certain holy father, being asked what duty

another as they lie in the book, or as he had determined upon beforehand when he prepared for his recollection.

'3. In meditating on each point let him act in this manner: (*a*) With his memory and understanding let him think on the subject-matter of the first point. (*b*) Out of it let him draw a reason or motive by which the will may be inclined some way or other towards God. (*c*) Then let him elicit an act of the will—as of humility, adoration, resignation, contrition, &c.—abiding in this application of the soul to God as long as he feels life, activity, and inclination for it, or in a word, *as long as ever he is able.* (*d*) When this fails and begins to be distasteful to him, let him proceed to the next point, and treat it in the same manner as he did the first; and then go on to the others in order, until he shall have spent a competent time in recollection.

'4. During meditation let him—avoiding the too common practice in which meditation is made rather a study and speculation than an exercise of the spirit—*spend no more time in inventing motives and in internal discoursings than shall be necessary to move the will to good affections;* and as for such affections let him abide in them as long as he can, for therein consists all the profit of meditation; and if upon one consideration or motive he can produce many acts of the will, let him not fail to do so, and to continue in each act as long as he finds himself able to do so. It is of no importance, if in the mean time his understanding should remain quiet, and, as it were, asleep without exercise.

'5. Those souls who have an effectual call to an internal life will make but little use of study or speculation in their meditations, for after a short and quick reflection on the matter, mystery, or motive, they will forthwith break forth into acts of the will; and their consideration of the matter is not so much by way of reasoning or inferring, as simply a calling to mind or thinking on a subject out of which the will may produce some act or other answerable to the point reflected on by the understanding. This method of meditating is suitable for many uneducated persons, and especially for women, who have not the gift of discoursing.

'6. A person who practises meditation will find at first that he stands in need of the consideration of many thoughts and motives to enable him to produce affections of the will. But in course f time the will will become so softened and pliable that fewer points will suffice to elicit good affections and purposes, and these will now take up almost the whole time appointed for recollection; and a soul brought to this state will then be ready and ripe for a more sublime exercise of immediate acts of the will' (*Sancta Sophia*, vol. ii. tr. iii. sect. 2, ch. iii. § 16-22).

Thus far the venerable F. Austin Baker. His teaching may be summed up in one sentence. Meditation can never be too much occupied with affections of the will, provided it roots out self-love, excites divine charity, and ends in sound practical resolutions—resolutions courageous and humble, which shape and control, impregnate and impel the thoughts, words, and actions of one's ordinary everyday life.

Here, perhaps, it will be well to guard the reader against imagining that the present writer has been actuated in what has been said by a desire to depreciate any one of those approved methods—and there are several—which lay greater stress upon the use of the understanding than that one which has been spoken of. Such is far from being the case. Every system which has received the sanction of the Church and has schooled saints is good and wise, and should be esteemed and respected. This is elementary. The ways and workings and dispositions of the human heart are strange and various beyond all count, oftentimes unsearchable. No two souls are exactly alike. The same method is not equally suited to all. What is salutary for one may be injurious to another. God's dealings with the loving and aspiring soul are not to be forced and straitened by the designs of man. The Holy Spirit breathes where He wills, and at the same time *how* He wills. And hence it is never right to compare one system of prayer with another, since all are equally well adapted to the hearts for which they were framed, and have sanctified the souls of thousands. Those persons who find that there is one method which suits them better than another—for example, the Ignatian method—and experience benefit from it, will do well to return God thanks for the knowledge of it, should cling to it faithfully, and exercise themselves diligently in all the rules it lays down. If, again, there are other souls who find this system distasteful, and experience greater attraction to those systems which lay greater stress upon the exercises of the will, they would do wisely to try the use of the old monastic method, as set forth by F. Baker. Whatever system, however, is adopted, let it be with a pure eye and a clean heart, and with the sole desire of thereby being the better 'rooted and founded in charity,' the more 'strengthened by the Spirit with might unto the inward man,' and more completely 'filled unto all the fulness of God.'

If what has been said should happily throw a gleam of

light upon the darkened path of any soul, and bring it to love and cultivate the spirit of prayer—that sweet and mighty spirit able to lift the soul up from the earth, unite it with God, and enrich it with a treasury of purifying, invigorating, and deifying grace—then the object of these few pages will have been fully realised.

With regard to the present edition, it has been carefully revised. Sections 2 and 3 of chapter vii. have been somewhat altered, and made in substance conformable to the more modern editions. Certain verbal inconsistencies and clerical errors which escaped notice in putting the first edition through the press have been rectified. A few expressions too concrete and realistic to be in harmony with the modern usages of ascetical language have been softened and toned down. The 'notes' remain, with rare exceptions, as they stood. Two or three, however, have been expunged, and their places supplied by citations from grave authorities, whose words, it is hoped, are not open to misconstruction.

With regard to the vexed question of the authorship of the *Spiritual Conflict*, since the publication of the first edition a learned antiquarian friend has brought under my notice certain facts and arguments maintaining Lorenzo Scupoli to be the author of the *Conflict*, which have led me to reconsider the controversy, and to conclude that the claims of Castaniza are not so clear and conclusive as I formerly believed them to be. The aim and scope, however, of the Preface to the first edition was not to decide the controversy once for all, but rather to point out the spirit, worth, and beauty of the two golden treatises of the *Conflict* and the *Conquest;* to show how highly these works had been prized by our old English

Benedictine fathers living in the days of persecution; to give a brief sketch of the life of the devout monk to whom the old editor ascribed the work; and in conclusion to state the grounds which had led the present writer to coincide with the old editor in attributing the original sketch of the treatise to D. Juan Castaniza. That the traditionary love of the *Conflict* amongst the Benedictines may be traced to Castaniza and sprung from his monastery at Oña is certain. Oña was one of those hospitable Spanish abbeys whither the young English aspirants to the monastic state used to betake themselves to make their novitiate and prosecute their ecclesiastical studies, and amongst the books which used to be put into their hands on entering the novitiate was a MS. copy of the *Spiritual Conflict*, which had been found amongst the papers of D. Castaniza after his death, 1599, and which soon became adopted as a text-book of Benedictine ascetical training. Of this little book, which they had now learnt to value so dearly, the young English monks took several copies with them on their return to England, leaving on their way home one copy in the Benedictine monastery of S. Germains at Paris, and another MS. copy at the English College at Douay, entitled '*Pugna Spiritualis* a J. Castaniza, Monacho Hispano.' These and other interesting matters are recorded by D. Gregorio Argaiz, who succeeded Yepez as chronicler to the Order, in the following words :—'The letters of Fra Juan Castaniza, which are preserved in the archives of the monastery of Oña, do not afford such a proof of the great piety of that excellent man as the little book which he wrote called the *Spiritual Conflict*, although he did not live to complete it. I must now say plainly how this came to my knowledge. When Fra Juan died in our college of S. Vincent at Salamanca, in 1599, all his books and MSS., amongst which was this one, were carried to Oña. In that monastery were some English monks for their studies, and on their way home to England they stopped at Paris for a course of sacred eloquence. Here they spoke to the monks of S. Germains about this book, and placed in the library a Latin copy which they had with them. Departing for Belgium, they remained some time in the English College of Douay, and there they left a MS. copy which they had brought from Oña. But since very great expectation of this book had been spread far and wide, it was often transcribed, and then printed, first in French and then in Italian. The translators, however, neglected to give the name [of the author], and as the book contained only six-and-thirty chapters, which were very short, they thought it preferable to say that it was the work of a certain anonymous religious man. Thus in the first edition, which was printed at Barcelona in 1610 by Juan Simeone, and with an approbation dated 1608, it is thus entitled: "Combate o Lucha Espiritual del Alma con sus afectos desordenados, compuesta en Lengua Italiana por un Servo de Dios, y traducido en la Castellana por Luis de Vera, Secretario del excellentissimo Señor D. Hector Piñatello Dugue de Monteleon."

'The same work, comprising thirty-seven chapters, was translated into Portuguese by order of D. Francis de Melo e Torres, Marquis of Sardien, whilst he was staying in Paris; it appeared enlarged, the work of the Venerable Laurence Scupoli, cleric regular of S. Cajetan, who added some chapters in the beginning and lengthened some of the shorter ones. A certain doctor of Paris also translated it into French and dedicated it to S. Francis de Sales, and stated that thirty-seven chapters had subsequently been added.

'Therefore it is easily proved that the first copy, containing thirty-six chapters, is to be ascribed to Castaniza. First, because with the Fathers of S. Germains at Paris, and in our monastery at Douay, there is found a MS. in Latin, with the title, "*Pugna Spiritualis* a J. Castaniza, Monacho Hispano." As soon as the monks of Paris discovered that this MS. was to be found in their library, they lost no time in communicating with their brethren at Douay, who on receiving this information could not contain their eagerness, but wrote to me at Madrid, where I then was, to make most diligent inquiry, whether by chance a copy could be found at Oña. It was actually found amongst the books which the novices were wont to use, and a Latin copy of it was forwarded to me, which I sent to Paris (y hallose entre los libros, que suelen tener los novicios, de que remetieron una copia latina que remiti a Paris). Hence it is easy to understand that the honour which is generally given to Lawrence Scupoli is due to our monk Castaniza.'

Yepez, who preceded Argaiz as chronicler of the Order in Spain, and who, being a contemporary of Castaniza and personally acquainted with him, must have had every opportunity of knowing the books and treatises that proceeded from his pen, also attributes the *Spiritual Conflict* to Castaniza. Not having the six big volumes of Yepez at hand to consult, it is right to add that this reference to Yepez is stated on the authority of De Feller. Mabillon lends the weight of his great name to this same opinion.

Nicholas Antonio in his *Bibliotheca Hispana Nova*, and Ziegelbauer in his *Historia Rei Literariæ*, O.S.B., also ascribe it to Castaniza, identifying it with his *Perfeccion de la Vida Cristiana*, a copy of which I have endeavoured to procure in vain. Gerberon, in his Preface to the French edition (Paris, 1675, 12mo), professes to have had the original Spanish MS. open before him whilst making his translation; and the translator of the present old edition (1652) states in his 'Advertisement to the Devout Reader' that he had consulted the 'originall Spanish' of 'our author.' Lastly, all through the seventeenth century editions kept coming out in French, English, and Latin from Paris, Douay, and London with the name of Castaniza on the title-page. Thus far for D. Juan Castaniza.

The arguments attributing the authorship of the *Conflict* to the devout Lorenzo Scupoli are also weighty. The main proofs alleged are briefly these. The first edition of the *Conflict* ever published was taken from an Italian MS., and was printed at Venice 1589, and edited by Count Gerolamo di Porcia the elder, who ascribes the second edition to a 'servo di Dio.' An Italian edition of 1594 contains an epistle dedicatory from Santo Milano of Milan, in which he says that the *Spiritual Conflict* is the work of one of the fathers of the clerics named Theatines, who to his knowledge had written it without the thought of ever publishing it; nevertheless it had pleased the Lord that for the help and comfort of souls it should appear in print. Fifty-three editions in various languages were published, many of them bearing only vague and indefinite titles, before the name of Castaniza was appended to it. S. Francis of Sales ascribes the book to a Theatine. Drawing one day from his pocket an edition of the *Spiritual Conflict* (whether an enlarged edition or no does not appear), he said to the Bishop of Belley: 'Le voila; c'est celuy qui avec Dieu m'enseigne dés ma jeunesse, c'est mon maistre aux choses de l'esprit et de la vie interieure. Depuis que j'estois escolier à Padoüe, un Theatin me l'enseigna et me le conseilla, j'ay suivy son avis et m'en suis bien trouvé. Il a esté composé par un sainct personnage de cette celebre congregation, qui a caché son nom particulier et l'a laissé courir sous le nom de sa compagnie, qui s'en sert en la maniere presque dont les Jesuites se servent du livre des Exercise de leur bien-heureux Ignace de Loyola' (*Esprit*, partie xiv. § 16: Gaume Frères, Paris, 1840).

Such is a condensed summary of the controversy on the authorship of the *Spiritual Conflict*, which, after all, is a question of only third-rate importance, and one that can in no way affect the value of the book. Whilst fulfilling the duty incumbent on an editor in retaining the title-page of the original edition, of which the present reprint professes to be a faithful copy, I do not pretend to pronounce any decisive judgment upon the question of the authorship. That the *Spiritual Conquest*, the second treatise of this volume, was from the pen of a Theatine, no one ever pretended. Of the two treatises it is by far the more beautiful and sublime, reaching to the loftiest heights of mysticism. Both treatises, whoever be their author or authors, are thoroughly patristic and monastic in tone and teaching, breathing that spirit of breadth, solidity, sweetness, and liberty which F. Faber looks upon as 'eminently the badge of the old Benedictine ascetics.' 'No one,' he says, 'can be at all acquainted with the old-fashioned Benedictine school of spiritual writers without perceiving and admiring the beautiful liberty of spirit which pervades and possesses their whole mind. It is just what we should expect from an Order of such matured traditions. It were well if we had more reprints and translations of them. S. Gertrude is a fair specimen of them. She is thoroughly Benedictine. There are whole treatises of the spiritual life which people living in the world read through, and feel quite honestly that the method proposed to them is a bondage which it would be a simple indiscretion for them to attempt. . . . A spirit of breadth, a spirit of liberty, that is the Catholic spirit; and it was essentially the badge of the old Benedictine ascetics' (*All for Jesus*, ch. viii. § 8). Bearing on its cover the thorns and 'Pax' of S. Benedict, this book goes forth again upon the world; and God grant that it may bring to many a weary and anxious soul the strength of liberty, the beatitude of peace, and the triumph of victory.

Feast of SS. Peter and Paul, 1875.
St. Michael's Pro-Cathedral Priory.

PREFACE TO THE FIRST EDITION.

In his *Spiritual Conflict and Conquest*, Juan de Castaniza has given to the world one of those undying spiritual books which contribute to form the inner life and character of all who aspire to love and serve God. The first part of this golden work is familiar to all. The *Spiritual Conflict* is of world-wide celebrity. There are few to whom it has not been, at one period or other of their spiritual course, a solace and a light. In many it awakens the memory of principles grasped, resolutions formed, passions rooted out, sins obliterated, darkness dispelled, graces cherished, and love inflamed. The souls it has rescued from the foul hands of the evil one, and brought weeping to the feet of their crucified Saviour; the souls it has kept steadfastly, in spite of the weakness and waywardness of fallen nature, in the strait and narrow path; the souls it has lifted out of the vanity of earth, made radiant with the charity of God and gently drawn into the mystic heights of divine contemplation,—what human tongue can count their number? Its fame is not confined to one hemisphere, but has reached to well-nigh every country under the sun, illuminated by the light of the

Cross and fortified by the life-giving grace of the Sacraments. To say that its fame is co-extensive with Christianity is hardly an exaggeration. No ascetical work, with the exception perhaps of the *Following of Christ*, has attained so many editions. Shortly after its first appearance, translations into Latin, Italian, French, English, German, Portuguese, Flemish, Greek, Armenian, Basque, and Arabic followed in astonishing rapidity. As early as the year 1599 there was published an 'Asiatic' and 'Indian' translation. A copy of the Armenian may be seen in the British Museum. The exact date of the original Spanish edition cannot be accurately determined. It was probably published some years before the death of its saintly author, which occurred in 1599. In the year 1598 it was clothed in an English dress, and introduced for the first time into this country. This translation, which was made from an early Italian version, was, however, in many ways defective. Thus, chap. xxxiii., '*Of the Perfect Oblation of thyself to thy Lord God*,' directed to Religious persons, and chap. xxxvii., '*How to Offer up Devoutly the Holy Sacrifice of the Mass*,' addressed to Priests, are both wanting in this edition. F. John Barnes, an English Benedictine Monk, who took the holy habit at Valladolid in 1604, and who possibly was personally acquainted with Castaniza, published a new translation some few years later. The work by this time had found its way into the Catholic homes of England, and during the dark days of persecution kept alive the flame of charity and the light of faith. The intrepid missionaries of these perilous times who, thirsting for the salvation of souls, had abandoned the security of the cloister, and crossed over the seas into England, there to expose themselves to the rack, the dungeon, and the gibbet, were warmly attached to the *Spiritual Conflict.* They had drunk deeply of its clear and invigorating waters, and drawn from its fountain those lessons of self-knowledge and self-sacrifice essential in an Apostle, and the first step to that perfection of charity, wherein God is the only Possessor of the heart, the only Mover of the affections, and the sole and supreme Ruler and Director of every thought and operation of the inward man. Some of them had enjoyed the privilege of knowing its author intimately. He was the dear friend and companion in religion of the Right Rev. F. Austin White, for ten years President-General of the Anglo-Spanish Congregation. It may have been from the burning lips of his eloquence that F. Mark Barkworth, the English Benedictine Protomartyr, caught that flame of divine love which transformed him into a glorious Apostle, and led him, like the good Shepherd, to lay down his life for his sheep, 1601. Many of the other monk-martyrs of this stormy period of the Church's history in England must have owed much to his spiritual teaching. F. Thomas Emmerson, F. Maurus Scott, F. John Roberts, F. Boniface Kemp, and F. Ildefonsus Hesketh, all missionaries of these times, had passed their novitiate amongst the Benedictines of Spain, and had there imbibed the loving and divine spirit of the Holy Rule. During the years they spent within the walls of the cloister, preparing for their future and eventful career—years of fruitful silence, solitude, study, psalmody, and prayer—they must frequently have heard of Juan de Castaniza, of whose praises all Spain was full. He must have been not unfrequently the theme of their conversations. His fame as a Director of souls, a Theologian, a Preacher, but, above all, as a Man of God, had shed fresh lustre upon the Benedictine Order. They must all of them, in one way or another, have come under the spell of his influence. It seemed to them but yesterday that he laid down his sickle in obedience to his Master's call, and passed out of the vineyard, bearing the golden 'sheaves' of a rich harvest. They had been carefully schooled in the Benedictine method of prayer, in which he was so deeply versed, and of which he was so skilful an exponent. Their spirits had been formed upon the same grand monastic masters as his had been—St. Anthony and St. Athanasius, St. Denis and St. Jerome, St. Gregory and St. Basil, St. Bernard and St. Bonaventure—masters whose lives here below were spent more in heaven than on earth, and whose works, reflecting the image of hearts divinely illuminated, breathe that spirit of discretion, freedom, fervour, and simplicity so distinctly characteristic of monastic asceticism, and so faithfully practised by the Saints and Fathers of ancient times. Any work, therefore, from the pen of the devout Castaniza would be welcomed by these Benedictine missionaries with the respect and veneration due to a great master. His *Spiritual Conflict*, together with the *Spiritual Conquest*, a book less popular than the *Conflict*, though apparently an integral part of the same work, and by far the sublimer and more mystical portion of it, they hailed as his profoundest treatise and the crowning glory of his literary labours. In the *Lives of St. Romuald and St. Bruno*, but, above all, in his *History of the great Patriarch of Western Monks*, he held up before the world the most perfect patterns of ecstatic contemplation and the highest models of monastic heroism. In the *Revelations of St. Gertrude*, he laid open to the Benedictine houses of his country the secret paths of the hidden life, and the sublimest mysteries of divine love. But in his *Spiritual Conflict and Conquest*, he reduced to theory what is seen in the lives of these Saints in practice, clearly elucidated and scientifically arranged the principles of Christian perfection, and compressed into two small volumes the whole Theology of the Mystical Life. Whatever weapon tends to secure the Christian warrior victory, and to lead him to the conquest of the 'Kingdom of God,' may there be found as in a spiritual armoury. The perils he will have to encounter from sensuality, pride, vanity, presumption, despair, self-love, self-esteem, self-seeking, and inordinate affection; the snares laid by the cunning enemy to entrap him in the steep and narrow path of perfection; the truths most potent to turn him from sin and lead him to conversion, silence, prayer, and recollection; the maxims to disentangle him from creatures, draw him from outward multiplicity, and imbue him with inward simplicity, peace, humility, and tranquillity; the principles to sustain him in dryness, darkness, desolation, and dereliction, curb his indiscretion in sensible devotion, guide him in subtle temptations, counterfeit visions, and satanic illusions; the exercises that will at length bring him to absolute abnegation, perfect resignation, spiritual death, and annihilation, and, finally, to transcendent contemplation, wherein the elevated soul, rapt out of itself and transported into the 'third heavens,' becomes ineffably united by seraphic charity to the uncreated Divinity, —all this is portrayed with marvellous lucidity in the *Spiritual Conflict and Conquest*, and brought home, in short and practical lessons, to the every-day life of the aspiring and struggling soul. This wondrous book, which I trust will do much to promote far and wide the spiritual life amongst us and to solidify devotion—unhappily nowadays too apt to become wild, fanciful, and sentimental—the old Benedictine missionaries of England held 'better than gold' and 'more precious than silver.' They felt that in its pages Juan de Castaniza, the Monk, the Apostle, the Ascetic, still lived. Like St. Francis of Sales, they carried it about their persons. They pressed it to their hearts. They ranked it next to their Breviary. It was a 'lamp to their feet' and a 'light in their paths.' When they themselves were suffering as Confessors of the Faith, they must often have filled their hearts from its pages with courage and fortitude, and wept hot tears over those thrilling chapters which speak so tenderly of the Passion of Christ and His intense love for souls redeemed with His precious Blood.

Through how many English editions this book passed after its first introduction into this country it is impossible to say. That the sons of St. Benedict were, of all others, the most active in spreading it in England, there can be little doubt. As early as the year 1598 an English translation appeared, of which the original was dedicated by Hierome Count of Portia the elder, 'To the Right Rev. Mothers, the Abbess and Sisters of the Monastery of St. Andrew in Venice, desirous of Christian perfection.' A few years later, another edition was brought out by F. John Barnes, O.S.B., who died in Rome, 1661. In 1612 there was published at Douai another edition, which was much used by the Secular and Regular clergy preparing themselves in the university of that town for the Apostolic Mission in England. In 1623 a second edition was called for. Nor was Paris behind Douai in its appreciation of this golden book. Some few years later there issued from the Parisian press a new English version, translated from the original Spanish, carefully collated with the Italian and Latin editions, embellished with the Theatine 'enlargements,' and enriched with numerous symbolical engravings, drawn from the famous *Emblems Divine and Moral* of Quarles, 1635. Whatsoever time, labour, and money could do to make this edition unique, was done. It eclipsed all previous editions, and has since been surpassed by few. With the exception of certain obsolete expressions and foreign involutions it calls for but little correction, and whilst embalmed in clear, sturdy, Saxon English, retains apparently all the fragrance and vehemence of the original Spanish. I have, unfortunately, failed in securing a copy of this first edition. A copy of the second edition, however, lies open before me, and bears the date 1652. It is dedicated, in common with most of the other editions of this early period, to members of the Benedictine Order viz. 'To the Right Rev. Fathers, Religious Dames, and devout Brothers and Sisters of the Holy Order of St. Bennet.' It bears the *imprimatur* of the learned Rudesind Barlow, a Benedictine Monk, Doctor and Professor of the University of Douai, and Brother of that Ambrose Barlow martyred in 1641. It is this translation, augmented with *Notes* and *Index*, and subjected to a few necessary corrections, which is presented to the public in the present volume. To some the *Notes*, appended to almost every page, may, perhaps, appear somewhat cumbersome and superfluous.

They have been added, however, in every case with a view either of illustrating, or expounding, or supplementing, or emphasising the text where it seemed called for, and with a hope of rendering this volume, as far as is possible, a perfect Manual of Christian and Religious Perfection. To secure due consideration for this fringe of *Notes*, I may remark that it has been spun, for the most part, not from my own heart and brain, but woven out of the golden traditions of the Church, and drawn from those standard works which embody the illuminated wisdom and accumulated experience of Saints and Doctors. The edition of which the present one is a reprint is exceedingly rare, and I have never yet met with it in any Catalogue. It bears an elaborate 'Approbation' from the hand of the Right Rev. F. President Barlow, O.S.B., concluding with these eulogistic words :—'Therein nothing is found dissonant to our Catholic Faith or repugnant to piety, but a holy, sound, and solid doctrine. To the perusal and practice whereof all they are invited who desire to be replenished with comfort, to overflow with joy, to be fervent in spirit, to aspire frequently towards heaven, to lift up pure hands in prayer, to preserve their consciences unspotted, and to follow the steps of the holy Saints.—Given at Doway January 17, 1652. Br. Rudesind Barlow, Doctor and Professor of Divinity in the Vedastin College, Doway.'

The spirit that dictated these beautiful expressions still lives green and fresh in the Benedictine Convents of England. Love of the *Spiritual Conflict and Conquest* has grown into a tradition amongst them. They guard their old copies with as great care and jealousy as they would a priceless heirloom. In those Houses where there exists only a single copy it is handed from one member of the community to another in succession, that all in turn may be encouraged by its fervour, guided by its wisdom, and refreshened by its unction. Nor is the interior spirit of this book confined to the Benedictine Convents. It has entered into the line of the English Episcopate, and sits this day in the episcopal throne of the Bishop of Birmingham. With the spirit of St. Benedict, the Right Rev. Dr. Ullathorne has inherited an ardent admiration for the *Spiritual Conflict and Conquest.* It is owing mainly to his counsel and encouragement that the present edition has been undertaken. His estimation of the book is expressed in the following words, written at a time when this volume was under deliberation :—'Of all the scarce old books I know, remarkable as being works of wide utility and of solid and safe teaching, I prefer the old Benedictine book, the *Spiritual Conflict and Conquest.* I think this work would be one of the most valuable, if not *the* most valuable, of the books remaining to be republished; and though not originally English, it was made thoroughly English by the old Benedictine editor.' Like St. Francis of Sales, Bishop Ullathorne has never failed to instil a love of this book into those many chosen souls whom he has guided along the higher paths of the mystic life. During her last years, it was the favourite book of his spiritual daughter and close friend, the Venerable Mother Margaret Mary Hallahan. As she advanced in years and sanctity she prized more and more the *Spiritual Conquest,* but especially its closing treatise, the *Maxims of Mystical Divinity,* answering to the unitive degree of prayer. The lofty and divine lessons of this book were constantly in her mind as she lay suffering tranquilly and joyfully on her bed of death. She kept it by her side. It was to her 'oil of the lamp of prayer.' She drew from it, as well as from her own large heart, sublime acts of resignation, and loving ejaculations. Its breadth and spirit of burning charity and angelic purity answered to a want in her beautiful soul, so that she felt it to be a friend that could always sympathise with her and help her on towards God. It was natural that it should be full of consolation for one whose love, as Bishop Ullathorne remarks, 'was a brave suffering love marked all over with the dints and scorings of the Cross of Jesus.' Mother Margaret's favourite prayer or aspiration, which she used to repeat more and more frequently as her end drew near, was drawn from its pages:—'Teach me, touch me, wound me, and win me unto Thee.'

Such were the words that fortified the last days of this valiant servant of God, uniting as she did in a singular degree the contemplative spirit of St. Benedict with the apostolic spirit of St. Dominic. Nor need this be matter of astonishment. For, the *Spiritual Conflict and Conquest*, which had so large a share in forming her spiritual character, breathes throughout its pages the broad, solid, sweet, peaceful, and governing spirit of St. Benedict. It is a mine of spiritual lore, a storehouse of practical and ascetical wisdom. It allows free scope to true religious ardour and heroism, whilst it holds in check unhealthy, wild, and spasmodic enthusiasm. The saintly Mother Margaret, with her keen spiritual discernment, soon detected the true worth of this masterpiece. With the advice of her Episcopal Director, she adopted it as the grand guide and model of her interior life. She derived all her strength from it. She left it to her devoted children as one of her most precious legacies; and it is in use amongst them to this day, and is put into the hands of every novice entering her convent, as the basis and groundwork of religious perfection. Moreover, Bishop Ullathorne, anxious to secure a succession of devout and devoted priests for his diocese, intends to put it into the hands of his young ecclesiastics, and introduce it into his new Seminary as their text-book of ascetic theology.

That St. Francis de Sales never met with the *Spiritual Conquest* appears nearly certain. What he thought, however, of the *Spiritual Conflict* is well known. With regard to the matter of spiritual reading in general, he started with this principle :—'To read well a man should have but one book, since those who pass lightly over many spiritual books profit little.' He used to say, that 'people who have no fixed plan of reading, but flit from one book to another, are apt to weary of them all, and to give up a habit which is one of the greatest enjoyments of life.' Hence, he advised everybody to select some good book, if possible to let it be a small and portable one, and to read it much, but practise what it teaches far more. He was very fond of a saying which is attributed to Thomas à Kempis :—'I have sought rest everywhere, and have found it nowhere, save in a little corner with a little book.' *His* 'little book' was the *Spiritual Conflict*—his 'favourite book,' his 'dear book,' the book he 'never re-read without profit.' He carried it for eighteen years and more about his person, and never allowed a day to pass without reading a chapter, or at least a page of it. Thence he drew, as from a treasure-house, those principles of Christian perfection which he has so beautifully dilated on and playfully illustrated in his ascetical writings. It was the voice that spoke to him in his tender years with irresistible force; the hand that led him on till he reached at length the loftiest heights of sanctity. When asked on one occasion, by the Bishop of Bellay, who was his director, he drew from his pocket the *Spiritual Conflict*, and said:—'This is he who, with God, taught me from my youth up; he is my master in all the exercises of the inward life. When I was a boy at Padua a Theatine made me acquainted with it; I followed his advice, and it has been well with me.' He was also earnest in commending to those who enjoyed his spiritual guidance this work, from which he had himself derived such extraordinary benefit. In a letter addressed to one of his penitents, he says:—'Read and re-read the *Spiritual Conflict*. This ought to be your dear book; it is clear, methodical, and most practical.' In a letter to St. Frances de Chantal, he speaks with equal emphasis:—'My dear daughter, read the 28th chapter of the *Spiritual Conflict*, which is my dear book, which I have carried in my pocket, it must be, these eighteen years, and which I never re-read without profit.' A work which had been the daily food of so many Saints could not fail soon to become popular. Vezzosi computes that within 190 years it had passed through no less than 260 editions.

And now it is time to bring these remarks to a close, and give a brief sketch of the life of our Author. Would that it were possible to draw something more than a mere outline of his personal history! Would that I could follow him in every step of his eventful life, watch every expanding virtue of his soul, and paint with bold strokes and in vivid colours the purity, the simplicity, and the love of his heaven-aspiring character! But, alas, for such a task the necessary materials are wanting. The monastic chroniclers have made no exception to their proverbial brevity, even in the case of the renowned Juan de Castaniza. In many cases the facts brought together in the present memoir have been culled from somewhat miscellaneous and inaccessible authors, whilst in other cases they have been drawn from the *Historia Literaria Ordinis S. Benedicti* of Dom Ziegelbauer, the *Annales* of Dom Mabillon, and the *Benedictus Redivivus* of Dom Bucelin.

Juan de Castaniza was born in Spain, probably, in the early half of the sixteenth century. His lot was cast in a turbulent century. The religious condition of the world at the time of his birth is not easily described. A state of religious anarchy and social conflict everywhere rife; the richest vineyards of the Church blighted by heresy; half Europe in revolt against the Holy See; license and immorality stalking abroad in open day; the Church, sorrow-stricken, groaning under the iron hand of her own children,—such was the state of Christendom when Castaniza first saw the light, when Catholic Spain was at the zenith of her greatness, and when Mary was endeavouring to restore in England the noble temple of religion shattered by the lust and avarice of Protestant Reformers. God, however, did not abandon the bark of Peter to the mercy of the storm and tempest. He raised up strong and valiant men to defend, guide, and illuminate it in the hour of its peril. Dom Juan de Castaniza was the contemporary of great and glorious Saints. St. Pius V., St. Charles Borromeo, St. Philip Neri, St. Camillus of Lellis, St. Francis Caracciolo, were all of them during his lifetime building up the Church in Italy, and restoring discipline to its primitive fervour; whilst in Spain his fellow-countrymen, St. Francis Xavier, St. Francis Borgia, St. Teresa, St. John of the Cross,

St. Peter of Alcantara, St. Paschal Baylon, were reënkindling the love of God in the hearts of the people, and renewing, by the brightness of their lives and the power of their preaching, the zeal and fervour of apostolic times. Whether Juan de Castaniza ever came in contact with any of these great servants of God cannot be positively stated. But it seems more than probable that he who was so attracted by the loveliness of virtue, and was himself the 'good odour of Christ unto God,' must have enjoyed the acquaintance, if not the friendship, of at least some of these Saints. Filled with a sense of the hollowness and vanity of all things transitory, and beginning already in his early years to taste of the contentment and joy experienced by those who take upon themselves the sweet yoke and light burden of Christ, Juan de Castaniza resolved whilst young to 'leave all things,' and dedicate himself wholly and completely to the love and service of God. That which was a source of attraction to other young men of his age and station had no charm for him. His spirit was pure, his senses guarded, his heart disengaged, his eye fixed upon God, his one ambition to love Jesus Christ perfectly, his only desire to possess Him totally. O ineffable bliss! O blissful possession! There was, however, still one tie that seemed to hold him to the world, and hinder him from flying freely into the arms of God—domestic affection. His tender heart was brimful of human sympathies, which made him cling to home with unusual tenacity. If it be a sweet thing to 'follow' Christ, it is a hard struggle to leave father and mother, and brethren and sisters, and lands, for a kingdom which neither the eye can see nor the hand feel. The youthful Castaniza was keenly sensible of this. Grace drew him in one direction, nature pulled him in another. The evil one cried :—'Eat, drink, and be merry; home-life is innocent; riches are from the hands of God; ease and comfort are not incompatible with prayer; and filial service is a duty that you owe those who have cared for you without stint, and loved you without measure.' The voice of God whispered :—*Yet one thing is necessary to thee: sell all whatever thou hast and give to the poor, and thou shalt have treasures in heaven, and come follow Me. He that loveth father or mother more than Me is unworthy of Me* (Matt. xix. 29). The struggle was sharp, but decisive. Grace triumphed, and Castaniza resolved to enter into holy religion. His next anxiety was about the Order which he should join. We may well suppose that the newly-founded Society of Jesus was one that attracted his attention. Only a few years had passed away since the warrior-saint of Loyola had gone to his rest. The odour of his sanctity was still fragrant in the air, his memory yet fresh in the minds of men, and his heroic deeds on their lips. God had raised him up in a time of urgent peril to save the Church, and establish an Order that was destined to be the breakwater against the flood of Protestantism, Infidelity, and Rationalism at that time threatening to sweep over the whole of Europe. The death of St. Ignatius did not diminish the fervour of his disciples, but seemed rather to increase it. Their zeal and holocaustic devotedness knew no bounds. In town and country, in city and village, in the houses of the great and the hamlets of the poor, they were found preaching Christ and Him crucified, carrying away the favour of princes and people, and showing themselves to be everywhere, in very deed as well as in name, the

Society of Jesus, the Company of Jesus, the conquering and unconquerable Squadron of Jesus!

Though Castaniza must have been struck by the practical sense, compactness, and unity of aim and action of the infant Society, yet his contemplative spirit was hardly fashioned for its mission of unwearied activity. We may, therefore, suppose, that he soon turned away his thoughts from the Society of Jesus, and fixed them upon the Order of St. Benedict, where he found in its calm operativeness and peaceful energy all that satisfied the cravings of his heart and filled the desires of his magnanimous soul. Juan de Castaniza, who succeeded as a Benedictine, would in all probability have failed as a Jesuit. There is a wide difference between the spirit of the two Orders, whilst the end of both is the same—the perfection of charity. This cannot fail to strike even the ordinary student of ecclesiastical history. The spirit of St. Benedict is contemplative; the spirit of St. Ignatius is active. The former is an interior spirit; the latter an ascetical one. The Benedictine loves silence, retirement, divine psalmody, and that peace of the cloister which surpasses all understanding. He is found among the waving cornfields, on the outskirts of the lonely wood, or upon the mountain-top, lifted out of the noise and turmoil of the world, and holding close communion with his God. The Jesuit, fashioned after another model, is formed for the arduous work of the apostolic life. His rest is in labour. He is to be seen moving with rapid step in the midst of great cities, instant in season and out of season, reproving, entreating, rebuking, in all patience and doctrine; mingling in the clash and strife of parties, healing discords, illuminating hearts, and apparently always flourishing most when 'smiting and being smitten.' Juan de Castaniza, doubtlessly, weighed the spirit of both Orders, and at the end his heart went out to St. Benedict. In his day the Benedictine was the dominant Order in Spain. It was laden with the glories of more than a thousand years. It had been introduced into his country as early as the sixth century, and had spread with well-nigh miraculous rapidity. Its abbeys and churches and schools covered the land as a network. More than one-half of the episcopal sees of Spain had been either founded or occupied by Benedictines. The bare record of the deeds of these men, whose early training in silence, obedience, stability, and self-mastery had well fitted them to become rulers of men and churches, fill seven folio volumes of Yepez, the monastic chronicler of Spain. The great Doctor-saints of Spain, that is to say, the grandest luminaries of their age—St. Leander, St. Isidore, St. Ildefonsus—were all Benedictines. Like England, Spain became the Apostolate of St. Benedict. Nor were the monks mere Contemplatives. To fasting, prayer, and psalmody they joined high refinement and extensive learning. They opened schools and established universities, which became centres of Catholic science and culture. Thither the flower of Spain eagerly hastened to drink-in wisdom from their calm and powerful minds. Their scholars regarded them with something more than mere feelings of reverence, and became deeply attached to them. Nor is this otherwise than might have been expected. The frank, simple, and loving spirit of St. Benedict is in a singular manner calculated to win the confiding disposition of boys, call out and ennoble their ingenuous and generous natures, and awaken those germs of latent power which but for some such genial influence, would, in many cases, for ever lie dormant and hidden in their souls. Thus the Benedictines became the educators of Spain. At the time Juan de Castaniza was resolving to join the Order, they occupied chairs in the universities of Salamanca, Valladolid, Orviedo, and Alcala, whilst the university of Yrache in Navarre was completely under their control. Don Gonsalvo de Illexas, the historian, and Dom Jerome Lauretus, in his day the first master of the Spanish tongue, were also flourishing at this time. Nor was monastic observance less cherished than learning. Mabillon's shrewd saying, that where studies are well cared for, there regular discipline will flourish, held good then as it does now. The lordly abbey of Monserrat, the metropolis of Benedictinism in the west of Europe, the Monte Cassino of Spain, stood as a city seated on a mountain—a beacon and a light to the tempest-tossed world that lay in confusion at its feet. There kings and princes had abandoned the world, and laid down their royal crowns at the foot of the crucifix; there countless hosts of lowly confessors had spent their lives hidden and unknown, and had died in the odour of sanctity; thence learned bishops and zealous pastors had gone forth to govern and feed the flock of Christ, and lead back into green pastures near the running brooks the wandering sheep who had gone astray; there the Mother of God had visibly appeared and taken up her abode with signs and wonders, healing the sick, restoring sight to the blind, giving hearing to the deaf, and dispensing priceless spiritual and temporal blessings to thousands of pilgrims who flocked to her sanctuary; there, in fine, the great St. Ignatius had been led by the Spirit of God to seek an asylum on his conversion, and during the course of two years had been befriended by the monks, and taught those deep principles of the spiritual life which he afterwards developed and so admirably systematised in his immortal book of the *Spiritual Exercises.* The soul of the young Juan de Castaniza was touched to the quick by the grandeur and simplicity of the Benedictine Order. He must often have visited Monserrat, and have poured out his heart before the statue of the Madonna. Perhaps it was there that the first seeds of his vocation were sown. He is claimed by Bucelin as one of the 'lumina' of that monastery; and though not one of its professed members, must have had some special connection with it. He found it in his day, as it had ever been, the nursery of Saints. One of the monks, D. Francis Levorotus, had, we are told, forsaken the world, and joined the community, in obedience to a distinct voice from heaven. He was possessed of the spirit of humility, poverty, compunction, and contemplation, to an extraordinary degree. After the hour of midnight matins until the morning dawn, he was rapt in prayer at the foot of the crucifix. The day he spent ministering to the wants of the pilgrims who thronged the abbey church, washing their feet, dressing their wounds, and healing their sin-stained souls in the sacrament of confession. During all these labours he remained fasting, however weary he might be, never eating anything until after sunset. After a long and fruitful life of eighty years, he was called to the home of his heavenly Father, dying on the feast of the Nativity of our Lady, 1581, with the reputation of a saint. Another monk who flourished about this time at Monserrat, and in all likelihood also known to Castaniza, was D. Alfonso de Burgos. This holy man had been in his younger days an intimate friend of Charles V.; but receiving at length a call from God to a purer life, he renounced the frivolities of the royal court, repaired to the abbey of Monserrat, and was clothed with the holy habit of St. Benedict. After spending there many years of cœnobitical life in the utmost piety, he was allowed, in accordance with the *Rule*, to become a hermit, and retire to one of the rocky caves that lay higher up the mountain, within the Abbot's jurisdiction. And there in this lonely spot, cut off from the society of men, he spent the remainder of his life, writing ascetical works, macerating his flesh, and holding sweet and familiar converse with God.

Such was the condition of the Benedictine Order in Spain when Juan de Castaniza turned his back upon the world, and journeying as a pilgrim into Old Castile, presented himself as a novice at the porch-door of the royal abbey of St. Saviour's, Onna. This monastery had been founded by King Sancho in the year 1011; and in choosing its secluded retreat for his home, Castaniza gave a pledge of how deeply he was in earnest.

St. Saviour's stood upon an eminence on the banks of the river Oca, a tributary of the Ebro, in a wild and inaccessible country, girded by a belt of rugged mountains, in the midst of which there lay stretched out a rich plain, bearing wheat, grapes, figs, and oranges, and sheltered from the keen winter winds by forests of pine and chestnut. The young postulant, upon making his appearance, was not received at once into the abbey. 'If any one come newly to his conversion,' says our holy Father St. Benedict, 'let not an easy entrance be afforded him, but, as the Apostle saith, *Prove the spirits if they be of God.* If he that cometh, therefore, shall persevere in knocking, and bear patiently for four or five days the injuries inflicted on him and the difficulties put in his way of entry, and shall still persevere in his petition, let him then be received into the monastery, and be in the cell of the guests for a few days; afterwards let him be taken into the novices' cell, where he may meditate and eat and sleep. And let such an experienced person be placed over him as may be apt in gaining souls, and may watch over him with scrupulous care, and be solicitous to discover whether he truly seeketh God, and whether he be anxious for the service of God, for obedience, and for hard usage. Let all those hard and bitter things—*dura et aspera*—be set before him by which one goeth to God' (cap. lviii.). Juan de Castaniza entered upon his probation with a heart full of unspeakable joy, seeking and embracing every opportunity of suffering, and kissing his holy habit with frequent tears of devotion, as the badge of Jesus Christ and the outward token of the interior consecration of his entire being to the love and service of his Lord and Saviour. Self-forgetfulness and self-oblation are the first lessons to be learnt by one who desires to live a cœnobitical life, in peace with himself and others. The first six months of his novitiate, therefore, were spent, in accordance with an old practice of the Valladolid Congregation, in waiting upon guests, ministering to the poor and forlorn, washing and kissing their feet, feeding and clothing them, and performing towards them the several corporal works of mercy. 'Let all guests that arrive,' says St. Benedict, 'be received even as Christ; for He will say:—*I was a stranger, and you took Me in.* And to all let fitting honour be shown, but especially to them that are of the household of the faith, and foreigners. And to all guests coming or departing, with the head bowed or with the whole body prostrated, let Christ be adored in them, Who with them is received as a guest. Let the Abbot pour water upon the hands of his guests; let the Abbot, equally with all the rest of the brethren, wash the guests' feet; which having been washed, let them say this verse:—*We have received Thy mercy, O God, in the midst of Thy temple.* But let the reception of the poor, and especially of those who are strangers, be made with all care and attention, because in them Christ is more especially received. For the fear of the rich by itself secures honour for them' (cap. liii.). With what devotion and tenderness Juan de Castaniza performed all these duties, words fail to describe. As he advanced in years, he became daily more and more supernatural and purified of the dross of earth. Humility, love, detachment, and conformity of his will to the will of God, were the four wheels on which the chariot of his soul sped along the road of God's commandments. Besides virtue, he was also gifted with no ordinary degree of talent. As a theologian he attained great fame, and was appointed Theological Censor to the 'Judges of Faith.' It would seem, from his title of 'Master,' that he must some time or other have held a chair in one of the universities. Beyond the languages commonly known by ecclesiastics of his day, he was a good German scholar, and devoted much time to the study of history—a branch of learning, as Dr. Newman remarks, especially Benedictine. What gained him the greatest celebrity were gifts, however, not so much of the head as of the heart—discernment of spirits and eloquence of speech. Purified by prayer, inflamed with charity, illuminated by close union with God, he had mastered the secret ways of divine love, understood by experience the multifarious impulses of the human heart, and became eminent as a Director of souls. Men and women of all ranks and stations sought his counsel, whilst those who were privileged to be under his guidance deemed themselves thrice happy. No one can read the *Spiritual Conflict and Conquest* without perceiving the rare power of psychological analysis which its author must have possessed. As a preacher, he was equally renowned. He was appointed 'Concionator Generalis' of his Order. In whatsoever town he entered, the people ran to the church to receive his blessing, catch a sight of his beaming countenance, and listen to the stream of eloquence that flowed from his burning lips. Nothing could resist the power of his earnest, fiery, piercing words. He is called by his biographers 'a second Paul.' Profligates, whose lives had been long steeped in sin, renounced their evil ways at his bidding, and came and cast themselves at his feet for pardon and peace, whilst others who had fallen into infidelity were brought back again into the one fold and into the tender embrace of the one Shepherd. *In the midst of the Church he opened his mouth, and the Lord filled him with the spirit of wisdom and understanding, and clothed him with a stole of glory* (Ecclus. xv. 5). The secret of his persuasiveness lay in this :—That his heart was inflamed with divine charity; his favourite reading were the Scriptures; his aim simply the conquest of souls; and his constant theme the Passion of Christ.

Juan de Castaniza was not allowed to remain all his life hidden within the walls of his cloister. God had poured into his heart and mouth and pen the heavenly dews of divine grace, and now called upon him to go forth and labour for souls, and become in his measure the 'light of the world' and the 'salt of the earth.' Like St. Gregory, St. Augustine, St. Boniface, St. Anselm, and hundreds of other Benedictine Saints, he must quit the narrow cell which long use had made so dear; he must forego the sweet labour of chanting the divine office; he must altogether abandon the abbey, so beautifully called by St. Benedict the 'Domus Dei;' in fine, he must, in deference to obedience, which makes all things easy and secure, exchange the fare and companionship of St. Saviour's for the high society, sumptuous banquets, and luxurious splendour of the glittering court of King Philip II.

St. Benedict says in his *Holy Rule* that 'the first step of humility is obedience without delay,' that 'this becomes those who count nothing dearer to them than Christ,' and that when anything has been commanded by the superior, it is to be obeyed as if it were a 'divine command.' In this spirit Juan de Castaniza bid adieu to all he held most dear and sacred at Onna, and hastened with the nimble feet of obedience to the royal palace in Madrid. There he was graciously received by the King, who had besought the Abbot to send him to the Court as his domestic chaplain and director. The Abbot could not easily have refused this request. King Philip had been a generous patron of the Benedictine Order. He had appointed the learned and saintly D. Athanasius de Lobera his historian, munificently assisted D. Ambrose a Gandavo in prosecuting his mathematical and scientific researches, nominated D. Placid de Iosantes his Legate at the Court of Rome for the purpose of urging the definition of the dogma of the Immaculate Conception, whilst in England he had been instrumental, in concert with Queen Mary, in restoring to the English Benedictines their time-honoured Abbey of Westminster, 1556. Castaniza's day was now spent in preaching, hearing confessions, giving advice to the numerous persons of rank who sought his counsel, and ministering to the poor of Christ. So striking was his love for these poor ones, that he was soon appointed the King's High Almoner. On several occasions Philip II. endeavoured to force upon him a bishopric; but the humble monk was proof against the glitter of a mitre, and persistently refused. Conscious of the unmonachising atmosphere he breathed, he devoted considerable time to spiritual exercises, fearing lest little by little the world should enter into his heart and undermine the temple of his interior man. His greatest pleasure was to repair to the royal abbey of San Martino in the city, and join his brethren in the choir, and renew his spirit in the solitude of monastic retreat. His closest friend was the Abbot of this monastery, blessed Sebastian de Villos Lada, one of the brightest ornaments of the Valladolid Congregation, and for many years Visitor-General of the Spanish Congregation. This saintly man, though full of gentleness and compassion towards others, was mercilessly austere to himself. He wore hair-shirts and fasted rigidly all the year, eating but three times a week, and then only partaking of bread and water. He was endowed with the gifts of prophecy and of miracles.

He possessed the gift of prayer in an eminent degree; and on one occasion, upon Ascension-day, whilst rapt in ecstasy, his countenance became suddenly illuminated with light of such dazzling brightness that the bystanders were obliged to veil their faces. He died in the odour of sanctity, on the eve of the Immaculate Conception, 1597, two years before his friend Juan de Castaniza. It was doubtless from his lips that our author gained much of that sublime wisdom exhibited in every page of the *Spiritual Conflict and Conquest.*

During his sojourn at the Court of Madrid, and the years spent in preaching in various towns, and travelling from one monastery to another with the object of collecting materials for a 'History of the Benedictine Order in Spain,' Juan de Castaniza had every opportunity of making the acquaintance of those English monks, already referred to, who in later years were so zealous in circulating the *Spiritual Conflict* amongst their fellow-countrymen.

How long he remained attached to the Court is not recorded by his biographers; but probably it was not more than a few years. Though still in the flower of manhood, his strength, as Yepez testifies, was already spent, and his frame weakened by incessant toil. He had grown weary of the noise and distractions of the city, and his spirit yearned once more for that peace of the cloister, where the dust of life is laid, its fever cooled, and all things are calm, fragrant, and restful. Gladly, then, he retired to the Abbey of St. Vincent's, Salamanca—the chief Benedictine centre of theological learning, supplying the famous university of the town with six professors—and there he gave himself, with greater ardour than ever, to a life of prayer and study. It was probably during this closing period of his life, enriched with the experience of years, that he completed his scheme of the *Spiritual Conflict*, by penning to it, as a sequel, his sublime treatise of the *Spiritual Conquest.* That he had from the first conceived some such sequel seems clear from the concluding words of his *Spiritual Conflict* :—'Much more might be said of these important matters; but let this which is here delivered, according to my poor talent, *suffice for the present.*' Several passages of the *Spiritual Conquest* bear traces of their having been written after his return from the royal court, and portions appear to have been suggested by things he had there seen and heard. Take, for instance, the following passage: —'They who faithfully and fervently addict themselves to spiritual recollection are neither sad nor solicitous except in appearance; for what can they want who are with God? In Him they find gardens to walk in, fountains to bathe in, palaces to dwell in, dainties to feed on, and all pleasures to delight in, with such infinite advantages that, ravished, they cry out, "My God and All!" These contemplatives need not your compassion, O worldlings! They are not so drowned in melancholy, so plunged in sorrow, so little enjoying themselves, as you imagine or complain of. No, your own poor souls are seriously to be pitied, which are so wide of wisdom and so wedded to sensuality as to relinquish true life and liberty, sincere comfort and content, for the shadows and smokes of the world. For this is most certain:—'That whosoever leaves recollection to look after earthly consolation enjoys neither God nor the world; whereas a soul that retires from the world to possess God enjoys truly both God and the world together' (*Maxim* 36). This paragraph, in conjunction with the words of the *Conflict* quoted above, and the declaration of the old English editor, that Castaniza was the author of the *Conquest*, leads me to believe that it may be so, and that this treatise was perhaps written by our author towards the close of his holy life.

This life, which had shed such light and warmth over the paths of others, was now fast declining. He lay during the autumn-fall stretched upon his bed of sickness, waiting patiently and prayerfully 'till the day should break and the shadows retire.' Like a true Benedictine, he continued writing, singing the psalms, teaching and guiding others almost to the last. On the feast of St. Luke 1599, the year after King Philip's death, he was called hence to his eternal rest, and was buried in the church of his monastery at Salamanca, regretted by none more than by the Primarius of the University, his devoted friend Ildefonso Curiel. Over his tomb was written the following inscription:—'Venerabili Magistro Frat. Joanni de Castaniza Benedictino; sermone aureo, ore facundo, in dicendo suavi, in persuadendo miro, Apostolo Paulo prædicatione simillimo; ob amabilem vitæ suæ sanctitatem, honori et decori omnibus: post oblatas sibi a Philippo II. præclaras dignitates, ac magnificè spretas, charissimi sui D. M. Ildefonsi Curiel petitione prope ipsum tumulato. Obiit xviii. Octobris, anno MDLXXXXVIIII.

The following is a list of his works:—

1. 'La Vida de San Benito, que San Gregorio Magno dexò escrita en Latin, traducida en vulgar con las Vidas de sus dos discipulos S. Mauro y S. Placido.' Salmanticæ, 1583, 8vo.

2. 'Approbacion de la Regla y Orden de S. Benito en

algunos concilios lugares del Derecho, y letras Apostolicas; con un Catalogo de Principes y Doctores Ortodoxos y Santos, que an florecido en Ella en todo genere de virtudes y ciencia.'

3. 'Historia de S. Romualdo Padre y Fundador del orden Camaldulense que es uma idea y forma perfecta de la vida solitaria.' Matriti, 1597, 4to. This work was translated into Italian by D. Timotheo a Balneo, a Camaldolese, and was published at Venice by Domenico Imbert, 1605, in 4to. A translation into French was published at Lyons, 1615, in 16mo.

4. 'Conceptus Evangelici.'

5. 'Vida de S. Bruno.'

6. 'Declaracion del Padre Nuestro,' not published till the year 1604.

7. 'Insinuationum Divinæ Pietatis.' Libri Quinque. Matriti, 1599, 4to.

8. 'De la Perfeccion de la Vida Cristiana;' more commonly known by the title of *Batalla Espiritual.* This book, in common with the *Following of Christ*, has been attributed to several authors. The anonymous editor of the *Erotemata de bonis ac malis Libris* (1665) claims it as the work of F. Achilles Gagliardi, a member of the Society. His theory, however, never found much favour with this Order. F. Brignon, S.J., in the Preface to his French translation (1714), declines to hazard so improbable an opinion; whilst the learned P. Xavier Feller, S.J., in his *Dictionnaire Historique*, attributes it to D. Juan de Castaniza, the Benedictine, and gives an account of the life of its author.

The Theatines, so named after Theate, the see of their founder, John Peter Caraffa, afterwards Paul IV., may with greater reason claim Lorenzo Scupoli, a member of their own Order, as its author. This devout priest translated it into Italian, enlarging the chapters with considerable additions of his own, and these in time becoming incorporated with the text, the name of the original author was thus, as some suppose, lost sight of, and the entire work attributed to Scupoli.

In the present volume the Theatine additions are indicated in the margin by the term 'Enlargement,' whilst the word 'Text' points out the original portion from the pen of D. Juan de Castaniza. In his Preface to the old English translation, the editor, speaking of the Theatines, says:— 'And because the endeavours of these pious men serve much to the elucidation of this subject and savour of a sincere spirit of devotion, I have also made use of their pains for your profit, and transferred hither (by way of "Explications"), whatever in that edition seemed pertinent and conducing to the illustration of our author; yet still punctually observing the "Text," and division of his own original Spanish, and the Latin traduction of some learned divines in the University Douai, where it was approved and reprinted in the year 1612.' On comparing this 'Latin traduction,'—entitled '*Pugna Spiritualis.* Tractatus vere aureus, de perfectione Vitæ Christianæ; olim Hispanicè a R. P. Joanne Castaniza Monacho Benedictino Monasterii Onniensis professo editus; postea Italice, Germanice, ac tandem redditus Latine, Duaci, 1612,'—with this old English edition, I find that the ancient Douai 'traduction' contains all those passages which the old English editor has indicated as 'Text,' whereas there are wanting to it those passages which he has marked 'Explications.' This shows that these 'Explications' formed no part of the original work, but were introduced into it by some other hand, namely, that of Lorenzo Scupoli.

The authorities which attribute the *Spiritual Conflict* to D. Juan de Castaniza are weighty and numerous. D. Antonio de Yepez, for many years President-General of the Valladolid Congregation, and a contemporary and intimate friend of Castaniza, in giving a list of his works, places the *Spiritual Conflict* amongst them. The erudite Antonio in his *Bibliotheca Hispana*, Ziegelbauer, Argaiz, Mabillon, and other writers, likewise ascribe it to this Benedictine monk, whilst Gerberon states in the Preface to his French edition (Paris, 1675, 12mo), that he had the original Spanish manuscript open before him while he was engaged in making his translation.

As regards solidity and spiritual discernment, the *Conflict and Conquest* may challenge comparison with the *Following of Christ*, whilst in method and arrangement it far excels it. Every age has had its great writers. As the thirteenth century witnessed the birth of the *Summa Theologica*, the *Divina Commedia*, and the *Imitatio Christi*, so the sixteenth beheld the birth of the *Opera* of Suarez, the *Dramas* of Shakespeare, and the *Batalla Espiritual* of Castaniza. The *Spiritual Conflict and Conquest* is as equally suited to the nineteenth century as it was to the sixteenth. One, grand, cardinal principle it teaches—a principle too apt to be lost sight of nowadays—is this: That it is the will which unites the soul to God and not the understanding. Humility and love are the burden of its spirit, the key-notes which vibrate through its every chapter. In no period of the world's history are these two great virtues more needed than in the present. Now, that men, instigated by intellectual pride, are foolishly denying the elementary dogmas of Christianity, and are allowing their hearts to be chilled and frozen up with indifference and infidelity, there is nothing but humility that can bring them back again into the narrow path of divine truth, and nothing but love that will keep them there. It is not light they require, but heat; not knowledge, but divine charity. These are the special gifts of the Sacred Heart, which may be best and most easily acquired by constant, fervent, and unwearied prayer and supplication.

May this volume have some share in promoting that sweet, affective, and monastic method of prayer which characterises the ascetical works of the Ages of Faith! May it fill souls with the inebriating wine of heavenly love, and casting out pettiness, narrowness, and exclusiveness, quicken in clergy and people that generous, self-forgetting, and all-embracing spirit of St. Benedict, which in every country and in all ages has identified itself with the larger and higher interests of the Church! May it draw all those who read it closer around the Sacred Heart of our Blessed Redeemer, and fortifying them in their Spiritual Conflict here below, bring them hereafter to the ineffable enjoyment of their eternal Conquest!

Whitsunday 1874.
St. Michael's Pro-Cathedral Priory, Hereford.

CONTENTS.

THE SPIRITUAL CONFLICT.

THE SPIRITUAL CONQUEST.

First Treatise.

OF THE DISCOVERY OF OUR ENEMIES' AMBUSCADES, ENABLING THE CHRISTIAN WARRIOR TO FORESEE AND AVOID THEM.

Second Treatise.

OF THE USE AND PRACTICE OF OUR SPIRITUAL WEAPONS.

Third Treatise.

OF THE STEPS AND DEGREES OF PERFECTION.

Fourth Treatise.

Of the Steps and Degrees of Divine Seraphical Love.

Fifth Treatise.

Of the Choicest Maxims of Mystical Divinity.

WORKS QUOTED IN THE NOTES.

Angela, Blessed, of Foligno, *Visions and Instructions of.*

The Ancren Riwle: from a semi-Saxon MS. of the thirteenth century. Camden Society.

Augustine, St. 1. *Confessiones.* 2. *Epistolæ ad Hieronymum.* 3. *Soliloquia.* 4. *Homilia in N. Testamentum.*

Anselm, O.S.B., St. *De Similitudinibus.*

Baker, O.S.B., F. Augustine. 1. *Sancta Sophia;* 2 vols. Douay, 1657. 2. *Notes* to the *Divine Cloud.*

Balduke, F. John. *The Kingdom of God in the Soul;* Paris, 1657.

Bellarmine, Card., S.J. *De Ascensione Mentis in Deum.* Coloniæ, 1850.

Benedict, Our Holy Father St. *Regula.*

Bernard, O.S.B., St. *Sermones in Cantica,* &c.

Bona, O.S.B., Cardinal. *Via Compendii ad Deum.* Romæ, 1866.

Bonaventure, St. *Stimulus Amoris.* Opuscula. Lugduni, 1619.

Blosius, O.S.B., Abbot. 1. *Spiritual Works of;* edited by Rev. John E. Bowden. 2. *A Mirror for Monks;* edited by Lord Coleridge.

Cassian. 1. *Vitæ Patrum.* 2. *Verba Seniorum.*

Climacus, St. John. *The Holy Ladder of Perfection;* edited by F. Collins.

Cross, St. John of the, *The Complete Works of;* 2 vols. Translated by Lewis.

Denis, St. 1. *De Mystica Theologia.* 2. *Epistola Caio Monacho.*

The Divine Cloud; or The Cloud of Knowing and Unknowing. Composed probably in the early part of the fifteenth century; edited by F. Collins.

Faber, F. *Spiritual Conferences.*

Fonseca, Christopher de. *A Discourse of Holy Love.* 'Done into English,' 1652.

Gregory the Great, St. *Moralium.*

Grou, Père. *The Hidden Life of the Soul;* Rivingtons.

Hilton, Walter. *The Scale of Perfection;* edited by Rev. Father E. Guy, O.S.B.

Instructions for Particular States; Anonymous, 1710.

Juliana, Mother, an Anchoress of Norwich, who lived in the reign of Edward III. *Sixteen Revelations of Divine Love.*

Mabillon. *Acta Sanctorum O.S.B.*

More, O.S.B., Dame Gertrude. *The Confessions of a Loving Soul;* 1658.

Nelson, Robert. *The Beggar and no Beggar, or Every Man a King if He Will;* London, 1716.

Palma, F. Louis de la, S.J. *The History of the Sacred Passion.*

Petersen, Master Gerlac. *The Fiery Soliloquy with God;* 1378. Richardson.

Sales, St. Francis de. 1. *Treatise on the Love of God*, Douay, 1630. 2. *The Spirit of;* Rivingtons, 1872.

Schram, O.S.B. *Theologia Mystica.*

Teresa, St. 1. *The Life of;* Lewis. 2. *The Book of the Foundations of;* Lewis. 3. *The Way of Perfection;* Dalton. 4. *The Interior Castle;* Dalton.

Thaulerus, Dom J. *Opera omnia.*

Thomas, St. *Summa Theologica.*

Vaughan, O.S.B., Right Rev. Archbishop. *The Life and Labours of St. Thomas of Aquin;* 2 vols. Longmans.

Whytford's Translation of *The Following of Christ*, 1556; edited by Very Rev. Cathedral-Prior Raynal, O.S.B.

THE SPIRITUAL CONFLICT.

THE

SPIRITUAL CONFLICT.

CHAPTER I.

Wherein Christian Perfection Consists; and of Four Things Necessary to Obtain it.

1. If thou heartily and seriously desirest, O dearly beloved in Christ, to reach the height of Christian perfection, and to be truly united to thy Lord God by becoming one spirit with Him, thou must, before undertaking this most profitable employment and noblest of all imaginable enterprises, understand, in the first place, wherein this perfection of spiritual life consists.

The importance of this knowledge.

2. For some there are who, for want of this necessary consideration, imagine that this high perfection is placed in leading an austere life, in the maceration of the flesh, in the use of hair-cloth, in much fasting, watching, and the like rigorous exercises and bodily afflictions.

Some place perfection in austerity;

3. Others, especially women, judge of their progress in spirituality by their daily recital of many prayers, their assisting at many Masses, their frequent confessions and communions.

others in reciting many prayers;

4. And there are very many, yea, even some of them religious and cloistered persons, who persuade themselves that perfection consists in frequenting the choir, in the exact observance of silence and solitude, and in well-ordered discipline.

others in strict observance:

5. Thus, some by their pious practices, some by other external exercises, tend to this desired perfection, but are all wide of the direct way leading unto it. For though these outward and devout employments conduce very much towards the attaining it, yet in them alone and their exact observance it consists not. It is true that the discreet use of them is undoubtedly a forcible means to obtain the grace of the Holy Ghost, to fortify us against the frailty of the flesh, to shield and arm us against the deceits and assaults of our common and cruel enemy, and finally, to perform our practices of piety, especially whilst we are new champions and novices in this spiritual conflict, with more sweetness and alacrity. Yea, they produce plenty of fruits in those also who are well-experienced and skilful combatants in this holy warfare; who afflict their body, because it has been instrumental in offending their Creator; who love silence and live in solitude, in order to shun all occasion of sin and attend to their heavenly meditations with the more quietness and tran-

all which means are good, but do not directly conduce to perfection.

quillity; who untangled from the impediments of the world, are therefore devout and diligent performers of the divine office, fervent and frequent in works of charity, prayer, and holy communion, and all this for no other reason than God's honour and glory, and to unite themselves to Him by the sacred bonds of sincere affection.

6. Yet they who rest here, and place their end in these outward exercises, do oftentimes endanger their own salvation; and this not by reason of the exercises themselves, which are truly and naturally holy, and warranted by the practice and example of many great and glorious saints, but because they are so totally attentive to these lower exercises as to leave their inward man in its natural affections, and unrescued from the snares of the devil. For the deceitful fiend, finding them gone astray in following their affections to these devotions, gives them not only peace, but also pleasure in the pursuance of them. They seem to taste the very sweets of paradise, yea, to walk and talk with God, and hear His divine whispers in their souls—such is their vain persuasion!—and are sometimes so absorbed in their curious and deep fancies of meditation, that they conceive themselves to be separated from the world, severed from all creatures, and even rapt into the third heavens.

And they that rest in these lower exercises are in great danger,

7. But how dangerously all such souls are deceived, and how widely they have strayed from the right way of perfection, will easily appear by the

as may appear by the rest of their actions,

rest of their actions. For they are commonly very singular, curious, censurers of their neighbours' lives and conversations, and prone to murmur at their proceedings; and when they themselves are warned of their own errors, or never so little hindered from their accustomed exercises, which they perform chiefly for fashion's sake, or debarred from the ordinary use of the Sacraments, you shall presently perceive them fall into passion, unquietness, and despair.*

8. And if it pleaseth God, to the end that they may truly understand their own state, to send them some infirmity, or permit some tribulation to befall them—for such trials are His touchstones,

especially by their want of resignation in time of affliction.

* St. Teresa, by way of warning, records the story of a pious lady, who was stricken down with a severe sickness, and in this state was in the habit of hearing Mass and communicating daily in her own house. Her illness lasting so long, the priest, a great servant of God, thought it not right to allow this frequent communion in a private house, and therefore refused on one occasion to communicate her. When she found Mass ended and herself without our Lord, she became exceedingly vexed and angry with the priest, and died immediately afterwards in this state, without ever again having gone to confession. Whereupon the Saint makes the following remarks:—

'Believe me, that love of God—I do not say it is love, but only that it seems so—if it stirs our feelings in such a way as to end in some offence against Him, or in so troubling the peace of the loving soul that it cannot listen to reason, is plainly self-seeking only: and Satan will not sleep over his work when he thinks he can do us the most harm, as he did to this woman; for certainly what happened to her alarmed me greatly, not because I believe it was enough to imperil her salvation, for the goodness of God is great, but the temptation came at a very dangerous time.

'I have spoken of it in this place that the Prioress may be on her guard, and that the sisters may fear and consider, and examine themselves why they draw near to receive so great a gift. If to please God, they know already that He is better pleased by obedience than by sacrifice. If that be so, and I merit more, why am I troubled? I do not

whereby He proves His servants' sincerity—O how soon shall you discover the false foundation whereon they built the edifice of their feigned devotion! How rotten is their inward man, and how full of secret pride! For they refuse to resign their wills, and to humble their hearts under God's powerful hand in all the changeable courses of prosperity and adversity, and will not, according to the divine example of God's humble suffering Son, subject themselves to all creatures, nor take their seeming enemies to be what in reality they are, true friends, as being instruments of God's goodness, promoters of their perfection, and helpers in the restoration of their unmortified passions; all of which are evident signs of their dangerous state. For the eyes of their souls are dazzled and corrupted by

say that they are not to feel a lowly sorrow, because all have not attained to the perfection of feeling none, merely by doing that which they know to be the more pleasing unto God; for if the will is perfectly detached from all selfish considerations, it is clear that there will be no sense of pain; on the contrary, there will be a great joy, because the opportunity has arrived for giving pleasure to our Lord by so costly a sacrifice; the soul will humble itself, and be satisfied with communicating spiritually. But as in the beginnings, and in the end too, it is of the goodness of our Lord that we have these great desires of drawing near unto Him, souls may be allowed to feel some uneasiness and pain when they are refused communion, yet they must possess their souls in peace, and make acts of humility because of that refusal. But if there should be any trouble, or anger, or impatience with the Prioress or Confessor, believe me the desire for communion is a plain temptation. Now, if any one is bent on communicating when the Confessor has forbidden her to go to communion, *I would not have the merit she may gain thereby*, because in such matters as this we must not be judges for ourselves. He is to be the judge who has the power of binding and loosing. May it please our Lord to give us light, that we may be wise in matters of so much importance; and may we never be without His help, that we may not use His graces so as to turn them into occasions of displeasing Him!' *The Foundations*, pp. 47, 48.

gazing upon these outward though good actions, arrogating to themselves I know not what degree of perfection, and from thence, falling into self-conceit, they judge rashly and condemn others. Nor can they be recalled or cured, unless God Himself strikes strongly at the door of their hearts, and dissipates the darkness of their interior with the Divine rays of His gracious light, making them see their own danger, and seek the remedy. For a great and open sinner is more easily reclaimed than a seeming saint, whose secret iniquity is shrouded under the appearance of virtue and piety.

True perfection consists in love, self-denial, resignation:

9. Thus, then, it is manifest unto thee, O my beloved, that spiritual perfection consists not at all in the aforesaid practices and persuasions. Know therefore that it is placed in no other thing than in the true knowledge of God's goodness and greatness, and of our own baseness, misery, and nothingness, and of the proneness of our natural affections to all malice: also, in the hatred of ourselves and the love of God; and lastly, in the absolute denying of our own will, and entire resignation of it to the Divine will and pleasure.* That is, that we totally submit ourselves, not only to Almighty God, but even to every one of His creatures for His sake; and this for no other end than only to please His Divine Majesty, Who

* 'Wherein lies the highest perfection? It is clear that it does not lie in interior delights, nor in great raptures, nor in visions, nor in the spirit of prophecy, but in the conformity of our will to the will of God, so that there shall be nothing we know He wills that we do not will ourselves with our whole will, and accept the bitter as joyfully as the sweet,

deserves to be purely served, highly honoured, perfectly praised, and glorified by all.

10. This is the abnegation which Christ our Saviour so often inculcated. This is the obedience to which the Son of God invites and directs His faithful followers, both by His words and by His example. This is the desirable cross which His diligent servants are to lay on their shoulders, and so follow the steps of their Saviour. This is that love which our Lord so seriously, frequently, and carefully recommended to the whole world, and especially to His disciples, as His particular friends and children, after His last supper.

this Christ hath taught us by word and example;

11. If, then, my dearly beloved, thou intendest to attain to this high perfection, thou must use violence to thyself, and vanquish thine own irregular affections, both great and small, and must diligently prepare and exercise thy mind to wage this holy warfare; for the crown of victory is conferred only upon stout and lawful combatants.

we must follow Him herein if we mean to gain the victory.

12. For as this battle we now treat of is the greatest and most difficult, so is the ensuing victory most glorious to ourselves, and most grateful to God, and so much so that if thou overcomest, subduest, mortifiest, and rootest out thine own

Nor is there anything more glorious than this or more grateful to God;

knowing it to be His Majesty's will. This seems to be very hard to do; not the mere doing of it, *but the being pleased in the doing of that which, according to our nature, is wholly and in every way against our will,* and certainly so it is; but love, if perfect, is strong enough to do it, and we fo get our own pleasure in order to please Him Whom we love.' *The Foundations*, p. 33.

disordinate and unruly affections, thou offerest up to God a more agreeable sacrifice than if, neglecting this, thou shouldst whip thy body till it were imbrued in its own blood, or fast beyond the austerity of the strictest anchorites, or convert thousands of infidels and sinners to Christ's faith and perfect penance. For though the conversion of souls be in itself more dear to our Lord God than the renouncing of our own wills in small matters, yet it is thy part to will and do that chiefly and most carefully which He most strictly requires of thee; and this is undoubtedly the serious mortification of thy untamed passions, wherein thou shalt better please Him than in any other highest and holiest employment.

but to do so we must make use of four necessary weapons.

13. Being thus instructed, O dearly beloved, wherein Christian perfection consisteth, and that to obtain it thou must adventure upon a cruel and continual war if thou intendest to be a conqueror, it befits thee, like a stout Christian champion, to arm thyself with four necessary weapons, namely:

1. Diffidence of thyself.
2. Confidence in God.
3. Continual exercise.
4. Devout prayer.

All which weapons I shall, by God's assistance, now briefly treat of, according to their several orders.

CHAPTER II.

OF THE DIFFIDENCE OR DISTRUST OF OURSELVES.

1. THIS diffidence of thyself may be obtained by three manner of ways. First, by a deep sense of thy own baseness and misery, truly acknowledging that of thyself thou canst not do the least good thing. For man can no more effect any good or meritorious work by his own power than a stone, if I may say it, is able of itself to ascend upwards; and he hath almost the like inclination to evil, as a heavy stone hath to the earth's centre.

Distrust of ourselves is acquired: 1. By a deep sense of our own nothingness;

2. The second way to get this self-distrust is to demand it of Him, Whose gracious gift it is, with humble and earnest prayer. And to prevail in thy petition, thou must first acknowledge that thou truly wantest it, and that of thyself thou canst never attain to it. Thus, totally naked, present thy prayers with a constant faith, and a courageous hope to be heard, and to obtain this desired diffidence of thyself. And let thy prayer increase in daily fervour, and expect, with perseverance, the Divine pleasure in the granting of thy petition, and then be confident it will, sooner or later, be granted thee.*

2. By humble and earnest prayer;

* God often bestows in one short hour what He has deferred granting for many years. He knocks at our door suddenly. When He seems to be furthest off, even then He is nigh unto us, and in one brief visit repays more than ten thousand times the labour, weariness, dryness, and downheartedness endured for His love. Blessed be His holy will in all things!

3. By often reflecting upon our own weakness.

3. The third is, that as often as thou failest and fallest into sin, thou perfectly turn the eye of thy soul towards thine own baseness, misery, and inability to do anything that is good; for until this be truly known, and humbly acknowledged by thee, never hope to be secure from falling.

Self-knowledge is a lesson which must needs be learned.

4. Whosoever therefore aspires to a blessed union with the uncreated Verity must first study this necessary lesson of self-knowledge. For God permits the proud and presumptuous to fall sometimes into some grievous sin, that so they may be forced to confess their own frailty and impotency; and according as their pride is greater or less, so is their fall more or less grievous, in so much, that if there were no pride in man—as was the case in the sacred Virgin Mary—there would likewise be no falling into any sin.

ENLARGEMENT. We must be careful to rise speedily after our fall.

5. Wherefore, presently upon thy fall, hasten thy thoughts to an humble reflection upon thine own nothingness, beg instantly and ardently of thy Lord God His true and inward light to see thy own frailty and infirmity, and to keep thee from more dangerous falls for the future.

The great necessity of distrust in our own strength.

6. This distrust of thyself, my dearly beloved, is so necessary for thee in this combat, that without it thou canst not only never hope to obtain thy so-much-desired conquest over thy enemies, but not so much as to surmount the least of thy passions or imperfections.

7. Thou art, therefore, seriously and frequently to reflect upon the corruption of thy natural inclination, which makes thee apt to conceive a good opinion of thyself and thine own actions, and to persuade thyself that thou art something, when, indeed, thou art nothing at all.

which is shown: 1. By the corruption of our nature;

8. Weigh further the vanity and presumption of such self-conceits, and the weakness of thine own powers.

2. By the weakness thereof;

9. Also consider how displeasing the one is to the Divine Majesty, and how pleasing the other. For our Lord loves a free confession of our own frailty, and a real acknowledgment of our total dependency upon His power and providence, from whose bounty and benignity all grace and goodness is derived into our souls, since being left to ourselves we can neither think nor act any one thing which hath the least degree of worth or merit.

3. By considering how pleasing to God this acknowledgment is, and how presumption displeaseth Him.

10. Wherefore, study well this first and fundamental lesson, as being a matter of highest importance, and yet the work of God's holy hand, which He teacheth His dear friends, sometimes by His heavenly inspirations, other times by permitting them to fall grievously and to be tempted violently, and by other ways unknown to themselves.* And be sure to make serious use of the four proposed ways in the

Therefore study this fundamental lesson.

* 'I consider,' says St. Teresa, 'one day of humbling self-knowledge, which may have cost us much sorrow and distress, to be a greater grace of our Lord than many days of prayer.' *The Foundations*, p. 37.

preceding chapter,* for by the due performance and practice thereof, and thy concurrenece with God's never-wanting grace, thou mayest confidently hope to attain it.

CHAPTER III.

Of Confidence in God.

1. Thou seest, then, how useful and needful this self-distrust is. But yet if thou enterest the field to fight with that weapon only, thou must look to be either speedily vanquished or basely put to flight. Wherefore, having fitted thyself with this first armour—distrust of thyself—let thy next diligence be employed in getting a pious confidence in God, begging, hoping, and expecting from Him all good and help whatsoever. In obtaining whereof, make use also of these three advices:

Confidence in God is obtained:

2. For, first, thou art to crave it instantly, ardently, and humbly of the Divine Majesty.

1. By prayer;

3. Then thou art to consider His wonderful power, and contemplate His infinite wisdom, from whence thou wilt conclude that nothing is either impossible to Him, or difficult. Then weigh His boundless goodness, which is ever ready to pour plentifully upon thee all necessaries for thy spiritual proficiency, and all things useful for thy gaining an entire victory over thy enemies.

2. By considering the Divine power, wisdom, and goodness, by which He can, knows how, and is willing to help;

* That is, 1. Diffidence of thyself; 2. Confidence in God; 3. Continual exercise; 4. Devout prayer.

For how can it be possible that this holy and heavenly Shepherd,* who, for full thirty-three years' space, hath so carefully run after this strayed sheep, so lovingly called it home to Himself, so painfully sought it, and so dearly bought it with the price of His blood and loss of His life, should turn away His eyes of compassion from it when it cries, calls, and turns itself unto Him? O, how can He forget His own promise, and not lay it upon His shoulders, and celebrate a feast of joy and jubilation with His heavenly citizens for its happy return! Or who can imagine that our loving Lord God, Who so much desires to dwell in our hearts and feast in our souls, and to this end is ever knocking at those doors for admittance, that so He may replenish us with the heavenly treasures of His grace, should then shut His ears when we open to Him our hearts, or should refuse to give us admittance when we humbly and earnestly invite Him to our banquet!

4. And thirdly, for the obtaining this holy confidence and trust in God make use of the infallible truth of sacred Scriptures, which frequently and manifestly tell thee that whosoever place their confidence in their Lord God are never confounded. 3. By meditating upon Holy Writ;

5. There is also another way to get this distrust of ourselves and confidence in God, which is—never to set upon any work before thou first makest reflection upon thine own frailty and 4. By thinking on our own frailty, and God's omnipotence at the

* Luke xv. 4.

beginning of each action. thy Lord's omnipotence. For if thou observest not this order in the beginning of thy enterprises, thou shalt find thyself oftentimes deceived, even when thou thinkest to have undertaken them in the best manner. For pride and presumption are so inherent in our nature, that the diligence of our whole life is scarcely sufficient to drive them out; and therefore thou must so order thine actions, that still the thought of thine own nothingness and God's all-sufficiency and readiness to assist thee go before them. And here look diligently to thyself, that thou be not deceived. For oftentimes when thou imaginest thyself to have truly attained to this diffidence in thyself and confidence in God, thou art far short of it, as thou mayest easily perceive by the remaining motions of thy mind and frequent fallings into imperfections.

Whereby we shall not be foolishly dejected at our frequent falls.

6. For if these relapses make thee sad, unquiet, and in a manner despair of thy spiritual progress, it is an evident sign that thy confidence is in thyself only, and not in thy Creator's goodness. And if thy sadness and despair be great, great also is thy confidence in thyself, and little is thy trust in God; as, on the contrary, if thou hast a true distrust of thy own self and a perfect confidence in God only, thou wilt not much marvel at thy own frailty, nor be vainly dejected at thy frequent fallings, which proceed from thy own weakness, and therefore hinder not thy confidence in the goodness of God. So that thou wilt conceive a holy anger against thyself for thy sins

and with an humble sorrow for thy offence, thou wilt trust hereafter less to thyself and more in God, and with a new enkindled zeal and greater courage than before, wilt continue the spiritual warfare thou hast begun, and pursue thy enemies even to death.

7. And would to God these truths were diligently dived into by some who seem to be spiritual; and yet they no sooner fall into defects but they presently become impatient, and cannot be quieted till they have recourse to their ghostly father, rather for their own solace than for any true devotion; whereas the prime motive of their coming to him should be to purge their souls from sin by absolution, and to obtain new strength against their enemies by the sacred communion.

A necessary caution for spiritual persons.

8. As we can promise to ourselves nothing but failings and fallings, because we are of ourselves nothing, so also we may certainly promise to ourselves from our God an entire victory over all our enemies, if we arm our hearts with a lively confidence in His Divine Majesty.

ENLARGEMENT. By God's assistance we can do all things.

9. But many deceive themselves in supposing that the pusillanimity and disquiet following their fall is an effect of virtue, because it is accompanied with a displeasure for their offence; whereas it springs from pride and presumption, and is founded in self-confidence and conceit of their own strength, which they trusting too much to, find by the woful experience of their fall that they are truly weak

The dejection following our falls is no virtue, but the effect of pride.

and really nothing; and thereupon they become troubled and astonished as at a new thing, and so lose their courage, seeing that prop which sustained their vain confidence fallen down to the ground.* But this befalls not those who are truly *humble;* for they confiding in God alone, nothing presuming of themselves, when they chance to fall into any fault feel indeed a true grief in their souls, but are neither disquieted nor astonished, seeing clearly by the light of truth that this proceeds from their own misery, frailty, and presumption.

CHAPTER IV.

Of Continual Exercise; and First that the Understanding is Carefully to be Kept from Ignorance and from Curiosity.

1. It hath been hitherto declared how much this distrust of ourselves and trust in God's goodness helpeth us on in the spiritual conflict; but they alone are yet insufficient to gain the vic-

The third spiritual weapon is continual exercise,

* St. John of the Cross teaches the same doctrine: 'Some there are who, when they detect their own imperfections, become angry at themselves with an impatience that is not humble. They are so impatient with their shortcomings that they would be saints in a day. Many of these form many and grand resolutions, but being self-confident and not humble, the more they resolve the more they fall, and the more angry at themselves they become. They have not patience enough to wait for God's help; this is also opposed to spiritual meekness. There are, however, other people who are so patient, and who advance so slowly in the desire for spiritual progress, that God wishes they were not so patient.' *The Complete Works of* S. John of the Cross, vol. i. p. 339.

tory and keep us from relapses, and therefore, besides these two, a third weapon is necessary, which we termed above *continual exercise;* and this chiefly consists in the rectified use of our understanding and will.

2. First, therefore, the understanding is to be kept from two great evils—ignorance and curiosity: from ignorance, that it may be pure and clear, and so we may see what is necessary for the taming of our passions and overcoming of our affections.

which consists in the right use of the understanding and will.

3. And this light may be obtained two manner of ways: first and chiefly by earnest *prayer,* invoking and imploring God's Holy Spirit to infuse this light into thy soul.

To be obtained, 1. By prayer;

4. And secondly, by *daily practice* of a profound and accurate search into all thine own actions and affairs, not only as they appear outwardly, but rather as they are truly in themselves. Do but make trial of this exercise for a time, and thou wilt come easily to understand what things and actions are good and what are evil; as also what are truly good and what are only in show, promising much by their outward splendour, but performing indeed nothing, nor any way conducing to the quiet of thy conscience.

2. By a diligent search into our own actions.

5. This point—which is to estimate all things according to their true and real worth and greatness—being well practised, will open our eyes to see the poorness of all such toys which worldlings most desire and delight in. It will show us that earthly honours and pleasures are mere

ENLARGEMENT. This search into the real worth of all things will betray the meanness of all worldly vanities.

vanities and afflictions of spirit; that injuries, infamies, and affronts, patiently suffered, are the harbingers of true happiness and glory; that afflictions are indeed friendships, and that seeming crosses are followed with certain contentments; that to despise the world is better than to be master of it; and that to be willingly obedient for the love of God to the meanest creature is a more magnanimous action, and the sign of a more generous spirit, than to command the greatest kings;* that the humble knowledge of our own nothingness, is more acceptable to the Divine Majesty than to dive into the height and depth of all sciences;† that to quell and conquer our own appetites and imperfections, though they be never so small, merits more praise than to force the strongest holds, than to triumph over the greatest enemies, than to work the greatest miracles, or raise the dead out of their graves. All which things, and others of like nature, are not sincerely discerned by us because, before we enter into ourselves to weigh them well as we ought, and as they truly are, we permit our fancy to be perverted, prepossessed, and surprised with

* 'The least work,' says the holy Abbot Blosius, 'done out of true obedience is more pleasing to God than a great work done from thy own will. It is better to pick up straws out of simple obedience than of thy own will to give thy mind to the sublime contemplation of heavenly things. And he obtains more of the Divine favour who, out of pure obedience, eats soberly and moderately to the praise of God, than he who of his own will undertakes the most rigid abstinence.' *Speculum Spirituale*, cap. ii. § 3.

† 'Truly, a lowly rustic that serveth God is better than a proud philosopher who pondereth the course of the stars and neglecteth himself. This is the highest and most profitable lesson:—truly to know and despise ourselves.' *Following of Christ*, b. i. chap. ii.

some sensual affection towards them, which so dims and darkens our understanding, that it is rendered incapable to judge of those objects rightly and impartially as it should, and as they truly deserve.*

TEXT.

3. By keeping the will from fixing its love until the understanding has weighed the object.

6. Wherefore, give an attentive care, O dearly beloved, to what I shall now tell thee, for it will much further thee to fight successfully. The means to know the true nature and properties of all things which occur in thy daily transactions, is by taking special care to keep thy *will* pure and free from all motion of love and affection which look not directly upon God Himself, or upon the means leading unto Him. To the end that thy *understanding* may rightly distinguish good from evil, it must first consider the object before thy will hath made its election or rejection of it. Because, when once the will hath fastened its affection upon an object, the understanding is hindered from a true knowledge thereof, by reason of the consent of the will intervening, and leaving it so involved and obscured, that it appears far fairer to the understanding than it is in itself. Hence it happens that the object being thus falsely represented to the will, it becomes too passionately beloved and embraced, without the due inquiry as to its real goodness; and by how much the desire or love of the will is more vehement, by so much the understanding is more grossly clouded in its judgment, and being so deceived, invites the will to an increase of affection towards it. So that these two chief

* See *Spiritual Conquest*, treat. v. Doubt xiv. § 8, and the *note*.

powers of man's soul, miserably deceived and misled, walk continually as in a circle, from this darkness into others, and fall from one great error into others more grievous.

7. Take heed, therefore, of fastening thy affection upon anything whatsoever, before it be well weighed and examined by the understanding; and recommend it to God in prayer, that so thou mayest truly discern whether it be good or evil. And to this I exhort thee, not only in all indifferent things, but even in those also which are good and holy. For though they are evidently good in themselves, yet they may prove otherwise to thee by reason of some circumstance of time, place, measure, or obedience.* Whence it often happens that many have endangered themselves in their most laudable and holiest exercises.

And the same caution is necessary even in spiritual things.

8. Thou must also warily refrain thy understanding from *curiosity*, lest it draw that into the soul which may retard it in its intended purchase of victory. For a curious inquiry after earthly things which are impertinent to thy spiritual purpose, though it may be sometimes permitted, yet is generally the poison of the spirit.

The understanding is to be also weaned from curiosity.

9. Restrain, therefore, thy understanding to thy utmost, and strive to make it simple and child-like. As for the changes and chances in the world, whether they be great or small, if they concern thee not, consider them not. And when thou needs must hear or behold them, let

and made simple and foolish as to worldly things.

* See *Spiritual Conquest*, Ambush ii., and the accompanying *notes*.

thy *will* always contradict them. Yea, even in the knowledge of heavenly things, be sober and humble, and content thyself in the only desire to know thy crucified Saviour, and His blessed life and death. Abandon all other things; for so thou shalt yield to thy Lord a most grateful service, Who puts those into the list of His best friends who desire no more knowledge than what is sufficient to inflame their hearts in the love of His goodness and hatred of their own wickedness; for in the search of all other knowledge, nothing but self-love and a certain pernicious pride lies secretly lurking.*

10. If thou thus weanest thy understanding from these curiosities, thou shalt happily escape many ambushes of thy enemies. For the wicked spirit, marking the unchangeable will and resolution of those travellers tending to spiritual perfection not to yield their consent to sin, lays his crafty plots first against their understanding, that so he may, by little and little, get the mastery over it, and then against the will together.

How highly this conduceth to perfection.

11. To this end, he suggests to the learned and sharp-witted sublime and subtle conceits, that they may think themselves already united to the Divinity, and so forget themselves, and give over the correction of their own consciences, the resignation of their wills, and study of their own nothingness. And thus they are inflamed with pride, and make to themselves a certain idol of their own wisdom

And how the devil plots by suggesting to the understanding thoughts of pride and conceit,

* In explanation, see *Conquest*, Ambush vi.

in their understanding, and are so highly puffed up and perplexed in their vain thoughts, that they now persuade themselves that they stand in no further need of others' counsel and direction.

which is far more dangerous, and cured less easily than that of the will.

12. O, the danger that these souls are in! and how hardly are they cured, by reason that the pride of the understanding is far more perilous than that of the will. For he that is proud only in will omits not all obedience, but submits his judgment sometimes to others, which he prefers before his own and believes to be better. But he that is puffed up with the pride of his understanding, and assuredly believes his own opinion to be better than that of others —ah! what hope is there of his cure? How shall he be brought to submit to others' judgment, since he thinks himself the wiser man? For when the understanding—which is the soul's eye, and should both see and correct its secret pride—is itself blind and blown out with presumption; when light itself is become darkness, and the very rule crooked, thou easily conceivest what follows, and what the end of those things is like to be which depend upon such principles. Wherefore, take timely care to prevent this pride before it pierce thee to the marrow. Yield not up the reins to thy understanding, but subject it to counsel, and submit thine own sense to others' judgment.* Become

* Our holy Father St. Benedict understood well the wisdom of submitting our own sense to others' judgment, and has a chapter of his holy Rule '*On taking counsel of the Brethren.*' 'Whenever any important matter,' he says, 'has to be transacted in the monastery, let

a *fool* in thy own conceit for the love of thy Lord, and by this means thou shalt be wiser than *Solomon.*

CHAPTER V.

Of the Will; and the End to which we are to Direct all our Actions.

1. If thou desirest, O dearly beloved, to become one spirit with thy Lord God, it is not enough to have a pious and prompt will to do good works, but even that good thou doest must, by His divine help and motion, be totally referred to God's honour, and to please Him only.* In this thou

A will to do well sufficeth not; but our actions must be performed only to please God.

the abbot call together all the brethren, and lay before them the subject upon which they have to give their advice. And having heard their opinions, let him weigh the matter attentively in his own mind, and then do what he shall judge most expedient. We have said,—let him call every one of the brethren to the council, and for this reason, that God frequently reveals what is wisest to the youngest. . . . If, however, any matter of minor importance has to be considered, let him seek counsel only of the elder brethren, as it is written: *Do thou nothing without counsel, and thou shalt not repent when thou hast done.*' *Regula S. Bened.* ch. iii.

* Spiritual writers draw a distinction between a pure and a right intention. A pure intention is when the beginning, prosecution, and consummation of an action is performed solely for the glory of God, without the alloy of any human motives, so that the action is altogether supernatural, and becomes as it were divine. Perfect purity of intention is of the utmost rarity, and is found only in perfect souls. F. Baker declares that 'the smallest act of love and service to God performed with a perfect self-abnegation is more acceptable and precious in His eyes than the working of a thousand miracles, or the conversion of nations, if in these there are mixed interests of Nature' (*Sancta Sophia*, vol. i. p. 320). A right intention is found where the main substance of an action and its chief aim are directed indeed to God, yet not so perfectly as to exclude the entrance of human or selfish motives, which detract from the supernatural merit of the good action, and render it proportionately impure and unpleasing to God.

must look to have a strong conflict with thine own nature, which, in all her actions and missions, seeks her own convenience and complacency, especially in things spiritual. Hence it is that, when any good thing is proposed to be performed as from God's will and pleasure, she readily undertakes to perform it; but yet not as a thing pleasing to God, or proposed by Him, but rather because she considers the gain and contentment which man reaps by doing the will of God.

To this end apply thy understanding to God's will,

2. When a thing is presented unto thee to be performed which is agreeable to the Divine will, first lift up thy understanding unto God before thou appliest thy will to execute it. Thus shalt thou clearly discern that it is His Divine pleasure thou shouldst perform it, and that thou shouldst do it solely for His honour and good-liking, and that thy will is drawn and moved by the Divine will to effect this work for this only end and intention, because God will have it so, for the honour and glory of His own most Sacred Majesty.

and take heed of being deceived.

3. So likewise, when thou wouldst omit or refuse the things not willed by God, resolve not rashly upon this omission until thou hast directed the eye of thy understanding to the Divine will, as hath already been declared.* And take particular care over thyself lest thou be deceived, because it may many times seem to thee that thou askest or omittest this or that for God's will or pleasure, when indeed it is

* See chap. iv. § 5.

otherwise. For Nature doth so secretly seek herself in our enterprises, that those very things which thou thinkest please or displease thee only for the love of God, are principally willed or refused for thy self-interest.

The intention of doing all for God is to be made at the commencement, and renewed during the progress of every action,

4. Wherefore, at the beginning of any action whatsoever, free thyself to the utmost of thy power of all intentions which have the least mixture of this self-interest, nor do thou venture to act or omit anything till thou feelest and findest thyself inwardly moved to begin and go on with it purely for the will and pleasure of God only. But if thou wantest time and leisure to make this *actual* intention, and to ponder the causes moving thee to do or omit anything, take care to do it when occasion gives thee an opportunity, and then content thyself for the time with a *virtual* intention of seeking only God's good pleasure and honour in every one of thy actions and omissions. Now, in other affairs, which admit of more deliberation, let this formal and express intention be made at the beginning of thy putting hand unto them, as also in things of longer continuance this intention is to be often renewed, lest, after a good beginning, some crooked intention may chance to creep and insinuate itself into thy mind. Thus shalt thou shun the secret deceits of thy own nature, which is too prone to seek herself, and to alter thy well-made intentions, and instead of God's honour, to strike in for her own interest.

5. So that a person who is not very watchful in this

lest self-love creep in, and so change and corrupt it.

doubtful conflict may, as you see, often begin a good work, and intend to perform it according to the Divine will, and yet afterwards, without perceiving it, may derive so much pleasure from the work, as at length to lose sight of his first pure intention of doing it only for the honour and glory of God; and thus, by little and little, he may become so changed, bewitched, and ensnared by the satisfaction, pleasure, profit, or honour redounding to himself from these works, that if he chance to be hindered from continuing them by means of sickness, or other accidents, he presently becomes troubled, dejected, and disquieted, nor can he without great difficulty be brought to his first pure intention of doing and suffering what God would have him, for no other motive than for His Divine honour and glory alone.

Therefore this right intention is of high importance.

6. In all thy actions, therefore, and omissions, carefully cherish this right intention; for it is not to be expressed what strength, efficacy, and comfort it will afford thee, in so much that the very least and meanest thing thus performed—*to please God, and for the honour of His name*—is of more merit and of higher value in His sight than the most heroic works which are done without it.

ENLARGEMENT. He who doth all things purely to please

7. From what has been said, it manifestly appears that whosoever followeth God's motion, and desireth to satisfy Him alone, fixeth not his affection upon one thing more than another, but is

ready to have this, do that, or leave the other thing in what manner, time, and circumstance it pleaseth God; so that he remaineth in such a state of indifferency, that whether he hath it or not, he is equally pleased and pacified, always quiet and content, because however it falls out he hath what he desireth, and enjoyeth the end he aimed at, which was no other than to be conformable to his Lord God.

God remains in perfect indifferency.

8. But if the hopes of eternal happiness, or the fear of punishment, which more particularly affects thine own interest, urges thee sometimes to perform certain good actions, yet even in this also thou mayest propose to thyself this end of the Divine will, since God is well pleased that thou shouldst not descend into hell, but enjoy His heavenly kingdom. And thus thou wilt keep alive in thy heart this holy motive upon all occasions whatsoever, of the importance whereof I need not here further enlarge.

This purity of intention may be even in things which directly affect our own interest.

9. For this, indeed, is an undoubted fact: that as the most holy and heroic work becomes not only defective but utterly lost, if it be not done for a good end, and may become even sinful, if it be directed to an ill end, so, on the contrary, the smallest and least action hath an inestimable price and value when done with an intention simply for God and His goodwill and pleasure; in so much, that a single penny bestowed on the poor is more acceptable to the Divine Majesty when given

That the best action without it is lost, and may be sinful, and the smallest with it most acceptable to God.

purely to please Him, than would be the most princely gift bestowed for any other end whatsoever, such as to gain the joys of heaven; though this end is not only good, but very much to be desired.

10. This exercise of performing all our actions purely and only to please God, of sighing always after God, of seeking Him in everything we do or omit, and of aspiring perpetually to Him with glowing and living affections, as to our most amiable and only good, Who deserves in Himself that all rational creatures should honour, serve, and love Him above all things, may seem at first very difficult, but use will render it easy. And the frequent consideration of God's infinite worth will so inflame the will in the production of the aforesaid acts of fervour and affection, that we shall with much ease and speed acquire a habit of doing all things for His sake only. Moreover, the ensuing reflections will in no little induce us to act thus purely for God in all things.

If this exercise seem hard at first, yet use will render it easy;

11. For who can but be persuaded to search and will God's pure honour, with an entire resignation to the ordinances of His Divine providence in all things, if he often call to his remembrance how much He hath first honoured and loved him? As in our *Creation*, He made us of nothing to be like Himself, and all other creatures for our use and benefit. In our *Redemption*, He sent no angel, but His only Son, to pay our ransom, not by the perishable value of gold and silver, but by the infinite price of His own precious

especially if we consider how dearly our Lord hath loved us.

blood, and by His dolorous and disgraceful death.* In our *Preservation*, each hour and moment fighting our battles for us against our enemies, preventing and accompanying us with His heavenly grace, and leaving with us His dear Son, always ready for our support and nourishment in the Holy Sacrament of the altar. These, verily, and many more, are evident tokens of the high price He puts upon our meanness and misery, and of the love which our great Creator bears to us, His poor and wretched creatures; and are in themselves such inestimable benefits, that none but His own Divine understanding is capable of comprehending the least of them. How much therefore are we bound in exchange to do for so excellent a Majesty, Who hath done such things for us! For if worldly potentates, receiving honour from private persons of lowest rank, think themselves bound to return them reciprocal honour, what ought our vileness endeavour towards the supreme Monarch of the universe, Who as highly courteth and cherisheth us.

* 'Knowing that you were not redeemed with corruptible things, as gold or silver, from your vain conversation of the tradition of your father; but with the precious blood of Christ, as of a lamb unspotted and undefiled.' 1 Peter ii. 18, 19.

CHAPTER VI.

OF THE TWO WILLS IN MAN; AND OF THE CONTINUAL STRIFE AND CONFLICT BETWEEN THEM.

1. THOU must take notice, my dearly beloved, of two wills in man: the one of *reason*, which is therefore called the rational or superior will; the other of *sense*, and so named the sensual or inferior will, and sometimes sensuality, appetite, concupiscence, the flesh, passion, and the like. And though both one and the other are in man, nevertheless, since we are only rightly called men when we act as rational creatures, so neither are we said to will anything which the sensual appetite chooses, until the superior will or reason confirms the choice.

Two wills, rational and sensual.

2. From this diversity, therefore, springs all our spiritual conflict; for our superior will, being as it were midway between God's will, which is above it, and our sensuality, which is beneath it, is perpetually invited, enticed, and pulled, first by the divine will and then by sensuality, each endeavouring to draw it to its own side, and subject it to its own control and command.

The rational is seated between God's grace and the sensual will.

3. But this battle is of no great difficulty to those who are either truly virtuous or downright vicious. For they who are virtuous come no sooner to the knowledge of God's holy will, but they presently yield their consent, and bridle their brutish sensuality.

The virtuous promptly yield to God's will,

4. The wicked, on the contrary, act straightway according to their appetite, checking the motions of the Holy Spirit which contradict it. the vicious to their sensuality;

5. They, therefore, chiefly feel the brunt of this battle—especially at first—who have been great sinners, and are now resolved upon amendment, and to this end sever themselves from worldly and fleshly delights the better to love and serve their Lord Jesus Christ for the future. For the inward feeling and strokes of God's will, which their reason receives from above, and the cruel contradictions and adverse motion of their sensuality, which it must necessarily suffer from below, are so powerful on either side, that between them the poor reason is brought into extreme straits and perplexities. but they who of sinners are become converts have the greatest conflict.

6. Wherefore, let no one think to gain the victory who is not instructed, prepared, and resolved to support patiently all such pains as he shall endure in leaving his past pleasures.* For this surely seems one of the chief causes why so few attain to true perfection; because, feeling grief and trouble in the Such as these must resolve to bear patiently the loss of their pleasures.

* In his *Confessions* (lib. viii. cap. 7, 8, 11, 12), St. Augustine draws a picture of the terrible conflict he experienced within himself upon his conversion. 'What did I not say against myself in this conflict? How did I lash and scourge my own soul, to make it follow Thee, O Lord? But it held back, it refused and excused itself; and when all its arguments were confuted, it remained trembling and fearing, as though it were death to be restrained from that unbridled custom of sin whereby it was wasting to death.' After this he went into a garden with Alipius, his companion, and then cried out unto him in these words, 'What is this, Alipius? What is this we have been hearing? What suffer we under the tyranny of sin? Unlearned men, such

beginning of their conversion, and in the quieting of their depraved affections and desires, they stand not fast to their resolutions, but yield to their enemies, who treacherously invade them, not making a manly resistance with the sword of reason, but rather, like cowardly soldiers, they skulk away, throw down their arms, yield

as Anthony and others, take heaven by storm; and behold we, with all our learning, cowardly and heartlessly, still lie groveling in flesh and blood.' After this he went a little further into an orchard, and there he underwent a still greater conflict. For presently all his past pleasures presented themselves before his eyes, saying, 'What! wilt thou depart from us? And shall we never after this moment be with thee any more? And shall it never be lawful for thee to do *this* or *that* again?' Then, dismayed with the recollection of these foul thoughts, he exclaimed, 'Turn away, O Lord, the mind of Thy servant from thinking of what they presented to my soul.' What filthy, what shameful pleasures did they set before his eyes! 'Presently,' he says, 'these evil thoughts became much fainter, so that I only half heard them; they now not openly showing themselves and contradicting me, but muttering as it were behind my back, and furtively pulling me by the coat, as one does to those going away to make them look back upon him. But yet in spite of my efforts they retarded me, so that I hesitated to break loose and shake myself free from them, and to bound forth whither I was called; the violence of vicious custom still saying to me, "Thinkest thou that thou canst live without them?"' At length, after enduring long and tedious combats, a marvellous tempest of weeping came over him, and being unable any longer to restrain his feelings, he ran away from Alipius, and casting himself on the ground under a fig-tree, gave free vent to his eyes, and poured forth an acceptable sacrifice in a torrent of tears. O, what strength and comfort may the sinner draw in his struggles against sin, by reflecting upon the savage assaults, fierce combats, and piercing anguish which the saints experienced upon their conversion to God! If even some of the greatest saints, such as St. Augustine, felt at times the iron hand of evil custom dragging them down from God to their former sinful life, and heard ever and anon the unclean whisperings of Satan in their ear, what right have miserable sinners, such as we, to hope that we shall escape the insidious attacks of the devil, when we turn from our wicked ways to serve the living God? Therefore it is written in the inspired Word: 'Son, when thou comest to the service of God, stand in justice and in fear, and prepare thy soul for temptation. Humble thy heart and endure.' *Ecclus.* ii. 1, 2.

themselves to the mercy of their enemies, and become again the bondslaves of those who will now more than heretofore tyrannise over them.

ENLARGEMENT. Divers sorts of unmortified souls.

7. And amongst these one may pick out some who indeed neither take away nor detain their neighbours' goods wrongfully, but yet have their affection fixed excessively upon those which they possess justly; so likewise they will not purchase honours unlawfully, but they love and desire them passionately; they will keep the prescribed fastings punctually, but care not to mortify their gluttony; they will live continently, but are loath to leave pleasing company, which hinders their union with God and greatly retards them in their tendance to perfection. From these things, and the like petty affections, it follows that their good works are performed with a certain irksomeness of mind, and are accompanied with divers self-interests and secret imperfections; yea, with self-conceit and good liking of their own actions, and with a longing desire to be lauded and loved by others. Such as these not only make no progress in the way of spirituality, but even return backwards, and are in imminent hazard of falling into their former follies, because they are neither enamoured with true virtue nor grateful to their loving Creator, Who hath freed them from the tyranny of the devil. They are, moreover, stricken with ignorance and blindness, since they neither understand nor see their own danger, but falsely and foolishly fancy themselves to be in a state of security.

D

8. And here thou mayest perceive a very perilous and pernicious deceit, which very few take notice of. For many beginners in a spiritual course, out of self-love, make choice of such exercises as are most pleasing to themselves, rather than most profitable unto their souls; whereas they ought to begin with the knowledge of their own natural affections, and the naughty desires of their sensuality, and to make their first and fiercest encounter with these enemies, and continue falling on and following them up till they be all entirely subdued to reason's empire, so far as it is possible in this life.

TEXT. A danger in the choice of spiritual exercises.

CHAPTER VII.

OF THE FIGHT AGAINST SENSUALITY, AND OF THE INWARD WAY OF THE WILL TO ACQUIRE VIRTUES.

1. As often as thou feelest thyself assaulted by the motions of thy sensuality, turn thy mind quickly to thy Lord God, and resist manfully; and that thou mayest become a conqueror in this combat, furnish thyself with these several ways and wards against thy foes. *First*, let the temptation be no sooner felt in the senses, but that thou forthwith put a precept of obedience upon the superior will or reason, that it yield no consent unto it.

When sensuality rebels, 1. Look to thy reason that it consent not.

2. *In the next place*, when thou hast happily vanquished and discomfited any such temptation,

2. Recall that motion

excite the same again in thyself and again repel it with the like fervour. Yea, do it yet again and again, that so thou mayest often have occasion more zealously to hate it, to reject it. This method may be used against all temptations and unruly affections of thy perverse nature, except only what concerns sensuality,* of which we shall treat hereafter in its due place.

again and again, and as often conquer it.

3. *Lastly*, let it be thy exercise to produce frequent and fervent acts of those virtues which are contrary to the temptations of these vices. For example: Art thou tempted to *Impatience?* Recall thy mind home into its inner room, and thou shalt there perceive that this temptation of impatience doth incessantly strive and fight with thy superior will or reason to terrify or drive it out of the field, or incline it to consent. Therefore thou must contradict and resist the said temptation with redoubled fervour of thy reason, and never leave off this resistance till thou seest thine enemy conquered at thy feet and become thy captive.

3. Produce the contrary acts of virtue;

4. But here thou art to be warned that our enemy, perceiving us so constantly and continually opposing ourselves against his suggestions, passions, and affections, ceaseth sometimes, out of his treacherous cunning, from stirring them

but beware of thy enemy, who sometimes suppresseth these motions.

* This method of coming to hate and eradicate sin should not be practised by all persons indiscriminately. In temptations against purity, it should never, as our author remarks, be made use of, while against envy, hatred, and the like, it is expedient only when the resolution to resist the emotion is so strong as to leave no fear of the passion gaining the ascendency and obtaining the consent of the will.

up. And what is more, when they are raised h ʒome-times suppresseth them, lest by the frequent fight of our reason against them we should get the habit of those virtues which are opposite to these passions.

for then it is thy office to excite them,

5. It imports thee, therefore, to be wary that thou lettest not slip this occasion of acquiring these virtues, and if thou hast made a truce with thy foe and art at peace with thy perverse nature, recall to thy memory those thoughts which excited thee to i.e. *impatience;* yea, and carry thyself so towards them as though thou seemest to consent and yield them the victory. And in that mark the motives, arguments, and reasons suggested by thy enemy; examine what he aims at, what he would have of thee, and to what thou art inclined; and when thou seest thyself sensibly stirred up and thoughts of *impatience* ascending, and almost domineering over thy reason—which is ever ready to give her consent—then draw back thy foot, and violently excite good thoughts in thy soul in opposition to those evil suggestions, boldly denying them farther entrance or longer continuance. And fight the battle over and over, so often and so long till thou feelest thyself to be at last a conqueror of thyself.

and to fight them till thou hatest them.

6. But we must yet furthermore take notice, that though we have gallantly fought and happily foiled our enemies, we are in no security till we *hate* our unruly passions perfectly. And to excite, increase, and perfect this our due hatred against them,

we must sometimes, as aforesaid,* stir them up and provoke them to the combat, thereby to take occasion of contemning, despising, and abhorring them with the greater indignation, till at length we come to have a true and constant hatred of them.†

7. Now, for the adorning of thy soul with virtues, the former fights and exercises against unruly nature and evil inclinations suffice not; but thou must frequently and fervently undertake the practice of those virtues which are contrary to those now-extirpated passions and conquered vices. For example: One gives thee occasion of *Impatience*. It is not enough for thee to conquer and quell this motion according to the now-delivered doctrine, but thou shouldst, moreover, desire that the same person may in the same manner more and more molest thee; yea, thou

The way to implant virtues is to practise acts contrary to their opposites.

* See above, § 2.

† 'They who, being still clothed with the mortal body, have undertaken the task of mounting up to heaven have occasion to do great violence to themselves, and to allow of no truce to their mortifications, especially at the commencement of their renunciation, until the love of those delights and pleasures to which they were formerly devoted, and the insensibility of their hearts, be changed into a true and sincere love of God, and a perfect purity of mind be established. Certainly it is necessary to undertake many and great labours, to expect many secret trials and contradictions, principally if we be slothful and deficient in fervour, until the spirit which previously resembled a dog that perpetually dwelt in the kitchen, and was obedient merely for the sake of its belly, becomes simple, meek, vigilant, a lover of purity and continual application to the great business of salvation. Nevertheless, let us take courage, however subject we may be to our passions, or however feeble we may be in virtue at the present moment. Let us offer ourselves to Jesus Christ with an unshaken faith, and acknowledge to Him our weakness and spiritual deficiency, and then we may hope confidently to receive the assistance of His grace, although we have not deserved it, if we but continually descend into the abyss of our humility.' St. John Climacus, *The Holy Ladder of Perfection*, p. 6.

shouldst force thyself to feel *content* in that trouble, and make resolutions to suffer more of the like nature, or greater of any other. And what is yet above all this, thou must constrain thyself to converse lovingly, speak sweetly, serve cordially that very person whose occasion thus moves thee to impatience.

ENLARGEMENT. The reason why such contrary acts are so necessary.

8. The reason why such contrary acts are necessary to perfect our virtue, is that the root from which the vice springs can by no other acts be so fully extirpated. Therefore—to continue in the same example — although, when we are slighted and contemned, we yield not to motions of impatience, but beat it down with the three fore-mentioned weapons, yet if we habituate not ourselves to make this contempt pleasing unto us and to rejoice therein, we shall never be freed and exempt from the vice of impatience, which, because of our natural proneness to seek the increase of our reputation, is founded in the abhorring of all contempt. And so long as this vicious root remains alive, it will be constantly pushing up, and will make our virtue languish and droop, yea, and sometimes choke it up, besides putting us to perpetual danger of relapses upon all occasions that are presented unto us. Hence it is clear, that without the practice of such contrary acts, we can never obtain true habits of virtue.

They must be made frequently, and be external as

9. And thou art farther to be instructed that these acts must be so fervent, frequent, and numerous, that they may be capable of destroying totally the vicious habit, which, having got possession of

our heart by many vicious acts, must be thence extracted by many acts of the contrary nature, that this desired virtuous habit may be let in and implanted. Yea, I moreover warn thee that more good acts are required to obtain a habit of virtue than vicious habits to get a habit of vice, because the former are not assisted, as the latter are, by nature corrupted with sin. I add to all this, that if the virtue which thou practise requires it, thou art to make outward acts conformable to the inward; as, in the aforesaid example, thou must use words of love and sweetness, and strive to find out and lay hold of some occasion of serving him whom thou takest for thy opponent and enemy.

well as internal.

10. And although these practices are full of pain, and are so coldly performed by thee that thou perceivest them to go against the grain, yet omit them not in any case; for if they are painful they are also profitable, making thee valiant and bold to fight these holy battles, and preparing thy way to the victory.

TEXT. Which, though painful, are profitable.

11. Thou art, moreover, to be advertised, that not only these great and grievous temptations and manifest wickednesses are to be stoutly resisted, but even the least and lightest passions and disordered motions; for these are but forerunners of the greater, opening the door for them to steal in upon us and oppress us unawares, and so to precipitate us into all vices. And it oftentimes falls out with them who slight these petty temptations, and care not to use dili-

This diligence must be used also against evil motions;

gence in resisting them, that when they afterwards least suspect it, much more grievous suggestions do suddenly, violently, and dangerously invade them.

yea, and against lawful affections, when not absolutely necessary.

12. Lastly, thou must also resolve to skirmish with thy lawful affections,* and deny thyself even in thy honest desires when they appear not to be necessary. This will render thee an experienced soldier in this spiritual warfare, and a most grateful servant to thy Lord and Saviour.

This is the way to become truly spiritual,

13. And now I tell thee plainly, my dearly beloved, if thou wilt try and train up thyself in the spiritual conflict according to this prescribed method, thou shalt soon feel, God's grace assisting thee, a happy and total change into spirituality. But if thou wilt needs follow other exercises, though seeming most excellent, and performed with such present gust and sweetness as if thou hadst the full and familiar conference and companionship of thy Crucified Jesus, never persuade thyself that such delicious ways are the direct path to perfection.

because vice springs

14. For as our vices spring from this fountain, that our superior will or reason submits herself to

* A monk, by virtue of his religious profession, is obliged to aim, without ceasing, at perfection. Now, since perfection, as St. Thomas teaches (2. 2. qu. 184, a. i.), consists in perfect charity, or in the love of God *above* all things and *in* all things, and since we come to this perfect love in proportion as we cast out of our hearts all human loves and in their place implant the divine charity of God, so it behoves those who are striving after perfection to mortify and destroy not merely such affections as are dangerous and pernicious, but even those that are lawful and honest, and this for no other end than to obtain greater purity of heart and a closer union with God.

the inferior feelings of sensuality, so, on the contrary, virtues are generated in our souls by due submission of this will to the Divine Will. And as our will can never be truly good and grateful to God—though it receive from Him never so holy and heavenly inspirations, and be driven by the impulse of His Will to all its works and omissions—unless it consent to the Divine operations working within it, so neither can it be termed bad and separated from God, though never so much tempted and troubled by sensuality, except by its consenting unto evil.

from yielding to sensuality, virtue from submitting our will to God's.

CHAPTER VIII.

What He must do who Feels his Superior Will or Reason Overcome by his Inferior Will or Sensuality.

1. If thou sometimes find, O dearly beloved, that thou prevailest nothing at all in the fight of the reason against sense, because thou feelest not an efficacious ardour to root out ill affections, be not troubled, but stand fast, and still pursue thy fight with courage and constancy; for as long as thy reason keeps herself from consenting to these motions of sensuality, so long hast thou the ascendency in this battle and art master of the field.

As long as thy reason consents not, fear not,

2. Nor is it necessary that all thy affections and motions of sensuality do entirely submit to the empire of thy reason; neither doth our victory

for victory does not consist in not feeling

temptations, but in not yielding; consist in feeling no perverse passions in our sensuality; but it sufficeth that our will and reason—though sensuality storm never so much—can always act or omit, do or not do, will or desire, when, how, where, and as she pleaseth, and even so that the devil himself and the whole world together can never alter this our resolution.

If thy enemies surprise thy reason, retreat to gain time and strength.

3. And if it sometimes happen that thy enemies suddenly and violently rush in upon thee, and so surprise thy reason as to give it no respite to have recourse to such wonted ways of devotion whereby it might suppress these motions, then briefly make use of the tongue in thy defence, and say: 'No, no! I believe thee not. I will none of thee. I will never consent unto thee.' And so behave thyself in this exigency against thy inward foes as one would do being oppressed unawares with outward enemies; for his sword proving useless in his defence, he strives to step backwards, that so he may get ground and time both to draw his sword and also to drive his enemy away therewith. And do thou in like sort, O spiritual champion, first retreat, thereby to gain time to think upon thy nothingness, and that of thyself thou canst never conquer thy cruel enemies, and then, buckling up thyself with hope and confidence in thy God, Who can do all things, make a gallant assault upon thy enemy, saying: 'Lord, help me. O my God, give succour to Thy servant. O Jesus! O Mary, the most worthy Mother of my Redeemer, deliver me from this danger.'

4. But if thou hast time, then thou mayest support thy will from consenting and yielding by the help of thy understanding, fetching strength from the consideration of those means which may help her against her enemies, as, for example, if a great and grievous impatience hath laid hold of thee, by reason of some accident or affliction, insomuch that it seems more than thou wilt or canst do to bear or dissemble it any longer, help thyself presently with these following thoughts: And if thou hast opportunity, consider:

5. *First*, whether or no thou hast in any way deserved or given just occasion that this adversity should befall thee. If so, rest contented: be no longer troubled, for it is most just and equitable that thou patiently bear the blow given to thyself by thine own hands. But if not, then turn thine eyes to thy other sins, for which neither thy loving Lord hath yet chastised thee as thou deservest, nor thou afflicted thyself as thou oughtest; and thence conclude, 1. Hast thou deserved this affliction.

6. *Secondly*, that thy meek and merciful Maker hath exchanged either the eternal pain which thou shouldst have endured in hell-fire, or else the temporal punishment due to thee in purgatory, into this easy and fatherly correction. And what, then, is more reasonable than that thou embrace it, not only with a willing mind, but also with a grateful acknowledgment for so boundless a benefit? 2. That it will lessen future punishment.

7. *Thirdly*, but if thou thinkest, which God forbid thou shouldst, that thou hast done sufficient 3. That suffering is the

way to heaven. penance for thy petty offences, then reflect within thyself that none can enter the heavenly kingdom but they must pass through the narrow gate of self-denial and of patience in tribulation, for thus God's holy Son Himself, and all His blessed saints, ascended to their glory.

8. *Fourthly*, nay, even in case thou couldst find out some other way to get to heaven, yet thou art obliged by the law of love and duty not to do or desire it. For the Son of God chose the way of thorns and crosses by which He would enter into His glory, and this for thy love; and that thou shouldst imitate Him who left thee this exact pattern of perfect patience.*

4. Love compels thee to choose the cross.

9. *Lastly*, know, for certain, that amongst all the pious motives and meditations which thou makest use of in these or the like events and necessities for the comfort and confirmation of thy will, this seems to be one of the most efficacious—to think what a joy and content it is to thy Lord God, how He likes and loves thee, when He beholds thee fight so stoutly for His sake. For nothing surely can be more grateful to thy Creator than that thou kill and cut up by the roots all depraved desires, and plant true virtues in their places; and this merely for that thou well knowest it to be His holy will and pleasure.

5. And that it is the most pleasing to God.

* 'I would always choose the road of suffering because I wish to imitate our Lord Jesus Christ, even if there were no other advantage than this; though there are always many others.' *The Interior Castle*, p. 128.

CHAPTER IX.

That We must not Shun the Occasions of these Combats.

1. And now, my dearly beloved, I add to all these means hitherto mentioned for the acquiring of virtues this, as a short and certain memorial: That thou neither fear nor fly the occasions of fighting against thy passions. For if thou art desirous to have the habit of any virtue—as of patience, for example—thy way is not to shut thyself up from conversing with men, or to shun those things—be they words, actions, or thoughts—which move thee to impatience. No, thou must not shun them, I say, but seek them out, desire them, and love their company and conversation who are the causes of this thy disquiet. And as often as thou shalt have occasion of intercourse with them, prepare thyself, and make ready thy will to receive joyfully and patiently all tribulations and troubles which they can any way bring upon thee. And this is thy only way to accustom thee to patience. In like manner, if thou art weary of any work which grows tedious and troublesome to thee—either because the person who commands it displeaseth thee, or because it is of itself offensive, or that thou art thereby hindered from some other employment which thou wouldst more willingly embrace—yet omit it not on any terms, but rather set sooner about that work than any other, be it never so painful or displeasing. And although

The way to acquire true virtue is not to avoid, but to seek the occasions of combat.

the leaving it undone seems to settle and quiet thy mind, nevertheless see that thou desist not from doing it; for thus thou shalt become more and more instructed in the way to get perfect patience. Nor is that imagined peace at all solid, because it springs not from a heart sincerely purified from all disorderly passions.

This applies to troublesome thoughts.

2. And I teach the same lesson concerning such thoughts as sometimes trouble and contristate thy mind: to wit, that thy aim be not utterly to expel them, but kindly to entertain them and treat them as pleasant guests, because the trouble of their company inures thee to the patient suffering of all contradictions. And whosoever shall otherwise instruct thee, O my beloved, commands thee to fly that very thing in affliction which thou seekest to obtain by fighting—that is, the virtue thou desirest to gain by conquering thy enemies.

Yet a novice must be wary in this warfare.

3. And yet a young and inexperienced soldier in this spiritual conflict must warily enter the list to wage this war with wicked thoughts. Therefore, I counsel him sometimes to oppose them, other times to exchange them for others, accordingly as he perceives this or that way best profits him in the acquisition of virtues; but never so to fly from them and totally leave them as to seek to be quit of all trouble and irksomeness which thence ariseth. For though by the flight he cuts off the occasion of impatience, yet he gets no strength or constancy of heart against the next rising motions thereof. Whence it follows, that if the

same risings of impatience do at any other time seize on him, he is soon terrified and quickly conquered, because he was unprovided with arms suitable to the combat—that is, he had not fortified his mind with customs, counsels, thoughts, and resolutions, to keep perfect patience in all events of adversity. This way of warring is very profitable, not only against impatience, but all other imperfections, except those of sensuality,* of which we shall treat hereafter.†

CHAPTER X.

Of the Fight against Sudden Temptations and Passions.

Foresee what cross is likely to befall you.

1. He that is not yet accustomed to receive sudden adversities and troubles with a calm countenance and quiet mind may thus inure himself thereto. Let him, first, diligently consider them with his understanding, then earnestly desire them with his will, and, finally, always expect them with a ready and prepared mind. The manner to ponder such adversities by the understanding is this:—Mark thine own state, calling, and condition, as also the place and person where and with whom thou art likely daily to converse. Thus thou mayest easily foresee what may probably befall thee, and how thou must carry thyself and fortify thy mind against any sudden surprisal of thy passions. And if some accident not

* See above, chap. vii. § 2, and *note*. † Chap. xi.

foreseen chance to happen, then, besides this former strength already gained by that first resolution to bear all crosses with an evenness of mind, thou mayest thus farther help thyself.

Fly to the thought of God's providence,

2. When thou perceivest that thou art slighted, scorned, or in any way injured, presently force thy mind towards thy Lord and Maker, and weigh His immense bounty and infinite love to thee. From this thought it will forthwith occur to thy understanding that He is the chief cause of this thy trouble and tribulation, and that He expressly permits it to befall thee that thou mayest learn to bear it patiently for His love, and mayest draw nearer and be more perfectly united unto Him.

who either sends or permits it.

3. And after thou hast thus concluded with thyself that it is His Divine will and pleasure thou shouldst suffer it patiently, then turn thy thought back upon thyself, and begin to chide thy soul and tell it:—'Ah, why strivest thou to cast off this cross, which neither this nor that enemy, but thy most loving Lord and heavenly Father hath laid upon thy shoulders?' Then turn to the cross or calamity which presseth thee; salute it, praise it, embrace it, and receive it with all possible joy and alacrity. And although the rising passions be so unruly and violent that they suffer not thy mind to elevate itself to God, but leave thee wounded and almost vanquished, yet persevere in thy well-made resolution, and proceed as if thou wert not worsted in the skirmish.

4. But amongst all the remedies against these sudden and unexpected motions, this seems most effectual:—To take away timely the causes from whence they proceed; as, if thou feelest thy mind much troubled when thou canst not obtain such a thing which thou lovest, presently away with that love, exclude that thing from thy mind. But if thy trouble and vexation ariseth not from the thing but from the person who hinders, helps, or procures it—and this party is so highly displeasing to thy humour that the least thing as coming from him is troublesome to thee—then the speediest and best remedy is to conquer thy own inclination, and compel thy will to yield him true love and affection.

But the best remedy is to cut off the causes of thy trouble.

5. For, besides that he is a creature framed as thou art by the all-powerful hand of God, and redeemed by the same precious ransom of thy dear Saviour's blood, he furthermore presents thee with a happy occasion—if thou canst love it and lay hold thereon—to make thyself even like God, Who is good and gracious to all.

Enlargement.

CHAPTER XI.

Of the Fight against our Flesh and Fleshy Concupiscence.

1. In this war with thy flesh, O my dearly beloved, thou must change thy weapons, and fight in a new posture, contrary to the former. And therefore thou art to take particular notice of

Shun the very occasion of lust: as, 1. Conversations.

three things; to wit, the time *going before* temptation, *accompanying* it, and *following* it. Before thou feelest the temptations of this kind, *fight not with them*, but diligently fly the occasions,* and cut off all causes which procure them: as, *First*, all conversation, though never so little dangerous.

For this enemy is not to be molested, but avoided
ENLARGEMENT. by all possible means; and we are to dread the encounter of any person whatsoever whose presence may put us in the least danger. Nor are we to trust our not feeling presently the stings of the temptation, for this accursed vice makes its approaches most commonly by stealth and underhand, and hurts us the more grievously in proportion as it the better feigns truce and amity, whereby we neither distrust its treachery nor stand upon our guard to defend ourselves vigorously. Hence there is oftentimes more cause of fear when the companionship and familiarity is continued under the pretext of lawfulness, as of kindred, of obligation, of complaisance, or even of virtue, in the party beloved. For then the poisonous pleasure of our sensuality intermixeth itself with this affection, which is in its own nature good and holy; and insensibly distilling into the heart, and penetrating by little and little into the very marrow of the soul, at last darkens and obscures

* It is the teaching of theologians that every proximate occasion of impurity, if it be unnecessary, must be avoided under pain of mortal sin. Here, in the warfare against the flesh, the old adage is inverted; the brave flee, and none but cowards face the enemy. *Qui amat periculum, in illo peribit*,—He who loves the danger shall perish in it. See *note*, p. 470.

the reason, till it be brought to slight all dangers, and so by degrees fall either into open ruin, or, at least, into such troublesome temptations as are afterwards very hard to be conquered.

Secondly. All pleasant aspects upon any such persons or things,* all show of familiarity, all loving salutations, all pressing of their hands with thine, or the like levities. But if thou hast some affair which must necessarily be transacted with such a one, despatch it with all speed and gravity. TEXT. 2. Looks.

Thirdly. Take heed of idleness, and take a particular and perpetual care neither to act nor think anything unbeseeming thy state and vocation. 3. Idleness.

Fourthly. Be punctual in obeying thy superior; never contradict him in anything, but be ever ready to execute his command. 4. Disobedience.

* 'Non licet intueri,' says St. Gregory, 'quod non licet desiderare,'—'It is not lawful to gaze upon that which we have no right to desire.' And St. Jerome, 'Oculi quasi quidam raptores ad culpam,'—'Our eyes are like ravishers which carry us off into sin.' The old proverb, 'Ubi amor ibi oculus,' also serves as a lesson. So great importance did our holy Father St. Benedict attach to the custody of the eyes, that he ranks it amongst his degrees of humility:—

'The twelfth degree of humility is that a monk should be humble not only in heart, but that in his very deportment he should always appear so to those who behold him; and whether he be working or praying, whether he be in the monastery or garden, on a journey or in the field, or wheresoever he be, sitting, walking, or standing, let his head be bowed down, and his eyes fixed on the ground, and always thinking of his sins, let him imagine himself standing before the awful judgment-seat of God already condemned, constantly repeating to himself in his own heart those words which were spoken by the Publican in the Gospel, with eyes cast down to the earth: "Lord, I, a sinner, am not worthy to lift up mine eyes unto heaven." And again, with the Prophet: "I am bowed down and humbled exceedingly."' *Reg. S. Benedicti*, cap. vii.

Fifthly. Judge not rashly of thy neighbour concerning this; yea, though his sin be manifest, and cannot admit of any excuse, do thou condole with him; but neither disdain nor despise him; and turning his imperfection to thy own profit, humble and contemn thyself, debase thyself even to the dust, and, trembling with awful fear, beg heartily the divine assistance that thou be not likewise tempted, lest thou likewise fall. For if thou art ready to judge and slight others, God will punish thee to thy cost, and permit thee to fall into the same vice, that so thou mayest learn truly to know and humble thyself, and suppress thy own pride and presumption. For if thou art proud and fallest not, thy salvation is much to be doubted of.

5. Rash judgment.

Lastly. Mark seriously, and beware of vain complacency in thyself upon the feeling of any sensible grace, or spiritual comfort, or inward delight in devotion; and persuade not thyself that thou art therefore more perfect, or that thou shalt henceforth have no enemies to fight withal, but still remain careful and ever fearful.

6. Vain complacency.

2. In the time *accompanying* thy temptations, weigh whether they proceed from an external or internal cause. By external causes are commonly understood conversation, speeches, reading, or whatsoever may provoke to this vice. The only present and perfect remedy against these external causes is to omit all such exercises, and fly from these

Mark if the causes of temptation be external or internal.

occasions; for there is no fighting with these temptations, as has been afore said;* but the best security is to fly far from them, lest they infect thy soul with their contagion. By inward causes are meant either the body, which is over full of sap and strength, or the mind, which is infested with filthy thoughts, coming either from our own evil customs and neglect of our senses, or else from the enemy's suggestion.

3. The first of these inward causes, which is from the body's fulness, must be prevented by fastings, haircloths, watchings, and the like chastisements and austerities, as reason dictates or obedience directs. The other inward causes, coming from filthy fancies, are best remedied by holy prayer, pious meditation,† diligent labour, and continual employment in affairs suitable to thy state.

Overcome them by chastisements and prayers.

4. Thy prayer may be made in this or the like manner. When thou first apprehendest the approach of thy enemy coming to assault thee with such fancies, run quickly to the sacred Crucifix,

ENLARGEMENT. A form of prayer.

* See above, chaps. vii. 2, ix. 3, xi. 1.

† 'This work and labour against the roots of impurity must be spiritual; that is, by prayer and spiritual virtues, *and not by bodily penance alone.* For be well assured, that if thou shouldst fast and watch and scourge thyself, and do everything else in thy power, thou wouldst never have purity and chastity without their being the gift of God, nor without the grace or virtue of humility. Thou wouldst kill thyself before thou couldst kill carnal motions and feelings of lust and impurity, either in thy heart or in thy flesh, by any amount of bodily penance. But by the grace of Jesus, the roots may be cut off and destroyed, and the spring almost dried up in a humble soul; and then there will be true chastity in body and in soul.' *The Scale of Perfection*, by Walter Hilton, p. 123; edited by Rev. R. E. Guy, O.S.B.

saying:—'O my Jesus, my sweet Jesus, succour me with speed, that I be not subdued;' and, embracing the Cross with thy Saviour upon it, kiss and cherish, again and again, His holy feet, and speak with heart and affection:—'O blessed wounds, O chaste and comfortable wounds, O sacred and sweet wounds. Wound this wretched and unworthy heart of mine with Thy pure and perfect love, and free it from these present and pressing motions of impurity.'

TEXT. Beware of meditations which may occasion impure thoughts.

5. But I would not advise thee to choose such points of meditation which many spiritual books prescribe for remedy of these temptations, such as considering, first, the foulness of carnal vices, and their insatiableness; then the great shame and danger which must of necessity accompany them; and lastly, the loss of fame and consumption of goods, temporal discontents, and eternal damnation. For though these are good meditations, yet they are not conducive to the conquering of these temptations; for since *flight*, in the judgment of all, is the sovereign remedy against this disease, every such thing is therefore to be avoided which gives any occasion to impure thoughts. But in these fore-mentioned meditations, however much the *understanding* tires itself in detesting these sins of the flesh, yet at the same time it fastens such fancies on the *memory* that there are just grounds to fear lest the *will* should fall into delight with these carnal sins.

Meditate on Christ's

6. Wherefore, let the matter of thy meditations for this purpose be rather taken from the Passion

and Death of our Saviour Jesus.* And if evil temptations of that nature do also in these pious meditations intrude themselves against thy will, so as to disturb thee, and, notwithstanding thy vigilance, yet still drive on their plots, and invent new devices against thee, as may happen to thee as well as to others, yet be not out of heart, nor leave off thy well-begun meditations; nor stay to dispute with these flying thoughts; but proceed constantly in what thou art about, leaving and laughing at the other fancies, as if they in no way concerned thee. And this is the only and best way to conquer impure thoughts, though never so importunate and troublesome.

death and passion.

7. And thou mayest conclude thy meditation with this or some such colloquy:—'O my sovereign Creator and sweet Redeemer, disentangle me from my enemies, for Thy bitter Passion's sake!' And be sure not to permit thy fancy to return or reflect on the vice, since the mere memory thereof is accompanied with very much danger.

ENLARGEMENT. A colloquy.

8. And take heed of holding any argument with them, whether thou hast yielded thy consent or not; for this is a covert deceit of the devil, who, under this mask of good, lies waiting to ensnare and entangle thee. These wiles of the evil one

TEXT. Dispute not with carnal temptations.

* 'Cum me pulsat aliqua turpis cogitatio, recurro ad vulnera Christi: tuta requies in vulneribus salvatoris,—When some foul thought assails me, I fly to the wounds of Christ: there is safe shelter in the wounds of my Saviour.' *St. Augustine.*

thou wilt be able to perceive at another time, when thou enjoyest peace, and art free from troublesome temptations; and thou wilt be warned of them by thy ghostly father, to whom thou art faithfully to discover every and all such thoughts, and not to be ashamed. For humility is here mainly necessary, if we mean to complete the victory.

and make no particular reflections upon these temptations.

9. As concerning holy prayer — another remedy against this carnal malady and all other spiritual diseases — know that it must be made with often lifting up thy mind to God, virtually intending to pray for victory over these thine enemies, without any actual reflection upon the temptations. Beware therefore of descending to particulars in thy prayer, or to show, as it were, their malice and thy misery, by reflecting upon special circumstances; for this will endanger thee to fall into new delectation. And this will suffice thee for thy defence in time of temptation.

After temptation, beware!

10. And after the carnal temptation is past, think not that thou art presently safe and secure from the like assault, but stand upon thy guard, and do not so much as ever remember those objects which occasioned thy temptations, though they be ever so much disguised with the appearance of virtue or piety. For all this is a secret perversion of our corrupted nature, and a craft of the devil to ensnare us and allure us to delight.

CHAPTER XII.

How to Fight against Sloth and Negligence.

1. That thou mayest secure thyself, O dearly beloved, from this pernicious vice, employ thy whole diligence and endeavours to correspond readily with all holy inspirations, and to decline all earthly comforts, curiosities, and superfluous affairs, not directly belonging to thy state and calling.

Follow holy inspirations speedily.

2. Concerning this prompt and speedy correspondence with God's holy inspiration, take this rule: Be sure not to defer the undertaking and beginning of that thing which thou art satisfied thou oughtest to do, beyond its due and fit time. For I assure thee this delay in the *beginning* of thy work will prove an unrecoverable loss in the progress thereof, because this first short lingering calls on a second, which invites a third, and that is attended by another; and so thou wilt pass on to admit of more, to which thy sense will consent more easily than to the first, as having now tasted the bait, and swallowed down the seeming pleasure of this procrastination. Whence it follows that thou either enterest upon thy exercise when it is too late, or wholly omittest it because thou art totally disgusted therewith. Thus little by little, and almost insensibly, creeps on this evil habit of *negligence*, and in the end we content ourselves with this conceit:—that we will do it another time more carefully and diligently!

Enlargement. Begin a good work speedily and in its due time.

Take heed therefore of this most subtle enemy—negligence—which not only infects the will by making it abhor action, but also blinds the understanding, that it apprehends not the vanity of these ill-grounded maxims, and so persuades us voluntarily to leave off our duty altogether, or negligently delay it.

Having begun courageously, prosecute thy good work,

3. Wherefore, having courageously begun thy good work, continue it carefully, prosecute it diligently; and yet not so hastily as to prejudice the perfection of it, or to imitate the error and idleness of those who out of slothfulness think of nothing but of making a speedy end of what they have undertaken, little caring to do it well, but only striving to despatch it quickly, that they may the sooner enjoy their overmuch-desired quiet and repose.

TEXT. the good fruit of which must be recognised,

4. And since there is no better remedy to recall one fallen into this sluggish vice than to set him at some good work—though the slothful man loathes all such employments, having more thought upon the labour which he must undergo than the fruit which follows it—therefore the fruit of this good work must be discovered and made apparent to him, and he must be given to understand that one hearty elevation of the mind to God, or only one bending of the knee humbly to the earth for His honour, is worth more than all worldly wealth and treasures.

ENLARGEMENT.

And that as often as we make diligent haste to speed a good work by using a certain force and violence to ourselves, so often the holy angels bring crowns of glorious victory from heaven to adorn our souls; and that God by little and little takes away from the tepid and negligent those graces which He had formerly given them, increasing them with respect to His faithful friends and followers.

5. And as for the pain which is to be taken in the prosecution of virtuous practices, it must be so dexterously hidden and disguised from him that it may seem less and lighter than it is. As: if thou shouldst employ thyself in the exercise of pious meditation for the space of one whole hour, and that should seem too long to thy lazy disposition, use a pious fraud and persuade thy sensuality that after half a quarter well spent in prayer thou wilt presently leave off. And again, when this short space is past, get thy body to have patience a little longer before thou ceasest thy devotion; and thus continuing from space to space, the whole hour will soon be spent and thy sloth easily shaken off. But if, indeed, thou findest a real disability of body to bear such labours, thou mayest lawfully leave it off for a time, till by degrees thy body becomes accustomed to perform these practices of piety with more fervour and alacrity.

TEXT. and the trouble disguised.

6. This I tell thee as condescending to thy sloth and weakness. But if thou wouldst habituate thyself to make all labour light, and all pains pleasant, the best though the most difficult way is to anticipate it, expect it, and cheerfully em-

ENLARGEMENT. The best way to endure labour is to prepare for and expect it.

brace it at the first encounter. Whence thou wilt find that all tediousness in the performance thereof will be turned into perfect quiet and content, since what thou dost, thou dost voluntarily and willingly; whereas, on the contrary, if thou seekest to shun labour, it will not only seem irksome when it comes to be performed, but formidable beforehand to thy imagination; so that thy very quiet will be subject to trouble, and the fear of a surprise will continually alarm thy fancy. Hence thou wilt abhor all painstaking as a thing loathsome, and still dread the occurrence of such occasions, persons, or objects as are likely to impose it upon thee.

Negligence is highly prejudicial to perfection.

7. Marvel not that I so much press this point and inveigh against this vice of negligence. I do it because it is seldom perceived and yet highly prejudicial; because it persecutes and pursues us most secretly and subtly; it falls upon us not by force but by flattery; it gnaws the very root of all spirituality, and insensibly gangrenes the marrow of our piety and devotion; and our enemy hath no better or more alluring bait to entice any one into his treacherous ambushes, especially those who aim at spirituality. Be thou therefore vigilant, O my dearly beloved. Pray heartily, perform good works diligently, and delay not the spinning of the wool for thy nuptial robe until the marriage-day be come, when thou shouldst be ready and arrayed to go before thy dear Spouse. Reflect that thy God, who gave thee the morning, doth not promise thee the evening. Therefore, improve each moment to

thy profit, and remember the strict account that will be exacted thereof. I conclude, and counsel thee to account that *day for lost*, though thou hast despatched ever so many affairs, wherein thou hast gained no victory over thy enemies, nor thanked God for His benefits.*

CHAPTER XIII.

How to Govern our Sensuality.

Keep thy heart disengaged from earthly creatures.

1. Thy sensuality, O dearly beloved, is the ordinary gate whereby the devil enters into thee.† Let it be therefore thy chief care so to keep and curb it, that it may rather be a door always open to let in the Lord God to thy soul. Therefore, in all thy commerce with earthly creatures, be sure to have thy heart free and disengaged from them, and often elevating the eye of thy affection to thy God, look upon Him hidden in that creature as in His own work.‡

* So also Thaulerus:—'Believe every day lost in which you have not resisted your own will for the love of God.' *Epist.* viii.

† Between love and concupiscence some put this difference:—1. That concupiscence aimeth at a supposed good that is absent; but love both at the absent and present. 2. Concupiscence, after the having and enjoying the thing desired, as being satisfied, groweth cold, or ceaseth for the present to desire; whereas, love, by possessing and enjoying, increaseth, and is more ardent towards the thing beloved. For, the possession or enjoyment of the thing beloved, serveth as fuel to continue and increase the flame or fire; whereas things desired by concupiscence, being enjoyed, die, and are often resolved into the smoke of disgrace, or the ashes of hate. *A Discourse of Holy Love*, p. 5.

‡ There is no method so efficacious for a religious person who desires to purify his heart of inordinate love towards creatures than to turn his eyes frequently upon Christ crucified, and to tell Him, on

Then reflect that thy same Lord's love is within thee also, and thou mayest begin to confer with Him in this sort:—'O my merciful Maker and eternal Lord God, Thou art ever present within me: Thou art more within me than I am in myself: and I, ungrateful and forgetful wretch, remember Thee not, love Thee not, honour Thee not!'

Contemplate thy Creator's greatness.

2. At other times, elevate thy thoughts to the contemplation of God's incomprehensible perfections, and rejoice in those His goods, greatness, and glories more than if they were all thine own. And be more glad that He is incomprehensible in His majesty than if He were within the reach of thy understanding and capacity.

Refer all perfection to Him the fountain.

3. And when thou remarkest any particular perfection either of grace or nature in any man or woman, as understanding, wisdom, piety, justice, and the like, lift up thyself to Him who is the

---

bended knee, with sighs, tears, and groans, that he desires to love Him with his whole heart, and Him alone, and all creatures for His sake, and in that degree only and manner in which He desires them to be loved. If, whilst thus engaged, the thought, desire, or love of some friend to whom he is over-closely attached should sensibly steal over his soul, let him turn upon it sharply and say resolutely:—'Ah, here thou art again, O foolish love, coming to interrupt my intercourse with God, and to rob Him of His due love. As long as thou entanglest my heart, so long, like a bird caught in the snare of the fowler, am I kept tied down to earth, and hindered from flying freely upwards into heaven. Away with thee, O deceitful love! Away with thee, and trouble me no more!' Then let him turn again speedily to God; and though he still feel this love lingering and lurking in his soul, let him not be disheartened thereat, but persevere in acts of the love of God, and wait with great confidence the hour when our Lord shall visit his soul in plenteous mercy, and absorb every human affection into Divine love.

bountiful bestower; and consider them not as they are in that creature, but referring them to thy Lord God, say:—'Behold these, O my God, are rivulets flowing out of Thee, the true, living, eternal, and uncreated Fountain. These are the rewards of Thy servants issuing out of the immense ocean of Thy ineffable bounty.'

From earthly beauty think of heavenly glory.

4. But when the beauty of any creature allures thee to any delight and complacency, pass presently from earthly beauty to the thought of supernal glory, and therein only take pleasure, say:—'O my God, when will the happy day come that I shall take in Thee only my whole delight!'

Mark the craft of the devil.

5. Another remedy against such-like surprises of pleasure may be:—To ponder presently with thy understanding how cunningly the devil—who only seeks to kill, or at least to wound thy soul mortally—lies lurking under this bait. When thou perceivest this, tell him boldly:—'Ah, thou cursed serpent, how craftily and covertly dost thou lie in wait to infect me with thy poison!' And then lift up thy mind towards God, saying:—'O, the goodness of my God! Be Thou eternally blessed and praised who hath discovered my hidden enemy lying in wait to destroy my soul.'

When things unpleasant befall thee, think of God's eternal decrees.

6. But in other accidents which go against the grain, and rather procure pain than pleasure, thou mayest thus exercise thyself: When something happens which is hard of digestion to thy sensuality—as heat, hunger, sickness, blows, or the like—elevate thy mind to that eternal

Will who would have it so, and even from all eternity decreed that thou shouldst suffer this or that calamity, at this very time thus grievously, and with these circumstances as thou now endurest. Therefore, full of hearty joy, say within thyself:—'Now is Thy divine will, O my eternal Lord and Love, accomplished in me, whereby Thou wouldst from all eternity that I now in this manner, measure, and number, should receive and carry this cross. And I acknowledge all this to be for Thine honour and glory, and my own soul's welfare and salvation.' And make use also of such-like thoughts upon all dismal occasions of wind, weather, and the like, which are out of man's providence, to hinder or prevent. So, when thou readest anything which tickles thy fancy, turn presently all thy delight to thy Lord God, and conclude that He infallibly is hid under those words, and now by them sweetly discovers Himself unto thee. And, in like manner, when good thoughts occur with complacency and delight, as proceeding from the reflection upon some good and virtuous action, turn thy mind suddenly to thy Lord God, and adoring Him with all possible humility and reverence, acknowledge that good to have sprung from His grace, and therefore thou gratefully returnest it to His glory.

ENLARGEMENT. The appetite seeks pleasure through the senses.

7. That thou mayest rightly study this useful science, and learn how to govern and regulate thy outward senses, it imports thee to make use of every means to that end—exactness of custody, every kind of care and diligence, and a perpetual

and never-intermitted exercise. For the appetite, which sits as captain and chief commander of our corrupted nature, is violently and inconsiderately bent on searching after worldly solaces, earthly pleasures, and outward contentments; but the appetite, being unable of itself to acquire them, makes use of the senses as its soldiers and natural instruments for apprehending objects, whose images it draws to itself and imprints on the soul. The unruly appetite then proceeds on to pleasure, which, by reason of the sympathy between it and the flesh, dilates itself through all those senses which are capable of such pleasure; and from thence is derived the common contagion which infects and corrupts both body and soul.

8. Now, if thou art truly sensible of the danger of this poison, apply speedily this antidote which The antidote. I have here prepared against it. Beware of giving up the reins to thy senses, or letting them run at random after the unruly fancy of their leading appetite, and never make use of them in things tending to mere pleasure, without any further good end, profit, or necessity; but if unawares they have broken loose, and have roamed too far abroad, either recall them back, or else so regulate and curb them that, whereas they had first basely yielded up themselves and were become wretched prisoners to vain pleasure, they may now bring home some noble spoil or other from each object, and place it as a trophy in thy soul, where she, recollected within herself, displays the banners of her

affections towards heaven in the contemplation of her Creator.

9. This thou mayest practise thus: As soon as any object is presented to one of thy outward senses, separate in thy thought the spirit which is in that creature from the creature itself, and conclude that it hath nothing of its own nature which can charm thy sense, but that all is the work of God, whose Spirit bestows invisibly this being upon it, gives it this goodness, and endues it with this beauty and with all its other prerogatives and perfections.* Then rejoice heartily that thy God is the only cause and source of so many and so great excellences, which He eminently contains in His divine essence, and whereof these are the least and lowest images.

Distinguish between the object and the spirit that is in it.

10. So, when thou findest thy sense fastened upon some creature, reduce it in thy mind to its first nothingness, looking with the interior eye of thy soul upon thy sovereign Creator there present, Who beautified it with this being; and taking pleasure in Him alone, thou mayest say:—'O divine and desirable

Be it a creature which only hath being;

* 'The spiritual man, whose eyes are open when he contemplates the external works of God, inwardly perceives how wonderful is the Maker of them; and from the fairness of those things which he is contemplating, he passes on to that Divine Beauty which is fairer than all other beauty, and from whence all beauty springs. To him who is occupied with this joyful contemplation all things are miraculous; so that in amazement he is forced to exclaim with the prophet, "How great are Thy works, O Lord! Thou hast made all things in wisdom" (Ps. ciii. 24). "Thou hast given me, O Lord, a delight in Thy doings; and in the works of Thy hands I shall rejoice" (Ps. xci. 5).' Blosius. *Canon Vitæ Spiritualis*, cap. xxviii.

Essence, how doth my heart leap for joy that Thou Alone art the Infinite Beginning of all created being!'*

11. In like manner, when thou takest notice of trees, plants, herbs, flowers, and such other things, (or hath vegetation and increase;) thy understanding will soon distinguish how they have no life of themselves, but from that quickening Spirit which falls not under the sense of thy sight; to Whom thou mayest thus break forth:—'Behold the true Life from Which, in Which, and by Which all creatures live and increase. O the lively and lovely contentment of my heart!'

12. Also beholding brute beasts, let thy spirit soar up to thy God, the free bestower of all their (or sense and feeling;) sense and motion, saying:—'O prime Mover of all

* This was the practice of all the saints, and preëminently that of St. Francis. So completely did this great saint see God in everything, that all creation was to him a mirror of God's love, and an exhortation unto praise and thanksgiving. His intense love of Jesus Christ and his extraordinary spiritual-mindedness is more touching, and overwhelms one with greater confusion, than anything I read of. 'He would preach to the birds of the air,' says F. Prior Vaughan, 'and remind them all what God had done for them. Then he would dismiss them with the sign of the cross, and they would fly away obedient to his voice. He would command the swallows which were building their nests, and twittering and circling round him, to stop and listen to his word. They remained motionless and attentive, till he dismissed them with incredible joy. He loved nature with all the tenderness of a little child. His prayer sums up his whole character. "O Most High Almighty, Good Lord God," he says, "to Thee belong praise, glory, honour, and all blessing. Praised be my Lord God, with all His creatures, and especially our brother the sun, who brings us the day, and who brings us the light. Fair is he, and shining with a very great splendour. O Lord, he signifies to us Thee.

"Praised be my Lord for our sister the moon, and for the stars, the which He has set clear in the heavens.

"Praised be my Lord for our brother the wind, and for air and

things, yet remaining in Thyself immovable, how great is my joy in Thy firm stability!'

13. Moreover, when thy sense is touched and tickled with some rare beauty, separate with all speed that which appears to the eye from the inward spirit, which appears not at all; and considering that all the outward fairness springs only from the invisible Fountain, say with a gladsome heart:—'O the jubilation of my soul when it thinks on that eternal and immense Beauty, Which is the original source and essential cause of all created comeliness!'

or is endowed with rare beauty;

14. Furthermore, upon the consideration of any perfection in creatures, still make the aforesaid separation; then break forth into these expressions:—'O rich Treasury of all virtues, what contentment do I feel that all good is derived from Thee and by Thee

or excellent perfection.

clouds, calm, and all weather, by the which Thou upholdest in life all creatures.

"Praised be my Lord for our sister the water, who is very serviceable unto us, and humble and precious and clean.

"Praised be my Lord for our brother the fire, through whom Thou givest us light in darkness; and he is bright and pleasant, and very mighty and strong.

"Praised be my Lord for our mother the earth, which doth sustain us and keep us, and bringeth forth divers fruits and flowers of many colours and grass.

"Praised be my Lord for all those who pardon one another for His love's sake, and who endure weakness and tribulation. Blessed are they who peaceably shall endure; for Thou, O Most Highest, shalt give them a crown.

"Praised be my Lord for our sister the death of the body: from whom no man escapeth. Woe to him who dieth in mortal sin! Blessed are they who are found walking by Thy most holy will, for the second death shall have no power to do them harm.

"Praise ye and bless ye the Lord, and give thanks to him, and serve him with great humility."' *Life and Labours of St. Thomas of Aquin*, vol. i. p. 81.

only, and that all goodness compared to Thy divine perfection is a mere nothing!'

15. Stretching forth thy hand to any action, imagine thy Lord God to be the first Cause thereof, and thou only the living instrument of His divine Majesty, to Whom thy soul may thus pour forth itself:—'O Sovereign Lord of this universe, how truly do I rejoice that I can do no one thing without Thee, and that Thou art the prime and principal Agent in all good actions!'

Also when thou undertakest any action;

16. Taking any refection of meat or drink, reflect Who gives it that gust and savour, and taking no other content than in Him only, say:—'Be joyful, O my soul, that there is no true satisfaction out of thy God, and that in Him only thou hast a full abundance of all pleasure.'

or refreshest thy body;

17. If some delicious smell be welcome to thy sense, stay not there, but ascend to Him Who is the source of all sweetness, and with a heart softened with comfort, say:—'Alas, O my Lord, as I am truly glad that all sweetness proceeds from Thee, so grant, I beseech Thee, that my soul, being truly despoiled and bared of all earthly pleasure, may purely soar up to Thy delicious Paradise, and render unto Thee a perpetually pleasing odour.'

or smellest sweet odours;

18. When thou art taken with the musical harmony of some excellent voice or instrument, turn thy soul to thy Saviour and speak to Him:—'O my Lord and my God, how do I joy in Thy infinite

or are charmed with music.

perfections! O what an admirable harmony do they make, not only in Thyself, but also in the heavenly citizens, and in all Thy other creatures!'* Thus mayest thou, my dearly beloved, raise up thy spirit from all sensible objects to the contemplation of the Divinity, as hath been hitherto declared.

How to raise up thy soul by the same objects to contemplate the Word Incarnate.

19. It remains that thou be now in like manner instructed how to pass from the same sensible objects to the meditation of the Word Incarnate, by frequent reflections upon thy Saviour's Life and Passion. And to this effect all things of the whole universe will conduce, by considering in them—as before—that Sovereign and Supreme Good Who is the efficient Cause of their whole being and

* It is related of St. Ansbertus, a monk and bishop of Rouen, that hearing on a certain occasion a choir of voices and instrumental music, he cried out in divine rapture, 'O glorious Creator, what will it be to hear that song of the angels who love Thee, which is to sound for ever in the celestial courts! How sweet and admirable will be that chorus of saints, since Thou ordainest that even the sounds of a mortal voice, and the skill of human instruments, should be able to excite the minds of the hearers to praise Thee devoutly, O Lord, their God and Creator.' St. Adalhard, Abbot of Corby, continually preserved such recollection of mind, and had his spirit and conversation so completely in heaven, that whenever he heard any sweet melody he was unable to refrain from tears, all music seeming to remind him of the sweetness of celestial harmony. *Vita St. Adal. Mabillon, Acta St. Ord. Bened.* § iv. St. John Climacus, writing for the instruction of those who are aspiring to perfection, says: 'They who love God are excited by secular and spiritual songs and melody to joy and divine love, and to tears, although they who are addicted to pleasure may gather from them matter of perdition for themselves. *Grad.* xv. And St. Chrysostom, in the same spirit, maintains that 'Nothing so exalts the mind, and gives it as it were wings, so delivers it from the earth, and loosens it from the bonds of the body, so inspires it with the love of wisdom, and fills it with such disdain for the things of this life, as the melody of verses and the sweetness of holy song.' *Hom. in Ps.* xli.

beauty; and thence passing on to the admiration of His immense goodness and greatness, Who being the absolute Lord of all these things would vouchsafe to descend so low as to become man and die for man, permitting His own creatures to arm themselves against Him their Creator. Many things will also particularly represent to the eyes of thy soul these sacred mysteries, and put thee in mind of the several instruments of His severe sufferings. *Poor cottages* will remind thee of thy Saviour's stable and crib. If it *raineth*, thou wilt reflect on that divine moisture, distilling from His Body in His bloody agony. The *stones* which thou beholdest will put thee in mind of the rocks rending asunder at His Death. The *earth* will seem to tell thee how it then trembled; and the bright shining *sun*, how its light was then obscured. If thou considerest the *water*, thou wilt fall into contemplation of that which issued out of His open side; and the like of all other objects. So, when thou tastest *wine*, thou mayest think of Christ's vinegar and gall: when sweet *odours* delight thee, how ill-savoured were the carcases upon Mount Calvary, where thy Saviour suffered. *Clothing* thyself, reflect how the Eternal Word put on our humanity to adorn thee with His Divinity: *unclothing* thyself, how He, naked, was nailed to the Cross. *Hearing a noise* or the acclamations of the people, remember those abominable outcries: *Away with Him, away with Him, crucify Him!** When the *clock strikes* the hour, think how

* John xix. 15.

thy Saviour's heart panted in the Garden at the apprehension of His approaching Passion; or seem to hear and count the cruel strokes of the scourges, or the blows of the hammer fastening the nails through the body to the Cross. *If sadness and sorrow seize* thee, whether by reason of thine own sufferings and sickness, or out of compassion for others, conceive, alas! how little is all this compared to the incomprehensible anguishes, distresses, and dolours which pierced the body and soul of thy dear Saviour.

Other ways to meditate upon sensible objects:

20. Having thus showed the way how to elevate thy understanding by means of all sensible things to the Divinity and to the mysteries of the Word Incarnate, I will now add other means and methods of meditation drawn from the same sensible objects; that as the soul's gusts are various, so the spiritual diet may be diversely dressed and served up for their sustenance. This variety may also be very useful, not only to the simple, but even to elevated souls well advanced in the way of the Spirit, which are not always equally disposed to sublime contemplations. Neither needest thou fear that this variety will in any way perplex thee, if thou art governed by the rule of discretion and the direction of thy ghostly father, whom thou art carefully and humbly to follow, not only in this, but in all thy other undertakings.

By considering how mean the best of them

21. When, therefore, objects most pleasing to the eye, delicious to the sense, and desirable to the flesh and blood shall be represented unto thee,

mark well how mean these things are in them- are in themselves; selves, though never so highly courted and cherished, extolled and esteemed by worldlings; how the best of them is no better than dirt and dung in respect of heavenly happiness, for which thou art designed, which thou desirest, and to which thou aspirest.

22. When thou gazest on the sun's glorious splendour, know for certain that thine own soul is as the sun's brightness; far more bright and beautiful than it, if she be in her Creator's grace and favour; otherwise she is more obscure and abominable than darkness and dismal hell itself.

23. When thou callest up thy corporeal eyes to the heavens, elevate those of thy soul to those the heaven's greatness; higher and holier mansions of the blessed saints and angelical spirits, and there fix and feast thy thoughts as in the happy mansion prepared for thy eternal abode.

24. When thou hearkenest to the birds' warbling notes, or other musical charms, soar up in the birds' melody; spirit to the sweet harmony of heaven, where alleluias do for ever resound, and beg of thy dear Lord that thou mayest become worthy to chant forth His perpetual praises amongst those heavenly choirs.

25. When thou walkest on the way, ponder how each one of thy paces is a step towards thy when walking; death.

26. When thou markest the fowls of the air, how swiftly they glide through the yielding element, marking the

flight of the birds; and the running waters hastening to their original ocean, think how thy life slips away and thy soul runs on to eternity with still greater speed and celerity.

27. When impetuous winds are raised, or thunder

in time of storms; and lightning rage in the sky, remember the fearful day of judgment, and prostrating thyself at the foot of the crucifix, adore thy Saviour and implore His gracious assistance that thou mayest now make such good use of the time He lends thee, that thou mayest be then prepared to appear courageously before His dread Majesty.

28. As concerning divers accidents which are per-

in sorrow; sonal and peculiar to thyself, thou mayest thus behave thee: When grief or sadness hath seized thy heart, when melancholy oppresseth thy mind, or when any ailment troubles thy body, raise up and resign thy spirit to the supreme and eternal Will of God, Who is pleased that this molestation should even now and thus touch and torment thee for thy good and His own glory, and be glad of this occasion to serve Him according to His own decree and disposition.

29. When thou castest thine eyes upon Christ's sa-

when thou lookest on Christ crucified; cred Cross, consider it as the banner of thy warfare, from under which thou mayest not step aside without imminent danger of being surprised by thy sworn enemies; but following it closely and valiantly, thou hast certain hope to conquer them and climb up to heaven, laden with their glorious spoils and trophies.

30. When thou seest the image representing the holy Virgin Mother, turn thy heart towards her now reigning in Paradise, and give her thanks for having been ever ready to perform the divine Will; for bearing and bringing up the Redeemer of the world,* and for never denying her favour and succour to thee and all spiritual combatants humbly imploring it.† or on the image of the B. Virgin;

31. So let the pictures of saints seem as so many representatives of stout champions and soldiers, who by their courage and conquests have made thee a free and safe passage to follow them, imitate them, conquer with them, and be crowned with them in eternal glory. and pictures of saints;

32. Let the churches which thou frequentest put thee in mind that thy soul is God's temple, and should therefore be kept most pure and prepared most perfectly for His coming. or enterest churches.

33. Finally, let each creature, all objects, and every accident be so spiritualised and distilled by thy understanding from their earthly and material dross, that they may serve thee as true Make *all* things instruments to thy perfection.

* All that we can say in praise of the Blessed Virgin falls short of what St. Matthew expresses in the words, *De qua natus est Jesus qui vocatur Christus.* The divine maternity of our Lady being the fountain and principle of her other prerogatives is that which commends her intercession so powerfully to the reason and heart of the children of the Church. Do you wish to inflame your devotion towards her? Meditate daily and more frequently upon this than upon all her other privileges—that Christ is God, and that Mary is His Mother. 'Run through all creation in your thought,' says Proclus, 'and see if there be one equal or superior to the Holy Virgin, Mother of God.'

instruments to the perfection of thy soul, and become powerful helps to thee—contrary to thine enemies' intention—in thy progress to divine union, which is the only end thou aimest at.

34. And because the tongue hath a near affinity with our senses—for we willingly discourse of those things wherein we take delight—I will here, before I descend to the following doctrine, briefly show thee how thou art to regulate, bridle, and master this unruly member. Much prattling proceeds ordinarily from a certain presumption, which persuades us that we are very knowing in the things we talk of; and so, priding ourselves on our own conceptions, we endeavour to imprint them in the hearts of our hearers, with superfluous repetitions and replications of the same subject, to appear thereby more masters of reason than others, and as if they stood in need of our instruction.* Few words cannot express the evil which ensues upon overmuch talking.† For it is the parent of idleness,

Much talk proceeds from presumption;

* '*Much and willing speaking* is the effect of tepidity, self-love, and pride. For commonly it flows from an opinion that we can speak well, and consequently out of a desire of gaining estimation from others by showing our wits and abilities. But such intentions and designs as these the disciples of true humility and spirituality will abhor. It is very requisite for an *internal liver*, therefore, at least to observe that moderate and qualified silence required in his community; not transgressing either in the appointed places or at the determinate times in which speaking is forbidden.' *Sancta Sophia*, 1657, vol. i. p. 294.

† We read in the *Vitæ Patrum* that on one occasion when some juniors were talking to one of the ancient Fathers and praising loudly certain of the brethren who were noted for being great prattlers, the holy man replied:—'Good indeed they are, but their dwelling hath no gate; their mouth is always open; and whoever will may go in and lead forth their ass, that is, their unwise soul.'

an argument of ignorance, the door of detraction, the instrument of falsehood, and the blaster of all true devotion and spiritual fervour.*

35. Wherefore I advise thee, in the first place, not to indulge thyself in long discourses before unwilling hearers, which is to break the laws of civility; nor yet before them who are willing to hearken thee, lest thou exceed the bounds of moderation.

therefore avoid long conversations,

* It will be well sometimes to ponder upon the following salutary *Maxims* of St. Teresa, and to examine ourselves as to how we have observed them:

'2. Speak well of all that is spiritual, such as religious, priests, and hermits.'—And I may add, be careful to speak well of *all* religious Orders. If one be more prominent and powerful than another, rejoice and give thanks that it has been found worthy to be chosen as a special instrument in promoting God's honour and glory. To feel a grudge at another's success is jealousy, and a sign of self-love and of great imperfection.

'3. Let thy words be few when in the midst of many.

'4. Be modest in all thy words and works.

'5. Never be obstinate, especially in things of no moment.

'6. In speaking to others be always calm and cheerful.

'8. Never rebuke any one but with discretion and humility and self-abasement.

'9. Bend thyself to the temper of whosoever is speaking to thee: be merry with the mirthful, sorrowful with the sad. In a word, make thyself all things to all, to gain all.

'10. Never say anything thou hast not well considered and earnestly commended to our Lord, that nothing may be spoken which shall be displeasing to Him.

'11. Never defend thyself unless there be very good reasons for it.

'12. Never mention anything concerning thyself which men account praiseworthy, such as learning, goodness, birth, unless with the hope of doing good thereby, and then let it be done with humility, remembering that these are gifts of God.

'13. Never exaggerate, but utter thy mind in simplicity.

'14. In all talking and conversation, let *something* be always said of spiritual things, and so shall all idle words and evil speaking be avoided.

'15. Never assert anything without first being assured of it.

36. Avoid also all pathetic and passionate expressions and an over-high elevation of voice; for both these are generally odious to the hearers, and are always arguments of thine own vanity and presumption.*

and passionate expressions,

37. Speak not at all of thyself, of thine own affairs, of thy parentage or kindred, unless in case of evident necessity, and then also with all possible brevity, simplicity, sincerity, and modesty.† And if another seem to overbound in such speeches concerning himself, be thou edified thereat, but imitate him not, though his words tend to his self-abjection and accusation.

and all talking of thyself

38. Discourse not of thy neighbour, nor of anything concerning him,‡ unless a just occasion urge thee to defend him, or speak well of him.

and of thy neighbour;

39. Show a willingness to talk always of God, and particularly of His love and liberality, yet still with profound reverence, lest even here thou

but speak willingly of God,

'16. Never come forward to give thine opinion about anything unless asked to do so, or charity requires it.

'17. When any one is speaking of spiritual things, do thou listen humbly and like a learner, and take to thyself the good that is spoken.

'44. Do not compare one person with another; it is a hateful thing to do.' *The Foundations*, p. 347, Lewis.

* So also our Blessed Father St. Benedict in his holy Rule: 'The eleventh degree of humility is, that when the monk speaketh, he speak gently and without laughter, humbly and gravely, few words and sensible ones, and that he be not boisterous in his speech—*non sit clamosus in voce*—as it is written, *A wise man is known by the fewness of his words.*' *Regula St. Benedicti*, cap. vii.

† See above, *Maxim* 12.

‡ See above, *Maxim* 44.

'When prudence and charity require of us to speak, we must be

slip and fall; and therefore take more content to hear others discourse than to talk thyself;* and preserve in the cabin of thy heart what good words are delivered.

40. As for all other discourses, let only the sound strike thy ears, but keep thy mind fixed upon thy God. And if thou needs must lend an ear because thy answer is expected, yet let thy soul's eye glance up to heaven, where thy Lord and Love is, and first examine briefly in thy heart what thou intendest thy tongue should utter, whereby thou wilt quickly resolve whether speech or silence be now more to the purpose.†

and ponder in thy heart what thy tongue is to utter.

very careful not to make the *imperfections* of *others* any part of the matter of our discourse; and especially not the imperfections of those for whom in our natures we seem to have an aversion. And principally we must take heed of speaking or doing anything to breed a dislike between any. Therefore all *secret informings* and accusations are most carefully to be avoided, as the ruin of Christian charity in communities. . . . The effects of it are the breeding of discontents generally in all, and the greatest mischief to the souls of private uncharitable informers. *St. Sophia*, vol. i. p. 295.

* See above, *Maxim* 17.

† Let no one imagine that our author condemns or disparages innocent recreations as destroying or hindering spiritual perfection. The devil sometimes fixes an idea of this kind into the mind of timid, scrupulous, and indiscreet persons, in order to disquiet their souls, to nourish pride, and bring about their spiritual ruin. The natural weakness and infirmity of the body is such, that relaxation is not only profitable, but also necessary, since without it the mind would soon lose its vigour and grasp, and become incapable of divine thoughts. This we find borne out by the practice of the saints. The Fathers of the Desert and the greatest Contemplatives were accustomed to have appointed hours for relaxation and conversation; for the soul cannot remain lifted up above itself beyond a certain time, but at length becomes exhausted and returns again to its ordinary state and condition. St. Teresa, speaking of the prayer of Union, says that a soul is 'never, in my opinion, *a full half-hour* immersed in the greatness of God, and united closely to Him' (*Interior Castle*, p. 105). In her *Constitutions*,

41. Lastly, thou wilt find by experience, my dearly beloved, that silence is an excellent and useful weapon for thy spiritual combat, giving courage to fight, constancy to continue, and confidence to overcome. It is the sure friend of him who distrusts himself and trusts in his God; it conserves us in devotion, and comforts us in the exercises of our duty. And surely the bare consideration of the disasters caused by inconsiderate talking is a sufficient motive to make us in love with silence; to which, that thou mayest habituate thyself, make frequent use of solitude, and retirement from fruitless company and frivolous conversation; whereby, instead of men, thou shalt have angels,

The praise and profit of silence.

this most discreet and glorious saint prescribes certain times and hours for the recreation of her nuns, and then adds: 'Let them be all together at recreation, for *this is time well spent.* Let them strive not to be wearisome one to another, though their words and merry sayings must be in discretion.' To attempt to lay down any rule according to which we could on all occasions regulate the exact measure of our 'words and merry sayings,' is impossible. The best guide on this point will be the instinct of religious sense, which in a soul that truly seeks God will never err or lead astray.

Whilst a monk should sedulously observe the rules of religious decorum during the hours of recreation, and shun all levity either of word or deed, he should at the same time carefully avoid oppressing his soul by the practice of a host of little self-imposed rules and maxims, which deject the mind, defeat the holy object of the prescribed recreations, and for the most part create a morose and pharisaical spirit. All such multiplicity is antagonistic to the sweet simplicity and joyful freedom of the Spirit of God; it straitens, cramps, and fetters the soul, gives rise to a thousand scruples and anxieties, and when performed without perfect purity of intention, engenders pride, vanity, and self-elation. F. Baker, in his chapter on *Silence*, gives some very sound advice respecting the manner, matter, and conditions of recreative exercises, which I think it will be found useful to quote at length:—

'It will be difficult to prescribe any set order or manner for the

saints, and God Himself for thy companions and comforters. Finally, reflect upon the conflict which thou hast undertaken, and, considering how much thou hast to do, thou wilt find little leisure to spend in idle talk.

---

talk, as not to speak unasked, not to exceed such or such a limitation of words, &c.; to omit many particular cautions which at other times are to be observed. Here some more freedom must be allowed, so it go not too far.

'Among women there can scarce be any recreation if the tongue be too much stinted. Neither is it to be expected that their talk should be *of spiritual matters;* both because such talk is far from being recreative, as likewise because none but expert persons ought to discourse of such subjects. Indeed, to make such the subject of ordinary discourse even between the most able experienced persons, either men or women, is not convenient at all, except some special occasion makes it expedient. For it usually proceeds from pride, or a willingness to interest oneself in the guiding of the consciences of others, and may produce inconvenient effects in both.'

'*The matter and conditions of recreative discourse*, therefore, may be, 1. That the matter do not particularly refer to the interior of any of the parties. But if it regard a religious state, that it be about less considerable external matters, as ceremonies, customs, &c. 2. That it may be something that may be apt to cause cheerfulness, though not (boisterous) laughter, which our holy Father would have banished from his communities. Now, discourses about such matters are not to be reputed *idle words.* 3. It were better to talk of the occurrences of former times than of the present, because our Holy Father forbids the inquiring or telling of news in the world, for fear lest the hearers, being interested, may become distracted with solicitudes. 4. It must not therefore be of anything that probably will leave in the mind any hurtful images. 5. The hearer is not to suffer the subject of the discourses to enter so deep into his mind as that it should raise any passions there. 6. It must by no means be of anything by which any one present or absent may be prejudiced or contristated, nor, indeed, afterwards distracted.' *Sancta Sophia*, vol. i. p. 298.

CHAPTER XIV.

Of the Order to be Observed in Fighting against our Enemies.

Mark which are thy greatest enemies.

1. In thy spiritual combat against thy disordered affections and passions, follow this method: *First*, enter into the cabinet of thy heart, and let thy inquisitive thoughts search and examine with exact diligence which be the affections that there bear the greatest sway, and with what thoughts and motions thou art most frequently tempted and troubled.

Single out the fiercest to fight with.

2. *Secondly*, and having found thy foes, turn thy weapons against that single enemy which then actually molests thee, most nearly endangers thee, and is now ready to grapple with thee, oppress thee, and ruin thee.

But when they appear not, seek them out.

3. *Thirdly*, but in time of peace with thy passions, when no enemy appears in the field to provoke thee to battle, begin thou with them, and make thy strongest onset on those which have chiefly wounded thee, most frequently foiled thee, and wrought thy greatest confusion before thy Lord God.*

CHAPTER XV.

What Course he must take who is Conquered and grievously Wounded by his Enemies.

When thou art

1. If thou chance to fall into some vice, either through frailty or weakness, or through wicked-

* See chap. vii. § 6.

ness and wilful malice, turn thee with all speed to God, and first reflect upon thine own baseness, and heartily hate thyself. Then gathering up courage, and converting thyself again to thy Creator, confess to Him thy ingratitude, and say with an inflamed heart: 'O my Lord, behold, I have acted just like myself. For what better could be expected from me than baseness, fallings, and sinfulness? I am sorry, O my God, with my whole heart, and I confess I should have done far worse and fallen more grievously had not the hand of Thy goodness kept me, stayed me, and upheld me; for which I render Thee most humble thanks. And now, O my loving Lord, do Thou like Thyself, according to the treasures of Thy mercies, and let me not live out of Thy grace, nor ever offend again Thy most sacred Majesty.'

fallen, rise with speed and pray fervently.

2. Having thus sincerely poured forth thy heart in the presence of God, be not solicitous and thoughtful whether He hath forgiven this thy sin or no; for such a curiosity savours of pride, endangers thee to fall into the snare of Satan, renders thee unquiet, and consumes time to little purpose. Therefore, cast thyself purely into the paternal bosom of thy merciful Lord, resume thy wonted exercises, and take up thy weapons again as though thou hadst not fallen. Yea, shouldst thou chance to fall many times a day, and receive many grievous wounds from thy enemies, yet never despair, never grow faint-hearted or over-fearful of thyself, but still stand

Be not over-solicitous or fearful,

upon thy accustomed guards against all new assaults, and do the same things with no less confidence the second, third, fourth time, and as often as thy need shall require, as thou didst at the first.*

* Let the pusillanimous and desponding frequently read over with a devout mind this beautiful passage of our author, and take heart. The following words of the holy Abbot Blosius will also afford a fruitful source of encouragement:

'Be always solicitous lest thou offend God by sin. But yet if thou hast sinned, distrust not His mercy. However many and erroneous may have been thy sins, thou shouldst never despair of pardon. Hast thou fallen? Arise, turn to the Physician of thy soul, and the bowels of His pity will be open to thee. Hast thou fallen again? Again arise, groan and cry out; and the mercy of thy Redeemer will receive thee. Hast thou fallen three, four times, yea oftener? Arise again, weep, sigh, humble thyself; and thy God will not desert thee. He never has despised, nor will He ever despise a contrite heart (Ps. l. 19). He never has rejected and never will reject those who fly to Him in true repentance. If thou cease not to arise, He will not cease to receive thee. Wherefore, if thou shalt have fallen a hundred, yea even a thousand times, within the space of one short hour, do thou arise as many times as thou hast fallen, with the holy hope of pardon; and arising, give thanks to thy Lord, Who has not permitted thee to fall more grievously, or to lie longer in perdition. And even if, after receiving innumerable gifts of grace, thou hast denied thy God (though far be it from thee), and hast trodden under foot His sacraments, do thou humbly acknowledge thy guilt, detest thy wickedness, heartily determine to sin no more, firmly resolve to lead a better life, and feel secure of pardon. For thy malice or thy infirmity cannot be so great as to surpass the mercy of God, which knows neither measure nor limit. God is omnipotent; He remits in one moment innumerable myriads of sins with the same facility as one single sin. He is most gracious; He is most willing to spare thee, to be propitious to thee, if thou wilt humble thyself, if thou wilt abstain from sin, and amend thy life. Therefore let not the memory of past sins disturb thee; but let these words of the Apostle console thee: "*And such some of you were; but you are washed, but you are sanctified, but you are justified in the name of our Lord Jesus Christ and in the Spirit of our God*" (1 Cor. vi. 2). Thou canst not put too much confidence in His goodness, if only thou dost not abuse it by sinning more easily.' *Canon Vitæ Spiritualis*, cap. i.

but use violence to thy own inclinations.

3. This kind of practice by so much the more displeaseth the devil by how much he well knoweth it is highly pleasing to God; and for this reason he moves all his engines to make us tepid and slack in making use of it. Do thou therefore use violence to thyself. And the more difficulty thou findest, by so much the more redouble thy diligence in doing it; and esteem it not a thing over-irksome to renew it divers times in one and the same fall. And if after the first, next, and third relapse thou feelest a grievous trouble, confusion, and diffidence in thyself, yet still endeavour, by all means, to recover the inward quiet of thy soul; and then reconcile thyself to thy loving Lord. For that disquietness of conscience remaining after the sin committed is not any sign of sorrow for having offended thy Saviour, but rather of fear for thy own private damnation, which thou hast thereby deserved.

The way to recover quiet of mind.

4. Now the way to recover this quiet of mind may be this:—Having turned thyself to thy God, and humbly craved pardon for thy sin, think no more of it, but forget it totally for the future; and fix thy thoughts only upon thy Lord's infinite love, by which He earnestly desires to unite thee to Himself, and make thee partaker of His eternal beatitude. And when by this, or the like considerations, thou hast settled thy mind and fixed thy heart in tranquillity, turn thy thoughts again to contemplate thy fall, and do as thou wert directed in the beginning of this chap-

ter. And when thou goest to confession—as thou shouldst frequently do—recall all thy falls and defects into thy memory, discovering them faithfully, and confessing them simply to thy ghostly father.

ENLARGEMENT. No accident can justly deprive us of quiet.

5. As when we have lost the quiet of our heart, we are to use all possible endeavours to recover it—as aforesaid—so thou must know that no accident whatsoever can, with any just reason, deprive us of the same. For it is most true—and thou hast been often told it*—that we must be angry with ourselves for our sins, yet our grief must be governed with discretion and accompanied with tranquillity, and our sorrow must produce acts and resolutions of amendment of our lives, not of disquiet and anxiety in ourselves. As for other painful and unpleasing accidents, as the sickness, death,† yea, and the eternal damnation of our dear friends, or the scourges of plague, famine, war, sackagings, burnings, and other evils falling upon ourselves; though, as they are things contrary to our

* See chap. iii. § 5; vii. § 6; xv. § 1.

† 'You must remember,' says St. Teresa, 'that there are pains directly produced by nature and by charity which move us to compassionate our neighbours, just as our Lord felt when He raised Lazarus. Our being united with God's will does not remove these sorrows, though they do not disturb the soul with a restless distressing passion. They quickly pass away; for, as I mentioned when speaking of the delights in prayer, they do not reach the interior part of the soul, but only the senses and faculties.' And a little farther on she says: 'Think not that if my father or brother should die, the matter consists in conforming myself to God's will in such a way as *not to feel* their death; or if sickness and troubles come, that I must bear them *cheerfully*. This disposition is good, and sometimes it arises from a certain discretion, because, as we cannot remedy the matter, we make a virtue of necessity.' *Interior Castle*, pp. 112, 114.

nature, we must needs reject them, yet we may, by the efficacious workings of God's grace, not only desire them, but even be delighted with them,* as being the just punishments of the wicked and exercises of virtue to the good, for which ends our loving Lord permits them to befall us.

6. Thus conforming ourselves to God's holy will, we may quietly and peaceably pass through the midst of all this life's bitternesses and contrarieties; and take this for a truth, that all disquiet of mind is displeasing to our dear Lord, because it is never without some imperfection, and evermore proceeds from some perverse root of self-love.†

Disquiet of mind is never without some imperfection.

CHAPTER XVI.

That we should Keep our Hearts ever Quiet and Joyful in the Lord.

1. To obtain quiet of heart in thy spiritual conflict,‡ thou must, O dearly beloved, appoint over thy-

To obtain quiet ap-

* Though it is never right to desire or rejoice at the misfortune, death, or damnation of any person, nevertheless it is lawful to rejoice when the justice and power of God is satisfied in the punishment of the wicked, and rendered glorious and adorable in the sight of men. It is in this sense that the words of our author are to be understood.

† Oh! if our hearts and desires were fixed upon God alone, then nothing would distress our minds nor disturb our tranquillity. He to whom all things are One, who aspires and longs after only One, who seeks only One, who finds no delight but in One, and who turns every trial into a means of drawing nearer and nearer unto One, such a man is securely established in peace, and cannot be moved by any accident whatsoever.

‡ 'He will never attain to perfection who will not labour to be

point a sentinel. self a faithful scout-watch, which, as soon as it discovers anything tending to thy trouble and disquiet, may suddenly shoot off the warning piece, that thou mayest timely betake thee to thy weapons for thy defence.

If taken by surprise, speedily quiet thy heart.

2. And if it falls out—as too often it doth—that through some sudden assault thou art grievously perplexed, presently setting all other things aside, pacify thy interior, and endeavour to regain a quiet and joyful heart. For this being done, thou wilt be better enabled to prosecute other affairs, which will take small effect so long as thy mind is troubled and unquiet. Besides, the enemy draws from thence an occasion to tempt thee more violently; for he fears this sacred quiet and peace of the soul, as God's tabernacle wherein He works His wonders,* and therefore he shadows his wiles with the show of good that he may the more deceive us, exciting in us sundry pious affections and holy desires, the cunning whereof

satisfied with this: that all his natural and spiritual desires should be satisfied in the absence of everything which is not God. This is most necessary for an abiding peace and tranquillity of spirit.' *St. John of the Cross*, vol. ii. p. 387. And again: 'If we forget all created things, there is then nothing to disturb our peace, nothing to excite our desires. These are they that disturb it; for, as the proverb says, "What the eye hath not seen the heart does not desire,"' p. 358. And the *Following of Christ*: 'Forsake all, and thou shalt find all; leave thy desires, and thou shalt have rest.' B. iii. chap. xxxii.; also see b. i. cap. vi.

* 'God reigns only in the peaceful and unselfish soul.' *St. John of the Cross*, p. 358.—It was in the retirement of her chamber when in prayer that the angel visited our Lady:—'Ave, Maria, gratiâ plena; Dominus tecum!' St. Arsenius, when praying to know the surest way to possess God, heard a voice from heaven, 'Arseni, fuge, tace, quiesce!'

is discovered by their fruits and effects, which is the bereaving our hearts of all their joy and content.

3. So soon, therefore, as thou hast understood by thy scout-watches signs of some new affection which demands admittance into thy heart, beware of opening unto it before thou hast blunted the edge of thy desire thereof;* and make an humble offering of it to God, with an acknowledgment of thine own ignorance and blindness, whereby thou art incapable—without the light of His heavenly grace, which thou now implorest—to judge of this good motion, and to determine whether it comes from His glorious majesty or from some earthly cause and consideration.

Admit no new affection before thou hast offered it to God,

4. And be ever mindful of mortifying the too great eagerness of thy nature before thou adventure upon any good desires, though sent from God Himself. For such works as are entered upon after self-mortification are more grateful unto Him than those which are done following the desires of thy greedy nature. And this mortification of thy will doth generally better please Him than the work itself.

and mortified thy will and desire;

5. Thus driving out vain and vicious affections, and not rashly admitting of the good, till first thy own nature, with all her passions, desires, and

which is the surest way to remain in peace.

* 'All the duties of mortification, and consequently the exercise of all virtues, may be reduced to *custodia cordis;* which is a wary guard of our heart, and it consists in not pouring forth our affections inordinately upon creatures, not admitting into our souls any inordinate love. It is a chariness over our interior, to keep it in as much quietness as we can.' *Sancta Sophia*, vol. i. p. 305.

natural impulses be stilled and mortified, thou mayest be sure to remain in peace, and to keep the bulwarks of thy heart in perpetual security from all thy foes without, and from self-reproaches and feelings of remorse within. These sad feelings of conscience, though they seem very good and to come from God, because they convict thee of some defect, yet they are sometimes suggested by the devil. But the only way to know their offspring is to examine their effects. For if such self-reproaches keep thee humble and quiet, and spur on thy diligence to good works without lessening thy pious confidence in God, then receive them as inspired by Him, Who thus knocks at the inner door of thy heart to teach thee self-knowledge. But if they make thee unquiet, pusillanimous, unapt to good works and diffident of God—especially at the time when thou feelest these interior reproaches and afflictions in thyself—conclude as a certain truth that they come not from thy Creator, but are suggested by the deceiver. Therefore hearken not to them, but persist merrily in thy devout and accustomed exercises, as if thou didst not at all feel any such suggestions.

CHAPTER XVII.

That Pious Purposes are sometimes the Deceits of the Devil to Hinder our Progress in Virtues.

1. Besides these hitherto discovered deceits of the devil, this yet remains, to wit: A holy purpose

The devil urges fight

and earnest desire to fight afresh against our former sins, which the devil suggests unto us, that our minds, being taken up with this employment, may forget their daily and more dangerous enemies, and wage no war against them. But he that will take due care of his own spiritual safety, must, in the first place, fall to work with his next neighbouring vices, and set them further off. For through the neglect of this we fall into many miseries, as they must needs do who are still suffering from fresh wounds, and yet think not of seeking for any salves to cure them.

against past sins to make us neglect present ones.

2. Because we esteem these purposes as real performances, we fall into self-complacency and secret pride;* and though we cannot digest a hard word, much less blows, yet we devote ourselves to high contemplations, and there we can make resolutions to endure patiently and purely for God's love all the pains of Purgatory. And because our inferior will or sensuality feels nothing in itself that troubles or grieves it, but looks only upon such calamities as are to come hereafter, we very foolishly and rashly pride ourselves to be of those who are perfectly patient, and imagine that we actually suffer many great matters for God's sake.

Thus we fall into self-complacency.

* 'Let us endeavour to know ourselves in *small things*, and not take much notice of those very great distractions, which come crowding upon us in the time of prayer, such as what we should wish to do for our neighbours, and even for the salvation of one soul; *and if actions do not follow conformable to these desires, we have no reason to think we shall perform them.* I say the same respecting humility, and all other virtues.' *In. Castle*, p. 115. Work, and don't sentimentalise.

3. Wherefore, O my beloved, that thou mayest avoid this deceit, resolve not only in thy mind, but buckle thyself actually to fight with thy nearest foes, which thou findest most troublesome, and which oppose thee most strongly. Thus thou shalt plainly perceive whether thy purposes be true or false, strong or weak. But I may not advise thee to wage war against those enemies which now trouble not thy quiet, unless thou plainly foresee that they are ready to assault thee. Then thou mayest lawfully and profitably fight them before they fall on thee, that so thou mayest have the more strength and courage at the time of the battle. Yet persuade not thyself that by this foregoing skirmish with thy enemies thou hast already vanquished them, unless thou hast been for a long time exercised and versed in the acts of that virtue. In which case thou mayest resolve to fight against past grievous sins, though thou canst not yet conquer some less defects; the Divine Providence so permitting this to preserve thee in the humble acknowledgment of thy own weakness.

Therefore fight with thy actual foes.

4. But whosoever is careless in overcoming small defects, and yet thinks he can easily vanquish the greatest, is notoriously vain and presumptuous, and even already falling into the snare of the devil.*

Be not careless of small defects.

* ' "Whoso despiseth small things shall fall by little things;" and "He that is faithful in that which is least, is faithful also in much; and he that is unjust in the least is unjust also in much." Carelessness in trifles leads to grievous falls, and our faithfulness in small

5. I advise thee here, my dearly beloved, to take special note of three principal occasions which render our designs fruitless, and defraud our pious resolutions of their desired and expected effect. And this doctrine will teach thee how to make good resolutions as thou oughtest.

ENLARGEMENT. Three things make our resolutions fruitless:

6. The *first* occasion—which was already touched upon briefly in the foregoing chapter—is: that we usually purpose to do a good action, or to avoid the doing of an evil one, trusting more to our strength than to God's assistance.* And this pride—from whence this deceit proceeds—so hoodwinks the eyes of our soul that we see it not at all, and are therefore justly permitted to fall and fail of our expectation, that we may thereby truly come to the knowledge of our own nothingness, and learn to ground all our good designs upon the Divine goodness, grace, and power, and not at all on our own strength or endeavours.

1. The relying on our own strength;

7. *Another* occasion is, that when our will enters upon a design it wants courage and efficacy to go through with it. Yet because our will eyes the beauty of that virtue which we aim at,

2. The want of courage to go through with them;

duties is a sure test of holiness in purpose and life. But when we speak thus, bear in mind that nothing is small or great in God's sight; whatever He wills becomes great to us, however seemingly trifling; and if once the voice of conscience tells us that he requires anything of us, we have no right to measure its importance. On the other hand, whatever He would not have us do, however important we may think it, is as naught to us. There is no standard of things great and small to a Christian, save God's will.' *The Hidden Life of the Soul*, p. 217.

* Read chap. ii.

rather than the difficulty which intervenes in the getting it, it seems otherwise to us. And hence it is no great marvel that such ill-grounded designs fall down to the ground, and melt away into nothing upon the first sight of the virtue.

3. The not aiming at the right end.

8. The *third* occasion is, that we address not our designs to their true and proper end, to wit, the pure service and honour of God.* For we make them oftentimes in our afflictions, and in time of distress and desolation, rather to find thereby some solace in such contrarieties than only to please our Lord God; and therefore He lets us fall afterwards that we may discern this deceit, and learn, to our cost, to aim at nothing else in all our actions than His holy will and pleasure.

CHAPTER XVIII.

How the Devil strives to Withdraw us from the Way of Virtue.

The devil often de-

1. Moreover, the devil makes use of another subtlety to draw us from the path of virtues into

* 'As works done only for God's honour will have a greater reward of glory, so good works which men do under the influence of other considerations will end in their greater confusion in the sight of God. The Christian therefore must keep in mind that the value of his good works, fasting, almsgiving, penances, and prayers, does not depend on their number and nature, but on the love which moves him to perform them for God; and that they are then most perfect when they are wrought in the most pure and sincere love of God, and with the least regard to our own present and future interests, to joy and sweetness, consolation and praise.' *St. John of the Cross*, vol. i. p. 275.

the precipice of vices. As thus:—A certain person falls into a sickness which he desires to support with patience. The devil, seeing that if he thus perseveres he must needs get the habit of patience, suggests unto him divers motions and desires to do this or that good work, if he could once have health restored; and that he could serve God better, advance his own perfection more effectually, and assist others more charitably if he were sound than he can do being sick. These conceits enkindle more and more in the breast of the sick person, till they make him weary and impatient of his sufferings, as being thereby hindered from doing such heroic actions.* And by this deceit the devil casts down a soul from the practice of patience—in which she first exercised herself—into open impatience against this infirmity; yet not as a thing which is in itself displeasing, but as it is a hindrance retarding her from the execution of those good works which she unquietly desires to perform.†

ceives a sick man by suggesting works of piety,

* 'Though in sensible devotion the good thoughts and affections given us are in themselves, and according to their substance, the effect of God's spirit, and ought with all security to be complied with—yet with discretion, so as that out of a gluttonous pleasure conceived by them we do not yield unto them so far as thereby to weaken our heads or prejudice our health—notwithstanding, the resolutions of undertaking any practices for the future, grounded on such sensible devotion, are to be mistrusted, as having in them more of nature and self-love, and wanting sincerity of resignation. Besides that, the senses being principal workers, the reason is rather obscured than illuminated thereby; yea, and by God's permission the devil may have some influence in such devotion and subsequent resolutions.' *Sancta Sophia*, vol. i. tr. i. sect. 2, chap. viii. § 6.

† The venerable F. Baker, speaking of how a soul should conduct

2. Nor doth the enemy rest here; but having brought the sick person to this, proceeds on in his plot, and takes away from him the aforesaid suggestions, when the sick person perceives it not, leaving in him only an ardent desire to recover his health; and if this follows not as he would, he falls into grievous sadness and great impatience.

and proceeds to make him over anxious about health.

3. The best remedy for this is, that when sickness or other adversity hath seized on thee, thou take care to admit no motion or desire into thy mind which thou canst not forthwith put into execution; otherwise it will make thee solicitous and leave thee in unquietness.

The remedy.

---

herself in times of sickness, says: 'She must particularly take heed of one notable temptation, which often befalls good but imperfect souls, by means of which they yield too freely to impatience in sickness; which is this. Nature, being soon weary of suffering, will suggest unto the soul, to justify impatience, amongst other incommodities of sickness this one—that thereby she is put in an incapacity to pray, or otherwise to serve God or her neighbour. Upon which she will be apt to desire health with impatience; falsely justifying herself for such impatience as if she did not so for the satisfaction of nature, but to the end that she may perform spiritual duties more perfectly. But this is a mere *delusion*. For *that is the true and perfect way of serving God which is suitable to the present condition wherein God hath placed a soul;* and an imperfect interrupted prayer made with resignation in the midst of pains or troubles sent by God is perhaps more efficacious to procure the good of the soul than the highest elevations exercised otherwise. It is no great matter though the soul herself do not distinctly and clearly see how her present sufferings, external or internal, may be profitable to her. She is to refer all things to the infinite wisdom and goodness of God, Who can bring light out of darkness; and therefore she must be contented—if such be His will—to be blindfolded, and humbly to remain in her simplicity, and in a reverential awe and admiration of the inscrutable ways of divine Providence.' *Sancta Sophia*, vol. ii. p. 194.

4. And thou art in this case to persuade thyself, with all patience, humility, and resignation, that perchance thy new-made resolutions would not have the effect thou imaginest, because thou art far weaker than thou thinkest; or that God, by His secret judgments, unknown to thee by reason of thy demerits, will not receive this good from thee, but that He would rather that thou humble thyself under the sweet and powerful hand of His holy will. So likewise, shouldst thou be hindered by thy ghostly father, or any other occasion whatsoever, from following thy own fancy in thy accustomed devotions, and particularly in receiving the Sacred Communion, trouble not thyself with over-earnest desires, but, truly divested of all self-will, clothe and content thyself with God's good pleasure, saying sweetly:—'If the all-seeing eye of Divine Providence found not in me so great ingratitude, and so many defects, I should not be now deprived of so great a blessing as is the receiving of my sweet Saviour in the Blessed Sacrament; but humbly acknowledging that my loving Lord doth thus discover unto me mine own unworthiness, His Holy Name be ever blessed and praised! O my God, I place my whole confidence in Thy Divine goodness, and hoping Thou wilt accept of my will, which I force and conform to Thy disposition, I here open to Thee my heart, ready to obey Thy holy command, disposed to do what Thou inspirest. Enter into it, I beseech Thee, and endow it with spiritual comfort and courage against

ENLARGEMENT. Trouble not thyself when thou canst not perform thy desires.

its enemies, and then do with it, O my Creator and Redeemer, that which is most agreeable to Thy Divine Majesty. Let Thy sacred will be now and always my only food and nourishment, since I desire nothing more, O sweet Spouse of my soul, but that, purged and freed from all things displeasing to Thee, I may be ready, adorned and prepared for Thy Coming, and willing to follow Thy blessed disposition in all things whatsoever.'

Rest secure that God accepts thy good will.

5. If thou punctually performest these precepts, rest secure, my dearly beloved, that all thy good desires to do well, which nevertheless thou canst not compass—either by reason of thine own nature, or the craft of the enemy, or God Himself not permitting it to prove thy resignation to His holy Will—will always minister some occasion of satisfying thy duty to thy Lord God in that manner which best pleaseth Him.*

Another

6. But I think it very convenient to give thee here another *caveat* against a most dangerous and

* 'A sick person is to account himself after an especial manner *in God's hands, as His prisoner*, chained, as it were, by his own weakness; disabled from the ordinary solaces of conversation, walking, &c.; debarred from eating what pleases the palate; become profitable to none, troublesome and chargeable to many; exposed oftentimes to bitter pains, and sharper remedies of such pains, &c. A grievous, indeed, but yet a happy prison this to a soul who will make good use of it! For *unless the internal taste of the soul also be depraved*, she may by this occasion infinitely increase in spiritual liberty, health, and strength, by accepting with indifference these incommodities, and mortifying her natural exorbitant desire of remedies, not desiring to escape but when and after what manner God shall ordain.' *Sancta Sophia*, vol. ii. p. 195.

subtle snare, into which many, blinded with self-love, fall; and this it is:—They so palliate and excuse their defects, that at last they themselves do scarcely perceive them.

dangerous snare.

7. And mark this diligently:—That oftentimes when a man falls into impatience, he imputes it, not to the pain which he endures, but to this:—That he is impeded from the practice of good works. So that the cause of his impatience relates, not to the sickness or adversity itself, but partly to himself as deserving it, partly to others whom he must be forced to trouble against his will, and partly to the omission of his spiritual exercises.

TEXT. Diverse excuses for our impatience.

8. Thus he who fails in his ambitious seeking of honours and offices will tell you he complains, not for his own sake, but for the necessity of his family and friends whom he might thus have helped. Now that such men deceive themselves is made manifest by this:—That they are not much troubled when the very same effects which seemed to afflict them, and under their concern for which they cloaked their own imperfections, come to pass by some other means or persons.

But all are vain,

9. For example:—Thou tellest me that thy sickness makes thee not impatient because it is in itself grievous to thee, but because they who are about thee are thereby overburdened. But should they whom thou so much compassionatest be as much overburdened in serving other sick persons, it would not much trouble thee. From whence it is evident that

as is explained by an example.

not the sense of their trouble, but thine own desire and self-love, was the true root of thy impatience. And in this manner thou mayest discover the hidden deceits in the rest of thy affairs.

ENLARGEMENT. Separate the pain from the circumstances.

10. To remedy this, I advise thee, my beloved, that as soon as thou doubtest of such a deceit, thou presently separate, by the help of thy imagination, the pain which presseth thee from those circumstances which are feigned excuses for thy impatience; and then reflect upon that alone, and force thyself to produce true and efficacious acts of patience and resignation to suffer it willingly. Thus thou wilt either become a true practiser of virtue, or, at least, thine eyes will be opened to discover thy own defects, whereof thou wert formerly ignorant.

TEXT. and desire not to be freed from thy cross.

11. Wherefore I exhort thee, that if thou art able to carry the cross with patience, thou never desire to be freed from it;* for this desire brings with it two great evils. The *one* is: That if it destroys not thy patience, yet it disposeth thee little by little to impatience. The *other* is: That it deprives thee of merit before God, Who esteems that only a work of perfect patience—though short in reference to time—which is done with the resignation of our wills to His divine pleasure.

* 'Embrace the cross,' says St. Teresa, 'which your Spouse carried on His shoulders, and remember that this should be your motto: *She who can suffer most for the love of Him will be the happiest.* Let everything else be secondary to this; if our Lord shall grant you this favour, give Him many thanks for it.' *Interior Castle*, p. 54.

12. In this therefore, and in all thy other works and proceedings, follow this rule:—Withdraw and purge thy heart from all other desires and demands than that only, purely and simply, which is comformable to God's will. This is the way to be no more disquieted with adversity, since no such thing can befall thee without His will and liking.*

but conform thy will to God's.

13. But when some lawful means must necessarily be used for the expelling of some overburdening adversity, take heed lest self-love creep into thy heart with them. See also that thou apply them, not so as to be thereby freed from thy pressure, but only because it is God's pleasure that thou shouldst make use of those instruments, and then thou canst not be discontented in case they should not conduce to thy deliverance from adversity.

Thou mayest use lawful means; but beware of self-love.

ENLARGEMENT.

§ 1. How to Oppose the Devil Striving to Deceive us with Indiscretion.

1. When the devil perceives that thou walkest on warily in the right track of virtue, so that

How to oppose the

* Disquietude of heart arises from our having the mind and affection extroverted, and taken up with creatures, instead of fixed and centred in God. He who is detached from created things, who has renounced all self-seeking and self-love, abides always in peace and is not disturbed by any adversity. Sickness, poverty, or the death of friends may disturb and agitate the faculties and senses of his lower nature, but they do not cause him any wild, harassing, or restless sorrow, since they cannot penetrate into the *interior part* of his soul, which is united to God, and lovingly conformed in all things to the divine will and pleasure. O blessed conformity, which makes things bitter to nature sweet and delightful!

devil pressing us to afflict our bodies indiscreetly.

his common cunning is become useless to his design of making thee go astray, he then transforms himself into an angel of light, and solicits thee with delightful thoughts, flatters thee with passages of Sacred Writ, and suggests examples of the saints; that so flattering thyself to have climbed up to the top of perfection, thou mayest fall more dangerously into the precipice which he hath digged for thee. To this end he urgeth thee to the punishment of the body with disciplines, abstinence, haircloth, and other extraordinary austerities;* that either thou mayest be puffed up with pride as thinking thou dost very much, or mayest destroy thy health and so become incapable to do good works, or lastly, that having endured much in this kind, thou mayest grow weary of doing penance and abhor thy spiritual exercises, and so become a prey to thine enemies and a slave to fleshy and worldly pleasures. This hath happened to very many, who having been led on by presumption, and left to the conduct and violence of an indiscreet zeal, have perished at last in their own inventions, and so become laughing-stocks to their enemies: all which disasters will never befall him who diligently observes this doctrine.

* 'Be well assured that for all men and women who occupy themselves with spiritual thoughts, great pain or hunger wilfully brought upon themselves, or bodily sickness, or pains in the stomach, or in the head, or in other parts of the body, which come from a want of proper self-treatment, as from practising too much fasting, or in any other way, will hinder the spirit very much, and prevent them from knowing and beholding spiritual things, unless they have much grace and are arrived *at a great height in the contemplative life*.' Hilton, p. 126.

2. For although these voluntary penances are sometimes praiseworthy, and may be meritorious, when strength of body and humility of spirit do correspond and accompany them, yet they must be tempered and moderated by discretion, according to each one's nature and quality.* Thus:—He that is unable in body to imitate the saints in severity of life, may right well be able to imitate their virtues by being fervent in devotion, frequent in prayer, continually aspiring to his Lord and Love, setting naught by the world and himself, and loving silence and solitude. He may be humble and affable to all, patient in suffering affronts, glad of the occasions to do good to his greatest enemies, and finally, resolved to perform his Lord's will and promote His honour to the utmost of his power,

All cannot imitate the saints in austerity of life;

* 'Thou shouldst not,' says holy Blosius, 'deny to thy body the necessary indulgence of food and sleep; thou shouldst not be very severe in that respect, unless thou hast learnt for certain by a revelation of the Holy Spirit that thou wouldst please God by a singular abstinence. For an excessive diminution of these refreshments' (and mark well that our author is only speaking of '*excessive* diminution,' and not of any slight and reasonable diminution, which purifies the soul without injuring the body), 'like too great exertion of a moderate intellect or too vehement use of the imagination, injures for the most part both the spirit and the weak body, and often causes madness. Fasts, vigils, and exterior works are indeed pleasing to God, when they are undertaken with discretion for the sake of God Himself; yet purity of heart is far more pleasing to Him, humility and charity far more acceptable. For these observances are commanded for the sake of the virtues, not the virtues for the sake of them. Therefore, as far as in thee lies, arrange, regulate, and dispose all things so that thou mayest never lose thy interior liberty, never confuse thy mind, never overtask thy strength, and yet never rashly omit those things to the observing or doing of which thou art bound by vow or by obedience.' *Canon Vitæ Spiritualis*, cap. xxiv.

and never to offend His divine Majesty in the least matter whatsoever.*

3. All which inward acts and mortifications are far more pleasing to God than the outward maceration of the flesh. Therefore I counsel thee to be very punctual in those things which concern thy duty and obligation, but as for extraordinary rigours, be rather backward and fearful than indiscreetly forward to embrace them.

but each may imitate their virtues.

4. Yet I speak not here to those delicate ones who, though in other things they are sufficiently spiritual, are overmuch inclined to indulgence

Yet beware of delicacies.

* The devil often impedes the advancement of beginners in the way of perfection by imbuing their minds with notions of false humility. He suggests to them that it is pride to have great desires, to long to imitate the saints or to wish to become an Apostle; whereas such desires, as long as they are accompanied with an exact performance of the obligations of our state, inflame the soul with love and conduce much to its advancement. If, however, a neglect of duty and carelessness in the observance of small rules should follow upon these high desires, they should quickly be repressed, and dealt with as springing from secret ambition, pride, or some unmortified passion. The evil one will also sometimes suggest that the saints are only to be admired by sinners, but not to be imitated by them. This notion is clearly erroneous. If we cannot follow the saints in everything, we should endeavour to walk in their footsteps at least from afar, and imitate them in those things in which we are able. God, indeed, does not require extraordinary mortification and heroic sanctity from every soul, but only from those chosen few whom He has predestined to be His intimate familiars, and to whom alone He has promised grace proportionate to such sublime perfection. To aim therefore at the marvellous would be, in the ordinary Christian, an act of presumption; but that he should strive to acquire purity of heart, conformity to the divine Will, and love of God above all things, is not only a highly commendable practice, but one of absolute obligation for all men. If, in spite of our efforts, we make but little progress in these virtues, believe me it is because we are lukewarm, have no spirit of sacrifice, little *love*, and are not as yet really in earnest.

towards themselves and to a punctilious doting on and diligence in the preservation of their health, under pretext of being thereby better able to serve God and perform their duty. For they strive to couple two capital enemies together, the Spirit and the Flesh; but unprofitably and with manifest danger to both, since this solicitude causeth oftentimes the loss of health to the one, and of devotion to the other.*

* Regarding this spirituo-valetudinarian class of religious, St. Teresa makes the following admirable remarks, which it will be well here to quote at length: 'The first thing we must aim at (in holy religion) is to banish from ourselves the love of this body of ours, for some of us are so delicate in our constitution, that no little pains are to be taken herein; *and we are so careful of our health*, that it is wonderful to see the war these two things (mortification and discretion) raise, especially among nuns, and even among those who are not religious. But some nuns amongst us seem to have come to the monastery *for no other object but to endeavour not to die*. This each one endeavours to do as far as she can. To speak the truth, there is little convenience in the house for accomplishing this object, and I do not wish you to entertain so much as a desire for such a thing. Remember, sisters, *you have come here to die for Christ*, and not to regale yourselves for Christ. This the devil suggests is necessary, in order to endure and observe the rule the better; and some so much desire to keep the rule by taking care of their health, that they die without even observing it for a month, or perhaps for a day!

'I know not, then, why we come here. Never fear that we shall want discretion in this respect. This would, indeed, be wonderful, for the confessors would immediately fear lest we might kill ourselves with penances; and this want of discretion is so hateful to us, that I wish we observed all the rest as exactly. I know that those who practise the contrary will not agree with what I say; nor need I mind what they say; for I judge of others by myself, that they speak the truth. But I believe, and indeed I know, that I have more companions than I have persons displeased with me, who act differently. I am confident our Lord allows us therefore to be more unwell and sickly; at least God has shown me great mercy in being so; for since I had to pamper myself (as I used), He would have it done for some reason. It is pleasant to see the torments with which some afflict themselves of their own accord. Sometimes a frenzy seizes them of doing penance,

Discretion must be used in mortification and in acquiring virtues,

5. Discretion, therefore, must be the chief director in this matter, which must distinguish between the diversity of temperaments and conditions; and since every one is not of the like temper, all cannot be regulated by the same precept. To this I add, that this discretion and moderation is necessary, not only in exterior things, but also in the acquisition of interior virtues, as I shall now declare. For though the true soldier of Christ, aspiring to perfection, must put no limits to his spiritual profit, yet there are some heats of spirit which need to be

---

without using any moderation or discretion, and this lasts for two days, so to speak. The devil afterwards suggests to their imagination that such mortifications do them harm, and hence they never do any more penance; no, not even what the rules of the Order command, having already found the mortifications hurt them. *Then they do not observe even the meanest injunctions of the rule*, such as silence, which cannot do us any harm; and no sooner do we fancy that we have a headache than we refrain from going to choir, which is not likely to kill us either! One day we omit going because our head aches, the next because it did ache, and three more days we keep away lest it should ache! We love to invent penances of our own, that we may be able to do neither the one nor the other; and even at times when we are not so ill, we think ourselves obliged to do nothing, *trusting that we satisfy for everything by asking leave.*

'You may ask, "Why does the Prioress grant leave?" I answer, did she know your interior, perhaps she would not do so; but as you inform her of your wants, and the doctor does not fail to support the account you give, and as there may be some friend or relation of yours who stands weeping by her side, what is the poor Prioress to do, though she sometimes sees you go too far? She is scrupulous lest she might be wanting in charity. She would much rather you would fail therein than she herself, and she does not think it just to judge evil of you. O my God, can such complaint be found among nuns? These things, it may be, happen sometimes; and I mention them here that you may be on your guard against them; for *if the devil once begin to terrify us with the idea that we have not good health, we shall never do anything.* May God give us light to be right in everything! Amen.' *The Way of Perfection*, chap. x. (The italics are my own.)

quenched with the dew of discretion, especially such as in beginners are kindled with overmuch fervour. Thou art therefore to know that virtues are to be acquired by little and little, and by degrees, that so they may take the deeper root, and become more durable in our souls. For example:—If thou art in the pursuit of patience, thou art first to study how to bear injuries and afflictions before thou fall to practise those higher degrees of delighting in them and desiring them.

6. Moreover, I advise thee not to apply thyself to obtain all virtues or many together, but first and principally to practise one, and then afterwards another, for by this means a virtuous habit is more easily planted and more firmly fixed in thy soul. For by this continual exercise of one only virtue, the memory is ready on all occasions, the understanding is studying new means and reasons to acquire it, and the will is more affectionately inclined to embrace it than if many were the objects of their employments.

which we must acquire separately, and not *in globo.*

7. And such is the conformity and affinity of one virtue to another, that the implanting of any one is the preparing of the ground for all the others. Hence, whosoever is a proficient in the practice of one virtue hath thereby learned the manner how to purchase another; insomuch that, as one is augmented, all the rest do by the same means increase in our souls, by reason of their inseparable nearness, connection, and concatenation together, they being all

The obtaining any one virtue is a preparation to all the rest.

beams proceeding from the same Sun, which is the Divine Light.

§ 2. FURTHER ADVICES FOR THE GETTING OF VIRTUES.

1. Besides the means formerly prescribed for the obtaining of virtues,* I will here give thee some brief and material advices concerning this important matter. First, it behoves thee to have a generous heart, a great courage, and a strong and resolute will, as being certain that thou hast to do with cunning enemies, and art to wrestle with many contrarieties, and suffer many crosses.

1. Re-olve to suffer;

2. In the next place, thou art to bring with thee a particular inclination and affection to virtue, which thou canst not want if thou truly weighest how pleasing it is to God, how excellent in itself, how profitable and absolutely necessary to the obtaining of all perfection.

2. Bear a great love to virtue;

3. Every morning make strong and efficacious resolutions and protestations to exercise thyself according to the probable occasions which may that day be offered unto thee. And sometimes in the day reflect upon thyself, and examine thy performance of this promise, and fervently renew thy desires and intentions.

3. Practise it on all occasions;

4. Apply all thy actions, spiritual exercises, reading, prayers, and meditations for the obtaining of that virtue which thou now practisest.

4. Apply all thy exercises to this end;

* See chapter i. 13, p. 8. Also chapter vii. § 3 and 7. Likewise the preceding § 5 and 6.

5. Endeavour so to accustom thyself to form acts of virtue, both internal and external, that they may by use become as easy and natural unto thee as were formerly their contraries, which were conformable to thy vicious desires.

5. Form acts thereof.

6. The sweet passages and sentences of Holy Scripture are of great service for this end; and therefore it will be convenient to commit divers of them to thy memory touching that virtue thou now aimest at, and to pronounce them often by mouth, or express them in thy heart, especially upon the occasion of feeling the passions and motions contrary to that virtue. For example, if patience be the virtue thou praisest, reflect upon that saying of Baruch: *My children, suffer patiently the wrath that is come upon you.** And that of the Psalmist: *The patience of the poor shall not perish for ever.*† Or that of Solomon: *The patient man is better than the valiant; and he that ruleth his spirit than he that taketh cities.*‡ And: *In your patience you shall possess your souls.*§ And: *Let us run by patience to the fight proposed to us.*‖

Meditate upon such Scriptures as commend it.

7. To the same purpose, thou mayest also make use of these ejaculatory prayers:

Frequently make use of ejaculations;

When, O my God, shall my heart be armed with the shield of patience?

When shall I, for Thy love, support cheerfully all contrarieties?

* Baruch iv. 25. † Psalm ix. 18. ‡ Proverbs xvi. 32.
§ Luke xxi. 19. ‖ Hebrews xii. 1.

O, sweet and dear sufferings, which make me like my meek Saviour afflicted for my sake!

O, only Life and Love of my soul, shall I never be able to content myself for Thy glory amongst thousands of crosses and calamities?

O, how happy were I, if, amidst the flames of tribulation, I could burn with an inflamed desire to suffer yet far more!

8. These and the like ejaculations and darts of affection have great power to excite us to virtue, and penetrate even to God's heart in heaven, especially when they are accompanied with two wings—a true knowledge of the *content* our Lord takes in our practice of virtue; and a lively and longing *desire* to obtain it, for no other end than because it is pleasing to His Divine Majesty.

which, being joined with two wings, will go up to heaven.

9. Thou art yet farther to be instructed, my dearly beloved, concerning this weighty and necessary matter of obtaining virtue, that one main point is to make a continual progress in the practice thereof.* For if thou leavest off this pursuit, it will necessarily follow that, through the violent inclination of thy sensual appetite, and the alluring impulse of outward objects, unruly passions will press in upon thee which will either destroy, or at least much diminish,

Above all things make continual progress;

* It is impossible that a soul who has begun to serve God in earnest, and who truly loves Him, should cease going on increasing in virtue; and for this reason, because *love is never idle.* Not to advance, therefore, is a very bad sign, and should make a soul tremble and fear exceedingly, and doubt the sincerity of its love.

the acquired habits of virtue, and will, moreover, deprive thee of those manifold graces and gifts of God which, by thy continuance and progress, thou hadst infallibly obtained.

10. For surely the way of the spirit walking to perfection is far different from that of earthly travellers, who lose nothing by their convenient stay, because they redress their weariness, which is caused and increased by the continuance of their corporal motion; whereas, in this way of the spirit, by how much more thou marchest onwards, by so much the more thy strength increaseth. For the inferior part, which by its resistance renders the path harsh and painful, is by this virtuous progress still more and more weakened; and the superior part, which is the habitation where virtue resides, is thereby fomented and fortified; so that, by the continuance of well-doing, thou still lessenest the repugnance which thou feelest in thy journey, and receivest a certain secret content in thy happy conquest.

for by going forward your strength increaseth,

11. Thus continuing thy designed course, and marching ever onward in thy journey, thou wilt arrive with less pain and more pleasure, ascending by the several degrees and steps to the top of the mountain, where thy perfected soul will perform her pious exercises, not only without contradiction, but with much quiet and content, having tamed and triumphed over her unruly passions, and completed her conquest over herself and all things

till thou reachest the mountain of perfection.

created, and being sweetly settled in the bosom of the Divinity.*

12. Neither is it sufficient, my dearly beloved, that thou strivest not to avoid the occasions which are offered in this practice of virtues, as was declared in the ninth chapter. But I would have thee *seek them out and joyfully lay hold of them,* though they appear never so little and at a distance, especially such as are most contrary to thy natural inclination.

Seek occasions of practising virtue;

13. To this hard combat, then, thou mayest encourage thyself by these following considerations. *One of these* is this: That all such occasions are the proportionate and probable, yea neces-

this being the best means to attain virtue;

* Our author seems to have drawn this and the preceding paragraphs from the following beautiful passage of St. Bonaventure:

'He who wishes to travel by the road of contemplation to the summit of the mount of God must never pause to take rest; but, by the elevation of his mind to God, ever persevere in climbing. For, in this ascent, *not to rest* is *to rest;* and he who thinks of resting becomes fatigued, and cannot afterwards continue his climbing with as much ease as before. Indeed it often happens that he who gives way to the idea of stopping to take rest becomes so weary as to be no more able to climb at all. In climbing a material mountain an occasional rest is necessary, for "the flesh is weak;" but since "the spirit is willing," in climbing the spiritual mountain, the very contrary is required, insomuch that the spirit must never rest; but when growing tired, must climb faster, and run more courageously; for so only will it be refreshened, and become more eager after loftier things; and so will its labour too seem lighter, and more easy and delightful; and hence more smoothly will he go who prefers exertion to rest.

'Foolish then are they, and ignorant of the very nature of contemplation, who take rest as a means of recruiting strength. Let them be quite certain that, in this resting, their strength is rather dissipated than recruited. The contemplative soul, as long as it runs at full speed, goes without difficulty; but as soon as it begins to walk at its ease, so soon does weariness begin; and as soon as it stops to rest, so soon is its strength gone. There is no other course, then, but, with the Virgin, "*to go up with haste into the hilly country*" (Luc. i. 39).

sary, means for the acquisition of virtue; insomuch that, when thou demandest virtue of God, thou also askest these occasions; else thy prayers would be presented in vain, and thy heart would contradict thy lips; yea, thou mightest seem to tempt thy Saviour, Who ordinarily gives not patience without suffering, nor humility without contempt. This is also true of all other virtues, which are all acquired by contrary accidents, whereby we best perceive our own wants, and therefore are most moved to desire their redress. And by how much these feelings are more sensible, by so much the more strong and generous are the acts by which we endeavour to

'But if there be any one who cannot apprehend this, and who, though he still persevere in his desire of going higher, yet wishes for some rest, although he cannot rise to the level of what has been said, there still remains this remedy:—at least let him not fall short of what they do who climb the material mountain. For such, if they grow tired halfway up the mountain, and feel the need of rest, do not dream of descending for the purpose into the valley; for thus they would never reach the summit, and, moreover, would be looked upon as fools by everybody. So are *they* fools, nor will *they* ever arrive at the summit of contemplation, who, by more or less of contemplation, climb up to a certain height to-day, and to-morrow, feeling weary, go down to rest at the place whence they started; and who think that amidst the valleys of sin and vanity, and on the flats of imperfection, they will grow stronger for the ascent—not knowing that with difficulty will they be able to ascend again even as high as the place they first reached. And this, it seems to me, is the reason why so few reach the brow of the hill of perfection. If a man would only climb as high as he could, and would take his rest *there*, without coming down; and if the next day he would go on a little higher, and there too would plant firm the foot of his heart, and so would go on afterwards, always in the same way—I say to you, that such a one would make more progress in one month than another that always went back to take his rest would make in forty years. And I am of opinion that such a one would, in a very short time, become perfect in his state, and glorious in the sight of God, and beloved by the whole court of heaven.' St. Bonaventura, *Stimulus Amoris*, cap. iv.

attain to the virtues we stand in need of. Thou art, therefore, to make high esteem of and improve thyself by the least occasion which is offered; as by a cross look or contradictory word, which will inure thee to the patient sufferance of more important difficulties.

and regard all adversity as from God's Providence.

14. The *other consideration* is that which hath been touched upon formerly:* To conceive of all things which befall thee as coming from God's Providence for thy particular profit. And though some of them, as thine own or others' faults, cannot be imputed to God, Who abhors all sin, yet they may be referred to Him, inasmuch as He permits them, and though He can, yet doth not hinder them. But all pains and punishments whatsoever which happen to us by and through our own defects, or others' malice, are from God and His Divine Providence, with which He concurs and wills us to endure; and which He would not permit—since they contain a certain deformity, a thing ever odious to His purity—but for the good we may draw from them, and for other just reasons best known to His all-knowing Majesty.

A mistake rectified.

15. Being, therefore, persuaded of God's will in all thy sufferings, and that He will have thee to support voluntarily all afflictions which befall thee either by others' faults or thine own, it follows that they are much mistaken who, to excuse their impatience, pretend that God wills not this or that thing because He hates all evil. For what is this but to seek

* See chap. x. § 2, 3.

a cloak to cover their own imperfections, and to refuse the carriage of that cross which Christ hath laid upon their shoulders.

16. And I yet further assure thee, that thy Lord God more values thy voluntary digestion of such difficulties as come from those persons whom thou hast obliged, than the enduring of those sufferings which come from other accidents. For by these former the pride of thy perverse nature is more suppressed, and by suffering them with patience thou very much increasest the glory of God by coöperating with Him in that wherein His ineffable bounty and power do so greatly appear. This, in effect, is to draw from the pestilent poison of sin and malice a most precious balsam of virtue and goodness.

To suffer patiently from those whom we have served is great gain.

17. For, believe it, my beloved, thy Lord God no sooner discovers in thy heart a lively and ardent love of well-doing, and a disinterested desire of getting this glorious conquest, than He forthwith prepares and presents this chalice of cruel temptations and harsh occasions, which thou art to take and digest, according as He best knoweth and pleaseth. Therefore, confident of His love, and careful of thine own profit, shut thine eyes and receive it from His holy hands, swallowing it down cheerfully, readily, and securely, even to the last and least drop, as a medicine made by a Physician incapable of error, and whereof the ingredients are by so much more profitable to thy soul by

Swallow cheerfully the physician's bitter cup.

how much they have less sweetness and savour to thy sensuality.

§ 3. How to Make Use of all Occasions in the Exercise of one Virtue.

Make use of all occasions to acquire the virtue thou aimest at.

1. Thou hast been already informed, my dearly beloved, that the single practice of one only virtue at once is more profitable than the laying thyself out for them *in globo;** and that all occasions and occurrences, though different in themselves, are to be directed to that end. Now take this Method for thy easier progress therein :—It may fall out that oftentimes in the same day or hour thou mayest chance to be unjustly reprehended for something which in itself deserves praise; that thou mayest cause anger by doing a good action, or be murmured against for some small matter; that thy reasonable demand may be harshly refused and rejected; that thou art suspected, contradicted, and calumniated without cause; that thy body is afflicted with pain, and thy mind with melancholy; that thou art employed in some annoying and ungrateful affair; that thy diet is ill-dressed; and finally, that thou sufferest in small matters of this sort, or in matters of greater difficulty, wherewith this miserable life is replenished. In all which accidents, though it be good to produce different acts of virtue conform-

* See Enlargement—'How to oppose the devil striving to deceive us with indiscretion,' § 6, p. 107.

able to the variety of the subjects, yet, following the rule already prescribed, thou art to exercise thyself in such acts as directly aim at that virtue thou then hast in hand.

2. As, for example:—If, at the time when these occasions are offered, thou art striving after *Patience*, Examples. thy way is to form acts of enduring those particular contrarieties with all willingness, joyfulness, and cheerfulness. If thy virtue be *Humility*, acknowledge thyself most justly deserving these and far greater indignities. If it be *Obedience*, yield readily, and submit to God's powerful hand, offering to obey, if it so pleaseth Him, not only all reasonable creatures, but even to sink below the brute beasts, and debase thyself under all things that in any way disgust or displease thee. If it be *Poverty*, content thyself with the want of all worldly comfort and conveniences whatever. If it be *Charity*, produce acts of love both towards thy neighbour, as being instrumental to thy purchasing virtue, and also towards God, as being the principal and loving Cause whence these crosses proceed, or, at least, are permitted to come upon thee for thy spiritual practice and profit. By this doctrine here delivered concerning the various accidents which may befall thee, thou mayest easily learn how to behave thyself, and make acts of the virtue thou art aiming at on any occasion of sickness, persecution, or other pains which are of longer duration.

3. As for the space of time which is to be employed in the practice of each virtue, it is not for me How long we should

continue practising the same virtue.

to determine.* This must be regulated by the condition, diligence, and necessity of each particular combatant, and according to their much or little progress in the way of the spirit; whereof none can be a competent judge but he who is the guide and director of their souls.

Signs of progress: 1. If thou lose not courage in time of aridity;

4. But whosoever shall heartily set himself to work with the devotion and diligence already treated of, may without doubt make great progress in few weeks' practice. And take this for one sure sign of thy proficiency:—If amidst all the dryness, darkness, and distresses of thy soul, and feeling thyself bereft of all spiritual sweetness and comfort, thou ceasest not to continue with courage in thy virtuous enterprises.

2. If thy sensuality be weakened.

5. Moreover, the contradiction of thy sensuality in the forming acts of virtue will afford thee a manifest testimony. For the more thy sensuality is weakened, the more is thy mind strengthened; so that to feel no rebellion in the inferior part, especially in unforeseen affairs, is a true token of thy having obtained the virtue. And in proportion as thy actions are accompanied with a promptitude and alacrity of spirit, in the same proportion thou hast just reason to think thou hast profited in this exercise.

* A few days' practice may serve for some persons; others will require many weeks; some again will find a whole year not too long; whilst others may labour a life-time, and at the end still appear to be far off the desired conquest.

6. Yet take heed of persuading thyself that thou art in sure possession of perfect virtue, or that thou art absolute master of any one passion, even though for a long time, and after many hot assaults, thou hast not felt its motion.* For here also the deceit of the devil and the subtle corruption of thy nature may deceive thee; since that thing may be really a vice, which secret pride clothes in the habit of virtue. If, moreover, thou steadfastly considerest the perfection to which God hath called thee, thou wilt easily grant that hadst thou made a far greater progress in the path of perfection than thou hast done, even then thou wouldst scarcely have yet entered upon the threshold thereof.

Yet never think thyself a conqueror;

7. And I must here put thee in mind, my dearly beloved, that thou art still to look forwards, and advance on courageously towards those many virtues thou standest in need of, without reflecting back on the progress thou hast made. For this is to be left to thy Lord God, the true Searcher and only Knower of hearts, Who lays open this secret to some and conceals it from others, according as His divine knowledge sees that it will lead to pride or to humility; and

but ever look forward to what is still to be achieved,

* 'I wish to warn you against one thing, viz. not to be too secure, because the Order is such, or because you have such a superior; for David was a great saint, and yet you know what Solomon proved. Neither should you make much account of the enclosure and penance in which you live; nor let your always conversing with God, or your continual exercise of prayer, make you secure, nor your being so much separated from the world, nor your abhorring worldly things—all this is very good, but not sufficient, as I have said, to free us from fear. Often, then, remember and meditate on this virtue :—*Blessed is the man who feareth the Lord.*' *Interior Castle*, p. 60.

so as a loving Father He removes a danger from one, whilst to another He gives an opportunity of increasing in virtue.

and pursue thy exercises with constancy.

8. Therefore, let the pious practitioner pursue his exercises with patience and constancy, though he perceives not his own progress; assuring himself that he shall in due time be sensible of it, when it pleases the Divine Providence to reveal it unto him for his greater good.*

CHAPTER XIX.

How our Enemy Endeavours to Make our Virtue Instrumental to our Ruin.

Our enemies strive to make us pride ourselves on our virtues;

1. Our deceitful and dangerous enemy the devil tempts us also by those very virtues which we have acquired, and casts them, as it were stumbling-blocks, in our way, to occasion our ruin.

* Be not too anxious to ascertain how far you have advanced in spirituality and holiness, and shun all restlessness and vain curiosity. Desire to love God with your whole heart, seeking Him alone in all your actions, and leave your progress in His hands, without troubling yourself whether it be little or great. Morbid self-inspection leads to self-deception, whilst it argues self-love and vanity, and betrays a want of holy Benedictine simplicity. The fact of your advancement, and not the knowledge of it, is profitable; yea, the knowledge of it is the occasion oftentimes of many dangers and temptations. Keep, then, the interior eye of your soul steadfastly fixed, not upon your own soul, but upon God; and if you turn it sometimes upon self, let it be but rarely and for a brief space of time, speedily lifting it up again to the contemplation of God, lest it should suffer from dwelling too long in the mire of your own misery, and become dimmed and tarnished. The Psalmist points out the excellency of this method when he says, *It is good for me to adhere to my God* (Ps. lxxii.). St. Teresa also teaches

To this end he strives to make us please and delight ourselves in them, that being puffed-up in our self-conceits, we may fall afterwards into the dangerous precipice of pride.*

2. But to secure thy soul from this fearful fall, stand always in the open and plain field, and persevere securely in the true and profound consideration of thy own nothingness; confessing that of thyself thou art nothing, thou knowest nothing, thou canst do nothing, and thou hast nothing else in thee of thyself but eternal damnation. And take a serious care to drive far from thee all such of thine own cogitations which seem to whisper against this self-knowledge. For they surely are suggested by thy sworn enemies, and therefore, if thou excludest them not from thy heart, they will either kill or cruelly wound it. Which truth that thou mayest apprehend, I prescribe this rule unto thee.

but do thou consider thy own nothingness.

the same lesson: 'We shall never be able to know ourselves except we endeavour to know God. By considering His greatness, we discover our own baseness; by contemplating His purity, we discover our own filthiness, and beholding His humility, we shall discover how far we are from being truly humble. Herein is a double gain. The first is, that as a white colour next to a black appears much whiter, and on the contrary, a black near a white colour, so are our imperfections better discovered by being contrasted with the divine perfections. The second is, that our understanding and will are ennobled thereby, and more disposed to every good, in meditating by turns both on ourselves and on God; for never to rise from the mire of our own miseries is very injurious to us. . . We must fix our eyes on Christ, our only good, and there we shall learn true humility.' *Interior Castle*, mans. 1, chap. ii.

* St. John of the Cross says, that they who rejoice in their good works are exposed to seven evils, and that because of their spiritual

3. When thou goest about to contemplate thine own baseness, think not of the benefits, blessings, gifts, and graces which thou findest in thyself; for these are none of thy goods, but God's gifts. Turn thee, therefore, to take a view of what is thine own, and so thou shalt rightly judge how great, or rather how truly nothing, thou art. This thou mayest do in the following manner:—Imagine the time before thou hadst a being, and thou wilt soon find that for an eternity thou wert an absolute nothing; that thou didst nothing, nor couldst contribute in the least manner to thy own life, or anything which thou now possessest.

What thou wert from eternity.

4. If, in the next place, thou dost ponder the time wherein thou didst begin to be something, thou wilt likewise understand that thou receivedst it from the pure bounty and benignity of thy God alone. For He created thee and gave thee this life, which He still continues and conserves unto thee; and He doth all other things thou now hast, knowest, and possessest, insomuch that thou canst not meet with the least occasion in thyself whereon to ground a thought of thy being anything, or of deserving any esteem above others for anything.

What thou art in time.

5. Now, as concerning thy state of grace, and

nature these evils are, of all others, the most fatal. They are: 1. Self-conceit. 2. Rash and contemptuous judgment of others. 3. Self-seeking. 4. Loss of supernatural reward. 5. A cessation from further progress in perfection. 6. A false estimation of good works, considering those to be of greater value which give delight than those which afford none. 7. Spiritual blindness and weakness. See vol. i. chap. xxviii., wherein these matters are treated of at length.

abilities given thee to do good, tell me—Can thy nature do the least good thing by itself, deprived of the Creator's divine assistance?

What good canst thou do of thyself?

6. If, further, thou turn thy thoughts upon thine own evil and sinful works, and others yet worse which thou hadst undoubtedly done and continued in, if God of His great mercy had not kept, stayed, and withdrawn thee with the right hand of His holy grace, thou wilt easily be brought to acknowledge that thine own wickedness—both by reason of the length of time in which thou didst lie drowned therein, and also of the multitude of thy evil actions and perverse affections—is so great, that it can neither be expressed nor numbered, insomuch that thou art, or surely mightest have been, like another rebellious Lucifer.* Therefore, unless thou wilt be a sacrilegious felon, and steal away the goods of thy Lord God, and attribute them to thyself, thou mayest justly esteem thyself every day worse and worse.

What evil hast thou or mightest thou have done?

7. Yea, thou hast good grounds to think thyself the most ungrateful and ungracious wretch in the world, and to be nothing but dirt and dung of the earth, or that which is more stinking and abominable, because the loathsomeness and stench of thy sins is far greater than this.†

ENLARGEMENT. Think thyself the worst of men.

* 'To attribute our good works to ourselves is to deny them to be God's, from whom all good works proceed, and to follow the example of Lucifer, who rejoiced in himself, denying to God what was His, and arrogating it to himself.' *St. John of the Cross*, vol. i. p. 279.

† It was no mock humility that made the saints confess them-

TEXT. Be just in thy accusation.

8. Yet here take this necessary *caveat:*—That justice be joined with the confession of thine own baseness, lest it bring thee more prejudice than profit. For if in this knowledge and humble confession of thyself thou excellest some one (who by reason of his own blindness thinks himself something, and desires to be esteemed as such by others), yet thou art far worse than he, if thou desirest that upon this score others should think well of thee, and esteem thee to be that which thou acknowledgest thyself not to be. Wherefore, that the acknowledgment of thy own baseness and vileness may be true and real, and render thee pleasing to God, thou art not only to acknowledge thyself base and wicked, but comport thyself as such a one, treat thyself as such a one, and desire to be so held and used by others.

selves the greatest of sinners. The nearer a soul approaches God, the more is it penetrated and overwhelmed with a sense of its own wickedness and vileness. St. Teresa tells us of a 'great servant of God' whose soul was pierced with such grief by the thought of her sins, that the pains of death itself would have been more supportable. '*She thought no one's sins could equal hers*, because she knew there was no one whom God had so patiently borne with and upon whom He had conferred so many favours' (*Interior Castle*, p. 170). F. Baker, speaking of the self-abasement of a contemplative soul, shows how this conviction of her own unworthiness is a necessary consequence of contemplation, and springs from an illuminated vision of God. 'The least imperfection in herself,' he says, 'being really a hindrance to her immediate union with God and perfect sight of Him, is, in so great a light as she then enjoys, perfectly seen and perfectly abhorred by her. Yea, such faults as to her natural understanding formerly appeared no bigger than *motes* do, in virtue of this supernatural light, seem as *mountains;* and defects which she before never dreamed or imagined to be in herself she now sees not only to be, but to abound and bear great sway in her.' *Sancta Sophia*, vol. i. treat. ii. chap. xiii.

9. And this thou canst do by abhorring all honours, rejoicing in affronts, and condescending on all occasions to perform the basest employments, and to be slighted and contemned by every one; yet still for the only end and intention to humble and exercise thyself, and not out of a certain pride and secret presumption of spirit. ENLARGEMENT.

10. And if it sometimes happen that for some good work, wherein the Lord God vouchsafed to make thee instrumental, thou comest to gain a good esteem, or beginnest to be beloved or praised by others, take heed, and be not drawn a tittle from the aforesaid truth of thine own baseness, but turn thy heart to thy Lord God, and there say to Him:—'O my God, let it never enter into my thoughts to steal from Thee Thine own divine goodness.' TEXT. And stick to this amidst all the applauses of men.

Or else:—'To Thee, O my God, all praise and honour is only due. To Thee only be given all the glory, and to me that which I truly deserve—which is only confusion.' ENLARGEMENT.

11. And afterwards thou mayest reflect upon him who praised thee, saying within thyself:—'Why doth this man think I am good, when, indeed, there is none good but Thou only, my good God?' If thou thus proceedest and practisest, thou renderest truly to God that which is His, and puttest thy soul in a disposition to receive greater grace. TEXT.

12. But if the memory of thy good deeds endangers thy soul to fall into vanity, looking upon them ENLARGEMENT.

If tempted to vanity because of thy good deeds, presently as none of thine own goods, but as God's gifts, reason thus with them :—'How can you appear and pretend to have a being in my heart, since I never gave you a beginning, progress, nor perfection? But my good God, by His only grace and goodness, created you. I therefore acknowledge Him for your principal Father, and to Him I return all hearty thanks, praise, honour, and glory.'

13. Then penetrate the best of thy good works, and ponder how imperfect are the best of them, thou wilt find thou hast not only failed in perfectly corresponding to the grace which God gave thee to perform them with, but also that they are far from that perfection, purity of intention, and due fervour and diligence which should have accompanied them; insomuch, that the whole matter being impartially pondered, thou mayest rather be confounded and ashamed than puffed-up with pride and complacency. For nothing is more certain than that the pure and perfect graces and gifts of God are destroyed and lessened by our imperfections when we put them in practice.*

* 'True purity of intention,' says F. Baker, 'is best discerned in the beginning of an action; for ordinarily we set upon external works out of a sudden impulse and liking of nature, and afterwards we cozen ourselves with a forced good intention fastened upon them, so thinking that in them we do purely seek the glory of God, and faintly renouncing our interests of nature. It is indeed better to do thus than to continue such actions upon the same motives upon which they were begun. But no actions are perfectly meritorious and pure but such as have for their first principle a divine light and impulse, and are continued in virtue of the same. Therefore, a certain ancient holy hermit was accustomed, before he set upon any work, to make a pause

14. And if thou wilt elevate thy spirit to thy Lord's supreme greatness and goodness, and truly reflect what service is due to so divine a Majesty, thou wilt soon conclude that there is no cause or colour for thee to glory in thine own merits, though thine actions had been far more excellent and renowned than they are; but accusing thyself of want of duty, and trembling at thine own deficiency, thou wilt become as a poor penitent desiring pardon, and saying:—'O my God, be merciful to me a sinner.' Thou mayest furthermore draw a comparison between thy works and those

and that thou hast more reason to weep than to glory.

for some time, like one whose thoughts were busied about some other matter. And being asked why he did so, he answered:—"All our actions are in themselves nothing worth; but like a rough unshapen piece of timber, they have no gracefulness in them unless we adorn and gild them over with a pure intention, directing them to the love and glory of God. Or, as one who is to shoot at a mark doth first carefully fix his eye upon it, otherwise he will shoot at random, so do I fix my eye upon God, Who is to be our only Mark; and for this reason, before I begin any work, I do seriously offer it to God, begging His assistance." Active livers have need in almost all their actions of moment to frame an *actual* intention: not so Contemplatives, who are always *habitually* united to God; for such iterations of actual intention would cause too much distraction to them. To conclude, how difficult and uneasy soever to nature the attaining to purity of intention be, because the very soul of corrupt nature—which is propriety—is rooted out; yet since it is absolutely necessary in an internal life, therefore considering God's promise that He will never be wanting to our endeavours, souls of good will will find it neither impossible nor of so great difficulty as at first it appeared, if they will attempt it with a strong resolution. To quicken and fortify which resolution, I will end this discourse with that piercing saying of Harphius: *O, how great and hidden deceits of corrupt nature will appear*, saith he, *and be discovered* (and consequently be severely punished) *after this life, for that souls have not here been purified and made dei form in their intentions.* God Almighty give us the grace to discover now and reform this perilous and secret self-seeking of nature, to the glory of His Holy Name. Amen.' *Sancta Sophia*, vol. i. 327-329.

of the saints and servants of God, and thou wilt, by that parallel, plainly perceive the baseness of thy best actions.

Learn therefore humility, the fountain of virtues;

13. Learn, therefore, O my beloved, this necessary lesson of humility, and acknowledge thyself, with thy whole bundle of good works put together, to be a mere nothing. For this is the firm foundation whereon thou art to raise the perfect structure of all other virtues; and the deeper thou layest this groundwork, the higher will be thy spiritual building.* Yet never think thou canst dig it deep enough, but rather imagine that if a creature were capable of infinitude, thy unworthiness would be infinite. This point—to wit, self-abasement—being well practised, gives thee the possession of all that is good, and without it thou art less than nothing, though thy actions be more perfect than those of the greatest saints, and thy heart be in continual recollection with thy Creator. O blessed abasement, which makes us happy on earth, and glorious in heaven! O true light,

* 'As much as thou hast of humility, so much hast thou of charity, of patience, and of other virtues, though they be not shown or made to appear outwardly. Be, therefore, earnest in getting humility, and hold fast to it, for it is the first and the last of all virtues. It is the first, for it is the foundation, as St. Augustine saith: "Dost thou think of building a high house of virtue, lay first a deep foundation of humility" (Serm. lxix.). It is also the last, for it is the maintainer and conserver of all other virtues. St. Gregory saith: "He that gathereth, and striveth to keep virtues without humility, is like unto one who would make or carry powdered spices in the wind. The deeds may be ever so good, thou mayest fast, watch, or do anything else, and yet, if thou hast not humility, it is all nothing that thou dost." Hilton's *Scale of Perfection*, p. 27.

shining out of our darkness! O great nothing, which rendereth us masters and monarchs of all things! No, my dearly beloved, I will never give over the pressing of this point, which thou art ever to practise.

14. If, therefore, thou desirest to praise God, accuse thyself. If thou wilt exalt His Divine Majesty, dive into thy own misery. If thou wilt find Him, climb not up to heaven, for He will fly from thee; but rather descend into the abyss of thine own nothingness, and He will there come to thee, and there embrace thee. Yes, He will court and cherish thee so much the more dearly, deliciously, and tenderly by how much thou seemest abject and vile in thine own eyes, and art well pleased to have all others shun and scorn thy company as a mere outcast, an object of derision, and a thing abominable.

It is the only way to praise, find, and please God.

15. Know, furthermore, and consider thyself most unworthy of so high a favour from thy Lord God as to be neglected and scorned by all; and fail not to render Him most hearty and humble thanks. Finally, thou art to be grateful and sensible of thy great obligation to those who have administered the occasion of this thy spiritual improvement, and to acknowledge thyself most bound to them who have most mastered and mortified thee.*

Therefore, give thanks when thou art scorned.

* On this point, Walter Hilton beautifully remarks: 'A true lover of Jesus, when he suffereth harm from his neighbour, is so strengthened through the grace of the Holy Ghost, and is made so humble, so patient, so peaceable, and that so really, that what harm or wrong soever he suffereth from his neighbour, he still preserveth his humility; he

16. But if, notwithstanding all these true and weighty considerations, the subtlety of the devil, thine own ignorance, or an evil inclination should have got the power over thee, so as to disquiet and trouble thy mind with fancies of self-praise, and to make some impressions in thy heart of thine own merits and defects, it is then that thou art chiefly and courageously to beat down and humble thyself, since thou findest by experience how poorly thou hast profited in the way of the Spirit and knowledge of thyself, and what deep roots thy pride and vanity have taken in thy entrails. This is the way to suck honey out of poison, and to draw health from wounds.

but be ever wary of the devil and thine own inclinations.

§ 1. Of Rash Judgment.

1. From this vice of self-esteem springeth up another no less dangerous, which is rash judgment concerning our neighbours; and this is commonly followed with contempt of their persons and detractions of their good name. This vice, as it hath its beginning from a peevish and proud inclination, so likewise it is nourished and fomented by no

This springs from self-esteem and pride.

despiseth him not, he judgeth him not; but he prayeth for him in his heart, and hath pity and compassion on him, and treateth him much more tenderly than another man who never did him harm. And, indeed, he loveth him better, and more fervently desireth the salvation of his soul, because he seeth that so much spiritual profit will come of the evil deed of that man, although, as being evil, it is against his will. But this love and this meekness are wrought only by the Holy Ghost, being far above the nature of man, in those whom He maketh true lovers of Jesus.' *The Scale of Perfection*, p. 290, edited by R. E. Guy, O.S.B.

other food. For pride and rash judgment increase together, comply with each other, and do both jointly, covertly, and insensibly concur to deceive us. For we presume to exalt ourselves by judging meanly of others, and we think ourselves free from those imperfections which we are fully persuaded are in our brothers.

The devil strives to keep our senses open to our neighbours actions.

2. Now, our wily enemy, the devil, no sooner discovers this perverse disposition in us, than he is busy in keeping our senses open to see, hear, examine, and heighten the faults of our neighbours. He is diligent to imprint *this* imperfection or *that* indiscretion of such or such a person on our spirits.

Be vigilant: 1. By refusing to pass judgment;

3. If, therefore, my dearly beloved, thy foe is so forward and watchful to entrap thee, be thou equally careful and vigilant to avoid his plots, and rescue thy soul out of his dangerous snares. And, in the first place, when another's defects are presented before thee, presently withdraw thy thoughts.* But if thou art solicited to give sentence, let it be a flat denial and short answer :—That thou hast no such power given thee; and that if thou hadst any such privilege, thou couldst hardly form a right and sound judgment, being environed and prevented with such a number of passions, inclining to think more amiss than there is just cause.

* Remembering the terrible saying of St. Bernard: 'Detrahere, aut detrahentem audire, quid horum damnabilius sit, non facile dixerim—I cannot well say which is the more damnable of these two things: to detract, or to listen to detraction.' *De Consid.* n. 22.

2. By looking upon our own-selves,

4. Then make use of this second and singular remedy:—Let the consideration of thine own wants and interior necessities so take up thy whole time and thoughts, that, seeing how profitable it is to look homeward, and how much thou art concerned to set in order thy own bleeding affairs, thou mayest recall thy mind from roaming abroad, and have no leisure left to lend away to others superfluously, who hast scarcely time enough to look after thyself in things of absolute necessity. And this serious search into thy own wants, will clear the inward eye of thy soul from those ill-humours which engender this pestiferous imperfection of rash judgment.

where we shall find some root of the fault we blame in them.

5. For know, when thou conceivest amiss of thy neighbour, there is some root of the same evil in thine own heart, which is apt to take the impression of that object which is like itself. When, therefore, thou feelest this itching desire to censure another's fault, grow indignant at thyself, as if thou wert equally culpable, and confer in these terms with thine own soul:—'Is it possible that I, who am so miserable, not only because I wallow in the same mire, but am also full of greater faults and imperfections, should, notwithstanding, be so proud and presumptuous as to take upon me to judge another?' Thus the weapons which first pointed at thy neighbour, but have thus pricked thine own heart, will prove a perfect cure of thy wounds, and a true comfort to thy soul.

6. But when the fault which is committed is become manifest, then excuse it with a charitable construction,* and piously conclude that thy brother hath many hidden virtues and perfections, for the custody whereof he is thus permitted to fall. Or that it is to humble him for a time, to make him see his own nothingness, and so, from this contempt of others, raise him afterwards to higher perfection in the sight of the Divine Majesty, whereby his gain may prove greater than his loss.

If the fault be manifest, put a charitable construction on it.

7. But if the sin be not only manifest, but even scandalous, and proceed from a perverse and obstinate heart, turn thy thoughts to God's secret and severe judgments, and you will find some who outwardly have appeared very notorious sinners, have yet afterwards shown ardent signs of holiness, and died with the reputation of sanctity.† And thou wilt also find others, who were thought to have reached the top of perfection, to have tumbled down

If scandalous, have recourse to God's secret judgments.

* 'Excusa intentionem, is opus non potest; puta ignorantiam, puta subreptionem, puta casum. Quod si omnem omnino dissimulationem rei certitudo recusat, suade nihilominus ipse tibi, et dicito apud temetipsum: Vehemens fuit nimis tentatio, quid de me illa fecisset, si accepisset in me similiter potestatem—Excuse the intention if you cannot excuse the action; think that there must have been some want of knowledge, some sudden surprise, or that it was purely an accident. But if an absolute certainty regarding the matter renders such an interpretation out of the question, at least mitigate the fault as far as it is possible, and say to yourself: "What a violent temptation this must have been! What should I have done, had it come upon me with equal violence?"' *S. Bernardi Sermones in Cantica*, ser. xl. p. 984, apud Migne.

† Witness St. Paul, St. Mary Magdalen, St. Augustine, St. Mary of Egypt, and St. Margaret of Cortona.

into the miserable precipice of eternal damnation.* It is therefore thy part to tremble at these imperceivable proceedings of Divine Providence, and to remain always careful and fearful of thine own condition,† not intermeddling with that of others, which is concealed from thy knowledge.

All charity is from God, all bitterness from the devil.

8. Finally, believe it for a certainty, that all the good and charitable constructions thou puttest upon thy neighbours' actions are the assured effects of the Holy Ghost, and that all contempt, rash censures, and bitterness of mind against them are derived from thy own malice and thine enemies' suggestion. Wherefore, erase out of thy soul with all speed and diligence such impressions as glance at thy brother's imperfections, and shut not thine eyes to sleep before thou hast excluded all such thoughts out of thy heart.‡

* Witness Lucifer, Judas.

† 'Dread continually thy weak nature, which is easily overcome, and say what the holy man said who began to weep when he was told that one of his companions had fallen with a woman into carnal uncleanness, *Ille hodie, ego cras*—"He to-day, I to-morrow;" as if he had said, I am of the same infirm nature as he is, and the very same may happen to me, unless God sustain me. Lo, thus the holy man had no overweening contempt of the other man that was fallen into sin, but wept his mishap, and dreaded that the very same might befall himself. In this manner, keep your heart humble and meek.' *The Ancren Riwle*, p. 279.

‡ 'The habit of not judging others is one which it is very difficult to acquire, and which is generally not acquired till late on in the spiritual life. Men's actions are very difficult to judge. Their real character depends in a great measure on the motives which prompt them, and those motives are invisible to us. Appearances are often against what we afterwards discover to have been deeds of virtue. Moreover a line of conduct is, in its look at least, very little like a

§ 2. Of the Means to Shield us against our Enemies at the Time of Death.

1. Though the whole course of our life is a continual warfare,* yet the most signal and important day of battle is the day of our death; and whosoever is conquered in that last and inevitable skirmish, remains hopeless of the victory for all eternity. Wherefore, that thou mayest be then ready to bear this fatal brunt with constancy, fight now, and fall upon thine enemies beforehand courageously; for he that is a stout combatant during his life is most likely to be conqueror at the point of death, as having by long practice acquired the true use of his weapon.

Fall now upon our enemies beforehand.

2. Thou art also to make death familiar to thy thoughts by frequent and attentive conference and consideration; for so thou wilt less fear it when it comes, and be freer to resist what will then so fiercely assault thee. Worldlings hear not willingly this doctrine, because it interrupts them in the career of their pleasure, which they follow with overmuch passion and affection, and consequently leave it not without great grief and affliction. But do thou, my dearly beloved, make timely preparation for a matter of so high importance. And to this end, imagine thyself sometimes to be all alone, helpless, and comfortless, strug-

Make death familiar to thy thoughts.

---

logical process. It is complicated with all manner of inconsistencies, and often deformed by what in reality is a hidden consistency.' F. Faber's *Spiritual Conferences*, p. 27.

* Job vii. 1.

gling hand to hand with death, and then represent to thy soul these following things, which, as I conceive, will then most afflict thee. Consult also with thine own heart how to remedy all things before it be too late, that so thou mayest readily make use thereof in thy last and greatest necessity. For that which can once only be acted, ought in all reason to be very exactly studied beforehand, lest a fault be committed which can never be redressed.

§ 3. Of Four Assaults which our Enemies make against Us at the Time of Death. And first, of their Assaults against Faith, and of the Means to Defend Ourselves.

The first assault is against Faith.

1. Our subtle enemies ordinarily make their strongest opposition when we are in the weakest condition. Therefore they raise four main batteries against us, from whence they let fly their impoisoned darts at us into our deathbeds, assaulting us with temptations against *Faith*, with *Despair*, with *Vainglory*, and with *Illusions*.

The remedy: Retreat from thy understanding to thy will.

2. As for the first: When the devil sets upon thee with false arguments to batter down thy Faith, make a speedy retreat from thy understanding to thy will, saying:—'Avaunt, Satan, thou father of all falsehood, I will give thee no audience! For it sufficeth and satisfieth me to believe that which the Catholic Church proposeth unto me.' Take heed therefore of admitting any fancies concerning thy Faith, though they appear never so friendly. But take them all, as indeed they are, for deceits of the devil to en-

gage thee in a dispute with him. But if thou art so suddenly entrapped that thou wantest time to retreat, stand strongly upon thy firm ground; and never yield either to the reason he allegeth, or to the authorities of Scripture he citeth, assuring thyself that they are either full of fallacies, or corruptly quoted, or ill-applied, or falsely interpreted, though they appear never so clear and evident.

3. And should the subtle serpent fall upon interrogations to entrap thee in thy answers, as:—'What doth the Church believe?' vouchsafe him no reply, but frame an inward act of lively and firm Faith, or tell him undauntedly:—'The Church believes the truth.' If he again proposeth:—'And what is this truth?' say:—'It is even that thing which this Church believeth.'*

Give no answer to thy enemy's questions.

* 'To this purpose Cardinal Bellarmine, in his book *De Arte bene Moriendi*, relates from Barocius Bishop of Padua a sad story of two doctors in that University famous for scholastic controversy; the one whereof, after his death, did, according to a mutual agreement formerly made, appear to his friend after a most affrighting manner, all burning in flames, giving this account of the causes that brought him to that woful condition: "A little before my expiring," said he, "the devil suggested to me doubts and arguments against the Divinity of our Lord; the which I, out of a confidence in my own abilities undertaking to resolve, found myself so pressed with new replies, that in the end, being quite overcome, I renounced the Catholic doctrine of the Church, and assented to the Arian heresy; and in this state—a just judgment of my pride—I expired, so receiving this reward of heresy." The living companion, astonished with this relation, revealed the case to some pious friends, from whom he received advices directly conformable to these here before delivered; and thereupon spending the remainder of his time more in prayer and penance than study, and not long after approaching to his end, the same temptation assaulted him. For the devil, requiring of him an account of his faith, could get no other ans-

but fix thy thoughts upon Christ crucified.

4. But, above all things, keep thy heart and mind fixed and attentive upon the contemplation of Christ crucified; when sweetly discoursing with thy Lord and Love, say :—'O my God, O my Saviour, O my Creator, succour me speedily, abandon me not in my necessity, let me not swerve one tittle from the truth of Thy Church; and grant me, I beseech Thee, this grace, that as I now live in it, so I may finally die in it, to Thy glory and my own eternal comfort.'

§ 4. Of the Second Assault of Despair, and the Remedy against it.

The second assault is despair.

1. The devil's next engine, wherewith he strives to ruin and destroy us, is the fright he puts into us upon the thought of our enormous offences, whence he would cast us down headlong into the gulf of Despair.*

wer from him but this: "I believe what the Church teacheth." And being thereupon asked what the Church taught, he answered: "The Church teacheth that which I believe;" the which words he often repeated in the hearing of those that assisted him, by which means he eluded the subtlety of the enemy, and so—as he told his wise counsellors on appearing to them after his death—passed in a glorious manner into heaven.' *Sancta Sophia*, vol. ii. p. 202.

* 'Fear without hope maketh a man despair; and hope without fear maketh him presume. These two sins, despair and presumption, are the devil's tristres, where the unhappy beast seldom escapeth. A tristre is where men wait with the greyhounds to intercept the game, or to prepare the nets for them. All that he driveth is to one of these two points; for there are his nets and there his greyhounds; despair and presumption are met together, and of all sins they are the *nearest the gate of hell.* These two sins are two fierce robbers; for the one, that is, presumption, taketh away from God His righteous judgment and His justice; the other, that is, despair, taketh away from Him His mercy. And thus they both are endeavouring to destroy God Himself; for God could not exist without justice, nor without mercy.' *The Ancren Riwle*, p. 335.

2. In which cruel danger stand fast to this certain rule :—That all reflections upon thy sins proceed from God's grace and tend to thy good, if they be followed with effects of humility, with true sorrow for having offended so good a God, and with a firm confidence in His goodness. But when this reflection disquiets thy mind, makes thee doubtful and distrustful, peevish and pusillanimous, then, although thy sins appear indeed sufficient to make thee think thyself justly and eternally damned, and that there can be no reason for thee to hope for salvation—assure thyself they are clearly the effects proceeding from Satan's suggestions. And therefore humble thyself so much the more, and be more hopeful and confident in thy God; whereby thou wilt confound and conquer thy enemy with his own weapons, which he prepared for thy destruction.

The remedy: Confidence in God,

3. When, therefore, thy sins are suggested to thy memory, conceive a perfect hatred of them, as of things detestable to the divine goodness. Yet be sure to have a hopeful confidence in thy Saviour's passion. And I tell thee yet more :—Shouldst thou seem to hear God saying unto thee :—'Away, thou art none of the number of My sheep;' yet thou art not to lose thy confidence in His mercy, but humbly to reply :—'Thou hast just reason, O my sovereign Lord God, to shake me off for my sins' sake. But I have greater reason to be confident of Thy goodness and mercy, and to believe that Thou wilt pardon me. Therefore, I humbly beg salvation for this Thy wretched creature; damned, in-

and trust in His passion.

deed, by its own merits, but redeemed by the dear ransom* of Thy Son's most precious Blood and Passion. Thou wilt save me, O my Redeemer, for Thine own glory's sake; and I resign myself freely into Thy hands upon the assurance of Thy infinite mercy. Do with me and dispose of me as Thou best pleasest. For Thou art my only Lord, and if Thou killest me, yet I will place my whole hope in Thy heavenly goodness.'

§ 5. Of the Assault of Vain-glory.

1. The third assault is that of Vain-glory and Presumption. Here thou art to be equally wary of the other extreme, and never to admit of the least conceit or complacency in thyself or thy actions, but to refer all goodness which seems to be in thee purely to God's great mercy and the merits of Christ's Passion. Abase thyself in thy heart, whilst there is the least remnant of breath in thy body, and acknowledge thy God as the true fountain of all thy goodness. Look not at all upon thy own merits, but rely totally upon His mercy. Distrust thyself and trust in thy Saviour; and think what poor provisions thou hast laid up in store for this passage of death and thy journey to eternity, and how vain and useless all thine own endeavours will prove, unless God will be pleased to put His helping hand and gather thee under the sacred wings of His divine protection.

Its remedy: Distrust of self and trust in God.

* 'For you are bought with a great price.' 1 Cor. vi. 20.

§ 6. Of Illusions and False Appearances which are Usually Presented at the Hour of Death.

1. If thy obstinate enemy, who is ever studying to supplant thee, should at this time set upon thee with false appearances, and transfigurations of himself into an angel of light, thy best way is to recur to the certain knowledge of thine own nothingness, and boldly to answer him:—'Depart, O thou accursed devil, into thy own darkness; I neither deserve nor desire any visions. I need no other thing than the mercy of my Jesus, the prayers of the Virgin Mary, and the assistance of the Saints.' Yea, though thou hast reason to guess by some evident signs that these are from heaven, yet still deny them all access unto thee, and drive them far from thee. Nor needest thou fear lest any such resistance—grounded upon thine own indignity—should displease God. For, if the visions come from Him, He knows well how to make them manifest, notwithstanding thy opposition. Thou art thereby secure to be no loser, since He Who gives His grace to the humble cannot be angry with him who practiseth such high acts of that virtue.

The remedy: Confession of thy own nothingness, and a turning away from illusions.

2. These are the common and ordinary engines which our enemy makes use of in this last passage. After which follow his other trained bands of temptations, according to each one's particular inclination and disposition. Stand, therefore, timely to thy arms, my beloved, before this

After these general temptations usually follow particular ones.

great day of battle steal upon thee. And fight now valiantly and generously against thy violent passions and imperfections, that thou mayest be prepared at that time which takes from thee all other time and power of preparing and fighting: for there is no work or understanding in the grave whither we are going.

CHAPTER XX.

THAT WE MUST NEVER FLATTER OURSELVES AS HAVING SUBDUED OUR ENEMIES; BUT MUST OFTEN RETURN TO OUR WONTED EXERCISES, AS IF WE WERE YET NOVICES IN THE SPIRITUAL CONFLICT.

Ever esteem thyself a novice,

1. I HAVE yet one thing, O beloved, to tell thee of, which is:—That thou never persuade thyself to have obtained a complete victory over any one of thy passions, though, perchance, thou hast for a long time together felt no motions thereof; but that thou often renew thy accustomed spiritual exercises, as if thou wert a beginner or a new-born babe now entering the list.

for perfection is high and difficult of attainment.

2. For if we behold and desire to follow the perfection whereunto God hath called us, we shall find it to be so high and so copious, that after our best endeavours we shall scarcely presume to say that we have learnt the first principles thereof. And besides this, that which seems to us a virtue may indeed sometimes be a vice, our judgment being deceived by some secret pride.*

---

* See chaps. xvii. xviii.

CHAPTER XXI.

Of Holy Prayer.

1. We have hitherto, O beloved, through the Divine assistance, heard and learned what concerns Diffidence in ourselves, Confidence in our God, and continual Exercise,* which are the three necessary means to get the victory of our passions, and to conquer the disordered motions of our sensuality. Now follows the fourth, which is devout Prayer; and this is the best and most efficacious means to obtain all good things from God's gracious and bountiful hands.†

The fourth weapon is Devout Prayer.

2. For prayer is the food and the support of the soul during its pilgrimage upon earth. It is a secure bridge for it to pass over the several seas of adversities and propensities. It is a wall of defence against vices and temptations; a key opening into the chamber of celestial treasures, the door of holy thoughts; and finally, an invincible citadel and sure retreating-place from the violent assaults of all our enemies. By prayer—if thou knowest how to apply it to its true use—thou puttest a sword into thy Lord's powerful hands wherewith He will fight thy battles for

Enlargement. A further description of prayer.

* See chap. i.

† So St. Augustine: 'Prayer is the key of heaven; prayer ascends and mercy descends; high as are the heavens, and low as is the earth, God hears the voice of man *Ser.* xlvii., *in app.*

thee, and vanquish all enemies which oppose thee in thy way of perfection.*

TEXT. Its conditions: 1. A desire to serve God.

3. But to make thy prayers grateful, useful, and acceptable, they must be accompanied with these conditions and properties. *First.* That an ardent desire to serve thy Lord God in such a manner as may best please His Divine Majesty do continually inflame thy heart.

ENLARGEMENT. How to obtain this inflamed desire.

4. To obtain this inflamed desire, consider that thy Lord God, by reason of His admirable excellences of goodness, majesty, wisdom, beauty, and other infinite perfections, is more than worthy to be served and honoured by thee and all creatures. That to serve and succour thee, this greatness hath condescended to compassionate thy weakness; and to suffer for thee in His Sacred Humanity for thirty-three years, during which time He cured and salved thy miserable sores—which were gangrened by the foul contagion of sin—not with medical oil, ordinary wine, and common plasters, but with the most precious balsam of His own sacred blood, and with unguents made of His purest flesh, torn from His body by scourges, thorns, and nails. Weigh, also, the importance of His service, since thou art thereby enabled to master thyself, to conquer thy enemies, and to become the child of God.

* 'With the cries of our prayers,' says St. Hilary, 'we must fight against the devil and his armed hosts.' *Hilar. in Psal.* lxv.

5. *Secondly.* That thou be possessed with a true an constant faith, whereby thou believest that thy loving Lord will give thee all things necessary for His service and thy salvation. TEXT. 2. Perfect Faith.

6. This holy confidence is the vessel which the Divine goodness fills with the treasures of His graces; and the greater it is, the richer and more laden will thy prayer return into thine own bosom. For how can our unchangeable Lord fail to make us partakers of His good gifts and graces, when He Himself hath commanded us to ask them, and promised His holy Spirit to them who petition Him for It with faith and perseverance?* ENLARGEMENT.

7. *Thirdly.* That thou have no other end in frequenting holy prayer than the accomplishing of God's will and not thine own; and this as well in asking as in obtaining. That is, let nothing move thee to pray, but only that which God will have TEXT. 3. Conformity to God's will.

* Confidence in prayer is based upon the attributes of the omnipotence and mercy of God. Whensoever our prayers are not heard, the reason is, in ninety cases out of a hundred, because we have prayed with a dull and wavering faith. There is nothing that is able to perfect the soul, or lead it to the heights of divine contemplation, except prayer. But in order that our prayer may ascend into heaven and pierce the ear of God, it should be informed with a strong, stable, and lively faith. For how can we expect that our Lord will grant our prayers if they be accompanied with misgivings as to whether He will hear them, or lavish His special graces and favours on those who manifest but little confidence in His mercy and goodness? To pray with these dispositions is to insult God, rather than to honour Him. Faith, as our Lord Himself testifies, is the first condition of prayer: *All things whatsoever you shall ask*, believing, *you shall receive* (Matt. xxi. 22). And St. James: *Let him ask in faith, never wavering.* And St. Augustine (*Epist.* x. *ad Hier.*), commenting upon the above words of our Saviour, declares: 'Without faith it is vain to pray.'

thee pray for; neither do thou desire to be heard for any other reason than that thou hopest it is His pleasure. Briefly, let thy intention and the whole purpose of thy prayer be this:—That thy will may be conformable to God's will, and strive not at all to bend His will, or draw it unto thine.*

ENLARGEMENT. Because the divine will is infallible, thine fallible.

8. And this thou art to do so much the rather because thy will, being infected with self-love, is subject to error and forgetfulness of itself, and so knows not what it asks. But the Divine will is ever accompanied with unspeakable goodness, and so can never fail, but is the rule and queen-regent of all other wills, deserving to be followed and obeyed by them all. Thou art therefore always to petition for those things which are conformable to God's holy will. And when thou suspectest whether some desire of thine be truly such, make thy demand conditional, and wish it not, but only so far as thy Lord God is well pleased thou shalt obtain it. In things also which are known to be certainly agreeable to His Divine Majesty, such as are virtues and graces, thou art to pray for them rather that thou mayest by their means better please, satisfy, and serve Him, than for

* St. Anselm, in his profound treatise *De Similitudinibus*, draws a distinction between the object of God's will, and that of our will in conformity with His. 'We ought not,' he says, 'always to wish what God wishes; but we ought to wish that which God wishes us to wish. For God wished that the blessed Martin should be taken from this life; but if his disciples had wished this they would have been cruel. They knew what God wished; but they wished what God wished them to wish.' Cap. clx.

any other end or consideration whatsoever, though never so spiritual.

9. *Fourthly.* That thy prayer and the aforesaid spiritual exercises be so joined together that they be wholly inseparable, and that they never go one without the other. For pray thou never so long and never so much to obtain any virtue, unless thou also labour and exercise thyself in the way to get it,* thou both temptest God, and obtainest not thy desire.

TEXT. 4. Conjunction of works with prayer.

10. *Fifthly.* Remember that before thou demandest new favours, thou art to render humble thanks for those thou hast formerly received, by these or the like expressions :—'O my good and gracious Lord God, Who hast made me, redeemed me, and rescued me from mine enemies oftener than I myself know or can conceive, succour me now also, and deny not to grant this my present petition, though I have been hitherto rebellious to Thy will and ungrateful to Thy goodness.' And if thy demand be for some particular virtue of which thou now standest in great need, by reason of some temptation, trouble, or contradiction which troubleth thee, forget not to thank Him for that occasion of thy trial and exercise, which through His gracious assistance may redound so much to thy spiritual good.

ENLARGEMENT. 5. Thanksgiving for favours received.

11. *Sixthly.* Since prayer hath its whole force, power, and hope of efficacy from God's good-

6. Based on God's good-

* 'Love, my daughters, must not be built on our own fancy, but proved by works.' *The Interior Castle*, p. 62.

ness and promises. ness and mercy, from Christ's merits and passion, and from the Divine promise, therefore thou mayest fitly usher in thy demands by some of these following sayings:—'O my God, grant unto Thy servant, I beseech Thee, this grace for Thy supreme goodness' sake, that Thy most dear Son's merits may obtain for me the request of my petition. Remember, O my Lord, Thine own loving promise, and incline Thine ear to hear my prayer.' At other times, thou mayest ask by the merits of the most glorious Virgin and the suffrages of the Saints, which are powerful to prevail in thy pious demands.

12. *Seventhly.* Thou art to pray with perseverance.
7. Perseverance. For if the continued importunity of the Widow in the Gospel moved the hard-hearted judge to give her what she asked,* how shall perseverant petitions be rejected by Him Who is mercy and goodness itself?

13. *Eighthly.* Therefore, after thy prayer, strengthen
TEXT. 8. Strengthened with hope. thy soul with a lively hope in God, that through His infinite love He will bestow on thee the asked-for grace or gift, or something that is better for thee, or both together. And although He so long delays His answer that thou mayest fancy He denies

* *And He spoke also a parable to them, that we ought always to pray, and not to faint. Saying: There was a judge in a certain city, who feared not God, nor regarded man. And there was a certain widow in that city and she came to him, saying: Avenge me of my adversary. And he would not for a long time. But afterwards he said within himself: Although I fear not God, nor regard man, yet because this widow is troublesome to me, I will avenge her, lest continually coming she weary me.*' Luke xviii. 1-6.

what thou askest, yet remain constantly in this hope, and never slacken therefore either thy prayer, or thy exercise, or thy confidence. Yea, though it may seem to thee that God rejecteth thee and thy prayer, yet do thou still humble thyself more and more before Him, increasing thy faith and comforting thyself with hope in thy Saviour. For the more fervently and frequently thou interposest this constant hope in God, even in such violent repulses, and, as it were, manifest rejections of thy prayer, the more thou becomest pleasing and grateful unto Him.

Give thanks even when thy prayer is denied.

14. And therefore thou art always to return grateful thanks to Him Whom thou acknowledgest no less good, wise, and loving in thy behalf when He seems to cast out thy petition, than when He grants it. Keep, then, an ever-constant, courageous, and joyful mind in all events, whether good or bad; and humbly submit to the infallible wisdom and all-ordering providence of thy Lord God.*

* And when your prayer is sometimes rejected, comfort your soul with that saying of St. Augustine: 'God denies some things in His mercy which He grants in His wrath' (*Init. Serm.* xxxiii. *de verb. Domini*). Yet deem not your prayer to have been on this account altogether in vain. God is a loving Father; and if you sometimes seek piously what would not be conducive to your salvation, He will in its place give you something that will be profitable. If He denies you high spiritual graces, it is because He sees your poor soul is still too weak and sinful to receive them with due fruit. He stores up for you, however, in heaven, reward a hundredfold for every petition that you make with a right heart. For, as blessed Blosius declares, 'It is impossible that the least prayer rightly offered, the least sigh, or the least aspiration to God, should fail to bring forth much fruit, or to redound to thy greater glory in heaven.' Pray on therefore fervently and frequently.

CHAPTER XXII.

What Inward or Mental Prayer is: what Contemplation; and the Use thereof.

Mental prayer includes either a virtual petition,

1. Inward or mental prayer is:—An elevation of the mind to God. It always includes either an actual or virtual petition of something. A *Virtual prayer* is when the mind is lifted up to God to obtain some grace from Him, showing Him our necessities simply and briefly, without any discourse or consideration of any other things. Thus, when I elevate my mind to God, and confess before Him my weakness both to do well and to defend myself from doing evil, this sort of prayer is properly termed virtual—because, when I thus briefly lay open my mind to God, He well knows what is wanting to me, and how much I stand in need of His help.

Enlargement.

And this virtually implies an humble supplication to His Divine Majesty that He will vouchsafe to supply thy necessities. And by how much the more this confession of thine own want and weakness is real and manifest, and thy desire efficacious and thy confidence lively, by so much also thy demand shall be of more force and value.

Text.

2. There is also another kind of virtual prayer, which consists in a simple beholding or contemplation of God in our minds. And this prayer is:—When we silently desire and, as it were, put our Lord in remembrance of that grace we formerly demanded.

Learn, O my beloved, this way of prayer, and make it familiar unto thee by the frequent use thereof. For experience will give thee to understand that it is the best armour against all enemies, adversities, and dangers. Have it therefore always in readiness, that where and whensoever need requires thou mayest make use thereof.

3. *Actual petition*,* or actual inward prayer, is:— When grace is asked by words expressed in the mind, in this or the like manner:—'Give me, O my Lord God, this grace, this benefit, for the honour of Thy most sacred name.' Or thus:—'I steadfastly believe, O my God, that it is Thy holy will I should beg of Thee this grace, which I stand in need of. Do Thou, therefore, O my God, accomplish Thine own pleasure in me.' Thus also thou mayest present before God's Divine Majesty thine enemy which annoys thee, or thy sins which afflict thee, joining therewith thine own weakness to resist them; and say:—'O Lord, look upon Thine own creature, made by Thy holy hands, and redeemed by Thy precious blood. Behold also Thine enemy and mine outrageously reaching at me, and striving to take me from Thee, and tear me in pieces. O my God, to Thee only do I fly, in Thee only I trust. Consider my weakness and the strength of my enemy, who will infallibly subject me to his tyranny, if I am left destitute of Thy powerful protection.'

or an actual asking by words expressed in the mind.

'Some there are who all their days abide in the exercise of acts. And they may well content themselves with such condition, which is both pleasing to God and sufficiently profitable to themselves.' *The Divine Cloud*, p. 248.

CHAPTER XXIII.

How we may join Contemplation to this Inward Prayer.

Take some points of Christ's passion, and apply them to the virtues you ask for.

1. If sometimes thou art willing to devote thyself to mental prayer for a certain space of time, as an hour or more, thou mayest join to this way of prayer certain meditations upon the *Life and Death* of our Saviour Christ, applying always His actions to that virtue thou then demandest, and so meditating upon them both together. For example :—Patience is the virtue thou art now in quest of. Choose, therefore, for the subject of thy meditation, some mystery of Christ's crucifixion, as: How cruelly He was despoiled of His garments, which were barbarously rent from His body, carrying away part of His sacred flesh, which cleaved fast unto them; with what outcries and curses He was crowned and uncrowned with thorns, His executioners iterating again and again that terrible torment; how this most innocent Lamb was fastened with nails to the wood of the cross, and lifted up into the air with unspeakable grief of His wounds, and new anguish of His whole body; and so of other like points.

The method of this exercise.

2. And in these considerations, *first*, apply thy senses to feel, see, &c., the pain which thy dear Saviour endured in these passages in all the members of His sacred Humanity. *Then*, elevate thy heart to His holy soul, penetrate into His patience and meekness, and see how pleasantly He passeth over these

so great and grievous afflictions; and how ready He is, for His father's satisfaction and our salvation, to suffer much more and far greater torments. *After this*, behold Him hanging on His cross and completing His sufferings by His death; stand thou close to Him and contemplate Him, and think with what an ardent desire He did all this for thee, that thou, by His example, mightest learn to endure with patience thy smaller adversities for His honour. And as He turned Himself to His heavenly Father, and prayed for thee, so thou shouldst implore His grace to bear and overcome this cross thou now groanest under, and all thy other grievances, with quiet of mind and constancy of resolution. And *lastly*, compel thy will to consent to these sufferings, and speak to it to take up this cross quietly and carry it constantly. *Then*, turn thee to God thy heavenly Father, and humbly beg of Him the virtue of patience, and that He will be pleased to hear the perfect prayer of His own dear Son poured out on the cross for thee.

CHAPTER XXIV.

Of another Certain Manner of Prayer by Way of Meditation.

Consider Christ's merits and the pleasure His Father took in His obedience.

1. There is yet another manner of praying and meditating together, as thus:—Having attentively and piously considered upon thy Saviour's bitter Passion, sustained for thy sake and to save thy soul, apply thine own senses, as aforesaid, and

endeavour to feel, as it were, the like dolours in thyself; and let thy thoughts penetrate into the promptitude of mind wherewith Christ thy Saviour suffered all this. And having weighed His exceeding pains and His perfect patience, proceed to these two following considerations:—*First*, of the treasure of Christ's merits; and *Secondly*, of the exceeding pleasure and satisfaction which the heavenly Father took in His dear Son's perfect obedience.

and present both of them to God.

2. *Then*, having filled thy mind with these pious points of meditation, present them to thy Lord God, and through them beg that grace which thou standest in greatest need of. And thus thou mayest put up thy petitions, not only in meditating upon any mystery of Christ's Passion, but also upon each particular act of His life, be it internal or external.

CHAPTER XXV.

Of a Way of Praying by the Intercession of the Blessed Virgin.

1. Fix the mind on the Eternal Father.

1. There is yet—besides these foregoing methods of Prayer and Meditation—another way; by the means of the most glorious and ever-blessed Virgin and Mother of our Lord Jesus Christ, and which thou mayest thus easily practise:—*First*, fix thy mind and meditation upon God the Eternal Father; *Then*, upon Jesus Christ His dear Son and our sweet Saviour; and *Lastly*, upon Mary the ever-blessed Virgin Mother. In thy meditation of the Eternal Father, take these two

points for thy subject, and offer them up to His Divine Majesty :—*First*, the great pleasure and satisfaction He had in Himself from all eternity concerning this perfect creature, the Virgin, before she had a being. *Secondly*, the wonders He wrought in her, and the pleasure He took in her, when she was born into the world.

2. And as for the *First* of these considerations, soar aloft and exalt thy thoughts beyond all time, and above each thing created, penetrating the very eternity of the Deity. And then consider what celebrity of joy and delight the Divine Majesty had within Himself concerning this sacred Virgin and her high perfections; and thou, finding thy Lord amidst these joys and delights, lay hold of the opportunity, and address thy petition unto Him with full hope and confidence that, for this His great joy's sake, He will impart bountifully some grace, strength, and courage unto thee, whereby thou mayest be enabled to encounter and conquer thine enemies, especially this vice which now chiefly tempts and troubles thee.

Considering the content He had in Himself (concerning her) from all eternity,

3. Hence, proceed to the consideration of those admirable virtues, great gifts, and singular graces conferred upon this most glorious Virgin; and sometimes present the whole bulk of them to the view of the eternal Father. Other times choose out some particular perfection to lay open before Him, imploring and entreating, for his own boundless goodness' sake, and in respect of these virtues and merits of this His dearly beloved Spouse, that He will graciously

and the wonders He wrought in her when she had a being.

CHAPTER XXVI.

How to Pray and Meditate by Means of the Holy Angels and Heavenly Citizens.

1. Address thyself to the Eternal Father.

1. Another powerful means to obtain thy petition is, by the Angels and blessed Saints in heaven. This also is practised two manner of ways. *First,* apply thy thoughts to the Eternal Father, and present before Him the love, honour, and praise wherewith His heavenly court worships and exalts Him. And withal, lay open all the miseries, labours, and molestations which His Saints suffered and by His grace surmounted here upon earth.

2. Unto the glorious Angels and Saints themselves.

2. *The other way* is by applying thyself to these glorious spirits, as to those who not only remember us amidst their joys, but earnestly desire our perfection. Beg, therefore, their faithful assistance in thy fight against vices, and sometimes implore their aid and assistance at the hour of thy death, against thy dreadful enemies. *Other times,* reflect upon those excellent gifts and graces wherewith their Lord God endued them; exciting in thy soul a lively feeling of love and joy that they possess these high perfections, as much, yea more, than if they were thine own, since such was the good will and pleasure of the Divine Majesty.

Dividing them into choirs, according to

3. And that thou mayest more easily and orderly perform and practise this pious exercise, divide the choirs of this blessed company according to

the week-days, in some such manner as followeth:— the days of the week.

1. Upon *Sunday*, meditate on the Nine Choirs of Angels.
2. Upon *Monday*, on the Choir of the Holy Apostles.
3. Upon *Tuesday*, on that of the glorious Martyrs.
4. Upon *Wednesday*, on that of the blessed Bishops.
5. Upon *Thursday*, on that of the holy Doctors.
6. Upon *Friday*, on that of the holy Confessors.
7. Upon *Saturday*, on that of the sacred Virgins.

4. But let no day pass, without some special devotion to the most glorious Virgin Mary, to thy Angel-guardian, and to that particular Saint and Patron to whom thou owest singular duty and veneration. But pray daily to the B. Virgin and thy Patron.

5. Amongst these I persuade thee to place St. Joseph, the dear spouse of the Sacred Virgin, who, as experience and contemplative persons testify, will assist thee by his holy prayers in all thy temporal and spiritual necessities, and particularly advance and direct thy soul in its spiritual exercises of Prayer and Contemplation. And surely, if our loving Lord so highly esteems His other Saints, because they paid Him His due honour and obedience upon earth, how much more doth He value this most humble and happy Saint; and how all-prevailing are his prayers likely to be with that Divine Son Who honoured, served, and obeyed him upon earth as His father. ENLARGEMENT. And to St. Joseph.

and compassion. Body, but the multitude of anguishes, griefs, and sadnesses of His most holy soul. For He, well knowing the eminent and infinite dignity of His heavenly Father, Whom He so highly loved, must needs be grieved above measure to see this benign and bountiful Creator of all things, after so many and so great benefits, to be so rashly, so maliciously, and so frequently offended and deluded by His own creatures. And this sadness of thy Saviour's soul was much augmented by the foresight He had of that vast multitude of men who, by their own sin and sloth, were to be damned eternally. The same grief was further aggravated by seeing the immense dolours of His dear and worthily beloved Mother; and the same sword spared not His which pierced her heart with sorrow. Moreover, Christ's sacred soul, which, by reason of the Divine union, was omniscient, suffered in all the Martyrs' and tender Virgins' torments, sustained for His faith and affection.

And acts of contrition for thy sins.

6. In these and the like meditations upon thy Lord and Saviour's Passion, thou must often reflect that thou, by thy grievous sins and defects, wert the cause and occasion of these His afflictions. And from hence conceive acts of true sorrow for thy shameful ingratitude, and humble thyself at the feet of His Majesty. And know that to be the best pleasing and most acceptable compassion when thou persecutest thine own disordered affections, and strivest to ruin and root out of thy heart those enemies which were the cause of thy Lord's so cruel pains and Passion.

7. And to move thee to a perfect hatred of thy sins, think seriously in running over all these points of thy dear Saviour's Passion, as if all these His sufferings were for no other cause than to stir thee up to detest all sin, and destroy thy unruly passions and affections: those especially which most disturb, defile, and distract thee, and most displease thy Saviour.

With a perfect hatred of them.

8. Lastly, that by these meditations upon Christ's Death and Passion thou mayest be moved to the admiration of His goodness; consider attentively, *First.* Who He is that suffereth these things? Surely, the only Son of the Almighty God, Who, to save thee, came from heaven and became man. *Secondly.* For whom He suffered? Surely, for us poor worms, the work of His own hands, and who are always prone to offend Him. *Thirdly.* By whom He suffered? Surely, by the vile and vulgar crew, and the very refuse of all nations. *Fourthly.* What He suffered? Surely, disgraces, contumelies, contempts, wounds, and torments, more than can be named or imagined. *Fifthly.* How He suffered all this? Surely, with a most patient, meek, and willing mind; neither showing any sign of distaste, nor speaking any word of reproach against His most ungrateful and malicious persecutors; but like an innocent lamb led on to the slaughter, He complained not of their violence and His own suffering, but laid down His life, His heart remaining full of sweetness. *Sixthly.* When and where He suffered? Surely, at the time of their paschal solemnity, and in their capital

Admire God's goodness by considering certain circumstances

and sacred city, and in the presence of His dearest Mother, and, finally, in the view, as it were, of the whole world.

ENLARGEMENT.

A Further Declaration of the Gain which may be Drawn from the Meditation upon Christ's Passion, and particularly of the Imitation of His Virtues.

1. Amongst the infinity of gains which may be
The first gain. drawn from this holy exercise, one is:—That thou must needs conceive, not only a sorrow for thy past sins, but feel also a shame and confusion in thy soul to see that those unruly passions, which put Christ Jesus to death upon the cross, do yet lurk and live within thy heart.

2. The other main gain, which flows from the
The second. former, is:—That being truly sensible of thy sins and ashamed of thine ingratitude, thou wilt heartily desire and humbly demand pardon for what is past, and grace to amend for the future. And by way of an acknowledgment of thy extraordinary obligation for thy Saviour's sufferings, undergone for thy sake, thou wilt resolve to serve Him, love Him, and suffer for Him hereafter.

3. The third gain is:—That thou wilt fall out with
The third. thy perverse inclinations and passions, and persecute them to death, be they never so little.

4. The fourth is:—That thou wilt force thyself to the
The fourth. utmost of thy power to imitate the virtues of thy dear Saviour, Who endured all this, not only to

save thee and satisfy for thy sins, but also to give thee an example to follow His sacred steps.

§ 1. Another Way to Meditate on the Passion.

1. And now, my beloved, I will here declare unto thee another method of meditating upon Christ's Passion, which thou mayest make use of as thy devotion or the occasion shall suggest unto thee. If thou desirest, for example, to obtain patience in imitation of thy Redeemer, consider these following points:

By considering: 1. How Christ's soul comports itself towards the heavenly Father;

First. What the afflicted soul of thy Saviour doth towards its heavenly Father.

Secondly. What the Father doth towards the soul of His Son.

Thirdly. What this soul doth towards itself and its sacred body.

Fourthly. What thy Saviour doth towards thee.

Fifthly. What thou shouldst do towards thy Saviour.

First, therefore:—Consider how the soul of Jesus Christ, being totally intent upon God, is amazed to behold this infinite and incomprehensible Majesty (in respect whereof all things created are as a pure nothing) subjected—though immutable in glory—to the suffering of such unworthy usages upon earth for man, from whom It never received anything but disloyalty and injuries; and how His soul afterwards adores, thanks, and offers up itself entirely to the disposition of the Divinity.

2. *Secondly*. Consider how God willeth and excireth the soul of thy Saviour to suffer for thy sake all those blows, buffets, scourges, spittles, blasphemies, thorns, and death upon the cross, giving Him to know how well He was pleased to see Him thus replenished with all sorts of affronts and afflictions.

2. How the Father towards Him;

3. *Thirdly*. Passing on to the soul of thy Saviour Christ, consider how with His understanding—which is all light—knowing how highly His Passion pleased God; and with His will—which is all fire—loving beyond measure the Divine Majesty, which thus invited Him to suffer for thee--He disposeth Himself readily, joyfully, and contentedly to obey God's sacred will and pleasure. And who can dive into the depth of those desires, which this pure and loving soul of thy Saviour had to suffer for thy sake? It found itself, as it were, in a labyrinth of troubles, casting about to encounter new ways of suffering; and therefore freely gave up itself and its innocent body as a prey to the pleasure and cruelty of the most lewd and worst sort of villains.

3. How the soul towards itself and its sacred body;

4. *Fourthly*. Consider, in the next place, thy sweet Saviour amidst His bitter torments, fixing His eyes full of tears and tenderness upon thee; and conceive thou hearest Him thus expostulating with thee:—'Behold, My child, whither thy immoderate desires and unmortified affections have brought thee, because thou wouldest not use a little violence to thyself. See and consider how much and how willingly I suffer for thy

4. How thy Saviour behaves towards thee;

love, and to give thee a pattern of perfect patience. I beg of thee, O My dear child, and I conjure thee by all these My sad sufferings and sorrows, that thou willingly embrace and cheerfully carry this cross, and any other which I shall think fit to lay upon thy shoulders; and that thou abandon thyself entirely into such hands as I shall permit to persecute thee in body or fame, how vile, contemptible, and cruel soever they be. O, didst thou but conceive the greatness of the comfort I should receive in this thy patience and courage! But thou mayest read it in these My wounds, wherein My love to thee is written in bloody characters, and which I willingly receive, as so many precious pearls, to enrich thy poor soul with all sorts of virtues and perfections, because I love it above all things created. And if I, thy Lord and Creator, am reduced to this extremity for thy love, why, O My dear spouse, wilt thou not consent to endure a little to satisfy My heart's desire, to supple My wounds, and to mitigate these My pains, caused by thy impatience, which more afflicts My soul than these grievous torments do My body.'

5. How thou shouldst behave towards thy Saviour.

5. *Fifthly.* Consider well who He is that speaks thus unto thee, and thou wilt find that He is the King of Glory, Jesus Christ, true God and true Man. Mark, also, the greatness of His grief, the variety of His torments, and the manner and indignity of His disgraces, too bad for the worst of men, or most infamous malefactor in the world. Yet, thou seest thy Saviour amidst all these affronts

and afflictions, not only immovable, mild, and patient, but even joyful and content, as if He now kept His marriage-banquet. And as a little water rather strengthens than extinguishes a full-kindled fire, so, by the increase of His torments—which were small in respect of His excessive love—His content and desire of suffering far greater was more and more enkindled and augmented. Consider, further, that He endured all this by no external violence,* nor for any self-interest; but, as He told thee, for thy love, and that thou mightest imitate Him, and exercise thyself in the virtue of patience. And then, penetrating into that which He desires thou shouldst do, and into the pleasure thou shouldst afford Him by this thy practice of patience, produce acts of a compassionate will, to bear not only this cross patiently and joyfully, but any greater; that so thou mayest imitate Him more perfectly, and please Him more abundantly. And imprinting in thy mind a lively image of these His sufferings, and of His constancy therein, be ashamed to think thy patience so much as a shadow of His, or that thy affections are really any at all being compared with His; and tremble that the least thought of not enduring for the love of thy Lord should remain in thy heart.

* As our Lord Himself testifies in these words: *I lay down My life that I may take it again. No man taketh it away from Me; but I lay it down of Myself, and I have power to lay it down: and I have power to take it up again.* John x. 17, 18.

6. Thy crucified Jesus, my beloved, is the best book thou canst read in, and the liveliest image thou canst look upon to draw the perfect portrait of all virtues.* For, it being the book of life, it not only informs thy understanding by words, but also inflames thy will by example. The world is full of books, yet all of them together cannot so speedily and perfectly teach the true means of obtaining all virtues, as doth the right contemplation of Christ upon His cross. But they who employ much time in deploring their Saviour's Passion and admiring His patience, and apply it not at all to their particular practice when occasions are offered, do like unto those soldiers who before the skirmish talk of great matters and speak high words in their tents, but who, at the first sight of the advancing enemy, take fright, quit their colours, cast down their arms, and utterly forsake the field. And, indeed, what thing can be more silly, cowardly, and untrustworthy than to contemplate, as in a most clear glass, the virtues of our Lord and Saviour, loving them and admiring them, and presently to forget them and disesteem them as soon as any occasion is presented wherein to exercise ourselves in their imitation.

Christ crucified is the best book to read.

* St. Thomas of Aquin, when paying a visit on one occasion to his friend St. Bonaventure, inquired of him what were the books out of which he derived the sublime thoughts found in his writings. 'Believe me,' replied the seraphic Doctor, pointing to the crucifix, 'from studying this book I draw all that I read, preach, or write, and my soul receives greater light at the foot of the crucifix than from all literary works whatsoever.' St. Philip Beneti, falling into his agony, called for his *Book*, and calmly expired embracing the crucifix.

CHAPTER XXVIII.

OF SENSIBLE DEVOTION, AS ALSO OF SPIRITUAL DRYNESS AND DERELICTION.

Devotion is best known by the effects it produces.

1. SENSIBLE devotion proceeds sometimes from a natural inclination, sometimes from the devil, and sometimes from God's grace.* And by the fruits of it thou mayest best judge from which of these springs it issueth. For if thence thou art no whit moved to amendment of life, thou mayest justly fear it comes either from thy enemy or from thy own nature; and the more sweetness thou feelest, the more shouldst thou be suspicious whence it floweth.

How to profit from spiritual sweetness.

2. When, therefore, thy soul is replenished with spiritual sweetness, question not whence it cometh, nor adhere much unto it. But still stick steadfastly to the acknowledgment of thine own baseness, abstracting thy heart from all other delights or desires than only that which it takes in God and His good pleasure. Thus will these short sweetnesses, whether they spring from thy own nature or thine enemy's suggestion, be truly turned to thy comfort and profit.†

* 'Sensible devotion which arises first in the bodily heart is to be held suspected, because it may be wrought by a good or a bad angel; but the devotion that descends from the superior will can only be wrought by God. If it be uncertain whence the sweetness came, a man may, by the exercise of the will, adjoining himself to God, remain secure from all harm. The same rule holds good in case of visions, revelations, and other extraordinary favours.' F. Baker's (O.S.B.) *Note* to the *Cloud of Knowing and Unknowing*, chap. xlviii.

† 'The desire of finding comfort in what we do is natural to all; but this being the desire of the natural man, they who proceed on

3. Dryness, or desolation of the soul, in like manner, may proceed either out of our own *natural Defect*, or from the *Devil*, or from *God*. From the *Devil;* who thereby strives to render the soul tepid and tedious in her spiritual exercises, and so to draw

Three causes of spiritual dryness.

better principles than those which nature suggests, never seek present comforts in what they do, but perform all duties with the hope of finding everlasting comfort in the possession of God. Hence, all their business is centred in this one point:—*What is the will of God; What duties He requires of them for gaining everlasting life:* and having settled this point, to make it the principal business of their whole lives, to perform such duties with the greatest fidelity, and in the best manner they are able, according to the circumstances in which they are. And whilst the end of all they do is to come at length to the presence of God, their great solicitude is so to perform all, that this may be the effect of what they do; but as to all other effects which regard this life only, whether in temporal blessings, interior peace, or sensible and present comforts, they endeavour to bring their mind to as great an *indifferency* as they are able, leaving these blessings wholly to the pleasure of God, to grant or deny them, as it shall seem good to His eyes. If He be favourable at any time in giving such encouragements to infirm nature, they receive them with thanksgiving, but without depending on them: and if He shows no favour in this way, they go on still with an equal fidelity; because it is not the present comforts of God they here work for, but *God Himself* in the life that is yet to come. Nature will never fail of desiring what is so pleasing to it; and piety, while yet imperfect, is ever solicitous for these encouragements; but he who is more advanced, is jealous of all sensible consolations, because he observes how ready self-love is to lay hold of them; and, therefore, being apprehensive lest the sense of these comforts become some motive in the exercise of prayer, he chooses rather to renounce or pass them by than rejoice in them; that so the love of God and duty may have the whole influence on whatever he does, and that he may perform no part of his duty, because of the comforts found in it, but because it is the will of God he should be faithful in it.

'This is the most perfect rule a Christian can follow in this mortal state, and those who are yet at a distance from perfection, though they cannot come up to it, ought yet to keep their eye upon it, so as to secure themselves against unreasonable disquiets, which otherwise will prove their discouragement in all duties.' *Instructions for Particular States*, 1718, pp. 72-74.

her by degrees to leave them, and look after earthly solace. From *Ourselves;* either because we stand in fear of ourselves by reason of our sins, or because we are negligent in the practice of our devotions. From *God;* Who therefore permits this dryness to excite us to more diligence, and abstract us from all other cares and curiosities but those only which concern our Creator, or have some relation unto His honour or our own perfection. Or finally, to teach us not to trust or rest in spiritual joys, but to depend wholly on His holy will and pleasure, as that resigned soul did who said: *The Lord gave, and the Lord hath taken away: as it hath pleased the Lord so is it done: blessed be the name of the Lord.**

Search out the cause thereof,

4. When, therefore, thou feelest this dryness of devotion, enter into thyself, and search out the cause thereof; and having found it, fight against it—not to recover that sensible sweetness of grace, but to expel far from thee whatsoever is displeasing to the Divine Majesty.

and keep on thy accustomed exercises.

5. And let it be thy continual care to keep on thy accustomed practices of piety, notwithstanding this dryness in thy soul. Yea, though thou seemest to labour in vain, yet prosecute them with greater diligence, and drink of that bitter poison of desolation with a prompt and peaceable resolution. And if it be so mingled with the thick dregs of a troubled mind, that thou knowest not how to swallow

† Job i. 21.

it, nor which way to turn thee, yet persevere with alacrity, and sit solitarily, thus deserted, under the shadow of the holy cross, seeking no outward solace, though the whole world should offer it, or any creature afford it thee.

Nor pray to have it mitigated.

6. For thou art to conceal this cross of thine from all persons,* except thy ghostly father, to whom thou art faithfully to discover it, not, indeed, to have comfort from him, but counsel how to carry thyself during this dryness, conformable to the Divine pleasure and good-liking. Nor art thou to make use of the Holy Communion, prayer, or any other spiritual exercise with intention to have the least mitigation of thy adversities, but only that thy good God will give thee strength of spirit to support thy cross with patience. And if through trouble and distraction thou canst hardly make use of thine understanding in thy meditations, keep only a willing mind to do it, and supply it with jaculatory prayers, and frequent elevations of thy mind to thy Lord God.

ENLARGEMENT. Suitable aspirations.

7. In this case thou mayest make use of these or the like sacred sentences:—

My heart is troubled, my strength hath left me, and the light of my eyes itself is not with me.†

* We may here draw attention to that shrewd maxim of St. Teresa's:—'Never make thy temptations and imperfections known to those in the community whose progress is only slight, for that will hurt thyself and others, but only to those who are far advanced in perfection.' *Maxim* 67.

† Psalm xxxvii. 11.

*Lord, I suffer violence, answer Thou for me.**

Return, return, O Sulamitess: return, return, that we may behold thee.†

How long, O Lord, wilt Thou forget me unto the end? How long dost Thou turn away Thy face from me? How long shall I take counsels in my soul, sorrow in my heart all the day.‡

Why, O Lord, hast Thou retired afar off? Why dost Thou slight us in our wants, in the time of trouble?§

O forgive me, that I may be refreshed before I go hence and be no more.||

O God, my God, look upon me. Why hast Thou forsaken me?¶

Or thou mayest say:—'O my God, O my Love, where, where dost Thou leave Thy poor servant thus all alone, who hath no comfort in himself, and desires none from any creature? O, what shall he do if he findeth it not in Thee? Whither wilt thou go, poor strayed sheep, if thou hearest not the voice of thy divine Shepherd? O living Fountain! O Source of all sweetness! shall I never more become worthy to taste one only drop of Thy delights? To whom shall I have recourse, if Thou, my God and only Refuge, keepest aloof from me? O unlimited Bounty! when shall I have a lively feeling of Thy effects? How is it possible for my dry soul to subsist in this desert earth, being deprived, O my God, of Thy heavenly dews?'

* Isaias xxxviii. 14. † Cant. of Can. vi. 12.
‡ Psalm xii. 1, 2. § Ib. x. 1. || Ib. xxxviii. 14. ¶ Ib. xxi. 1.

8. When thou findest thyself thus abandoned, remember how thy dear Saviour was also left comfortless by the same heavenly Father in the Garden, upon the Cross, and in His greatest afflictions. Therefore pronounce with Him oftentimes those hard words:—*Non mea voluntas, sed Tua fiat*—'Not My will, but Thine be done:'* which, proceeding from the depth of thy heart, will sweetly wound the heart of thy Lord God, and move Him to compassionate thy misery, either by sending thee comfort, or giving thee courage, constancy, and resignation to endure it.

In thy dryness, think of thy Saviour's desolation on the cross.

9. For know assuredly that to *do* or *suffer* for God's honour is to Him the most acceptable prayer. And, therefore, to endure this dryness with perfect patience and humble resignation, makes thee truly devout. For true devotion consists in no other thing than to have a ready will to follow Christ thy Lord with thy cross on thy shoulders, whither and which way He pleaseth, having and desiring God only for God, and sometimes leaving God for God.†

TEXT. Suffering is a prayer that makes thee truly devout.

10. If, therefore, spiritual persons, especially religious men and women, would seriously examine and measure their progress in the way of perfection and piety by this rule, and not by the feeling of

And not sensible devotion;

* Luke xxii. 42.

† See the *Third Treatise of the Conquest*, the Fifth Degree of Perfection; also, the Sixth, § 6; likewise, the *Maxims of Mystical Divinity*, Maxim 37.

sensible devotion—which many do chiefly regard—they surely would make better use in their exercises of devotion of sensible comforts, which their loving Lord affords, to make them more zealous in submitting to that sacred Will which disposeth all things in order to our salvation and benefit.

wherein many are deceived.

11. And in this also many are much deceived, that when they are troubled with impure and perverse thoughts, they presently become fearful and faint-hearted, and, as if God had utterly forsaken them, think it impossible that His holy Spirit should inhabit a heart so troubled and tormented. And they so entangle themselves in these fancies, that by degrees they fall into a grievous dislike of themselves, and, lastly, into a certain dangerous despair; and this they no sooner apprehend in themselves, than they presently run to their wonted prayers to recover their quiet. But hereby they show themselves little grateful to God. He therefore permits them to be thus troubled and tempted, to bring them to the clear knowledge of their own nothingness; that so, as wretched, frail, and desolate creatures, they may more seriously seek Him, and more diligently draw near unto Him.*

* 'When the Lord suffereth us to be tempted He playeth with us, as the mother with her young darling; she flies from him, and hides herself, and lets him sit alone, and look anxiously around, and call "Dame! Dame!" and weep awhile, and then she leapeth forth laughing, with outspread arms, and embraceth and kisseth him, and wipeth his eyes. In like manner our Lord sometimes leaveth us alone, and withdraweth His grace, His comfort, and His support, so that we feel no delight in any good that we do, nor any satisfaction of heart; and

12. Wherefore, O my beloved, that which thou must do in such a distress is this:—Enter straight into a profound reflection upon thine own baseness, and then humble thyself, and confess thy peevish affections and passions, and acknowledge thy proneness to fall, if left to thyself, into all manner of wickednesses; and that without thy loving Lord's care and custody,

What thou art to do in this distress.

yet, at that very time, our dear Father loveth us nevertheless, but doth it for the great love that He hath to us. And David understood this well when he said: "*Non me derelinquas usquequaque*"—"Lord," quoth he, "do not Thou utterly forsake me." Observe, he was willing that He should forsake him, but not utterly. And there are six reasons why God, for our good sometimes, withdraweth Himself: *One* is, that we may not become proud; *Another* is, that we may know our own feebleness, our great infirmity, and our weakness; and that is a very great good, as St. Gregory saith, "*Magna est perfectio suæ imperfectionis cognitio*;" that is, "It is great goodness in a man to know well his own wretchedness and his weakness." When two persons are carrying a burden, and one of them letteth it go, he that holdeth it up may then feel how it weigheth. Even so, dear sister, while God beareth thy temptation along with thee, thou never knowest how heavy it is, and therefore, upon some occasion, He leaveth thee alone, that thou mayest understand thy own feebleness, and call for His aid, and cry loud for Him. If He delays too long, hold it well up in the mean time, though it distress thee sore. For he that is certain that succour shall soon come to him, and yet yields up the castle to his enemies, is greatly to blame. Think here of the story how the holy man in his temptation saw opposed to him, on the west, such a large army of devils, that through great terror he lost the firmness of his faith, until the other holy man said to him, "Look," quoth he, "towards the east. *Plures vobiscum sunt quam cum illis*—We have more than they are to help on our side." The *Third* reason is, that thou be never quite secure; for security begetteth carelessness and presumption, and both these beget disobedience. The *Fourth* reason why our Lord hideth Himself is, that thou mayest seek Him more earnestly, and call and weep after Him, as the little baby doth after his mother. After this is the *Fifth* reason; that thou receive Him the more joyfully on His return. The *Sixth* reason is, that thou mayest the more wisely keep, and the more firmly hold, Him when thou hast got Him, and say with His beloved, "I hold Him, and I will not let Him go" (Can. iii. 4).' *The Ancren Riwle*, pp. 231-235.

help and defence, thou wouldst be cast down headlong into ruin. This done, raise thy heart with a good hope and confidence in thy Creator; seeing that it is He only who permitted thee to fall into this adversity, that thou mightest take hold of the occasion to draw nearer unto Him by humble prayer; and therefore thou art obliged to render grateful thanks to His Divine Majesty for these like troubles and temptations. And take this for a certainty:—That all such perverse thoughts are sooner expelled with meek sufferance and patience than with much solicitude and study.

CHAPTER XXIX.

That the Worthy Frequenting of the Blessed Sacrament is an Efficacious Means to Conquer our Passions.

Meditate the day before Communion on thy Saviour's desire to come to thee,

1. The sacred Communion, or most Holy Sacrament of the Eucharist, is received by devout Christians for divers ends. But if thou desirest to take it for the particular strengthening of thy soul against the assaults of evil inclinations, attend to what I shall now teach thee:—The day before thou intendest to communicate, meditate, if thy leisure give thee leave, on the great desire thy dear Saviour hath to unite Himself to thee by the means of this Sacrament and thereby to root out thy vicious

affections.* For this His desire is so immense that no created understanding can comprehend it. But that thou mayest have a small glimpse thereof, consider these two things. *First.* What pleasure our Lord takes to dwell in us, since the holy Scripture calls this *His delight*;† and in requital of this love He only requires our hearts.‡ *Secondly.* How much He hateth our sins, which hinder His nearer union with us, and are directly opposite to His incomparable perfections. For He, being the only chief Good, the purest Light, and most perfect Beauty, cannot but detest that which is mere darkness, frailty, and the corruption and canker of our wretched souls. And that this loving desire of thy dear Lord may make yet deeper impression on thy mind, meditate often on His marvellous works, related in the Old and New Testament; especially upon His most bitter Passion and cruel Death, which He did expressly suffer to deliver thy soul from sin, and to cleanse it from such affections as are contrary to His Divine Majesty. Concerning which point, all the illuminated doctors of God's Church do unanimously conclude and teach:—That Christ our Saviour would again, if it were needful, expose Himself to a thousand deaths to free us from the least evil passion or affection.§

* 'The morning of Communion remember in thy prayer that, notwithstanding thy wretchedness, thou art about to receive God; and in thy prayer at night, that thou hast received Him.' *Maxims of St. Teresa*, 58.

† *My delights were to be with the children of men.* Prov. viii. 31.

‡ *My son, give Me thy heart.* Prov. xxiii. 26.

§ See *Note* to chap. xxxiii. § 5.

2. By such considerations thou wilt easily gather the great desire thy dear Saviour hath to dwell with thee. And from thence conclude how fitting it is that thou shouldst reciprocally stir up in thyself an ardent affection to receive and entertain Him. This thou mayest do by these and the like ejaculatory prayers :—'Come, O my Lord and my Love; help Thy vile creature to conquer her enemies. When, O when, my dear spouse, will that happy hour come, that I may receive Thee, the Bread of life; and being comforted and encouraged by Thee, may fully conquer myself, and totally subdue my own evil passions and disordered affections?'

And move thy soul to a reciprocal desire towards Him.

3. And when thou art strengthened with the hope of thy sweet Saviour's Coming into thy soul, then provoke thy passions to battle, call up thy affections and curb them again and again with perfect hatred and horror.* This done, produce acts and desires of the virtues which are opposite to these vices; and let this be thy evening's entertainment and morning's employment.

Then provoke thy passions to battle.

4. But when the hour of sacred Communion draws near, think seriously of thine own faults, failings, and unfaithfulness to thy Lord God since the time of thy last approach to the sacred table, and for which ingratitude and unfaithfulness thou tremblest with fear and confusion before His dread Majesty. But then, again, encourage and comfort thyself

Near the time of Communion, fear, yet have confidence.

* They should be stirred with great caution. Compare chap. vii. xi. xxx. § 9.

with the consideration of His goodness, His readiness to pardon, and His inclination to mercy. And with a pious confidence that He will have thee receive Him, notwithstanding thine own indignity, go on with alacrity of spirit to the holy banquet, and joyfully embrace thy Lord God in thy soul.*

5. The sacred Communion thus received, presently shut up thyself within the closet of thine own heart, and discover to thy Saviour thy wants and thy weaknesses, saying in thy mind:—'Thou seest, O my sweet Saviour, how I am possessed with this passion and pestered with this perverse affection. Thou also well knowest, O my Lord, my weakness to resist it, and that it is not possible for me by my own diligence to be delivered. Therefore, this battle is Thine. I resign this my quarrel against these enemies into Thy powerful hands, and from Thee alone I look for the victory.'

After Communion discover thy wants,

6. After thou hast thus silently prayed, turn thyself to the eternal Father, and piously present His dear Son Jesus unto Him, for the same grace for which thou now receivest Him into thy soul. And expect with constant hope His divine help, which, although thou presently perceivest not, yet thou shalt infallibly and plentifully receive, when it shall be most expedient for thee.

and constantly hope for the divine help.

* 'Each time of communion,' says St. Teresa, 'beg some gift of God, by the compassion wherein He has entered thy poor soul.' *Maxims*, 64.

CHAPTER XXX.

How to Excite in us Affections of Love by the Sacred Communion.

Consider God's love and liberality in the Holy Communion.

1. If thou desirest to stir up in thy soul, by means of this most Holy Communion, that fervent love of thy Lord God which destroys and consumes all self-will and self-love within thee, devote thyself, in the evening which precedes thy Communion, to meditate upon thy Lord's immense love and liberality towards thee, unworthy wretch, the work of His own hands. How, not content to have formed thee of nothing to His image and likeness, and to have sent His only Son from heaven to inhabit our earth, and to serve thee for the space of three-and-thirty years in continual labours and travails, and, lastly, to undergo His most bitter Passion and ignominious Death for thy redemption, He would further bequeath this His Son unto thee in the most holy Sacrament of the Eucharist, for the perpetual food and refreshment of thy soul.

Weighing: 1. Who it is that comes unto thee;

2. And that by the due consideration of this special benefit of sacred Communion thou mayest become all fire and love, thou shalt thus order thy devout exercise:—Consider, in the *first* place, Who it is that confers on thee this so large and liberal gift. Surely it is thy Lord God Himself, the divine and uncreated Wisdom and Goodness, Whose worth and perfection infinitely exceeds the reach of all created capacity.

3. *Then* look upon the gift itself, which is the true

and only Son of God,* of equal height, nature, and substance with the heavenly Father and Holy Ghost. Now, if a small gift proceeding from a king hath its high value because of the giver, how highly is this gift to be valued by us, which is God, and given by God Himself as a token of His true love and a perpetual memorial of His tender affection towards us.† 2. What He gives thee;

4. *Again*, reflect upon the eternity of this love, by which it was decreed by His most divine, most hidden, and most holy wisdom that He would thus give thee Himself for thy food and refection. And hence begin with joy and jubilee of heart to sing and say within thyself:—'O infinite goodness of my God, and is it even so that Thou lovest me in Thy endless eternity? Didst Thou, O my Lord and my God, so much value me, Thy poor and unworthy creature, that Thou rememberest me in Thy blessed eternity, and hadst an ardent affection and desire to give me Thyself for the food of my soul?' 3. The eternity of His love;

5. And *finally*, look into the purity of this love,

* In this lies the preëminence of the Holy Eucharist above the other sacraments: that whereas in the others we receive the gifts of God, in the Eucharist we receive God Himself, the Author and Fountain of every grace; the gift and the Giver being one and the same. Hence the early Fathers of the Church call this sacrament:—'the Salve of immortality:' 'the Pledge of eternal health:' 'the Defence of faith:' 'the Hope of the resurrection:' 'the Food of immortality:' 'the Conservatory of everlasting life.'

† *He hath made a remembrance of His wonderful works, being a merciful and gracious Lord: He hath given food to them that fear Him.* Psalm cx. 4. And in St. Luke: *Do this for a commemoration of Me.* xxii. 19.

4. The purity of His love.

which so great a Lord shows unto so mean a worm. How different it is from all earthly affection! how free from the least mixture of gain and self-interest! How far is it above thy merits, and how purely is it a work of His only mercy and bounty!

Hence break forth into admiration

6. Having thus seriously and sweetly, with affection and admiration, meditated on the Divine goodness, thy heart may break forth into these raptures:—'Whence is it, O my God, that Thou so lovest me, an abject creature? Why, O King of glory, wilt Thou so nearly join me to Thyself, who am but a little dust and ashes? I will conceive Thy design, O my dear Lord, in this Thy excessive love towards me! It is to win me reciprocally to Thy love. O, the purity of divine love! Thou lovest me, O my God, and givest Thy whole self unto me, for no other end but that I may in gratitude give Thee my love, life, and will entirely; and this for no need Thou hast of me, but merely for Thy mercy's sake, and for my advancement and profit, that by this sweet tie and happy union of love my earthly heart may be raised up to become one with Thy divine heart, O my Lord and my God!'

ENLARGEMENT, and ravishment, making an oblation of thyself;

7. Here, all ravished with joy to see thyself so highly prized and beloved of thy Lord God, withdraw into the most secret part of thine own heart, and there acknowledging that all this powerful love is to entice thy poor and inconsiderate self unto His Divine Majesty, make so absolute an oblation of thyself unto Him, that thy me-

mory may scarcely think of anything but thy God, thy affection may abhor all content which comes any way without Him, and thy understanding may admit of no other object for its continual entertainment than Him, Who is the only satiety and satisfaction of all thy inward faculties and outward senses. And since there is no action amongst all those which concern our religion and loyalty to God which can, either in appeasing His anger or uniting us to His love, compare to this—the receiving Him worthily in the most Holy Sacrament—force thyself, to the utmost of thy power, to prepare, purify, and open thy heart unto Him, and to shut it against all things created.

8. Then offer and dedicate thyself humbly and wholly, with heart and affection, to the divine pleasure, and retain an ever-ready and inflamed desire to please God and follow His blessed will. And when this holy desire and affection shall be thoroughly enkindled in thy soul, thou wilt seem to move thy Lord God also to be so much enamoured with thee, as to desire thou shouldst freely open thy heart to Him, that He may the next morning enter in unto thee, feast with thee, and take His full delight in thee. Then do thou also declare thy mutual desire to receive Him with these kind of ejaculatory prayers:—'O heavenly and divine Manna, when will that wished-for hour come when I shall, to Thine own content, receive Thee into my soul? Ah, when shall I be surely united unto Thee by sincere affection? When shall I,

TEXT. dedicating thyself wholly to Him.

O only life of my soul, relinquish all self-will, and vanquish all my passions and imperfections?'

9. In these, and the like devotions, thou mayest spend the evening and the morning to excite, cherish, and increase thy desire to receive thy dear Saviour, that so thou mayest perfectly please Him, and be most happily united unto Him. And in thy pious practices of these things take this *caveat:*—Be sure to keep each power and faculty of thy soul pure and free from all curiosity of worldly things, and from all idle and vain thoughts. Take also the like care of thy outward senses, lest thy heart steal out by them, and so thou lose all thy devotion.

But take heed of vain thoughts.

10. The time of the sacred Communion drawing nigh, think thou art to receive the Lord, Who created this great universe, and thee to His own likeness; the Son of God, Who died for thee naked on the cross—that uncreated Goodness Which hath so often freed thee from danger, death, and damnation, which thy sins deserved.

ENLARGEMENT. Near Communion, think what thou art going to do.

11. Thank Him with most profound humility, and, uniting all thy faculties and powers of body and soul together, adore Him as true God and true Man. Beg also His pardon for thy faults, and that the same love which moves Him to grant thee this great gift may also induce Him to purge thy soul from the stains of all sin and uncleanness, thereby disposing it to a more pure and perfect union with His Divine Majesty.

Thank. Adore. Implore.

11. When the priest pronounceth these sacred

words:—'*Domine non sum dignus*—O Lord, I am not worthy,' accompany him with these following, and speak to thy Lord and Love from the bottom of thy heart:—'I am not worthy to receive Thee, O my great Lord, before Whose Majesty the angels of heaven, trembling, confess their own nothingness. I am not worthy, O my Lord, that Thou shouldst lodge with me, because I love Thee not, and I remember Thee not, though these are the chief reasons of Thy instituting and remaining in the most blessed Sacrament.' Thus humbled, confound, and abase thyself at the serious consideration of thy sins, malice, and misery. But then raise up thy heart with hope by the following words:—'*Sed tantum dic verbo et sanabitur anima mea*—Do Thou only speak the word, O my Lord, and my soul shall be saved. Enter, O my Love, into this unworthy harbour, and make use of Thine infinite power and goodness in pardoning my sins, supplying my defects, and protecting me from my enemies.'

At the *Domine non sum dignus* humble thyself.

12. And after thou hast received this Divine Sacrament, betake thee presently to the innermost closet of thy heart, and there enter into sweet communion with thy holy Guest, using these or the like loving and respectful expressions:—'What hath moved Thee, O great King of kings, to enter into me, who am nothing but a miserable, despicable, vile, blind, and naked creature?' And He will answer thee:—'Love, for thou art My dove, My friend, My sister, My spouse, and My dearly beloved.' Then thou mayest reply:—'O

TEXT. Entertain thy Guest with amorous expressions.

uncreated Love, O sweetest Dilection, O friendly and faithful Charity! what wouldst Thou have me do? What demandest Thou? What desirest Thou?' He saith:—'I ask nothing but love. I would have nothing burn on the hearth of thy heart but the fire of My love; that it may devour all foreign love within thee, and destroy all self-will and seeking. This, this is My desire, because I would be truly thine, and would have thee likewise be totally Mine. This can never be accomplished until thou freely deliverest up thyself to My good will and pleasure. For, without this entire resignation, thy fancy will be always fastened to the loving and liking of thyself and thine own actions, be they never so mean. I desire, therefore, that thou shouldst hate thyself that thou mayest have the love of Me. I demand thy heart for My habitation, that I may join and unite it unto Mine; for to this end was My heart opened to thee upon the altar of My Cross. My will is, I say, O My dearly beloved spouse, that thou desire nothing, think nothing, understand nothing, see nothing, feel nothing, but Myself only; that so I only may be in thee and thou totally turned into Me; and that thou mayest possess in Me perfect quiet, and I in thee pleasant content.'

Offer up the divine Son to His heavenly Father.

13. *Lastly*, thou shalt offer the Holy Son to His heavenly Father for thyself, for the whole world, and for the souls departed; in memory and union of that Divine Oblation which He offered upon the Holy Cross, presenting in like

manner all the unbloody sacrifices to the Divine Majesty, which are that day offered up in His Universal Church.

CHAPTER XXXI.

Of Spiritual Communion.

1. Although, my beloved, thou canst receive thy sweet Saviour sacramentally only once a day, yet thou mayest receive Him spiritually every hour and moment; nothing can hinder thee from this but only thine own fault and negligence. And this spiritual communion may sometimes prove more profitable to thy soul and pleasing to thy Saviour than the Sacrament, especially if there be a defect in thy due and diligent preparation. For as often as thou desirest to receive thy loving Lord God thus spiritually into thy soul, thou shalt find Him ever ready to feast thee with His own sacred hands: and thou mayest easily dispose thyself unto it thus:—Turning thyself unto thy Saviour to this end, reflect upon thine own frailty and frequent failings, and conceive an inward sorrow and detestation of thy defects. Then make thy supplication with a loving affection, that He will not disdain to enter thy poor cottage and feast thee with His own true body and blood.

Frequently receive Christ spiritually by desire.

2. So, also, when thou art moved by a pious zeal against any perverse passion, and desirest efficaciously to mortify it, or to plant some virtue in thy soul, make use of this spiritual com-

It is an excellent exercise against passions.

munion by converting thy thoughts to thy Lord God; and invoking His aid with ardent prayers, beseech Him to enter and possess the secret part of thy soul. Or, calling to mind thy last sacramental communion, speak to Him with an inflamed desire:—'When, O my good God, shall I again welcome Thee into the closet of my heart? Come now, O my Saviour, and comfort me spiritually with the like strength and virtue.'

ENLARGEMENT. How to make great use of this exercise for thy spiritual profit.

3. If thou wilt practise this pious exercise of spiritual communion with more reverence and profit, make thy intention over-night to apply all the mortifications of thy vicious passions, all the acts of virtue, and whatsoever good thou shalt in any way perform, for the obtaining of this happy effect, and that thou mayest worthily open the gate of thy heart to give due entertainment to so Divine a guest. And in the morning, fix thy thoughts upon the serious consideration of the great happiness of that sweet soul, which worthily receives this most holy sacrament, whereby sin's breaches are repaired, lost virtues are restored, languishing forces are recruited, and each good returns to its first beauty, by the communication of Christ's merits and Passion. Then force and excite thy heart to an ardent desire of these comforts by thy Lord's coming; and, turning towards Him, say:—'O my God and my Love, I am not worthy to receive Thee sacramentally; but do Thou, O Uncreated Goodness and Unlimited Power, pardon all my imperfections, and make me worthy to receive Thee spiritu-

ally, to the honour of Thy holy Name, and the true comfort of my poor soul.'

CHAPTER XXXII.

Of Thanksgiving.

1. All our good actions are of God and from God; and, therefore, a thankful gratitude is due to Him for all our well-performed exercises, for each victory obtained against our enemies, and for all and each of His blessing and benefits. And that thou mayest not be defective in this point of duty, remember that the chief motive why our omnipotent Creator confers His mercies upon His creatures is, that they should correspond to Him in pious, perpetual, and worthy thanksgiving.*

All good is from God, and to Him all gratitude.

2. And because our Lord God, in bestowing His benefits, intends principally His own honour,

Acknowledge His

* They who neglect to thank God for the daily graces He mercifully lavishes upon them, rob Him, as far as it lies in them, of the honour which is His due, and are guilty of base impiety. The spirit of thanksgiving moves and constrains the sacred heart, as with a holy violence, to new acts of mercy; whereas a spirit of ingratitude closes up the fountains of grace and calls down destruction upon the soul. 'Ingratitude,' says St. Augustine, 'is the root of every spiritual evil. It is a burning wind that scorches and dries up all holiness, and shuts up the fountains of the divine mercy against men' (*Soliloq.* cap. xviii.). Have you received any signal favour from God? Hasten and return Him thanks for it: acknowledge the divine clemency, and be not like the ungrateful lepers of the gospel, whose ingratitude wrung from the meek and tender heart of our blessed Saviour that reproachful complaint:—*Were not ten made clean? and where are the nine? There is no one found to return and give glory to God save this stranger.* Luke xvii. 17, 18.

goodness and thy unworthiness. and secondly our profit, do thou likewise in receiving them acknowledge, in the first place, His power, wisdom, and goodness, which most gloriously shine in each of them. And in the next place, reflect upon thine own unworthiness of so great favours, who art nothing else but ingratitude, misery, and baseness. And lastly, submit thyself to obey His Divine will and pleasure, and study to perform what thy Lord, in lieu of these benefits, expects from thee; which is, to love Him chiefly, to serve Him carefully, and to offer and dedicate thyself to Him freely and totally, as I shall now teach thee.

CHAPTER XXXIII.

Of the Perfect Oblation of Thyself to thy Lord God.

To move thyself to this oblation, consider: 1. God's greatness and glory;

1. After thanksgiving for received favours, the soul presently breaks forth into that delicious affection of the Royal Prophet:—*What shall I render to the Lord for all the things that He hath rendered to me?** That therefore thou mayest do something seeming like satisfaction, by offering up to His Divine Majesty all that thou art, hast, and canst, and that entirely, absolutely, voluntarily, and by an efficacious act of thy inward man, consider first, with a serious attention, the greatness and glory of thy Lord God, for upon this depends the perfect oblation of thy-

* Psalm cxv. 12.

self, and thou wilt find that there is a *reverence and fear* due to this His greatness and glory; that there is a *love* due to His goodness; that there is a *hope and confidence* due to His mercy; and so of His other attributes and perfections. And thou shalt congratulate and rejoice with thy Lord God that He is what He is; to wit, the best, greatest, most wise, most holy, most happy, most powerful, most infinite Being, and that He hath all the perfections which He possesseth: thus multiplying many such amorous acts of complacency in thy heart.

2. Adore and acknowledge Him;

2. Then, bow down the knees of thy soul and body with most profound reverence before thy Lord and Maker, adoring His Divine Majesty, and acknowledging Him to be the supreme Governor of all His creatures. And particularly, that whatsoever good thou hast by nature and by grace is His own gift, since He also conferred it upon thee, and He alone conserves it in thee. And thus thou must needs confess thyself to be His debtor, though thy offering be never so great, because thou canst present Him with nothing which is not already His own, and first proceeding from His liberality and bounty; neither does He lose His dominion thereof by conferring it upon thee.

3. Offer up all the interest of thy works to Him;

3. In the next place, pass on to the oblation itself, and deliver up all thine own interest in whatsoever thou hast, or mayest have, into the holy hands of thy heavenly Creator, with all possible cheerfulness and integrity; that is, offer up unto Him all that He hath given thee, and so restore thy whole

self to thy God in perpetual bondage, to dispose of thee both in time and in eternity as He best pleaseth. Neither shall it suffice thee to make this oblation general, by presenting unto Him the root or beginning of all thy thoughts, words, and works; but thou shalt do it in particular, by presenting even those also which, by reason of thy state, thou art obliged to exercise to the honour and glory of His sacred Name.

4. Uniting all to the merits of Christ, present them to the eternal Father.

4. Lastly, thou shalt unite this entire oblation of thyself and all that belongs to thee unto the merits of Jesus Christ, the sweet Spouse of thy soul; that from thence it may have that value and esteem which from itself thou canst not hope nor expect. And thou shalt end thy exercise thus: —By presenting the eternal Father with thy whole self and the holy merits of His only Son joined together, and with all His actions and sufferings from the crib unto the cross. For all these are thy treasures, which He at His Death bequeathed by His last will and testament unto thee, whom He left entitled to all His merits.* But remember that thou makest not this oblation for

* St. Teresa tells a story of a certain holy person who, being in great distress at the thought that she had nothing to give to God, or to abandon for His sake, prostrated herself before a crucifix, and was presently comforted by the voice of our Lord speaking to her from the crucifix and declaring:—'That He gave her all the labours and pains which He suffered in His Passion, and that she was to consider them as *her own*, and offer them to His Father.' 'The soul,' adds the saint, 'immediately became so rich and so comforted (I heard it from the person herself) that she can never forget it; and every time she finds herself thus desponding, the remembrance of these words animates and consoles her.' *The Interior Castle*, p. 158.

thyself alone, but also for the Universal Church and her members. Thus it will be far more acceptable to God, being sweetened with the incense of perfect charity. In like manner, when thou wilt offer up thy sufferings, prayers, or other pious works to thy Lord God, consider that His holy Son, thy sweet Saviour, hath already presented them, together with His own, to His eternal Father, and so hath conjoined and united them both together. Do thou, therefore, offer up the same in the same manner, by which thou shalt know that thy oblations proceed from a sincere heart. And if thou practisest this in time of adversity, thou wilt easily master all misery, anguish, pain, and perils whatsoever, and duly fulfil God's holy pleasure.

How to offer up Christ's actions for our offences.

5. If, furthermore, thou desirest to make an oblation of Christ's actions for thine own offences, behave thyself in this manner :—*First*, cast an eye upon thy sins, and perceiving that thou canst not hope to pacify God's wrath, nor satisfy His divine justice by thine own endeavours, address thyself to thy Saviour's Life, Passion, and Death, and fix upon some one or other action or suffering of His, as upon His fasting, or His praying, or the effusion of His precious blood. *Then* reflect that He offered this His action or Passion to His eternal Father for *thy* sins, and to reconcile Him to *thee*, as if He said :—'I do now, O My heavenly Father, fully satisfy Thy divine justice for the sins of this Thy servant, N. ... O, let it please Thee to spare him, and to receive him into the number

of Thy elect.'* Do thou also make the same oblation of thy dear Saviour to the eternal Father, and humbly beg for thyself and others that, in virtue of this offering and for His own glory's sake, He will in His mercy pardon both thine and their offences. And thou mayest piously and profitably make use of this manner of spiritual exercise in any action or passage of our Lord and Saviour's Life or Passion.

* 'Without doubt Christ loved much more than He suffered, and there remained far greater love shut up in His heart than that which He showed outwardly in His wounds. And if, as they ordered that He should suffer one death, so they had ordered Him to suffer a thousand deaths, He had love enough for all; and if, what they ordered Him to suffer for the salvation of all men, that same they had ordered Him to suffer for *each one of them*, He would have done it for *one* as for all; and if, as He remained three hours hanging on the cross, so it had been necessary for Him to remain there until the end of the world, He had love enough for all had it been necessary for us.' *The History of the Sacred Passion*, p. 148, by F. Luis de la Palma.

This same truth was declared by our Lord in the following revelation to Mother Juliana, an Anchorete of Norwich, who lived in the reign of King Edward the Third:—' Then said our good Lord, asking, "*Art thou well afraid that I suffered for thee?*" I said, "Yea, good Lord, gramercy [great mercy]; yea, good Lord, blessed mote [must] Thou be." Then said Jesu, our good Lord, "*If thou art afraid, I am afraid: it is a joy, a bliss, an endless liking to Me, that ever I suffered passion for thee: and if I might have suffered more, I would have suffered more.*" In this feeling my understanding was lifted up into heaven. . . . And in these words, "*If I might suffer more, I would suffer more,*" I saw truly, that as often as He might die, as often as He would, and love should never let Him have rest till He had done it. And I beheld with great diligence, for to wit, how often He would die if He might; and truly the number passed my understanding and my wits so far that my reason might not nor could not comprehend it, ne take it. And when He had thus oft died, or should die, yet He would set it at naught for love; for all thinkest Him but little in regard of His love; for though the sweet manhood of Christ might suffer but once, the goodness of Him may never cease of profer [proving that] every day He is ready to the same if it might be; for if He said He would for my love make new heavens and new earths, it were but little in

6. To the end that the oblation of thyself may be acceptable to the Divine Majesty, consider that whilst our Saviour sojourned here upon earth, He perpetually offered up to His eternal Father, not only Himself and all His merits, but also all us mortals together with Himself.

ENLARGEMENT. Christ offered Himself and us to His Father.

7. Make, therefore, thy oblation in virtue of and in union with His; yea, make the selfsame oblation of Jesus Christ, in which He also comprehended thee. And let this thy oblation be without the least touch of propriety or self-will; neither regarding earthly goods nor heavenly graces, but purely and precisely looking upon the divine pleasure and providence, to which thou art entirely to submit and sacrifice thyself as a perpetual holocaust. And forgetting all things created, say unto thy Lord God:—'Behold, O my good

Make thou the same oblation.

regard: for this might He do each day if He would without any travel. But for to die for my love so often that the number passeth creatures' reason, this is the highest profer that our Lord God might make to man's soul, as to my sight. Then meaneth He thus; "*How should it then be, that I should not for thy love do all that I might, which deed grieveth me naught, sithen* [*since*] *that I would for thy love dye so often, having no regards to my hard pains?*" And here saw I for the second beholding in His blessed Passion the love that hath made Him to suffer, it passeth as far all His pains as heaven is above earth; for the pain was a noble, precious, and worshipful deed, done in a time for the working of love: and love was without beginning, is and shall be without end; for which love He said full sweetly this word: "*If I might suffer more, I would suffer more.*" He said not, if it were needful to suffer more, but, "*If I might suffer more.*" For though it were not needful, and He might suffer more, He would. This deed and this work about our salvation was ordained as well as God might ordain it; it was done as worshipfully as Christ might do it; and herein I saw a full bliss in Christ; for His bliss should not have been full, if it might any better have been done than it was done.' *Sixteen Revelations of Divine Love*, Rev. ix. ch. xxii. pp. 51-53.

God, O my great Creator, a small lump of mire and earth mixed together in the hands of Thy eternal providence. Do with me what best pleaseth Thee, in my life, at my death, and after my death, in time and in eternity.'

How to know the sincerity of thy oblation.

8. And thou mayest give a probable guess concerning thy own oblation, that it proceeds from a sincere and disinterested heart, if thou canst perfectly practise it in time of adversity; bearing it with true patience, and being then ready to execute God's holy will in all thy desolations and distresses. This is the right way, O my dearly beloved, to make a beneficial truck and traffic of thyself for thy Saviour, Who will give thee Himself in exchange, if thou bequeathest and sacrificest thyself thus totally to His Divine Majesty.

CHAPTER XXXIV.

How to Petition for Divine Grace.

1. Encourage thyself with confidence in His goodness;

1. Having made this perfect oblation of the most precious treasure—which is no less than Christ Himself with all His glorious merits — to the eternal Father, thou mayest appear with confidence before the throne of His mercy, to petition for the supply of thy necessities. And that thou mayest do it with the more decency:—*Firstly.* Encourage thyself with confidence, remembering His benefits, bounty, and liberality towards thee; for nothing can more strengthen

thy hope of obtaining new supplies than the reflection upon God's former favours in times of necessity. And know that this confidence gives the whole efficacy to thy petition, so that, without it, never expect to obtain from God anything which thou demandest.*

2. *Secondly.* Take special care that this confidence be coupled with humility, distrusting totally thine own merits, and relying boldly upon Christ's mercies; not that I advise thee to become fearful and pusillanimous upon pretence of humility, so as not to beg large benefits from God's bounty. For though it behoves thee to know thine own baseness, and to consider how little thou deservest, yet thou must beware of mistrusting the divine Bounty, or undervaluing its liberality. No; be not dejected. For as thou deservest nothing, so thou hast greater occasion to demand much; since God's gifts are not grounded upon thy deserts, but upon Christ's merits, which are of infinite worth and dignity. 2. Join humility with it;

3. *Thirdly.* Endeavour to press thy petition with frequent and fervent desires: that is, that thou ardently wish to obtain what thou askest. For since thou petitionest a most pious Father for a supply of thy necessities, Who not only bids thee ask great things, but is also angry if thou askest not, and hath made a promise to perform thy petition, why shouldst thou not have inflamed desires to obtain what thou demandest? 3. Press thy petition with fervent desires.

* See chapter xxi. and *note* to § 6 of the same.

4. And, indeed, we most commonly fail in the efficacy of our demands, because we want this *fervour in our desires,* and make our petitions tepidly, rather because faith and reason dictate unto us that such things are needful to us than that we zealously covet to receive them. The true cause of which tepidity is, that our affections being fastened to earthly things, we prize them in our wills, though we slight them in our understandings; and, consequently, though we know in our judgment that our minds are to be raised up to higher objects, yet we do not seriously seek to be separated from them; whereas, if we verily and vigorously, humbly and heartily desired it, our prayers would soon return us happy fruit.

The want whereof hinders the efficacy of our prayers.

5. *Lastly.* Provide that thy petition want not, First: *Affection of charity* to thy neighbours. For it should not suffice thee to pray fervently for thyself, but to extend thy piety in petitioning the divine grace for all others. Secondly: *Perseverance.* For our loving Lord is accustomed sometimes to prolong and to put off the fulfilling of our petition for our greater profit, and the better increase and enkindling of our holy desires, as may be exemplified in the Cananean woman,* and the Widow in the Gospel.† Thirdly: *Resignation* of thy will. For thou art to represent thy desires to thy dear Lord as if thou rather expectedst the fulfilling of His divine pleasure than

4. Pray with charity, perseverance, resignation.

* Matthew xv. 22-29. † Luke xviii. 1-8.

of thy petition.* So Christ prayed in the garden, not to have His own will, but His heavenly Father's accomplished.

CHAPTER XXXV.

Some short Observations concerning Meditation.

1. Before thou betakest thyself to thy night's rest, read attentively and considerately that mystery of thy Saviour's Life or that argument which thou meanest to meditate upon the morning following; and condensing it into two or three points or heads, commit it to thy memory.

Read overnight the meditation.

2. When thou awakest from sleep, shut out all other thoughts from thy heart, and let thy employment be to reflect upon and repeat the points prepared overnight for this morning's exercise; and think that thou art presently to talk with thy Lord God.

Reflect on it in the morning.

3. Wherefore, making, as it were, a stand for a short space before thou art in the place of prayer, imagine that thy great Creator, Whom the angels adore, is present in the oratory, expecting thee to enter upon thy discourse with Him, and beholding thy behaviour in thy prayer. Let this truth make a deep impression on thy mind; and thereupon yield Him most profound reverence with body

Weigh His Majesty with Whom thou conferest.

---

* This may be done by making our petition conditional; and not desiring it, except so far as it may be God's holy will that we should obtain it. See chapter xxi. § 8.

and heart, as craving permission to confer with His Majesty.

Begin with oblation and petition.

4. Then, with bended knees, begin thy prayer; first offering up to thy Lord God all the thoughts, words, and actions of thy whole life; particularly presenting unto Him this present exercise, to His honour and glory; and humbly implore His gracious assistance, that thou mayest perform this thy practice with such attention, devotion, and reverence, as befits one who speaks to his Lord and Saviour.

Then apply thy senses to the mystery,

5. Immediately after this, imagine thyself present before the mystery thou intendest to meditate on, and in the very place where it occurred; for this will fix thy fancy from wandering.* As—if thy theme be of Christ's *Incarnation,* think that thou seest the glorious archangel entering the secret chamber of the sacred Virgin, and there listen to their mutual discourses. So, if thy subject be of thy Saviour's *Scourging,* suppose a pillar before thee with thy dear Lord fastened thereunto, and eye those inhuman executioners, how cruelly they whip and beat

* The first difficulty that is commonly experienced in meditation is to quiet the imagination and keep it from wandering upon creatures. The *compositio loci*, or the picturing to one's mind the scene of the meditation, is a useful means, especially for beginners, for keeping the imagination fixed upon the subject of consideration. This method, however, should not be adopted by all persons indiscriminately, since to some it may prove a hindrance rather than an assistance to their advancement in prayer. In judging of matters of this sort, much will depend upon the nature, character, and spiritual progress of the individual soul. Let each person follow the practice which leads him straightest to God and most excites him to *love*, and he will then be very secure.

Him. And thus thou art to vary thy fancy, and conform it to the manner of the mystery.

6. And when the mystery is thus present to thy mind, make thy petition, and beg that which thou proposest to obtain by this exercise. As —if thy meditation be concerning Christ's *Incarnation*, let thy prayer be for spiritual light, that thou mayest clearly penetrate and perceive that ineffable love which moved Him to be made man for thy sake. If it be of His *Passion*, ask the grace of compassion and condoling with thy dear Saviour's sufferings. And so let thy petitions be for such pious affections as are ushered in by the argument of thy prayer.

and beg what thou intendest to obtain.

7. This done, begin with thy first point; and if that alone furnish thee with fuel sufficient to inflame thy affection, persevere therein for the whole space assigned to thy prayer; but if otherwise, then pass on to the second. And briefly take this for a maxim in all meditations :—That whensoever thou feelest thy affection enkindled, stay there and digest well that consideration till thou hast therein fully satisfied thy devotion.*

Then begin with the first point.

* 'In meditation I would not tie the will that it should not go beside or beyond the understanding; on the contrary, my advice and request is that the will, so it be carried towards God, should be suffered to go as far as it can, and that scope should be given to any good affection, not caring whether such affections be pertinent to the present subject to be considered on at that time, upon condition that the soul find that she bestows herself more efficaciously upon God by such affections than by those which would properly flow from the present motives considered. Neither would I that when a soul has chosen one point or mystery to meditate on she should strictly oblige herself to proceed on with it, but that if, without a voluntary roving and seeking,

8. And suffer not thy understanding to roam after
Beware of inquiring into high mysteries, high and delicate mysteries; but make use of its discourse so far only as may help to treat thy will with pious affections and solid resolutions. Wherefore, from each consideration extract some affection, and from every affection draw some determinate and particular resolution to do this very day this or that thing for thy Lord's honour, to reform this or that fault, and to mortify thy sensuality in this or that occasion. And this is the true fruit and profit of prayer.

9. Be resolute also in staying out the full time
and of leaving off before the allotted hour be expired. allotted for thy prayer, and stir not from it through any dryness in devotion, or any trouble of distractions. For such a prayer is, for the most part, more profitable to a soul using diligent re-

any other should offer itself to the mind more grateful and more justful to the soul, she should entertain the latter, holding herself to it as long as the virtue of it well lasteth; and it ceasing, then let her return to the first proposed subject. Nevertheless, in case that the new matter or affections occurring be such as that it doth feed some over-abounding humour or passion in the soul, as fear (even of God Himself), tenderness, shedding of tears, scrupulosity, or dejection of spirit, I should by no means permit a soul to entertain her mind with such matter, because she will thereby only plunge herself more deeply into nature and immortification, and not at all purify her inordinate affections. Such souls, even in the beginning, ought not to choose such matters for their prayers, and much less ought they to be permitted to quit other good matter for that. Now, such freedom of spirit and permission to change the present matter or affections, is to be supposed to be allowed only when the said change proceeds, not out of sloth, inconstancy, a vain pleasing of the fancy or affection, but out of a judicious election, or from an interior invitation proceeding probably from the Spirit of God. Here may be applied that saying of S. Bernard, *Modus diligendi Deum, est diligere sine modo*—The measure and manner of loving God is to love Him immeasurably and freely, without a prescribed manner.' *Sancta Sophia*, treat. 3, § 2, chap. iii.

sistance and patient expectance of God's grace than when it sensibly partakes of the sweets and abundance of devotion.

10. Thy exercise being ended, insist a while in the examination of thyself, and reflect how thou hast behaved thyself in prayer. If thou findest all well, give thy good God all the thanks. If thou hast been negligent, resolve upon amendment; and take notice of the cause of this ill success, that thou fail not for the future. Let the matter or mysteries thou meanest to meditate upon be well arranged; as, if thou proposest to thyself thy Saviour's Life and Passion, make thy entrance at His Incarnation, and duly proceed in the rest of the ensuing mysteries; and leap not inconstantly from one to another.

In the end, reflect how thou hast behaved thyself.

CHAPTER XXXVI.

AN EXERCISE BEFORE THE SACRED COMMUNION.

1. THE above-named *compositio loci* for the composing of thy mind, may be to imagine thy Saviour Christ encompassed with His angels and saints, who all adore His Divine Majesty with all possible reverence. Make thou also thy humble address unto Him, and since He vouchsafest to come into the harbour of thy poor heart, entreat Him to send before Him such ornaments as are necessary for His worthy entertainment; because thy poverty is incapable to provide what is suitable to so great a Majesty.

Beg of Christ to make thy soul a fitting abode.

Think what Guest is to lodge in it.

2. Then, reflect Who it is that intends to lodge with thee. It is surely He Whom the angel named Jesus,* the Saviour of mankind; He Who only can cure thy wounds; He Who so dearly loves thee and takes such care of thy salvation, that He came purposely and personally to procure it, interposing His authority, hazarding His honour, and losing His life for thee upon an ignominious cross. And be sure to insist upon this pious consideration, as being very proper to prepare thy soul for the receiving of this most holy Sacrament, according to our Saviour's precept:—*This is My body which is given for you. Do this for a commemoration of Me.*†

Why He comes to thee.

3. Consider to what end thy dear Lord comes unto thee. Surely, to conclude a union between Himself and thy soul, whence results a certain divine life which thou henceforth enjoyest by this sweet union with thy Saviour. For the food we take begets humours of the same quality which itself is of. And, consequently, no marvel if this heavenly food and divine nourishment do, in some sort, deify thy soul:—*He that eateth Me, the same also shall live by Me,*‡ saith our Lord.

To whom He comes.

4. Let the next consideration be, to whom He comes. To a little worm of the earth; to a vessel full of filth and rottenness; and perhaps, which is far worse, even to His enemy; to the contemner of His commands; to the wilful transgressor of

* Luke i. 31. † Ib. xxii. 19. ‡ John vi. 58.

His laws; to a base runaway, who hath forsaken the colours of His Lord God, and taken part with the devil.

5. Make, therefore, thy humble supplication to thy sweet Saviour, that since He vouchsafeth freely to come unto thee for His own mercy's sake, and not for any merits of thine, He will also be pleased to prevent thee with His grace and adorn thee with the gifts of His holy Spirit, that thou mayest become a worthy receptacle for His sacred body; as He formerly, by a like prevention, prepared for Himself a happy and holy habitation in the virginal womb of His most blessed Mother.

Make thy petition.

CHAPTER XXXVII.

How we may Devoutly Offer up the Sacrifice of the Mass.

1. When thou feelest thy heart inflamed by this foregoing exercise or the like, free thy fancy of all sensible objects, and shutting the windows of thy senses, soar up to thy Lord God, and fix there the eye of thy soul upon Him only, purely, freely, and quietly, excluding all tumults of outward thoughts; and implore the assistance of the Holy Ghost, by reciting the hymn of the holy Church, *Veni Creator Spiritus* Then coming to put on the sacred vestments, mark with attention those mysteries which they mean and signify; and from that very instant, take upon thee *Christ's person,* Whom thou representest in this holy action, that so thou mayest be moved to conform each outward and inward deed to Him Whom thou now personatest.

Free thy mind from distracting thoughts.

2. And as for the outward deportment of thy body, see that thy going forth of the vestry be with all decency and gravity. Let thy countenance be cheerful, thy eyes humbly cast down, and not curious to pry into anything that is being done in the church. Let thy voice be low and sober, reading the sacred words neither precipitantly nor over pausingly, but beseemingly between both these extremes. Let the holy ceremonies be piously and punctually observed; and let all be attentively performed, taking more care in the *Canon*, and, most of all, when thou comest to the words of *Consecration*.

Let thy outward deportment be decorous;

3. Let thy inward composition also correspond with thy outward carriage. Therefore, coming to the foot of the altar, look upon Christ thy Lord and thy Love, sitting in His throne of glorious majesty, attended by His angels and blessed saints; and think that He is presently coming down from His throne to the altar to enrich thy poor soul with the treasures of His divinity; and considering so high a Majesty, confess thine own misery, meanness, and nothingness; and so humbling thyself both inwardly and outwardly, begin the action of the Sacrifice. And keep this presence of thy Saviour, sitting in His throne and beholding thy devotion, until thou comest to the Consecration; which done, thou hast Him then before thee upon the altar; thou touchest Him with thy hands, and embracest Him in thy heart, there present in the Sacrament.

As also thy inward composition.

What thou shouldst contemplate in thy first memento.

4. In thy first *Memento*, contemplate thy Lord Jesus crucified, reposing in thy heart, and lay all thy necessities and wants in His sacred and sweet wounds. And first offer up thy whole Mass to His *holy Head*, intending it to the eternal honour of the most blessed Trinity, and for the increase of the accidental glory of His dear Mother, thy Angel Guardian, and thy particular protectors and patrons in heaven. All of these thou shalt join together in the wounds of thy Lord's venerable Head; and beseech, then, that as thou in this vale of misery strivest to augment their glory, so they in their heavenly and happy mansions will be pleased to remember thee, and join with thee in the oblation of this divine sacrifice to thine and their Creator. Coming, then, to the *wound of His right Hand*, pray for the entire state ecclesiastical; that is, for the Pope, Cardinals, Bishops, and Pastors of the Church; for all religious persons and their prelates; and for them all offer up this present sacrifice. At the *wound of His left Hand*, pray for the laity; for kings, princes, magistrates, and the rest of their people; and, in particular, for thy parents, friends, familiars, and all who desired to be made partakers in thy devotions. At His *most sweet Heart*, offer up thy whole self only, humbly representing to Him thy life past and begging His pardon; thy present being, and desiring His direction; thy spiritual necessities and corporal needs; thy health, thy temptations,

loving embraces, thou mayest sweetly intone the *Nunc dimittis*.

3. In the next place, consider that He Whom thou hast now within thee is thy same Lord God of Whom before Communion thou conceivedst such high things; and render Him humble thanks for this immense benefit of communicating and uniting Himself unto thee, entreating Him that it may not be a slight and, as it were, a passing visit, but a permanent abode with thee.

Consider Whom thou hast within thee.

4. After this, look upon thine own unworthiness to receive such a guest; how homely is thy habitation; how beggarly, yea, how beastly, is thy heart; how full of the noise of passions and perplexities; and draw from hence acts of sorrow for thy sins, or shame for thy negligence, and of confusion for the uncleanness of thy soul.

Mark thy own unworthiness.

5. And lastly, ask with a most fervent desire that He Who is the King of glory and goodness, and the source of all sanctity and purity, will garnish thy soul with His virtues, and wash away all thy filthiness with the water of His celestial grace; and so inseparably unite and join thee to Himself, that nothing created may evermore make a breach between thee and Him; but that He will strongly lock up the closet-door of thy heart, and mark it for His own habitation with the signet of His sacred love; that so He alone may there peaceably and perpetually take up His rest, without the least disturbance of any foreign guest.

Make thy petition.

CHAPTER XXXIX.

A Daily Examination.

1. For the keeping clear of thy conscience, it will be necessary for thee to go down daily into it, and sweep each darkest corner thereof with the besom of diligent examination, that all uncleanness may be speedily cast forth out of doors. Wherefore thou art to do three things every morning:—*First,* give God thanks for all His benefits bestowed upon thee in the night past, and particularly for thy delivery from sudden death and from the deceits of the devil. *Then,* make a hearty oblation of all things thou shalt think, speak, or do in the day following; and entreat the Blessed Virgin, that she will be pleased to present with her purest hands this oblation of thyself and thy actions, together with thee, to her only Son. *And lastly,* conceiving a confidence in the divine assistance, make a firm purpose by His grace not to offend Him that day in the least venial sin.

Every morning thou art to do three things.

2. And at night, a little before thou betakest thyself to thy rest, examine thyself how stoutly thou hast stood to this good purpose. But before thou descendest to particulars, think of thy Lord's presence, to Whom thou art now ready to give in a reckoning of that day's transactions. And endeavour to feel a certain shame and confusion in thyself, like a bad servant before his most indulgent master; or like

At night thou art to examine thyself.

a perfidious soldier before his pious sovereign, who raised him from the dunghill to the highest degree of honour; for how much more reason hast thou to be ashamed in the sight of thy God, Whom thou hast served so negligently and offended so impudently?

Begin with a general acknowledgment of God's favours;

3. Begin, therefore, with a general acknowledgment of thy Lord's love and favours conferred upon thee from the first instant of thy being to that present hour; rendering Him particular thanks for the benefits that day received from His bounty. And invite all the angels and saints, and chiefly the sacred Virgin, to help thee to make a worthy thanksgiving for thy Creation, Conservation, Redemption, Vocation, Remission of thy enormous crimes, and so long Expectation of thee to repentance.

then beg light and grace.

4. Secondly, demand light and grace to see thy defects and negligences which thou hast that day committed, and to feel a true sorrow and contrition for the same. For they are so secret, that without this light thou canst not discern them, and so enormous, that without this aid thou canst not truly judge of them.*

Next, descend to particulars.

5. Thirdly, run over each hour of the day, and discuss with diligence what were thy thoughts, words, actions, or omissions in each of them, that thou mayest punctually perceive wherein thou hast particularly transgressed.

---

* Therefore the Prophet David cries out in the anguish of his soul: *Who can understand sins? From my secret ones deliver me, O Lord.* Psalm xviii. 13.

6. Fourthly, endeavour to exercise a true sorrow for thy sins—which is the main drift of this examen—and let this grief touch thy heart, rather because thou hast offended so good a God, than for any other inconvenience which thereby thou incurrest. Let it proceed, I say, not from any fear of punishment which thou hast deserved, but from a true reverence and high esteem which is due from thee to the divine Majesty of thy Lord God, Whom thou desirest to love and respect above all things, and resolve to practise this sorrow for the time to come.

Excite sorrow for thy sins.

7. Fifthly, therefore, and lastly, beg His pardon for thy past negligence and His assistance for thy future amendment; promising particularly and resolving effectually to shun, for His love, this or that occasion of sin; and to lay hold of this or that opportunity for the correction and bettering of thyself. And if thou happily findest by this serious discussion of thyself, that thy transgressions are not so grievous as to excite thee to this sorrow and shame, refer all this to the divine mercy, and not to thy own diligence or virtue. And reflect upon thy former faults, and the grievous failings of other worldlings; and conclude that thou hadst surely fallen more foully, had not His heavenly grace upheld and prevented thee.

Implore pardon for the past and protection for the future.

8. Or else, question thyself concerning three things. First, wherein thou hast that day fallen and offended. Secondly, what occasioned it. Thirdly, how diligent thou hast been in the practice of

ENLARGEMENT. Another method of examination.

virtue. Concerning thy *fallings*, read the fifteen foregoing chapters. Concerning the *occasions*, resolve to cut them off for the future. And for thy *practice of virtue*, strengthen thy will with these three cordials: Distrust in thyself, Trust in God, and Prayer. Suspect thy past victories, and rely not upon thy former good works; but rather forget them, lest thou fall into self-complacency. Look always forwards upon what thou yet wantest, and how much remains to be done. And acknowledging God's grace to be the source of all goodness, thank Him for all His benefits and blessings, for the inspirations He hath sent thee, and the good desires of virtue He hath given thee; for His deliverance from dangers and defence against thy enemies.

CHAPTER XL.

Being a Conclusion of the whole Work.

This short book well practised is sufficient.

1. Much more might be said of these important matters; but let this which is here delivered, according to my poor talent, suffice for the present; which surely, if thou endeavourest to keep in thy memory and accomplish in thy actions, thou hast learnt and laboured sufficiently. But in respect of thy weak capacity and my proposed brevity, it will be necessary that thou use a studious diligence in often revolving and meditating upon these foregoing precepts. For by frequent consideration and continual exercise

thou wilt certainly increase thy inward strength, whereby to conquer all thy enemies.

ENLARGEMENT. Pray ever for perseverance.

2. Above all things, beg incessantly of the divine goodness the gift of *Perseverance* in thy unwearied endeavours against thy passions and imperfections, it being the chief weapon in this spiritual warfare against thy never-dying enemies, which, like ill weeds, are ever budding and breaking forth so long as the earth hath any life in it to nourish them.

TEXT. Fight manfully,

3. Resolve, therefore, to betake thyself to these pro posed arms of defence, and to fight stoutly, manfully, and constantly; because no man can avoid this combat without endangering the loss of the conquest. Nor can there be any hope of peace with such enemies, for they trouble those most who most desire to enter into league and friendship with them.

and be not terrified at thy enemies' power;

4. Neither be thou terrified at their seeming power and cruelty, since all their force and fury is in the more powerful hands of that supreme Captain for Whose honour thou art engaged in the battle, wherein none can be vanquished but they that will themselves. And if thy Lord, for Whom thou wagest this war, doth seem sometimes to withdraw His assistance and delay thy conquest over thy enemies for a time, yet be not thou faint-hearted, but fight on courageously, being most certain and secure that His goodness, power, and providence direct all events, and more especially all adversities, to the best profit of His soldiers.

though thy victory seems to be slowly achieved.

5. These thoughts will beget in thee a generous spirit and a constant heart to resist and fight with courage. Therefore, though the victory comes slowly on, believe firmly that this deferring is *either* to free thy soul from secret pride, and preserve thee in true humility, or *else* to perfect thee in virtue, and to teach thee to become a tried soldier, by these long-continued conflicts; or *surely*, for some other good of thine, which thy Lord then conceals from thee, for thy greater merit and improvement.

A final exhortation.

6. Go on, therefore, O my dearly beloved, and enter these lists with a cheerful and heroic mind, lest thou seem ungrateful to thy loving Lord God, Who so much cared for thy good that He suffered death for thy sake. And attend carefully to every counsel and command of thy Captain Christ Jesus, that thou mayest totally rout and ruin all thine enemies. For if thou permittest but one only to live and lurk in thy soul, it will be as a moat in thy eye, and as a lance in thy bowels, and prove a perpetual impediment in the progress of so glorious a victory.

To him that overcometh I will give to eat of the tree of life (Apoc. ii. 7).

Thou shalt fight against them until thou hast utterly destroyed them (1 Kings xv. 18).

In omnibus glorificetur Deus

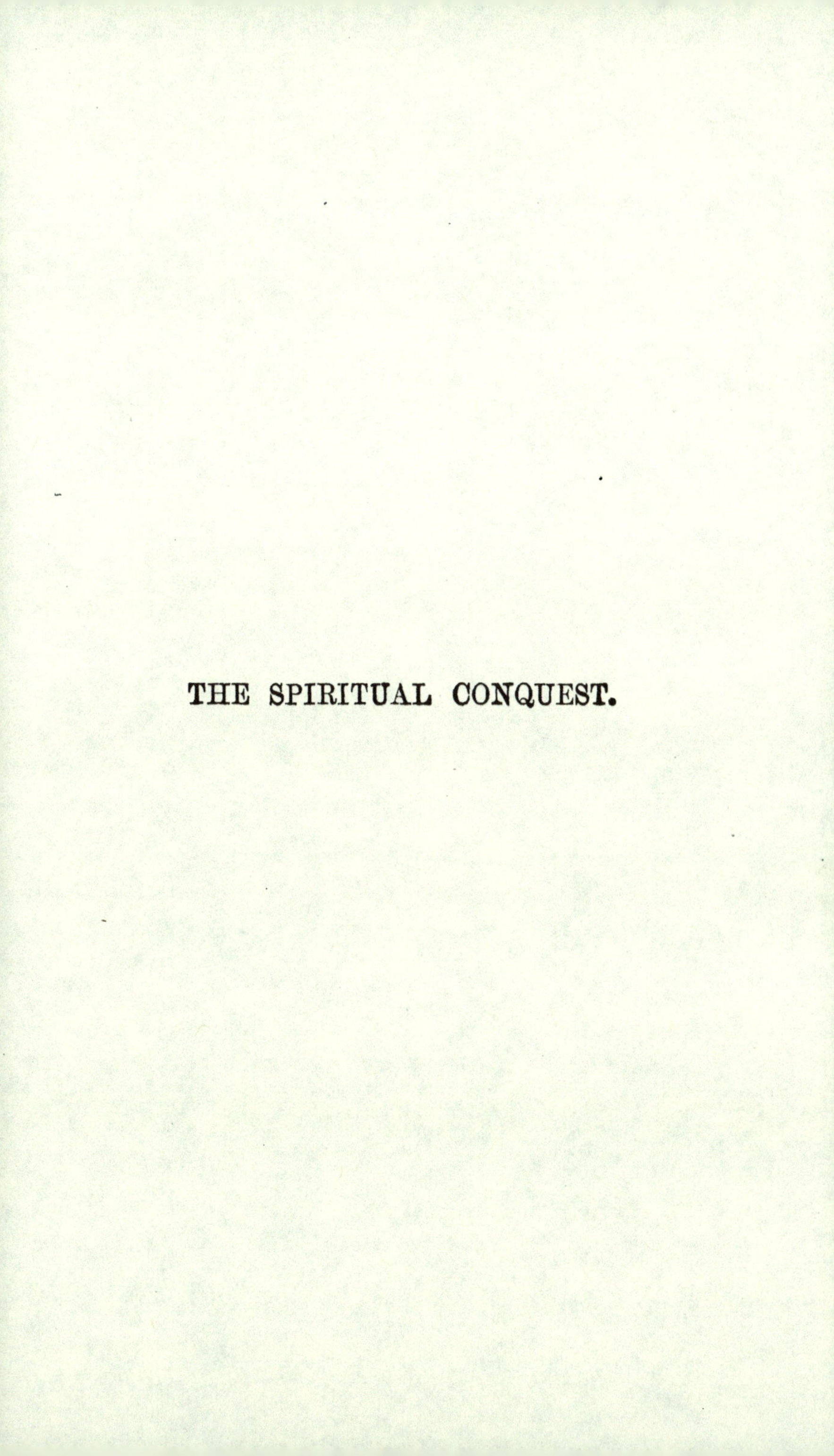

THE SPIRITUAL CONQUEST.

First Treatise.

OF THE DISCOVERY OF OUR ENEMIES' AMBUSCADES, ENABLING THE CHRISTIAN WARRIOR TO FORESEE AND AVOID THEM.

They prepared a snare for my feet (Psalm lvi. 7); but
The snare is broken, and we are delivered (Psalm cxxiii. 7).

THE FIRST AMBUSH.

Self-Love.

Self-love is the root of all sin and cause of all inproficiency in the way of perfection.

1. This, in St. Austin's* opinion, is the root of all sin; and we may fitly add and vouch it to be the cause of all inproficiency in the way of perfection. For our subtle nature so constantly seeks herself in all her actions and omissions, that even the spiritual man, who treads in the pleasant paths of piety, is subject to be drawn into this dangerous ambush. He will find upon due examination

* 'If by loving himself man is lost, surely by denying himself he is found. The first ruin of man was the love of himself. For if he had not loved himself, if he had preferred God to himself, he would have been willing to be ever subject unto God, and would not have been turned unto the neglect of His will, and the performing of his own will. For this is to love one's self, to wish to do one's own will. Prefer to this God's will; learn to love thyself by not loving thyself. For that we may know that it is a vice to love one's self, the Apostle speaks thus: *Men shall be lovers of themselves* (2 Tim. iii. 2). And can he who loves himself have any sure trust in himself? No; for he begins to love himself by forsaking God, and is driven away from himself to love those things which are outside of himself; and to such a degree that when the said Apostle saith, *Men shall be lovers of themselves*, he immediately adds: *covetous*.' St. Augus. *Hom. in N. T.* xcvi. See also *De Lib. Arbit.* iii. § 48; *Confessiones*, lib. iii. cap. viii.

some sinister intention and self-interest creeping in and corrupting his sincerest endeavours; and perceive, unless highly illuminated, that there is more of private commodity than pure and perfect charity in his most transcendant and heroic exercises.*

Few are found free from it.

2. Who is not generally more diligent in the performance of his duty for the fear of hell and hope of heaven than for the sole and substantial love of his Creator? Who hath not rather some small clause and secret condition of self-interest in his actions than the only fulfilling of God's holy will, and the following of His divine inspirations? Whom shall we find, though they be never so great pretenders to perfection, so totally disentangled from the net of self-love, that they neither hover after human respects and praises nor look upon rewards or punishments, nor over-value their own ways and exercises, nor solace themselves with the sweets of sensible devotion, nor pride themselves upon their high-towering contemplations and raptures into God's immediate perfections; nor, finally, dress up devotion after the pattern of their own passions, and so fall in love with their own conceptions, and make to themselves *in Bethel golden calves*, instead of the *cherubim in Jerusalem?*† Whose will is so truly divested of all *self* as to remain untouched, unmoved, undisquieted, resolute, and resigned in all temporal chances and changes, and in all spiritual dryness, desolation, dereliction, and affliction whatsoever?

* Read chapter ii. of the *Conflict.*

† 3 Kings xii. 28.

To avoid this snare we must seek God's honour in our actions.

3. To avoid this pernicious snare, we must strive to direct all our actions to God's pure honour and pleasure as the only end we aim at, the only object of our love, life, and labour; in Whom only, and not in the best of His creatures, is found true quiet and content.

To self-love belongs unmortified sensuality;

4. Unmortified *sensuality* is the darling of *self-love*. It proposes nothing but pleasure and pastime to our seduced appetites, roamings abroad to our affections, makes us careful to satisfy our fancies, anxious to content our curiosities, to hearken unto vanities, to glut our tastes with dainties, and to waste our precious time and talents in extravagant love to creatures.* What hope, alas, of internal repose and recollection, where such tumults and troubles prepossess the spirit! What place remains for the holy entertainments of heavenly love, when such affections have filled up each corner of the heart!

which must be tamed by cutting off superfluities.

5. Wherefore, a soul that seeks God must scorn to rest in these seeming goods. She must banish all superfluities, and be content with the mere supply of her necessities; she must admit of no excess in meat, drink, sleep, attire, talk, or other solaces whatsoever, if she really intend to make the body pliable to the spirit, and the spirit proper to tend to perfection.†

* Read chapter vii. of the *Spiritual Conflict*.

† Yet in all these practices and strivings after perfection a certain discretion must be exercised, lest the spirit, unduly taxed, succumb at length to the weakness of fallen nature. Hence F. Baker says:—' Dis-

To the same belong pride, self-conceit, &c.;

6. Pride, presumption, vanity, self-esteem, self-complacency, self-praise, self-seeking, self-delight, with all the rest of like nature, are but several nooses of the same net, and sprouts out of the same main root—*self-love*. And whosoever hopes for honour, praise, preferment, or profit from others—for any goods of nature, gifts of grace, or prerogatives of virtue—is fallen into this snare of the devil, robs God of His proper due, is rotten at the heart, and hath already received his full reward.

which must be remedied by the practice of humility.

7. The remedy of all this, O dear souls, is unfeigned *humility*. Cast one glance of your soul's eye upwards upon your Creator's might and mercy; all your perfections come out of His treasury, and are lent you to be improved for His service, not to be proud of for your own satisfaction. And look down with your other eye upon your bottomless nothing; see

cretion is to be held in all bodily needs, and in all our other outward doings, so as neither to do too much nor too little. But the same discretion is best practised, not by reflecting on those things themselves with a solicitude to hold a mean in them, but by tending towards God by the exercise of love. A soul thus disposed takes external things, as it were, by the way, with no love to them, but only to be able to hold on his journey. If any, through forgetfulness, should take more meat, drink, sleep, or other thing, than perhaps nature did need, let him not mind about it, or suffer it to distract him; but let him hold on his way towards God, and let it pass as if he had not done it, and all will be well. If that cannot be gotten which perhaps nature desireth to have, still be content; or if it is not at such time, or of such quality, or so dressed, as nature would have it, hold thy peace. If obedience or providence offer thee things that are more liking, precious, or dainty, eat without fear what is fitting. Take what comes in thy way without thought, not resting in anything but only in Him.' *Note* to the *Divine Cloud*, p. 250.

there your own base indignity and brutish ingratitude, your great impurity and gross impiety, and be ashamed to desire any temporal esteem, who so truly deserve eternal damnation.

8. Other knots of the same snare are all those passions which have their residence in our inferior nature; love, hatred, joy, grief, hope, and fear, with their several attendants. These raise up broils to disturb our inward tranquillity, to discompose our reason, and interpose their earthly exhalations between our superior will and the grace of God.

To self-love appertain also all the passions of our inferior nature, love, hatred, &c.;

9. *Peace of heart* is the secure refuge against all these peevish passions. Do but cast your whole care upon your Creator, and call away your inordinate affection from creatures; and what, then, can punish or perplex you? Remit and refer all accidents, whether adverse or prosperous, sweet or sour, good or bad, to God's high power and holy providence; comfort yourselves in His mercy, content yourselves in His all-sufficiency, and quiet yourselves in His love. Ah, how poor, how vain, how vile, how unregardable are the best of worldly blessings!* How is it possible that things in themselves so contemptible can have the least entrance or admittance into a soul settled in God's pure love and presence? O, let the children of this world, who place their final felicity in such fading fooleries, who have their souls buried in this earth and swallowed

to which we must oppose peace of heart.

* Read chapter iv. § 3, of the *Conflict*.

up in sensuality, be solicitous to seek them, to glut themselves in the enjoying of them, and be dejected to be deprived of them; but we, O souls aspiring to perfection, whose Master is God, whose aim is virtue, whose reward is heaven, what have we to do with these inferior passions? Away with these mammons! My heart is signed with the signet of God's love; my hatred is only bent against sin and myself; my joy is in God my Saviour; my grief is that I am not all His; my fear is to offend Him; and my hope is to enjoy Him.

The adhering to our own will and preferring our own judgments are also points of self-love;

10. Lastly, all adhering to our proper will and judgment appertains to this ambush of our enemy.* This draws us off by degrees from doing our duty, diverts us from following divine motions and superiors' commands, daunts us from relying entirely on God's providence, and fulfilling

* Independence, self-assertion, the spirit of criticism, and all things that directly tend to subvert authority, are hateful in a religious person, as being antagonistic to his state and profession, and to that spirit of humility and subjection which is the guarantee of peace and happiness in the cloister. The devil, knowing man's proneness to vanity, and wishing to compass his ruin, is always on the alert to fill the mind of a religious with false and foolish notions of his own importance, talents, dignity, and position; so that, puffed up with conceit and vainglory, he may come at length to contemn his superiors, disregard their commands, and fall, it may be, even into open rebellion. Wherefore, O devout religious, stand on your guard against these wily snares of the evil one, and manfully resist the first beginning of these vain thoughts and emotions. Why do you so frequently feel the spirit of rebellion rising in your breast? Because you have not yet subdued your pride and become as a little child for the love of Christ. O, if you were truly humble of heart, and sincerely placed yourself below all men for God's sake, accounting yourself as mere dust, and reputing yourself unworthy to tread the earth or to breathe the fresh air of the heavens—O, with what meekness and docility you would behave yourself towards all! How changed would be your conduct and comport-

perfectly His holy pleasure. We dare not disobey this master, nor will we venture to destroy this idol of our hearts.* It is death to be crossed in our conceits or contradicted in our exercises, which we have chosen according to our private fancy, practised with self-complacency, and keep with unpardonable propriety.

11. Perfect *obedience* breaks through this snare, and a total resignation to God's good will and pleasure is the secure refuge against this deceit. How can a soul be disquieted to receive or refuse, act or omit, that which she truly conceives to proceed both in substance and circumstance from the divine providence and permission? How can that person go astray who is perfectly obedient to God and his

which must be cured by obedience, submission, and resignation.

ment; how sweet would be your conversation; how readily would you seize every occasion of obedience, no longer reckoning it a hard thing to obey, but deeming it a privilege to submit your will to another for the love of your crucified Redeemer! And recollect well, that what our Lord prizes most in your obediences, is not the outward action, but the inward conformity of will and submission of judgment which should accompany their performance. For if, whilst doing the command of obedience, your mind is in a state of rebellion and uttering protests against the decision of your superior, then your obedience will profit you little, and you shall never attain that perfection of charity and Divine union which consists in making your own will one with the will of God—the end of the religious state, and one most securely acquired by the constant practice of perfect obedience. 'The more we subject ourselves to men,' says St. Teresa, 'having no other will but that of those who are over us, the more we shall master our will so as to conform it to the will of God' (*Foundations*, v. 14). Moreover, F. Baker declares that 'unless the commands of a superior be obeyed in purity of heart, *as for God's sake*, and with submission not only of the outward but inward man also, that is, *both the will and the judgment*, such obedience is not at all meritorious nor conformable to the general design of a religious life, and to the vow of profession' (*Sancta Sophia*, vol. i. treat. 2, chap. xiv.).

* Read chapter v. of the *Conflict*.

superior, gives up himself wholly to the guidance of God's holy Spirit and the government of a discreet Director, observes each beck of the divine call—first examined and approved by those who are encharged with his soul—and waits upon the divine will, as the shadow on the body?

12. Whence you are to take notice of a triple obedience: one is of vow; another of conformity; and a third of union. The first concerns all *Religious people*, and imports an external, exact, and necessary performance of that which is commanded.

Note a triple obedience: 1. Of vow;

The second concerns all *Spiritual souls*, and consists in their inward promptitude and readiness to execute God's will—manifested by faith and by their ghostly guide—purely for Himself, and precisely for His own sake, without the least touch of proper interests or self-seeking.

2. Of conformity;

The third concerns all *Perfect persons*, and consists in so entire a connection of their wills with the will of their Lord God, that they seem both one. Hence it is that they embrace all that happens to themselves or others, good or bad, life or death, for time or eternity, as immediately proceeding from His divine goodness, and as the very best that could happen. Here the soul, elevated above itself and all things into God, and steadfastly fixed in divine contemplation, patiently expects and obediently attends to what He speaks, wills, and acts within it, remaining ever ready, and really resigned to suffer outward pains or inward pressures, to

3. Of union.

receive comforts or endure crosses, as the Supreme Providence best knows, permits, and pleases; being fully content with all and faithfully constant in all.*

THE SECOND AMBUSH.

Immoderate Affection to Creatures.

1. This infects, distracts, disquiets, and diverts our minds from their pure and perfect attendance to our Creator. Ah! what have we, whose inheritance is heaven, to do with the poor and perishable commodities of this world? Yet our subtle enemy strives to make us serious in searching after them, solicitous to keep them, and impatient to part with them.

This affection to creatures distracts us from our Creator;

2. Against this we must provide *true poverty of spirit*, which consists in a perfect denudation

against which we

* 'If we will do as we ought, and as is best for us, we must be subject to the will of God in all things without exception. And this is the benefit of an internal life, that it makes Religious capable of seeing and knowing God's will, and also most ready to perform it, which way soever He signify it to them; and makes them obey as readily and willingly—merely for God's sake and out of obedience to Him—a simple or imperfect superior as they would an angel, or the wisest creature in the world. Yea, if it were possible, that a worm or any other creature were ordained by God to rule over them, they would with all their hearts embrace His will by them. For without this *total subjection to God* it is impossible to become truly *spiritual*. For if we resist His will in our *superiors*, in vain do we pretend to please *Him*. This virtue, therefore, of obedience, we must learn of Him; and it must be grounded on true humility. This must be our stay in all things. And these two virtues of humility and obedience, together with the divine virtue of discretion, He will teach us, if we do our parts in seeking to become more and more humble and subject to Him.' *The Confessions of a Loving Soul*, p. 251, D. Gertrude More, O.S.B., 1658.

must provide poverty of spirit. of our souls from all inordinate love to corruptible creatures; we must use them only, and not rest in them; we may enjoy them, but take no joy in them. If superiors command them from us, we must cheerfully part with them. If any accident bereave us of them, we must willingly let go our hold, saying:—'Our Lord gave them, our Lord hath retaken them; His name be ever praised, His will always performed. Farewell, uncertain and unsatisfying profits; welcome, sweet and secure poverty!'* We must throw away courageously all such clogs as retard our soul's flight to perfection. Away with such superfluities! O, that we could live with the only love of our naked and crucified Jesus! That we could support our feeble nature without the supplies of any creatures, that so our souls, disengaged from the depressing necessities of flesh and blood, might soar aloft, and sweetly repose in the bosom of divine love!

3. Nor is the overmuch tenderness of affection to any person whomsoever, under what pretext soever, any other thing than a mere ambush of our enemy; for it corrupts our purest actions and vitiates our most pious intentions; it is the bane of God's love, the poison of our hearts, and the venom of our souls.† For when human favour and respect

Affection to persons, corrupts our judgments.

* Read chapter xiii. of the *Conflict*.

† There is no true, lasting, and profitable friendship but that which is founded upon God and maintained without impediment to His love. That affection which so fills and possesses the heart as to weaken in it the love of God, though in ever so slight a degree, and

strive to oversway the love of God, and strike in for a part of that which is due to God only, we do or leave undone, say or unsay, what we neither should nor

rob Him of that plenitude of love which He demands of us, is inordinate and sensual, and should therefore be destroyed, and cut out as a most insidious enemy of the soul, and a certain obstacle to all further advancement in perfection. The signs whereby we may detect inordinate affection are principally these: 1. *Constant* distractions respecting the person loved during times of prayer. 2. A continual hankering and languishing after his bodily presence. 3. Disquietude of heart, and feelings of envy, that destroy interior peace and recollection. 4. Remissness in the observance of rule. 5. Disrelish for spiritual duties. 6. Waning in the desire after perfection.

'As for tenderness of nature,' says F. Baker, 'distracting solicitudes, and unquiet images in the mind touching those we love, the best and safest course would be to mortify and diminish them as much as may be, as proceeding from a natural sensual affection; the which, in as far as it does not flow from the superior soul, and is not subordinated and directed to the love of God, is defective. An internal liver ought to mortify all sensual affection to creatures—I mean, all particular friendships and intimacies which are not grounded upon the necessary foundation of the Divine Love; and as for such affections as are necessarily due by virtue of some respects and relations that God has put between ourselves and any others, such a one ought, as much as may be, to root them out of the sensual portion of the soul, because there they will cause great distractions and hindrances of our most necessary love to God.' *Sancta Sophia*, vol. i. treat. 2, sect. 2, chap. v.

F. Baker, in common with other spiritual writers, strongly deprecates all particular and over-tender friendships in religious communities, especially where such communities are small. 'A serious care to practise according to this advice is very necessary, especially in religious communities, both for our own good and others'. For besides that sensual friendships grounded on external or sensual respects are most unbecoming persons that have consecrated themselves only to God, and infinitely prejudicial to abstraction and recollectedness of mind, and much more if they be between persons of different sexes, such particular intimacies cannot choose but cause partialities, factions, particular designs, aims, &c., to the great disturbance and harm of the community.' *Ibid.*

St. Teresa is still more precise and emphatic on this matter. After pointing out how important it is that members of the same community should love one another tenderly, she proceeds:—

'It is thought that excess [of affection for one another] among ourselves cannot be an evil; and yet the evil and imperfections in its

would, but for their sakes. Our kindred corrupt our judgments, and courtesies blind our reason; so that we neither discern their follies nor correct their faults,

train are so serious, that I am certain nobody will believe it who has not seen it with his own eyes. By means of it, Satan lays many a snare of which their consciences are hardly aware whose efforts to please God are rude and rough; these look upon it as a virtue! But those who aim at perfection know well what it is, because it gradually weakens the will, so that it cannot give itself wholly to the love of God. I believe it to be even worse among women than among men, and in a community it works other and most manifest harm; for out of it, comes it that a sister does not love all her sisters, that she resents a wrong done to her friend, that she wishes she had something to give her in order to please her, that she seeks opportunities to converse with her, and that very often for the sake of telling her of her love of her rather than of her love of God. Satan never directs these grand friendships to the greater honour of God, but rather as a beginning of factions in Religious Orders. When they help us to serve our Lord, we find it out at once, for then the affection is without passion, and helps to overcome other passions; and I wish there were many of these friendships in every large monastery; but in St. Joseph's, where the sisters are not, and must not be, more than thirteen, none.

'All the sisters must be friends; all must love one another; all must cherish one another; all must help one another; and for the love of God, let them be on their guard against these private friendships, however holy they may be, for even among brothers they are usually poison. If there be those who do not think so, let them answer the story of Joseph; nor do I see any advantage whatever in it. If the religious be of kin one to another, it is much worse; it is then a plague.

'And though, my sisters, you may think this an extreme course, believe me it is in this extreme course that perfection lies, and great peace, and thereby many occasions of sin are avoided by those who are not very strong. If our affection be drawn towards one more than towards another—it can hardly be otherwise, because it is but natural, and nature often leads us to love that which is most worthless, if endowed with more natural grace—we must strive and struggle not to be mastered by that affection. Let us love goodness and inward purity, and earnestly labour to keep aloof from all respect for that which is only on the surface.

'Let no one with our consent have dominion over our will, except Him who purchased it with His blood. Let people look to it, for they will find themselves in a bondage out of which they cannot escape. The follies that have their source here are not to be numbered; but

but rather comply with their imperfections, and sometimes wink at their open wickedness, for the continuance of our own content.

I will enter into no details, lest the weaknesses of women, which are so many, should be discovered, and lest they should harm them who know nothing about them. But certainly, as for myself, I have been at times amazed at the sight of them, while, by the goodness of God, not so much in their power, but that may have been, because I was under the power of other things which are worse. However, as I have said, I have seen much of this, and I am afraid it prevails in most monasteries; for I have seen it in some, and I know it to be of all things the most ruinous to high religious perfection. In the prioress it is the plague. This I have said before. But in rooting out these particular friendships, it is necessary to be careful the moment they are observed, and it must be done with a skilful patience and affection, and not with sharpness.

'In the way of correction, it is a great help if the sisters are never together, not speaking to each other except at the settled times, according to the custom we observe when we meet in common, and according to our rule, which orders every religious to be by himself alone in his cell. Let the sisters in St. Joseph's be exempt from having a common workroom where all assemble, for though it be a praiseworthy custom to have one, yet silence is more easily kept when every sister is alone and makes it a custom to be so. Solitude is a great help, and for persons given to prayer the habit of it is a very great blessing. As prayer must be the foundation on which this house is built, and as we are gathered together in it for that end more than for anything else, we must strive to have an affection for that which helps us to our end.' St. Teresa, *The Way of Perfection*, chap. iv.

Lest these passages should sadden, perplex, or unnecessarily distress the soul of any warm-hearted person earnestly aiming at perfection, I will add the following words of the loving and discreet St. Francis of Sales:—

'Man gives himself entirely by love, and he gives himself in proportion to the ardour of his love; as he loves God sovereignly, he consecrates himself sovereignly to His Divine Majesty. He may love other objects, provided that, in giving them his heart, he does not take it from God; no love removes our heart from God, except such as is opposed to charity.

'We cannot have a doubt of our power to advance in the paths of divine love; nor can we hesitate in believing that the saints, who always loved God with their whole heart, love Him more ardently as the termination of their career approaches.

The remedy is, love all impartially in and for God.

4. O, how far is this from that pure love which obligeth us to love all—without exception of persons—only in and for God, as bearing His image, as being truly virtuous, and as far as

'Those who are still novices in the art of loving their Divine Spouse, love Him sincerely; but they are frequently diverted from this affection by distracting amusements and employments. Though they love God above all things, they are still occupied with many objects which they do not love for God, nor refer to His greater glory.

'There are other souls, who have made some progress in the exercise of divine love, and renounced their attachment for unprofitable and dangerous objects, but who still retain useless affections and inclinations. This is because they attach themselves to the objects which God permits them to love with an excessive tenderness and a kind of passionate ardour which displeases God.

'Souls which are inordinately attached to the objects which God wills they should love may certainly be said to love God *above* all things; yet they do not love Him *in* all things, since their affection for many objects is founded on other motives, in which God has no share, though they are not opposed to His divine will. These persons are like the phœnix when, having but a few feathers, which are beginning to get strength, it attempts to soar into the air, and being unable to support itself long on its wings, is obliged frequently to return to the earth and rest. These souls, though weak and imperfect, have a share in the favours of the heavenly Spouse; but they do not enjoy these favours as spouses, because their excessive affection for objects which are otherwise lawful often prevents them from being admitted to union with their divine Spouse, Who finds them occupied in loving, without any reference to Him, objects which should only be loved in Him and for Him.

'There are other persons who only bestow their affections on the objects which God permits them to love, and according to the measure of love prescribed by His divine will; thus admitting no inutility, either with respect to the object of their attachment or their manner of loving it. These souls are truly happy; they love God ardently; they love their friends in God, and their enemies for God. They love many things with God, but their attachment to them is entirely referred to the love of God; consequently, they not only love God above all things, but they love Him in all things, and all things in Him. They may be compared to the phœnix after its existence has been renewed; when it is only to be seen in the air, or on the summit of the highest mountain. The Divinity is the element which these souls never quit, not even when their love extends to other objects beside

they are furtherers to our soul's salvation and perfection. Fie upon all friendships and affections which are attended with such dangers, accompanied with such distractions, and followed with such disquietudes; which busy our fancies, and bend our imaginations to things so unprofitable and impertinent, and so much impede us in our intended progress to the perfection of God's love.

5. So, also, all disordered delight, pleasure, and propriety in spiritual sweetnesses, and inward Spiritual sweetnesses

God; for whatever its object may be, its centre is the Almighty. They deserve to reign with Christ, since they love Him without reserve or division, since they love nothing out of Him, nothing independently of Him, and everything in and for Him.

'Finally, the most perfect degree of love is that of a soul who not only loves God above all things, and in all things, but who loves *God alone* in all things; who, to speak more correctly, amidst many things which are the objects of her affection, loves but one, which is God. As it is God alone Whom she loves in the objects of her affection, she loves Him equally everywhere, independently of circumstances, and according to the will of Him she loves. Such is the state of those favoured souls who have attained the perfection of love; accurately speaking, they do not love creatures in themselves, but in their Creator, Whom they also love in His creatures. If the law of charity sometimes attaches them to a created object, it is not with a view of reposing therein that they form this attachment; their repose is centred in God alone, Who is the sole motive and term of their love. When they consider God in His creatures, and creatures in their Creator, it is God alone Whom they love, and not His creatures; as those who seek for pearls only value the oysters they find for the pearls they contain.

'It is not probable that any mortal being has ever attained this state of perfectly pure love except the ever-blessed Virgin, who was at once the Mother and Spouse of her God. As for other creatures, they cannot remain long in the same disposition; they advance or recede, they ascend or descend, and consequently, they pass from one to the other of the four degrees of perfection, distinguished in the love of God above all things.' *Treatise on the Love of God*. pages 224-234.

may be sometimes snares of our enemy. solaces of devotion are mere traps of the enemy, laid to catch and ensnare our unwary souls, and to make them rest with complacency in things which are not God Himself—the end of our desires—but only His creatures, gifts, and graces.

6. You must not stay here, O devout souls, but We must not stay in them, but transcend them. pass on your way, and transcend all for His sake, Whom you only seek, and not His solaces. These are helps and encouragements in your course, not the goal you must touch. These are neither security nor sanctity, but only baits of the divine pity to strengthen you in climbing the steep mountain to His perfect charity.*

THE THIRD AMBUSH.

Extroversion, or an Inordinate Application of the Soul to External Things.

1. This chokes up the spirit of devotion, quenches Extroversion chokes up devotion; the soul's ardour in her holy exercises, hinders her hastening to perfection, and buries in mean and inferior employments the whole heart and mind, the whole time and talents, which should be totally taken up in divine contemplation.†

2. Take heed of being drawn into this dangerous

* Read chapter xxviii. of the *Conflict*.

† 'The less attention I give to business, the more advanced I find myself in my interior. Though I know this very clearly, yet I often neglect using care to be released from business, and doubtless I receive some harm thereby.' *Letters of St. Teresa*, no. viii.

ambush, O dear soul, and intrude not yourself into any business. When *necessity*, *obedience*, or *charity*—the only pretexts which can make extroversion lawful and laudable—urge you abroad, keep your heart still at home, converse there with your Lord and Love, and commune with Him concerning the more important affairs of eternity; abstract yourself from all outward multiplicity, and there treat sweetly and secretly with Him of your soul's union to that '*one thing*' which is only and absolutely '*necessary*.'

therefore we must not intrude ourselves into employments,

3. Curb, therefore, your fancy from fruitlessly roaming abroad upon all occurring objects, for this proceeds from instability of heart, and argues a neglect of your interior.* Curb and suppress all wanderings of your mind, not only from sinful, but from superfluous and unprofitable conceptions, which nothing advance your soul in its progress to perfection, but contaminate it with the dust of vanity, and grieve the holy Spirit of God within you.

but curb fancies.

4. Perform such works as concern your calling, without solicitude of mind or engagement of affection, lest your senses become darkened, your soul distracted, your fervour diminished, your prayers neglected, and you, sliding insensibly into negligence and a total discomposition in your *inward man*, be hardly ever again reclaimed and recollected. For how can a soul which is totally environed with worldly impertinences have any leisure left for

Perform works of obedience, necessity, and charity without engaging your affections;

* Read chapter iv. § 7, of the *Conflict*.

the entertainments of piety? How can a mind dulled and astonished with the continual noises of the world, hearken attentively to God's holy inspirations?*

and strive to enter into your interior,

5. Wherefore, strive timely and diligently to enter into your interior; prevent your soul, which is ever active and never idle, with pious thoughts, lest evil habits press in first and prepossess it; apply yourselves speedily and seriously to introversion, spiritual silence, and inward attendance to God alone; adhere to Him only, and remain immovable from this maxim:—*To desire nothing, demand nothing, think of nothing, love nothing, labour for nothing, but Him alone, that One and All Who is needful for you.*† Do this

* St. Teresa likens worldly solicitudes and external distractions to 'serpents, lizards, vipers, and venomous creatures.' As long as a religious man allows his heart to be engrossed by multiplicity, so long will he be unable to draw near and behold clearly with the spiritual eye of contemplation the Face of God. For 'these *filthy vermin* are an impediment that blind his eyes in such a way that he sees nothing else but them.' And a little further on the saint says:—'It is very important, in order to enter into the second Mansion, that every one should endeavour, according to his state, *to give up every business which is not necessary.* This is so essential for arriving at the principal Mansion, that unless one begin to do this, I consider it impossible to arrive.' *The Interior Castle*, p. 47.

† Our author appears to be quoting here, as from memory, the celebrated maxim of the Pilgrim in Walter Hilton's *Scale of Perfection*:—'I am nothing, I have nothing, I covet nothing but One.' Hilton's explanation of this maxim of the poor Pilgrim journeying to Jerusalem is so full of divine beauty and perfection that I shall give it *in extenso.* 'Humility saith, "I am nothing, I have nothing;" Love saith, "I covet nothing but One, and that is Jesus." These two strings, well fastened by the recollection of Jesus, make good music in the harp of the soul when they are cleverly touched by the finger of reason, for the lower thou strikest one, the higher soundeth the other. The less thou feelest that thou art, or that thou hast of thyself through humility, the more thou wilt desire to have

as if nothing else concerned you, and as if there were nothing but Him and yourself, and you and Himself considerable in the whole world.

6. The surest way to compass this happy and heavenly design, is to keep your eyes and heart fixed constantly and continually upon Christ crucified. This is the solid ground from whence the highest contemplatives take their first rise; hither—into this sacred *Ark* of our Saviour's humanity—they must again return after their lofty soarings into the Divinity, and here they must settle when elsewhere they can find no footing. And surely a soul that seriously considers His sufferings, contemplates His mercies, and reflects upon His virtues, will find its whole time too short to visit each room of His several perfections, and none at all left to be lost upon extravagant and worldly fancies.

by fixing your heart upon Christ crucified.

THE FOURTH AMBUSH.

Bitterness of Heart.

1. Bitterness of heart comprehends all kind of sadness, melancholy, frowardness, restlessness, indignation, despitefulness, proneness to impatience, discontent, tediousness of mind,

Bitterness of heart comprehends all sadness, frowardness, &c.;

Jesus through love. . . . And since this alone is truly precious and noble, therefore, whatever else thou hast or whatever thou dost, hold and esteem it as nothing, *at least to rest in*, without the sight and the love of Jesus.' *The Scale of Perfection*, p. 209, edited by R. E. Guy, O.S.B.

aversion, distaste of all things, dislike of others, suspicions, sinister interpretations, unpleasantness, murmurings, detractions, rancour, malice, rash judgments, and the like.

all which proceed from perverse nature, &c.,

2. The source of these bitter streams is either perverse nature, or indiscreet austerities, or an over-serious application of the mind to study and thoughtfulness, or a secret presumption of self-perfection and sufficiency, or an immortification of passions, or a reflection upon past injuries, or an envying at others' virtue, praise, preferment, and prosperity.

and must be sweetened with charity,

3. And all these anguishes of mind and harshnesses in conversation are great impediments to our progress in spirituality, and must necessarily be sweetened and seasoned with the sugar of perfect charity. For if we truly love our Lord God, how can we scorn His image stamped in the souls of our brethren? Do they cease to be God's amiable creatures because they displease, despise, or neglect me?* May they not be God's friends, though they are my foes? Are they not more likely to love God because they dislike me, who am so truly unworthy to be loved by any one? Are not my seeming enemies, upon due consideration, my surest friends, since by mortifying me they increase my stock of merit, occasion my more serious application to the practice of virtue, and egg me onwards in the way of all perfection?†

* Read chapter xvi. of the *Conflict*.
† Read *note* to chapter xix. § 15, of the *Conflict*.

4. You must therefore buckle yourselves, O dear souls, against all these bad and bitter dispositions, by loving all in and for God, by being amiable to all, affable to all, meek to all, merciful to all. Strive to be gentle in words, cheerful in countenance, pleasing in your actions, patient in enduring, compassionate to others in their failings, charitable in assisting them, ready to pardon them, pious to interpret their actions for their best advantage, far from troubling or thwarting them, free from contristating or confounding them.

and by being amiable and affable to all.

5. There is also another private and perilous corner in this ambush of bitterness of heart, which is a certain grudging at the proceedings of God's providence, and a repining at His permission of adversities to befall us.

To this ambush belongs a certain repining at God's providence;

6. Take heed, dear souls, of slipping into this sad and dismal gulf of discontent and murmuring against God, in the least thought, word, or gesture. Be not dejected or disquieted at anything, but say cordially, cheerfully, faithfully, and resignedly:—'It is the Lord! let Him do what seems good in His own eyes. Alas, can self-love so blind my understanding as to make me think I deserve not to suffer this and much more? I offer up myself to Thy sweet pleasure, O my God; my heart is ready and prepared to perform what Thou pleasest, and to endure what Thou permittest; and I am wholly resigned to Thy holy will in all things which shall befall me for time and eternity.'

which must be corrected by a cordial resignation.

THE FIFTH AMBUSH.

Scrupulosity.

Scrupulosity

1. Which includes all inward affliction, fearfulness, perplexity, vexation, and trouble of the soul, and is an evident effect of some secret pride and self-love.

aims at the destruction of our Faith and Confidence.

2. This dangerous ambush is designed by our enemy to cut off all succours of Faith and Confidence in God's mercy and goodness from us, that so by degrees he may lead us on, and cast us headlong into the precipice of despair!*

To avoid this we must rely upon God

3. To avoid this deceit, which aims at your utter ruin and destruction, your only secure and short way, O dear souls, is to cast yourselves really,

* Scrupulosity usually springs from one of three causes: 1. The Dispensation of God. 2. Pride. 3. Ignorance. The scrupulosity which arises from the Dispensation of God is sent as a trial to prove the fidelity of the soul, purge it of self-love and confidence, and lead it by interior afflictions to higher perfection and closer union of charity. In this case, it becomes an instrument of sanctification, and as such should be regarded as a signal grace and token of God's special predilection. Every soul called to a high degree of prayer will have, as a rule, sooner or later to pass through this harassing torture, which darkens and envelops the soul in a cloud of fear, doubt, and desolation. Whilst in this state, a soul should remain in the hand of God like an earthen vessel in the furnace, enduring patiently its sufferings in silence and resignation until the Good Shepherd shall be pleased to release it from its cruel bondage, and leading it into green pastures near the running brook, restore it to peace, refreshment, and the joy of the Holy Ghost. When, however, scrupulosity proceeds from pride or perverse nature it is displeasing to God, and should be made a matter of sacramental confession. It may be known by its fruits:— 1. Vanity, which regards as unsound the advice of our spiritual director. 2. Disobedience, which wilfully neglects his commands. 3. Obstinacy and Presumption, which makes us trust to our own reason

and our ghostly father.

resignedly, cheerfully, and confidently into the bosom of the divine bounty, and on the guidance of your ghostly father; for there is no other hope of shelter or safety from these storms of trouble and temptations. There you may make a happy exchange of your servile and slavish fear for sweet and filial love; there you will drown and destroy these dismal, dreadful, and desperate imaginations and fancies in the abysses of God's infinite mercy; there you will admire, adore, and implore His power, wisdom, and goodness, whereby you will confess, yield, and confide that He can, knows how, and is willing to help and heal your sick and sorrowful souls in His own good time and liking; there you will truly see that you are nothing of yourselves, but are all things, have all things, and can do all things in Him, your all-sufficient Creator and Comforter.

4. And you may securely stand to this infallible verity:—That you can never err in overmuch

We can-

and abilities, and not submit to the wiser judgment of our divinely-appointed guide. 4. Self-love, which supplies subtle excuses for disobedience under the counterfeit cloak of fear and care of our souls. Sometimes scrupulosity arises from ignorance, whilst this again may spring from some flaw or weakness in the critical faculty that distinguishes good from evil. This species of scrupulosity is more common to women than men. It is a misfortune, not a sin, unless it be occasioned by culpable neglect.

To souls troubled with scrupulosity I commend a careful perusal of 1. *Sancta Sophia*, treat. 2, chap. x. 2. The *Spiritual Conquest*, treat. 5, doubt 21. 3. F. Faber's *Growth in Holiness*, chap. xviii.; *Spiritual Conferences*, Self-deceit iii. p. 204. 4. P. Marin's *Perfect Religious*, p. 397. 5. St. John of the Cross, *Complete Works* of, vol. ii. p. 321. 6. Premord's *Rules of a Christian Life*, chap. xxviii. 7. *God's Safe Way of Obedience*, by Rev. S. Jenks, a missionary in England of the seventeenth century. This is, perhaps, one of the best and most exhaustive treatises on the subject.

not err in confidence so long as we fall not into negligence. trust, hope, and confidence in God, and in His mercy and bounty, so long as you slack not in the punctual performance of your duty, cease not in the serious mortification of your passions and sensuality, continue your practices of patience in adversity, of gratitude in prosperity, and of indifference and resignation to the divine will in all occurrences.*

THE SIXTH AMBUSH.

Excessive and Unnecessary Study.

Which busies the understanding, but leaves the will barren.

1. This busies the understanding about curious notions and useless speculations, and leaves the will barren of all true devotion and affections. For there are some who study to know much that they may become *learned*, and it is a foolish *curiosity;* some study that they may *sell their skill*, and that is a foolish *avarice;* some strive to know that they *themselves may be known*, and it is a foolish *vanity;* some study knowledge that with it they may *edify others*, and that is *charity;* and finally, some desire knowledge that they themselves may be *edified* and their own souls *bettered*, and this is *wisdom.*†

* 'Confidence in God is beset by two enemies, both of which must be guarded against; on the one hand presumption, cowardice on the other. Both extremes arise from self-love and distorted views: the true course is to trust wholly to God, neither presuming nor desponding. As a general rule, men are most liable to err on the side of presumption, and women on that of fearfulness and distrust.' *The Hidden Life of the Soul*, p. 129.

† Our author is quoting here a passage of St. Bernard, which it may be useful to give in full:—

'*Qui se*, inquit S. Paulus, *putat aliquid scire, nondum scit quomodo*

2. Wherefore, all such study as aims at the bare knowledge of things, without any further relation to piety and proficiency in the way of the spirit, is a mere trap of our enemy, thereby to puff us up with pride and vanity,* to take up our time and fill up our souls with self-conceits and presumption. It maketh a great noise, and furnisheth our tongues with fair expressions concerning the spiritual life, divine feelings, and the secret ways of God's proceedings with His faithful friends and servants, but hath no true taste at all of that of which it talks so much; it is an empty discourse void of all inward experience, a mere hypochondriacal wind.

Puffs us up with vanity, but leaves us empty of true piety.

3. The remedy against this is to rectify our in-

oporteat eum scire (1 Cor. viii. 2). Vides quoniam non probat multa scientem, si sciendi modum nescierit. Vides, inquam, quomodo fructum et utilitatem scientiæ in modo sciendi constituit? Quid ergo dicit modum sciendi? Quid, nisi ut scias quo ordine, quo studio, quo fine quæque nosse opporteat? Quo ordine, ut id prius, quod maturius ad salutem; quo studio, ut id ardentius, quod vehementius ad amorem; quo fine, ut non ad inanem gloriam, aut curiositatem, aut aliquid simile, sed tantum ad ædificationem tuam vel proximi. Sunt namque, qui scire volunt eo fine tantum, ut sciant; et turpis curiositas est. Et sunt qui scire volunt, ut sciantur ipsi; et turpis vanitas est. Qui profecto non evadent subsannantem satyricum, et ei qui ejusmodi est decantantem:

'*Scire tuum nihil est, nisi te scire hoc sciat alter!*

'Et sunt item qui scire volunt ut scientiam suam vendant, verbi causa, pro pecunia, pro honoribus; et turpis quæstus est. Sed sunt quoque qui scire volunt, ut ædificent; et charitas est. Et item qui scire volunt, ut ædificentur; et prudentia est. Horum omnium soli ultimi duo non inveniuntur in abusione scientiæ, quippe qui ad hoc volunt intelligere ut bene faciant.' *S. Bernardi Sermo* xxxvi. *in Cantica.*

* 'Eruditio absque dilectione inflat, dilectio absque eruditione errat—Learning without love inflates, love without learning leads astray.' *S. Bernard. Serm. in Cant.* lxix.

The remedy is to rectify our intention.

tentions. Read not, dear souls, nor study to be accounted learned, but to become perfect.* Desire rather to love God's goodness than to know much of His greatness, to lead a holy life than to speak high words concerning it. Confess your own ignorance in all things, and content yourselves with the sole knowledge of your Saviour.† This is the sum of all science, and this alone will suffice for your salvation.

THE SEVENTH AMBUSH.

Tepidity and Coldness in Devotion.

This is the bane of all spirituality.

1. This is the bane of all spirituality, nor hath the devil any more alluring bait than this, which is seldom perceived and highly prejudicial, namely, lukewarmness in devotion, want of vigour in our spiritual exercises, and defect of fervour in our tendency to perfection.‡

2. Think not, therefore, dear souls, that it sufficeth

---

* Love to be unknown and of no account. Believe me, said one, he hath lived well that hath lain well hid. Be not too forward to show your knowledge, though you think yourself to be more knowing than others. *Let not the wise man glory in his wisdom; but let him that glorieth glory in this, that he understandeth and knoweth Me* (Jeremias ix. 23). Read *Following of Christ,* book i. chaps. 1, 2, 3, and also book iii. chap. 43.

† It will be understood that our author does not here censure the right use of study, but its abuse; nor does he mean that those who are obliged by their vocation to aim at learning should neglect it. *The lips of the Priest shall keep knowledge, and they shall seek the law at his mouth* (Mal. ii. 7).

‡ Read chap. xii. of the *Conflict.*

you to perform your accustomed practice of piety, but rather you are continually to aim at a further and daily increase of charity. Consider that *not to advance in the way of the Spirit is to recede,** and that it is not the multitude of your good works which makes them considerable, but the fervour wherewith they are performed. Be sure to keep your heart and soul always—as much as human weakness and the rule of discretion will permit—elevated to your Lord and Love.

We must always go forward towards perfection,

3. Cry continually for His grace. Knock incessantly at the gate of His mercy. Sigh after Him perseverantly. Seek to perform His will diligently, and follow His pleasure purely and perfectly. Give that day for lost wherein you have not made some progress in the way of perfection. And finally, rouse up yourselves, and prick forward your sluggish dulness in devotion with some brief and burning aspirations, which you are to have always ready in your heart and mouth, as :—

and sigh after it perseverantly.

'O my Lord, O my God, the life of my soul, and the only love of my heart, when shall I love Thee as I desire and as Thou demandest!

'O my Jesus, when shall I die perfectly to the world, myself, and all things, that I may live purely and entirely in Thy only charity!

'O when shall I be nothing to any creature, and

* 'Nolle proficere, est decipere.' *S. Bernard. Epis.* 254.

every creature nothing to me, but only in Thee, and for Thee alone!

'O that I could go out of myself and get into Thee! That I could thrust my caitiff heart out of this breast to establish Thine, O my sweet Saviour, in its place!

'O let Thy true love transform me totally into Thee! Let me not live any longer but in Thee! Let me not love any creature but by, in, and for Thee, my Creator!

'O incomprehensible bounty, either take my soul out of this world or take the love of this world out of my soul! Either bereave me of my life or bestow on me Thy love!'

In all which raptures and affections the Holy Spirit is the best Director, Whose inward impulse and dictate you are diligently to follow—though still according to discretion and obedience—with a perpetual longing and loving, sighing and seeking, to advance your soul to divine union.

An excellent counsel of St. Anthony.

3. Finally, I conclude with this hearty and heavenly counsel of St. Anthony to his disciples against this dangerous coldness in devotion:—*My brethren, let this be my general and particular precept unto you; never to lose your first fervour and good purposes, nor to grow slack in your observances, but to go always forward, and renew daily your devout exercises, as if you daily were new beginners in the way of perfection.** This he often repeated and inculcated; and being on his deathbed, that his last words might remain more vividly

* See *Vitæ Patrum*, lib. i. cap. xv., Migne, *Patrologiæ*, tomus 73.

imprinted in their minds, he bequeathed unto them, as his final and never-to-be-forgotten testament, this piercing and pithy document, able to win, wound, and melt a flint into fervour and compunction:—*O my loving children, I go the way of my forefathers; our Lord calls and invites me, and my soul thirsts after Him and heaven. But you, O my beloved ones, what will you do? I have often admonished you, and do at this last gasp leave unto you for my will and testament this warning—That you grow not tepid, and go not backward, and so on a sudden lose the pains and profit of so many years past. Think still you are to begin anew, as though what you had already suffered for Christ were nothing. Let your good-will and desires get every day new strength and vigour. Forget what is past, and run to what is before you. Live and labour with such fervour and purity, as if it were your first work that ever pleased God, or the last service you should ever render Him in this mortal life.*'*

O devout souls, our days pass away swiftly, death is always at our heels, eternity approaches, wherein our God, Whom we have served and loved, will wipe the tears from our eyes, the sweat off our brows, and the blood off our wounds, and crown us with glory, peace, security, and immortality. Let us not lose heart in His service, nor hope in His goodness. He expects and invites us. Angels and saints offer their helping hands. The question is of eternal life, eternal light, eternal liberty, and eternal love!

* See *Vitæ Patrum*, lib. i. cap. lviii., Migne, *Patrologiæ*, tomus 73.

Second Treatise.

OF THE USE AND PRACTICE OF OUR SPIRITUAL WEAPONS,

HERE METHODICALLY ARRANGED AND DRAWN INTO SEVEN EXERCISES, AFFECTIVE ACTS OR ASPIRATIONS, ACCORDING TO THE DAYS OF THE WEEK.

Give me understanding, and I will search Thy law: and I will keep it with my whole heart. Ps. cxviii. 34.

MONDAY.

Of the Knowledge of God and Confidence in Him.

The First Exercise.

1. To know Thee, O divine Fountain of goodness, is to be truly happy; and yet none can know Thee, O boundless and bottomless Sea of all perfections, but through Thy own manifestation and mercy. Vouchsafe, therefore, I beseech Thee, O most loving and liberal Lord, to enter this poor and empty heart of Thy meanest servant, to inform my ignorant soul with a glimpse of this necessary science, and to inflame my cold affection with a small spark of Thy love.

O omnipotent Creator of heaven and earth, both of which Thou fillest with Thy goodness and glory; O God of infinite power, excellent wisdom, immeasurable goodness, and incomprehensible love, my soul thirsts after Thee, the essential Source of all felicity; my heart seeks Thee, the proper Place of its repose; it sighs to Thee, the natural Centre of all its hope and happiness. In Thy blessed mind, O my God, it first rested in its eternal possibility and similitude; thither it must again return, and there it must either rest eternally or perish for evermore. O let it now find Thee that it may ever love Thee!

2. O Lord, most good, glorious, and gracious, most blessed and bountiful, most high and holy, most excellent and ineffable, what words or thoughts can express Thy purity and perfection! Let me know Thee, O Thou Life of my soul. Let me see Thee, O Thou Light of my eyes. Let me seek Thee, O Thou only Solace of my spirit. Let me find Thee, O Thou Desired of my heart. Let me embrace Thee, O my heavenly Spouse. Let me possess Thee, O Thou sovereign Sweetness and full Satiety of all my inward and outward senses. O that my heart could always think on Thee, my will ever love Thee, my mind still remember Thee, my understanding continually conceive Thee, my reason perpetually adhere to Thee, and my whole man incessantly praise Thee. O hide not Thy face from me, my Joy, my Light, and my Life. If I may not see Thee and live, O let me die that I may see Thee. I desire to die here, and be dissolved, that I may see Thee, know Thee, come to Thee, live with Thee, and love Thee eternally.

O ever blessed and glorious Divinity; O Father,

Who of Thine own substance bringest forth an ineffable Goodness, coequal, consubstantial, and coeternal with Thyself, which is Thy Son; O Father and Son, Who loving each other with infinite charity and content, are united together in the Holy Ghost, equally and unspeakably proceeding from You both; I admire Thee, adore Thee, and worship Thee with all the powers of my body and soul.

3. O sacred Deity! O Tri-Unity and Uni-Trinity! O Father, Son, and Holy Ghost! Holy, holy, holy, Lord God of hosts, Who wert, art, and shalt be for ever Almighty! I, Thy poor creature, prostrate before the throne of Thy Divine Majesty, from the abyss of my own nothingness invoke, adore, and acknowledge Thee the abyss of all perfection. I present Thee with all Thine own gifts, goods, and graces, which Thou hast plentifully poured out upon all Thy creatures. I offer up to Thy praise the affections of angels and men, the properties of the elements, the beauty and motion of the whole universe, and the essence of all being. O that my soul were capable of comprising unitedly all their several affections and perfections. How joyfully would it employ them in Thy praise! How sweetly would it melt away in Thy presence! Behold, O my God, I make an entire oblation of them all, I acknowledge and adore Thee with them all, and desire to do it as frequently as I breathe, and as often as there are minutes in time, stars in the firmament, sands in the ocean, and numbers in all nature.

O my Lord, whose love is the life of my soul, increase my knowledge of Thee, that I may enlarge my love to Thee. Alas, I love Thee not, O amiable Lord God, because I know Thee not. I know Thee not, because darkness and sin hath covered and encompassed my understanding. Wherefore, O bright Light, Who illuminated all things, expel this darkness from my soul, drive off these clouds from my understanding, and draw the curtain from off the face of the abyss of my mind, that I may see and know Thee, and then I shall not choose save to love Thee.

O my dear Jesus, show me Thy divine Father. Dart a beam of Thy heavenly splendour into my dull heart, that I may have some degree of that holy science which may help me in Thy love, make me obedient to Thy will, and resolute in Thy service.

To know all things of this world, O Jesus, and not to know Thee, is but ignorance and folly. Let me, therefore, know Thy eternal Father, and Thee, Whom He sent for my salvation, and it sufficeth me. O give me this knowledge, that I may give Thee my love, and I ask no more. Let me be unknowing, ignorant, and a fool in all other things, so I may wisely know Thee, O my Lord and my All.

4. O King of Glory, I acknowledge Thy perfections to be above all knowledge, save that of Thy own divine understanding. I confess that Thy height is unreachable, Thy goodness unchangeable, Thy greatness incomprehensible, Thy light inaccessible, and all Thy

other divine attributes and perfections are so mighty and so many, so good and so glorious, so excellent and so admirable, so worthy and so wonderful, that were all the power and prerogatives, all the virtue, wisdom, and qualities of all creatures united in one individual nature, it were not so much in respect of Thy glory and greatness as the least drop of water is in comparison to the vast ocean. Wherefore, I beg of Thee, O immense and inaccessible Godhead, only so much to know, conceive, believe, and understand of Thy hidden Majesty as may efficaciously move my will to Thee; and I content myself with so much light of Thy divinity as may force me to love Thee ardently, effectually, and perseverantly.

O my Lord and my Love, fill my heart with the sweet influence of Thy heavenly grace, that I may in some measure discover how good and gracious Thou art to me and to all Thy creatures. O let me still remember Thy mercy, ever dread Thy justice, and continually admire and adore Thy power and providence.

Ah! my noble soul, stamped with thy Creator's lovely image, endowed with the excellences of understanding to know Him, of will to love Him, of memory to rest in Him, why adherest thou not fast to Him only in pure and perfect delight, forgetting and foregoing all sensible and worldly objects?

5. O that I were so ravished with Thy love and liking, my only amiable Lord God, that through joy, jubilee, and admiration, I might feel no self at all, no sense, no

change, no inequality; that no prosperity might puff me up, no adversity deject me, no accident separate me from Thee, O my God of infinite love and liberality!

O that I could be ever joyful in Thee, ever grateful to Thee, and ever mindful of Thy inhabiting presence within me.* Thou art always nearer to my soul, O my God, than my soul is to my body, always conserving, counselling, disposing, directing, inciting, and inspiring it to Thy love. And wilt thou not, O my senseless and sinful soul, be always cautious and circumspect how thou behavest thyself in thy Lord's presence, Who is so tenderly careful of Thy safety? O let His love be no longer neglected, His sweet invitations

* '*Lo, the kingdom of God is within you* (Luke xvii. 21). These words are very clear, and are, both by St. Thomas, St. Bonaventure, and others, understood of the internal kingdom in the soul. This "Kingdom" the soul obtains when, as in due order, she hath subjected the inferior man to the superior, and the superior man to God, Who then doth live and reign in her, as in His "Kingdom." In confirmation whereof, St. Cyril, St. Jerome, and St. Augustine understood these words of the *Paternoster*—"Thy kingdom come"—of the spiritual kingdom in the soul; whereof St. Augustine had particular experience, as appeareth by his own words when he said: "O great depth! O sweet intimacy!" An intimacy without the bitterness of wicked thoughts, without fear, remorse, or sorrow. This is the joy whereof our Saviour said: *Enter thou into the joy of thy Lord* (Matt. xxv. 21).

'Truly, if to one who with great labour did fetch water afar off we should show the fountain from whence it did flow within his own house, would he not spare the labour of fetching it from abroad and enjoy that which he has within doors? Where the kingdom of God is, there is God, Who is the Fountain of all good, beauty, and perfection, which man seeks out of himself with great labour. Yea, by the "Kingdom of God" we understand nothing else but a perfect union of the soul with God. And therefore, understanding that the "kingdom of God is within him," each one ought to be inflamed with a great desire to seek the same.' *The Kingdom of God in the Soul*, by Father John Balduke, p. 29-31, 1657.

no longer slighted. O that thou wouldst henceforth walk before Him as His dear, chaste, and holy Spouse, with all respect and reverence, fear and fidelity, courage and constancy, preparing thyself diligently for his divine embraces.

6. Grant, I beseech Theé, O mighty and merciful Creator, that my whole time and thoughts may be totally taken up in the contemplation of Thy unmeasurable benefits and bounty towards me. For I know, Lord, that I am truly nothing, and yet Thou carest for me, O my loving Maker, as if Thou hadst no other creature in heaven and on earth. Thou deliverest me from innumerable dangers, adornest me with many gifts and graces, givest me leave at all times to have free access to Thy throne of mercy, so that with one holy thought, one humble sigh, one devout desire, I may draw near to Thee, and enjoy Thee, and in Thee all comfort and content—O divine privilege!—and discover to Thee my wants, lay open my wounds, and boldly declare my wishes as to my nearest, dearest, and trustiest friend and familiar, and be sure of supplies, salves, and succour in all my necessities! O what goodness, what grace, what mercy is this!

O my soul, how loving and liberal a Lord have we! How loving in mercy, how liberal in bounty! Ah, our unthankfulness to requite, our unworthiness to deserve His favours!

Up, my heart, be no longer ungrateful and unfaithful to so great, good, and gracious a benefactor. Yes,

O blessed and bountiful Giver, I now say cordially, and will ever stand to it courageously :—' I will henceforth love Thee, O my Lord, my love, my life, my strength, my support, my home, my harbour, and my happiness.' I will remember Thy sweet words to all sinners :—' Why will you perish, O children? *As I live, I desire not the death of the wicked, but that the wicked turn from his way and live.*'* I will behold Thy sacred wounds suffered for me, able to move a rock to love and compassion. And though I am ashamed to think what I have been, and how little I have done, how much Thou hast endured for me, how long Thou hast expected me, how lovingly Thou hast besought me, and how poorly I have corresponded to Thee; yet I know, O my Lord, Thou ceasest not to be God and good, though I am weak and wicked. Therefore, I will yet take courage in Thy service, and confidently hope that Thou, Who soughtest after me, a lost sheep, wilt mercifully receive me now I seek after Thee, my loving Shepherd, with a right intention, real resolution, and inflamed affection.

7. Yes, O my Lord and my Love, heaven and earth shall sooner perish than my confidence in Thy sweet mercies and my Saviour's merits. If Thou repel me, I will run after Thee. If Thou shut Thy door against me, I will never cease knocking. And if Thou killest me, yet I will trust in Thee.† I wholly cast myself upon

* Ezechiel xxxiii. 11.

† '*Although He should kill me, I will trust in Him.*' Job xiii. 15.

Thy holy will, providence, and protection. I protest with heart and mouth that I now am, and henceforth will be, entirely Thine; that I have nothing, seek nothing, fear nothing, desire nothing, demand nothing, want nothing, will nothing, but Thee only, my Lord, my Love, and my All!

And I firmly purpose to serve and love Thee, O sacred and supreme Majesty, simply, sincerely, purely, and perseverantly, not for any fear of pains or punishment; not for any self-interest of what this world can offer, or the next afford; not for the least hope of heaven or happiness; but I will Thee, seek Thee, and love Thee for Thyself only, O my all-sufficient Lord God, Who art the sole object, sweet completement, and solid contentment of my soul. Pardon me, protect me, and provide for me; for Thou art my only hope and happiness.

TUESDAY.

To Obtain Knowledge of and Diffidence in Ourselves.

The Second Exercise.

1. What is man, O omnipotent Creator, what is this man, that Thou shouldst be mindful of him? He is nothing, O Lord, and I am the worst and least of these nothings, because I have least corresponded to Thy grace, and made worst use of Thy gifts. O, give me light; reach forth Thy hand to this blind creature crying after Thee, O Thou true Light of the world and

Life of my soul, that now at length I may duly, diligently, cordially, and abyssfully dive into my own baseness, weakness, misery, nothingness; that, knowing what I truly am, I may really loathe, hate, distrust, despise, and deny myself and all my own proceedings, sincerely love Thee, only trust and hope in Thee, and rely wholly upon Thy divine providence and protection.

I am not only content, O my Lord God, but even willing and desirous, that all Thy creatures should take me and treat me according to my true condition and unworthiness. And I am resolved by Thy grace to humble myself, not only under Thy mighty hand, but also under the feet of all creatures, as their servant and slave, to be trodden on, abhorred, avoided, and detested by them all as a sink of sin and filthiness.

I will be desirous to be esteemed and used as dross amongst metals, chaff amongst grain, a wolf amongst sheep, and as Satan amongst the children of God.

I acknowledge myself as unworthy of all grace and comfort from God or man, and worthy of all pain, punishment, crosses, contradictions, confusion, desolation, death, damnation. I will be henceforth ashamed to complain of any grievance, and be content to suffer whatsoever the world, the devil, and hell itself can inflict upon me.

2. And to strengthen this my resolution, I will rationally consider before Thee, O my Lord, what I really am, what I was, and what will become of me, both touching my body, my soul, and my whole being.

Ay me! I have a body all clay, a soul all sin, a life all frailty, and a substance all nothing. And this is all I have to vaunt of in Thy presence, O my Lord and my Maker.

My material part is but slime of the earth, the very worst part of the basest element. Ah, poor man! and canst thou look so big, who camest from so low an extraction? Be ashamed to lift up thy head, vile mud and dirt, since thy pedigree is so well known, and the ingredients of thy being are so mean and contemptible.

And when I consider what this my body was in the womb, how it was conceived in concupiscence, nourished with infirmities, and brought up in darkness, I am ashamed to own my own beginning, which is so mean and so very low. Who, then, can justly boast of state, strength, beauty, or nobility, since the groundwork of all is but a little dust and clay?

Ah, poor worm! what a dismal prison wert thou detained in for nine months' space of thy time, how weak and fragile wert thou in body, how weak and woful in thy nature! And what art thou in thy best and most flourishing condition in the world, but a clog and a cage to thy enthralled soul; a painted sack or plastered* sepulchre, full of wretchedness and abomination! O my Lord, give me grace to frame an impartial judgment of what I am, and then how soon shall I check all risings of pride and presumption!

3. I came into this world, O my Lord, with groans

* Original text—'Pargetted.'

and tears; I live in it with griefs and cares; I shall go out of it with pangs and fears; and lastly, I must become a horror to the eyes of my dearest friends, a prey of vermin, and a companion of rottenness. Ah! how canst thou be proud of thy perfections, poor clay and ashes? Why shouldst thou look to be so highly prized and so daintily pampered, thou corruptible one? Dust thou art, and to dust thou must return. Hast thou not always before thy eyes these ashes for thy glass, and death for thy mistress? Why, then, dost thou suffer so many sparkles of vanity to arise from this thy caitiff condition?

And thou, my poor soul, the spiritual part of my composition, O what shall I say of thee to thy great Lord and Maker? What thou hast *hitherto* been I well know—wretched, wicked, sinful. What thou *now art* I know not, being uncertain of God's grace and love. What thou *shalt be hereafter*, I am altogether ignorant of, because doubtful of thy correspondency with grace, and fearful of thy perseverance in goodness.

Ah, sad condition! I came, O my Lord, into this world in original sin, I am bred up in actual sin, and if death and deadly sin meet together, I shall feel the smart of them both eternally. O how much need, then, have I of Thy grace, O merciful Lord God, to avoid sin, since I cannot eschew death! O let me rather admit a deadly wound than commit a deadly sin!

4. What art thou, then, O my whole man, consisting of body and of soul? What art thou, O N...., from all

eternity, before thy conception in the womb and birth into the world? Nothing. Ah, poor nothing! What is less than nothing? Where dwells this nothing? Who can describe a nothing which more differs from the least atom in the sun, than God's infinite greatness from the least of his creatures? O proud thing! what hast thou that thou hast not received? Nothing. Why, then, art thou puffed up with it as if thou hadst not received it? I acknowledge my whole being to be from Thy bounty, O my great, good, and glorious Maker; and since I possess nothing but what I have from Thee, since I shall also necessarily fade away into my first nothing if Thou withdraw from me Thy conserving hand for a moment, I will no longer glory in that which is none of mine, but I will here lay the foundation of my spiritual edifice upon this sure and solid foundation of *Thy All, and my own nothingness.* I will endeavour to frame a true conceit of my own misery, frailty, insufficiency, and nothingness, that so I may fully, speedily, and solidly come to this desired self-knowledge and humility.*

* '*All our works, O Lord, hast Thou wrought for us* (Isaias xxvi. 12). In all things nothing is left for man to boast concerning himself, either concerning his own virtue or his own operation; but all his glorying is in the wholeness of God, and that the only thing which belongs to himself is nothing. By this means he becometh wholly lost in himself, and cannot in any way find himself, but in God he findeth himself whole, in Whom he dwelleth with enough of quietness and security. And for this he exulteth greatly, namely, that all occasion hath been taken from him of glorying in himself, that *God may be all in all* (1 Cor. xv. 28). And in that he thus stands, he needeth no glory or praise, for he is full, and the plenitude of God Himself is in him. But wheresoever he desireth glory, there he is convinced he is altogether empty and without glory; for nowhere doth he seek anything,

I will run over my lesson, repeat my questions, learn my answers, and strive to grow skilful in this necessary and sacred science.

What have I received that I have not abused? Nothing; body, soul, will, judgment, memory, understanding, affection, senses, meat, drink, company, habit, books, prayer, sacraments, all creatures.

Can I, then, be proud of sin, filthiness, rottenness, labour, grief, infirmity, blindness, obstinacy, corruption, death, and damnation, which are worse than nothing?

Shall I boast of Thy gifts, O my God, which are not mine, or of my own abuses and ingratitudes? The one is to rob Thee of Thy honour, the other is to be honoured for Thy dishonour.

5. What creature ever sinned so grievously as I have done, and yet sorrowed so little and suffered less?

Who ever forsook so great and good a God for so little and vain a toy as I have done?

What sinful soul is there now in hell that would not have been a glorious saint in heaven, if it had had the helps, favours, feelings, and visits which I have both had and abused?

Who ever received so many mercies, so sweet com-

save where he is vain or empty. Thus it behoveth a man to be ever weak in himself, and to be strong in our Lord, and frequently to give all things for all, if he will not be straitened; because whatsoever he keepeth for himself and for his own possession, he is convinced that for this he hath sold God, since God giveth all gifts for the one gift, which is *Himself*, in order that He may become all ours, and that we be henceforth in no wise beggars, but full.' *The Fiery Soliloquy with God*, chap. x., by Master Gerlac Petersen, 1378.

forts, and so great graces from Thee, O bountiful Lord God, and made so little and bad use of them as I have done? If I deny all this, my conscience witnesseth against me. If I confess it, O, why am I not more humble?

Finally, if such great troubles, temptations, and tribulations had happened to me as have done to others, I should by consenting have burned, ere now, in hell-fire. But Thou, O meek and merciful Creator, hast spared me because Thou knowest my weakness, and sent me small crosses because I cannot bear greater.

Wherefore, not unto me, O Lord, but to Thee be all honour for time and eternity.

O that I could know Thee and know myself! O that I could see my own nothingness, and total dependency on Thee; my misery and malice, and Thy perfection and total goodness!

Ay me! weak and wretched N...! What are my powers, that I should rely on them? I have nothing, O my Lord, but what is Thine; my merits are Thy mercies, my goods Thy graces; yet I neither have been thankful for receiving them, nor faithful in using them.

O, when did I trust in my own strength and was not foiled and confounded? Grant, therefore, O my Lord, O my only Hope and Help, O my sole Safety and Security, that I may totally trust to Thee, and distrust myself; truly acknowledge Thee, and deny myself; entirely love Thee, and hate myself.

6. I confess, O my Lord, that I am the poorest, ungratefullest, unprofitablest, and unworthiest worm of

the earth, — a thing altogether useless to the world, and only active to offend Thee and to do wickedly in Thy sight; and is it possible that I can harbour any thought of self-love or self-liking?

O God of infinite glory, greatness, and majesty, before Whom the powers of heaven do tremble, what are all creatures in Thy sight, and what am I, the meanest of them all? O, what proportion is there, great God, between Thee and me, between Thy all and my nothing! And yet have I infringed Thy laws, disobeyed Thy commands, contemned Thy counsels, resisted Thy callings, and contradicted Thy will, to prefer my own. O monstrous impiety and ingratitude! And shall I not willingly submit to all pain, punishment, contradiction, and contempt, which Thou, O my highly-offended Creator, shalt suffer Thy creatures to inflict upon me? Behold, O my Lord, I debase, humble, and annihilate myself under all things that have a being. I will henceforth utterly hate, distrust, and detest myself, and wholly love Thee and rely upon Thy mercy.

O holy self-knowledge! O sacred humility! thou art the key of all perfection, the door of all solid virtue, piety, and devotion.

7. I now clearly see by the light of Thy divine goodness, O gracious Lord God, what hath hitherto been the cause of my non-proficiency in the way of the Spirit, and why the path of virtue seemed so unpleasant, thorny, tedious, and troublesome to my deceived soul. It was because I had not learned to leave, loathe,

deny, and distrust myself, and to rely wholly on Thee, O my only comfort and support.

I will, therefore, henceforth faithfully practise what I perceive so necessary. I will profoundly humble my soul both inwardly in Thy presence, O my Lord, and outwardly to the whole world.

I will joyfully and voluntarily embrace all injury, indignity, contempt, correction, and confusion, which can befall me, with as much pleasure as I have formerly any cherishings and kindnesses.

I will utterly destroy, ruin, and root out all self-love, self-liking, self-seeking, self-praise, and self-complacency.

I will cast myself under the feet of the vilest creature, take pleasure in the meanest employments, and obey them most willingly whom my nature most distastes and dislikes.

I will walk before Thee, O my Creator, as the needy, naked, desolate, and destitute vassal, acknowledging myself void of all virtue, and attributing to myself nothing but sin, ingratitude, defects, failings, imperfections.

I will fully persuade myself that no one can contemn, confound, persecute, and punish me as I deserve.

I will not regard whether I am honoured or hated, but imagine myself as a thing dead and forgotten, or as that which never had a being, and is now truly nothing.

I will be contented to be accounted a hypocrite in

my sincerest actions, and to be thought full of inward impatience, secret grudgings, and desires of revenge against those who shall any way mortify or misuse me, though my heart be never so free from it.

Finally, I will have these and the like thoughts and words always in my heart and mouth:—'I am nothing, I have nothing, I do no good, I am an unprofitable servant, I utterly hate and distrust myself, and totally rely upon Thee, O my Lord, my Love, and my All.'

WEDNESDAY.

To Obtain Remission of our Sins.

The Third Exercise.

1. *Who will give water to my head, and a fountain of tears to my eyes? and I will weep day and night** for my sins, which cover me all over, like an incurable ulcer, from the sole of the foot to the crown of the head.

Where art thou, O my wretched and wicked soul? In what labyrinth dost thou walk? In what sinks of sin and puddles of uncleanness dost thou wallow? Awake, arise, lament, repent! How long wilt thou sleep? Why wilt thou die? When wilt thou shake off thy fetters? Ah, return, silly sheep, to thy good Pastor; return, poor prodigal, to thy pious Father, whose goodness so lovingly invites thee; whose mercy has so long expected thee.

---

* Jeremias ix. 1.

O great and glorious God, the mighty Monarch of heaven and earth, King of kings and Lord of lords, behold a poor penitent publican who is ashamed to lift up his eyes to heaven, and unworthy to take Thy sacred Name into his sinful mouth, humbly knocking at the gate of Thy mercy, clasping Thy holy feet, and craving Thy accustomed pity and compassion.

O merciful Lord, hide not Thyself from me; shut not the door against me. O, one crumb of comfort, one dram of devotion, to my sad, sick soul, to my dry and desolate spirit.

2. I am conscious of my ingratitude against Thee, O supreme Majesty, *and my sin is always before me** and confounding me. But *whither shall I flee from Thy face?* † To whom should I have recourse but unto Thee? Art not Thou my Father, a Father of mercies, which have neither limits nor measure? Art not Thou my Maker, my Preserver, my Governor, my Deliverer, my King, my Pastor, my Physician, my Priest, and my Sacrifice?

If Thou art not all this and more to me, and if I am nothing to Thee, refuse me, reject me, and leave me a prey to be swallowed up by Thy enemies. But it is time, O my Lord, that heaven and earth take notice of what Thou art to me, and what I am to Thee. It is time Thou enter into Thy right; and I must now either give myself to Thee, or Thou must take me unto Thee.

Not that I aspire to those excellent prerogatives of

* Psalm l. 5. † Ib. cxxxviii. 7.

Thy dearest servants. No, my Lord, it sufficeth me to be in the outer rank of Thy meanest slaves; to be only stamped with Thy mark and linked fast to Thy chains, that I may never more have the power to fly from Thee. O grant me this favour, most merciful Father, which Thy dear Son hath purchased for me by the price of His Death and Passion.

I am fallen without Thee by my own frailty, but can never hope to rise but by Thy mercy, O my Lord and only support. I am sick without Thee, but cannot be cured without Thee, my heavenly Physician. I am dead without Thee, but can never be revived but by Thee, O Life of my soul. So true it is that to make me come to Thee, Thou, O most gracious Lord God, must first come to me.

O the amiable goodness of my loving Lord! Even this little I am doing is rather Thine own work than mine. Thou, O Lord, puttest repentance into my soul, desires into my heart, sighs into my breast, confession into my mouth, prayers into my lips, remorse into my memory, resolutions of amendment into my will. It is Thou, O gracious God, Who chiefly actest all this good in me, by me, and for me.

O my All, do Thou all in me that Thou desirest, and particularly overwhelm, I beseech Thee, my whole interior with perfect contrition, not coming from a slavish and servile fear, but from a faithful and filial love. Grant me a true and entire grief for having offended Thee, not because of Thy promises or threats, but because Thou art in Thyself good, amiable, adorable.

3. Or, if mercenary interest do still more move thee, O my sensual and sinful soul, how seriously dost thou take a small injury, how deeply dost thou resent a little disgrace, the loss of a dear friend, of health, of honour, or the like temporal and perishable commodities! O whence is it, then, that thou so little apprehendest thy loss of grace, and thy eminent and imminent danger of eternal damnation?

Is it a small matter to be God's enemy, to lose the good-will of all heaven, to destroy God's image, to cut up life, root and branch, to side with the accursed devils, thy Creator's sworn enemies, to hatch treason and enter into conspiracy with the damned, yea, and to kill, as far as in thee lies, Him Who by His own Death gave thee life? O brutal and unnatural ingratitude!

Surely the annihilating of heaven, earth, angels, men, and all nature, cannot be compared with this malicious, evil, and wilful destruction of Thy grace, O Lord, in my soul. O eternal God, what a monster, then, have I been in grace, what a prodigy in nature, who have so little cared to commit such enormous sins!

But, O my Lord, I will even now change my life. I here detest all sin, I make firm purpose of amendment, I have a full confidence in Thee my Creator, a good will to make satisfaction, and a total resignation to Thy divine pleasure.

4. I am the woful criminal, O just Judge of my soul, and I will be also the accuser and witness, the advocate and executioner, in this tribunal.

I summon you, therefore, O detestable pride, O abominable envy, O execrable avarice, O beastly brutality, and all you accursed crew of sin. How long will you reign on earth? how long will you dispeople God's inheritance? who brought you in amongst God's children?

It is the perverted will of man, O dread Sovereign, which hath done all these mischiefs. Rectify, O my Lord, I beseech Thee, this my crooked will, and murder these horrible monsters in me, and grant that I may henceforth rather expose my body to a thousand deaths than my soul to one deadly sin.

Thy saints will rejoice, O God, at my amendment, and Thy angels will make a feast, but Thy own resentment of joy will be infinite, because Thy love is infinite, which goes hand in hand with Thy essence, and comprehends all love in supreme eminency.

I will, therefore, expect from Thee, O heavenly Father, the exact remembrance; from Thee, my Redeemer, the perfect knowledge; from Thee, O Holy Spirit, a true repentance; and from Thee, O sacred Trinity, an entire absolution and plenary indulgence from all my iniquities. The grief I feel for my past offences, the hatred I have against each sin at this present, and the resolution I make to avoid all iniquity for the future, are not equivalent in me to their enormity and heinousness. I therefore humbly crave, O holy Lord God, that Thou wilt accept Thine own hatred against sin for that which I should and would have; and instead of the sorrow that is wanting to me, I offer that of Thy Son, my sweet Redeemer, with the sacrifice of His immaculate Life and innocent Death.

And since I cannot be impeccable by nature, O my Lord, nor dare presume to ask to be so by grace, give me leave to prostrate myself before Thy infinite bounty and clemency, and beg by the merits of Jesus Christ, Thy dear Son, and by the desires of Thy essential love, the blessed Holy Ghost, that though I may not be impeccable, yet I may never sin more; and if I must sometimes sin through my frailty, yet that I may never sin mortally.

This Thou desirest, O Lord, this Thou demandest, this Thou commandest. O give me what Thou commandest, and command what Thou pleasest.

5. O my good Lord Jesus, Who art Lord of my life, and Who—had I not, like an ungracious and ungrateful wretch, given my heart and sold my affections to fond, frail, filthy, and fading creatures and comforts, which are so far from bringing me either quiet of mind, peace of conscience, purity of soul, or perfection of spirit, that they leave me nothing but trouble, confusion, and remorse, with a world of disquiet and desperate thoughts, violent passions, and vicious inclinations—shouldst be the love of my soul, I find no other refuge or remedy but to return to Thee my Creator; to convert myself

to Thee, O my good Lord and Master; to cast myself in all humility at Thy sacred feet, and heartily to beg Thy mercy, pardon, and reconciliation.

O merciful Father, I truly acknowledge my prodigality, and humbly confess my treachery, and am sorry from my heart that ever I offended Thee, Who deservest so much love and service from me, beseeching Thee as a guilty prisoner to be pitiful to Thy poor creature, and mercifully to forgive me the manifold rebellions and grievous iniquities that I have committed against Thy Divine Majesty and Goodness. And for the love of Thee, I freely forgive all those who have in any way offended or contristated me, sincerely acknowledging that I deserve no comfort from any creature, but all contempt and confusion, and not only to be troubled by all on earth temporally, but even to be tormented by the devils in hell eternally.

6. O how ungrateful a child have I been to offend so often and so grievously so loving and liberal a Father, so meek and merciful a Redeemer, and so sweet and sovereign a Majesty, Who hath always showed Himself so benign and bountiful to me, tolerating me in my sins, and expecting me to His mercy, wooing me to His love, and calling me to His service by a thousand means, all of which I have either rejected or neglected, and Who hath still, nevertheless, given me time and opportunity to do penance!

O blindness, O folly, O frenzy! would to God I had never sinned! O that I might never sin more! O my

God, what have I done? Would I had suffered on the cross pains of body and pangs of soul, when I thus miserably sinned!

O, what can I say or do more? I abhor and detest whatsoever I have done, said, thought, or desired contrary to Thy holy will, O my Lord and my Love. I renounce all company and occasions which may induce me to offend Thee.

7. I cast myself at Thy sacred feet, to be Thy slave for ever, with a firm resolution to bear Thy cross till death, and to do penance and satisfaction for my past pride and pleasure, desiring nothing but to live at Thy feet, like the penitent Magdalen, in solitude, silence, submission.

O good Jesus, out of Thy infinite mercy, merits, and meekness, suffer not me, Thy poor creature, to be damned and separated from Thee eternally. O amiable eternity! O eternal amity of God! shall I leave and lose thee for filthy pleasures, frail creatures, fond friendships, fading honours?

No, dear Lord, no! Let it please Thee rather to take my soul out of my body than Thy love out of my soul; let me rather die miserably than sin mortally.

Let me pass on through the rest of my pilgrimage in Thy grace and fear, that I may end my days in Thy friendship and favour. This I beseech Thee to grant me, O most powerful and merciful Saviour, by the love of Thy sweet heart, by the merits of Thy bitter Death and Passion, by the intercession of Thy blessed Mother, and by the suffrages of all holy, happy, and devout souls.

Upon all of which relying, as upon so many sure anchors of my hope, I commit and resign myself to Thy disposition and providence for time and eternity, O my Lord, my Love, and my All, fully trusting that Thou wilt mercifully pardon my sins, carefully assist me in my wants and weaknesses, and in the end happily bring me to eternal bliss by such means as Thy divine wisdom knows most convenient for me.

THURSDAY.

To Subdue Sensuality to Reason.

The Fourth Exercise.

1. My spirit is willing, O most glorious and gracious Lord God, to serve Thee, love Thee, honour Thee, and follow Thee; but my flesh is weak, frail, and refractory. *I do not that good which I will,* O my God, and that which Thou demandest; *but the evil which I hate, that I do,** and what Thou forbiddest.

I feel, O my Lord, a law of sensuality contradicting the law of my mind, captivating my reason, clouding my judgment, and continually striving to cast me down headlong into sin and perdition.†

Unhappy man that I am, who shall deliver me from

---

* Romans vii. xv.

† '*But I see another law in my members, fighting against the law of my mind, and captivating me in the law of sin that is in my members.*' Rom. viii. 23.

the body of this death?[*] Ah, my brutish body! ah, my burdensome flesh! thou art my dangerous and deadly enemy. It is thy weight that depresseth my soul, thy earth that clogs and corrupts my spirit, thy contagion and perversity which infecteth and debaseth my better part and heavenly portion, thy sensuality which draws on, endangers, and almost destroys my reason.

2. Ah, sensuality! the source of all my misery, how justly do I now hate thee, and how willingly would I leave thee!

At my first acquaintance with thee, thou didst defile me with original sin; in my infancy thou madest a beast of me; and now in my riper years thou still pursuest me, proclaimest open war with me, blindest my understanding with darkness, ignorance, and errors; makest my will refractory to good, and ready to all evil; distractest my memory with vain and vile fancies; and perpetually tossest me to and fro between love and hatred, joy and grief, hope and fear; and the rest of thy numerous and enormous, irascible and concupiscible powers and passions. Ay me! how sad is my state! how deplorable my condition! O, how long must I dwell with these devils? how long must I endure the violence of these passions?

O my Lord, my strength and my salvation, break these fetters for me. Command a calm, O Thou only Ruler of sea and winds, and appease the surges of these my unmortified appetites. O, restore me to myself

[*] Rom. vii. 24.

again, reduce reason to her lost dominion in my soul, and me bring back, Thy poor creature, to Thee, my powerful Creator. O, let not this passenger perish amidst these boisterous billows, nor suffer utter shipwreck in these fearful tempests.

I suffer violence; O my Lord, answer for me. The companion which Thou hast given me hath deceived me;* sense hath corrupted and conquered my judgment. O how I am dragged up and down by my all-mastering appetites, commanded by my servants, and fettered by my slaves! O tyranny! O indignity!

Ah, my soul! O noble spirit, fair as the angels, formed to thy Creator's lovely resemblance, stamped with His divine character, and heir-apparent to His glorious kingdom, and yet to be thus subject to the base and brutal desires of flesh and blood! O intolerable bondage! O unworthy servitude!

3. O Father of mercies and only Physician of my soul, Thou art all might and all mercy, and I am all weakness and all misery. There is no part left sincere in my whole body and soul from the contagious poison of passion, from the infectious leprosy of sin and sensuality.

All is out of order, O my Lord: I acknowledge it to my own shame and confusion: each sense is gone astray, each member of my body is corrupted, each power of my soul is perverted.

* '*And Adam said: The woman whom Thou gavest me to be my companion gave me of the tree, and I did eat.*' Genesis iii. 12.

My understanding is obscured with self-love; my memory distracted with sensual objects; my will possessed with peevish inclinations; my affections are vain, my passions violent, my disposition vicious; my body is burdensome, my imagination troublesome, my life irksome.

These are my wounds, O my heavenly Surgeon. O, put to them Thy helping hand, I beseech Thee; see, sear, and search them before the gangrene enter, and the grief grow incurable. My soul is sick even to death; if Thou wilt, O my Lord, Thou canst both cleanse and cure me.

To this end Thou descendest from Jerusalem to Jericho, O pious Samaritan—from heaven to earth, O compassionate Saviour, where Thou findest me in this pitiful plight, sore, beaten, wounded, half dead, and utterly despoiled of all natural and spiritual riches by thieves and robbers, which are the senses of my body and the faculties of my soul. O, pass not by me, sweet Jesus, but mercifully bind up my bleeding wounds with the swathing-bands of Thy Death and Passion; pour upon them the wine of Thy precious Blood, and supple them with the oil of Thy heavenly Grace.

4. I intend, O my Lord—strengthen me in this hour—I intend, O sweet Saviour, a total reformation of life and manners, an entire mortification of my corporeal senses and spiritual faculties, an absolute change in my whole man.

O, grant me, I beseech Thee, my loving Lord, the

powerful assistance of Thy special grace for the performance of this great and good purpose. Teach me now, O my blessed Master, to live inwardly, piously, spiritually, as I loved formerly to live outwardly, vainly, sensually.

O, let me henceforth yield to Thy divine motion, obey Thy call, imitate Thy example, and follow Thy will.

O, let me never more act or omit anything—be it ever so little—for my own liking, but purely and perfectly for Thy love.

5. Grant, O good Jesus, that, at each word of my mouth, at each glance of my eye, at each morsel I eat, at each member I move, and at each inward and outward action I undertake, I may first ask Thy leave and permission, and so do it, or leave it, accordingly as Thy holy inspiration answers and allows me.

O that I could perform each natural and necessary work with an actual reflection upon Thy praise and pleasure, and with a pure intention to be united to Thee, my Lord and my Love!

Thy outward senses, O my sweet Saviour, were exactly subject to Thy reason, and perfectly obedient to Thy sacred soul. O, let mine be swallowed up, I beseech Thee, gracious Jesus, and sanctified by the merits of Thine. Let me live, love, move, and make use of my senses purely and only in Thee, for Thee, and by Thee.

Thy sacred hands, O holy Jesus, were harshly nailed

to the tree of the cross: preserve mine, I beseech Thee, from all sinful touching.

Thy blessed feet were likewise pierced and fastened to the same rood: O, fix my steps that I run not to evil actions; direct them in Thy paths, and make me speedy in all works concerning Thy honour and the assistance of my neighbour.

Thy holy mouth was free from guile, full of wisdom: put Thy words, sweet Jesus, into mine; let it always speak of Thy love, and only sing Thy praises.

Thy divine ears were filled with blasphemies and derisions: let not mine be open to hear vanities and detractions.

Thy sweet eyes poured out floods of tears for me: O, give unto mine tears of compassion for Thy sufferings, and of compunction for my own sins.

Thy taste was tormented with the noisome potion of gall and vinegar: O, take from me, I beseech Thee, all desire of delicacies; let me not eat or drink but for mere sustenance and necessity.

Thy whole humanity, O gracious Jesus, was martyred and murdered: O, grant that I may be truly and totally mortified; let me not see, feel, hear, taste, smell, eat, drink, do anything, or make use of anything as following my own gust, sensuality, and self-seeking, but in pure conformity to Thy will and pleasure.

6. O merciful Redeemer, how great and grievous were the inward sufferings of Thy soul! O, for these Thy sorrows and Thy tender mercies' sake, cleanse,

cure, enlighten, inform, reform, and transform all my inward man.

O, permit not my understanding, where the knowledge of Thy greatness and goodness should be only seated, to be overspread with ignorance and error.

Let not my memory, which should be totally taken up with Thee, be stuffed with vain fancies or impertinent curiosities.

Let not my will, which Thou gavest me to desire and love Thee above all Thy creatures, O my only Lord and Love, be enslaved to any inferior affection.

Repair, O gracious Redeemer, this lively image of the lovely Trinity, which is almost defaced by my brutish sensuality. Grant, O dear Saviour, that my understanding, will, and memory may be incessantly busied in knowing, loving, and remembering Thee, and that they may forget and forego all other objects, save only in Thee and for Thee.

7. O that my heart were perfectly disengaged from the love of all creatures! Drain it, sweet Jesus, and deliver it from all foreign and domestic affection, and fill it up again with Thine own, that it may never love, desire, nor will anything but Thee alone, O my Lord, my Love, and my All.

O that my will were conformable to Thine without reservation or retraction! Take it unto Thee, dear Lord, freely and fully, for time and eternity. I will have no will but Thine; dispose of me as Thou pleasest here and hereafter.

O that my memory were disencumbered of all imaginations, and purged from all impressions but of Thee only! Empty it, O Thou only amiable object of my soul, and then replenish it with such holy and heavenly notions as may best please Thy Divine Majesty.

O that my understanding were imbued with some measure of the knowledge of Thy Divinity! O my Lord, infinite in goodness, dreadful in majesty, and unspeakable in all perfection; O my great, gracious, and glorious God, quicken it, sharpen it, elevate it, and illuminate it, that, knowing Thee, I may not choose but love Thee, and that, knowing and loving Thee, I may be eternally happy. Behold, Lord, I make an absolute divorce from all self-love, sensuality, and affection to creatures, and give Thee myself by an irrevocable donation.

Behold, Lord, the keys, the lodging, the treasure, and the master prostrate at Thy sacred feet. Enter freely, possess all fully, dispose universally, and command absolutely. Put me where Thou wilt, give me what Thou wilt, treat me as Thou wilt. Thine I am, O my Lord, my Love, and my All, for time and for eternity!

FRIDAY.

To Obtain Mortification and Perfect Abnegation.

The Fifth Exercise.

1. O eternal and ever-blessed Lord God, Thou hast framed me of soul and body, and fitted me with faculties proportionable to attain the end of my creation, which is to love Thee entirely, and to live with Thee eternally. But, alas, how far am I from observing Thy blessed and beautiful order!

Thou, O Lord, gavest me a *soul* to bear all the sway in my body, *reason* to have the chief regency in my soul, the *law* to be the guide of my reason, and Thy *Self* to be the sole mover and governor of my whole man.

But, O how have I wilfully crossed Thy sacred design, contradicted Thy intention, and swerved from this perfection! My body is all brutish, my soul all animal, and my reason all sensual. I am all blindness, self-love, and immortification.

Yet I know well, and Thou, O eternal Verity, hast expressly told me, that unless I renounce all, deny myself, take up my cross and follow Thee, I can never become Thy true disciple.*

Ah, harsh words to my carnal ears!—'If thou wilt be My disciple, deny thyself; if thou wilt be perfect, sell all, give away all, reform all, renounce all, relinquish all; if thou wilt possess life eternal, contemn

* Luke xiv. 27; Matthew xvi. 24.

this life temporal; if thou wilt be exalted in heaven, humble thyself in the world; if thou wilt wear a crown with Me, bear thy cross with Me.'

But, O my soul, how wilt thou brook that more dismal sentence:—*Depart from Me, you cursed, into everlasting fire!**

Wherefore, O my Lord, my Love, and my All, since Thou hast taught me these things by Thy sacred word, and showed them by Thy holy example—and Thou art *the Way, the Truth, and the Life*—grant, O infallible 'Truth,' that I may courageously walk in this Thy perfect 'Way,' that so I may happily come to Thee, the only true and eternal 'Life' and love of my soul.

2. What dreadest thou, O my fearful and faithless heart? Behold, Christ, thy King and Captain, has marched on before thee. Take up thy cross and travel after Him. He leads thee to a kingdom. Heaven is worth thy pains. O take courage to mortify thyself, deny thyself, and die to thyself, that thou mayest live to Jesus, and with Jesus eternally.

Learn, O my soul, this short and secure lesson: *Leave all things, and thou shalt find one thing which is all in all.* Take courage and fight valiantly against thy own bad nature; pray, suffer, stoop, bear repugnances, swallow down contradictions, digest injuries:—*the kingdom of heaven suffereth violence.*† The end thou aimest at is perfection, the reward of thy conquest is eternal love, eternal life, eternal happiness.

* Matt. xxv. 41. † Ib. xi. 12.

Behold, O my Lord, my strength and my salvation, I am fully resolved to lay the axe to the root of this wicked tree. Help me, I beseech Thee, with Thy grace from above, that I may hew myself out of myself, that I may kill, crucify, and mortify my inveigling sensuality, cut off my evil inclinations, rectify my disordered passions, and root out each thought or desire which tends not directly to Thy honour, will, and love, O my Lord and my God.

3. I know, Lord, that it is foolishness to study perfection without the practice of mortification. I confess I can never love Thee truly, but inasmuch as I hate myself really; such is the antipathy between self-love and Thy holy affection. Ah, how can a spirit, distracted with contrary inclinations, be freely and fully open to Thy divine contemplation! Put therefore, I beseech Thee, a sluice to my unmortified passions, put a bound to my crooked heart, and powerfully keep back those innumerable concupiscences and corrupt imaginations violently succeeding each other, that my united affections may regard Thee only, the only object of all happiness.

Gather, O Lord, the dispersed forces of my soul from all multiplicity of worldly affections to the union of Thy only love.

Keep, I beseech Thee, my understanding, will, memory, imagination, and all my inward and outward senses from roaming abroad; that, carefully attending and entertaining Thy divine presence in my soul, I may attain true introversion, simplicity, and union of my spirit with Thine.

Reform, O my Lord, all the natural corruptions of my outward man, and redress all the spiritual infirmities of my inward man; destroy and disperse all internal and external enemies and opposers of Thy holy love; possess me perfectly, and dispose of me entirely according to Thy divine will and pleasure.

4. To this end O bless my weak endeavours, almighty and all-merciful Lord God. I will subtract all superfluities from my body, and accustom it to all sorts of sufferings, that so I may fit it up for Thee, O holy Spirit, Who dwellest not with them that are sensual and subject to sin.

Alas, I have not yet 'resisted' to the effusion of my 'blood;' and should I spill each drop of blood in my body in this holy quarrel, how little ought I to regret it in respect of the great good I expect!

I will therefore crucify thee, O my flesh, with all thy concupiscences. I will mortify my outward senses, the windows by which death steals into my soul, the hinderers of my heart's tranquillity, the destroyers of true devotion, the dispersers of inward recollection, and the utter ruiners of all the good desires which I conceive and kindle in my prayers. Ah, how soon is this divine fire cooled and quenched, not only by sin, but also by the distracting images of outward objects!

I will keep a special and strict watch over my tongue, on which depends my spiritual life or death, and cherish Thee, O blessed silence, which art the key of piety, the keeper of innocency, and the preserver of purity.

I will trample down my inferior nature, with all its evil affections and motions of love, hatred, joy, sadness, desire, fear, hope, anger, &c. I will order, dispose, and direct it according to the laws of reason and Thy divine inspirations, O my Lord and my God. Grant me courage, I beseech Thee, to quell and curb this my most dangerous and greatest enemy, which is the source of all my miseries, the citadel from whence sin assails me, and Satan fetcheth forth his forces to fight against me. Grant, good Lord, that I may never yield to this wicked *Eve,* persuading *Adam* — my superior will—to eat the forbidden fruit, and consent to unlawful pleasures.

O that I could tame these cruel beasts, my natural passions! How soon, then, should I be master of all moral virtues!

O that I could so till this vineyard, so delve this garden, so purge it of all ill weeds of affections, and prune all superfluous shoots of passions, that only the seed of Thy grace, O heavenly Husbandman, might there take root and fructify!

5. I will also mortify my superior and rational part, with all the curious and fruitless speculations of my understanding, all conceits of self-wisdom, natural prudence, proper judgment, and good liking of my own proceedings: all vain and foolish reflections of my me-

mory, and all petty desires and affections of my will which relate not to Thee, the only object and lord of my love.

I am resolved, O my Lord, to nip off each budding passion as soon as it peeps up in my soul to trouble it in its true repose, and to hinder its liberty and tendency to Thy love.

I will, by Thy gracious assistance, proceed faithfully and sincerely in the hatred, denial, and mortification of self, and in the prosecution of Thy divine love. And in order to this one end and aim, I make in Thy presence, and from the very bottom of my heart and soul, these following particular acts:—

I renounce, O my Lord, for the pure love of Thee, *all affection to worldly things.* Give them unto me, O gracious God, or take them from me, as best liketh Thy divine Majesty. I resign up all my interest in anything, though never so near and dear unto me. Behold, O my Lord and Lover, I unclothe my soul from all affections whatsoever to creatures, and desire nothing but Thyself alone. O happy nakedness! O rich poverty of spirit! O pure obedience to the divine Will in all things! Be you my heart's delight, my whole pleasure and patrimony.

6. I renounce all *self-seeking.* Ah, my corrupt nature! I abhor Thee. Adieu all private interest, profit, praise, and preferment. I will henceforth perform all my actions and exercises, O my Lord God, for Thy only pure and perfect love. I will seek to please and praise

Thee with an inward, ardent, and amorous affection for Thyself only, and not for Thy gifts or graces.

I renounce all *sensuality*, whether it be in meat, drink, sleep, apparel, curiosity of my five senses, or anything else whatsoever. O my Lord, I will make no other use of any of Thy creatures than I am absolutely compelled to by necessity of nature. I look for no solace but from Thee alone, my only comfort and content.

I renounce all *disordered love* to any worldly person: no favour or friendship, O my only amiable Lord God, no greatness or goodness of any one, shall make me swerve from my exact duty towards Thee. No carnal affection to kindred, no tenderness of amity, no private or public respect, no connivance or participation shall make me partial in the reproof of vice, or praise of virtue. O, take up my whole heart with Thy holy love, that Thy perfect image and perpetual memory may blot out all kinds of foreign objects.

I renounce all *vain, vicious, idle, and unprofitable thoughts, fancies, and imaginations*. O, let my mind not only yield no consent, but give no entrance to them. O, let me never more contristate Thy holy Spirit with these vanities, nor hinder my soul's advancement and union with Thee by distractions. I will henceforth compel my heart to some good employment. I will no longer permit it to wander and waste itself in any idle and superfluous curiosities. No, my Lord and Saviour, Thy bitter and blessed Passion, Thy blessings and benefits, shall be the continual occupation of my interior. O, what have I to do with transitory things who am made for eternity?

I renounce all *care and solicitude* which necessity, obedience, and charity do not oblige me to. No natural passions of joy, sorrow, hope, fear, love, hatred, anger, or shame* shall make any impression in this heart of mine, which is preëngaged in Thy affection, sealed up and settled in Thy contemplation. No pretext of lawfulness, no show of fittingness, nor conceit of compassion, nor excuse of necessity, shall procure the admittance of such passions into my soul as may any way distract, darken, or dull the point of my affection and devotion towards Thee, my only Lord and Love.

I renounce all *bitterness of heart* against any one. Is he good; be Thou eternally praised in him and by him, O bountiful Bestower of all blessings. Is he wicked; correct him, O merciful Creator; comfort, encourage, and raise him to amendment. Hath he offended, affronted, injured, or slighted me; I deserve, O great God, to be trodden on by all creatures, and therefore I freely forgive him for the past, and give him free leave to add stripes to his injuries for the future. Am I denied the grant of my most lawful and just demands; Thou best knowest, O eternal Wisdom, what is best for my state and condition. O, deny not Thy love to my soul, and let me be refused in all my other requests whatsoever.

I renounce all *vain-glory, all self-liking and pride* which may arise from worldly praises, all delight spring-

* Original text, 'Shamfastness.'

ing from any gift of nature or grace which is in me. *Not to us, O Lord, not to us; but to Thy name give glory.** Alas, what am I, what have I, what can I? All is Thine, O my bountiful Lord God. Nothing is mine but sin, and therefore I deserve only shame and confusion.

7. I renounce all *desire of delight in my devotions*, all sensible gusts of grace, and all sweetnesses and solaces in the inferior faculties of my soul. Ah, my heart, what are all these to thee? Follow thou thy Saviour. Thou seekest thy crucified Jesus. These are not Himself, but His gifts. O my Lord, it is Thyself I seek and sigh after. If Thou sendest me comforts for the encouragement of my weakness, be Thou ever praised, for Thou actest like a most benign and bountiful God. If Thou withdrawest them, still blessed be Thy providence, which hath secret and several ways of conducting souls to Thyself. And if Thou wilt make trial of my fidelity by permitting me to be dull, dry, and desolate in my devotions, be Thou equally and eternally praised.

I renounce all *scrupulosity of conscience*, which in any way betrays the least diffidence or distrust in Thy mercy. I am a sinner, O Jesus, but Thou art a *Saviour*. I have great reason to dread Thy justice, but greater to hope in Thy goodness. Heaven and earth shall sooner fail than my confidence in Thee, my merciful Maker. If Thou kill me, I will trust in Thee;† and if

* Ps. cxiii. 1.
† '*Although He should kill me, I will trust in Him.*' Job xiii. 15.

I had formerly hated Thee, and betrayed Thee as Judas did, I would now with penitent Magdalene run to Thy blessed feet, weep and bemoan my misery, and hope to obtain Thy mercy.

And finally, O my Lord, I absolutely, entirely, and irrevocably renounce *my whole will in all things*, and totally resign whatsoever concerns me to Thy holy will and pleasure. I offer up unto Thee the full sacrifice, both principal and accessory, of all that I, by Thy gift and grace, am, have, and can; my self, goods, graces, body, soul, senses, heart, will, all. I leave no right or title to anything whatsoever that savours of *self*. I am no longer my own, but Thy slave, O Lord; not my will, but Thine be done, for time and eternity! O, let me will what Thou wilt, or not will at all. Let all my desires be involuntary if they swerve never so little from Thy divine pleasure. *Die* self-will! *Live* Jesus! my Lord, my Love, my All!

SATURDAY.

Of Conformity to Christ Crucified.

The Sixth Exercise.

1. Crucified Jesus! Thou only art Lord of my life, life of my love, and love of my soul. O that I could reform my life, deiform my love, and conform my soul to Thee, the absolute pattern of all perfection.

O that I could imprint Thy lively and lovely image

in my heart, fasten all my affections and imperfections to Thy sacred cross, drown all my desires and defects in Thy dear wounds, put off myself totally, and put Thee on intimately, O sacred humanity, O my suffering Saviour.

O that I could perfectly imitate Thee, the pure Exemplar of all virtues; that I could give up my whole self to Thee by an act of irrevocable donation, as Thou demandest and commandest.

But, alas, I am yet, O my Jesus, all self-love, sin, and sensuality. I acknowledge, O my Lord, what I have and what I want; I know what I desire and what I deserve. I confess I am wounded, I am wicked, I am wretched, and I tremblingly come to Thee, my heavenly Physician, to be cured, converted, comforted.

O sweet Saviour, for Thy mercies' sake, and for Thy Passion's sake, forget and forgive what I have been, pity what I am, satisfy for what I deserve, and supply what I desire.

2. Behold, most merciful Jesus, I first cast myself at Thy sacred feet, pierced and fastened to the cruel cross for my transgressions; *pierce Thou my flesh, O Lord, with Thy fear,** and fasten my soul to Thy love. O, let not pride and presumption nestle any longer in that heart which Thou, O meek Saviour, lovest so tenderly, and redeemest at so dear a rate. O my vainglory and arrogance, what have I to do with you; how

* Ps. cxviii. 120.

much do I now detest you? Wash off these stains, O Jesus, from my poor soul, in these sweet streams flowing from Thy wounded feet. O, drown these my imperfections in these sacred seas of piety.

Give me, O gracious Lord, such true humility of spirit, that I may perfectly perceive the abyss of my own nothingness and naughtiness, and rightly conceive the immensity of Thy greatness and goodness, whereby I may depress myself unfeignedly, and exalt Thee only in my soul. Let me be content to be contemned by all creatures, desire to be despised, be willing to be trodden on as dirt and dust, and the very outcast of the whole world. O, let me really hate all honour, and humbly pronounce with mouth and mind :—*I am nothing, have nothing, deserve nothing, desire nothing, but only to please Thee perfectly, my Jesus, praise Thee perpetually, love Thee purely, and live with Thee eternally.*

3. Grant me also, good Jesus, by the merits of these Thy wounds, the virtue of perfect obedience. O, let me never tire in trampling down self-will, in forsaking my own sense, in subduing self-judgment, in submitting my spirit inwardly to Thy inspirations, and outwardly, not only to my superior's injunctions, but even to the commands of all Thy creatures. O, let me have no propriety, affection, or affectation in my own proceedings, but wholly mind Thy holy pleasure in all things.

Let me lay down all my desires at Thy sacred feet, O my Jesus, saying :—*Lord, what wilt Thou have me to* *do?** so transforming my will into Thine by an absolute forsaking, denying, and annihilating my whole self.

Let me receive, O my Saviour, as from Thy secret providence and permission, not only patiently, but thankfully, all pain, all poverty, all shame, all sickness, and all sufferings whatsoever; acknowledging that I truly deserve worse, and desiring willingly to endure more, that so I may have a more perfect resemblance to Thee, my crucified Lord.

Let me learn, O my Lord, by Thy blessed example, the holy lesson of discreet silence, not only from ill and idle talk, but even from all needless and unprofitable discourses. Let me rather edify by the purity of my life and conversation than by multiplicity of words and conceptions.

O, give me, sweet Jesus, a free and frequent access to Thy sacred feet during the whole course of my life, and a sure comfort in them at the hour of my death.

4. From Thy blessed feet, O my dear Lord, I raise my humble devotion to Thy all-holy hand, and beg leave to cast into the sweet fountain issuing from Thy powerful right palm my manifold sins of malice and injustice, with all my faults of hypocrisy and ingratitude, falsehood and infidelity, rancour and revenge.

Renew, O Lord God, a right spirit within my bowels. Let exact justice be the square of all my actions, truth the touchstone of my words, and sincerity the subject of my thoughts.

* Acts ix. 6.

Let me be punctual in performing my duty to Thee, zealous in punishing myself, and charitable in compassionating my neighbour. Let me ever yield first unto Thy sacred Majesty all honour and glory, reverence and respect, praise and love, gratitude and obedience, with my whole heart, soul, and strength; next, to my superiors, equals, and inferiors, and lastly to my own body, soul, and senses, that which is my duty, and each one of their respective duties. O, let me fully perform what I am bound to, carefully eschew what is forbidden me, and uprightly walk according to my calling.

O, let me never presume to slight, scorn, suspect, judge, or condemn any person, but sincerely serve, succour, and seek the temporal and spiritual good of all men whatsoever, even of my professed and most peevish enemies.

Lord Jesus, give me grace to imitate Thy virtues, to be grateful for Thy gifts, and to make use of Thy goodness in order to my soul's advancement in the way of Thy dear love and desired union with Thy Divine Majesty.

5. And in the sacred wound of Thy left hand, I humbly intrust all my offences of negligence and tepidity, sluggishness, cowardice, and pusillanimity, all my covetous desires, all impurity, and all intemperance. Cleanse me, O my powerful Lord! Purify me, O my merciful Saviour! Give strength, comfort, and courage to my feeble and frail nature, that I may pass undauntedly through all difficulties and dangers, to come

to Thee, my Jesus, to lay hold on Thee, and to repose in Thee, the only centre of my desires.

Grant me, O my Lord, chastity of body and cleanness of heart, temperance in my appetites and sobriety in my senses, gravity in my deportment and moderation in all my proceedings, that nothing may displease Thee in my soul, nor dissolve the sacred knot wherewith Thou hast fastened me unto Thee.

Give me also, O Jesus my Lord, perfect poverty of spirit. O, permit not my soul, intended to enjoy Thee, the only solid and satiating riches, to be entangled with the least affection to the poor and perishable trifles of this world. Behold I cast myself, disengaged of all creatures, into Thy sacred embraces. O crucified Saviour, I desire to embrace nothing in my folded arms but a breast burning with desires to please Thee, my Creator, and a heart melting away in Thy love. I make choice of Thy bare cross, O Christ, for my best inheritance. I stretch out my opened arms to meet Thy holy and heavenly embraces. O, let me never more be unclasped from Thy blessed bosom! Be Thou, O my own best beloved Jesus, my rest during the short time of my life, and my refuge at the dreadful hour of my death.

6. And now, O merciful Saviour, I humbly turn my eyes and contemplation to Thy sacred Head crowned with thorns, and Thy divine Face, all besmeared with gore and spittle for my sake. Here I implore strength, O Jesus, for the weaknesses of my head, and pardon for

the wickednesses of my five senses. O my Lord, I desire to bury in these Thy innumerable wounds the enormous number of my iniquities; and I beseech Thee for these Thy sufferings' sake to adorn my weak capacity with so much solid wisdom as may fitly suit with my condition. O, let me never think, speak, or act anything which is not seasoned with the salt of discretion. Let me seriously weigh each circumstance, and patiently wait Thy leave and leisure before I leap into any work.

Enlighten me to see clearly Thy will and pleasure, and empower me exactly to fulfil and follow it. Open the eyes of my understanding to behold my own baseness and wickedness, and give me Thy gracious assistance to reform it. Help me to form a right judgment of the real vileness and vanity of all transitory things, and endow my heart with courage to contemn them.

Inebriate my affection, O amiable Jesus, with the sweetness of Thy love, and let all worldly solaces savour of bitterness to my soul. Let me be deaf, blind, and dumb to all things which are not Thyself, O my crucified Saviour.

Let me prudently discern and piously perform each portion of my duty in its due circumstance of time, place, order, measure, and manner. Let that holy innocence and simplicity which is the virtue of the saints shine in all my actions. Let me not be curious to know much, but careful to practise much, and cordial to love Thee much, O my only Lord and Love.

Cleanse my will from all self-seeking, keep my

memory from all superfluities, close up my senses from all vanities, that my happy soul, separated from all sensible images, may quietly tend to Thee only, sweetly repose in Thee, and continually enjoy Thy blessed presence.

O, let Thy pure and perfect love, dear Lord Jesus, be the faithful scout-watch over all my proceedings, that no foreign affection, no sinister intention, no self-liking or self-seeking, may steal into my heart, and defraud or disturb its happy enjoyment of Thee, and its holy union with Thy divine Spirit.

Grant, O my Lord, that I may prudently turn all good events and all bad accidents to my spiritual profit, by reflecting wherefore they befall me, of what they warn me, and how far they concern me. Let me learn thereby gratitude to Thy goodness, fervour in prayer, contempt of myself, humility of spirit, care of my actions, resignation to Thy will, amendment of my life, or what else Thy holy Spirit shall please to intimate by these fatherly visitations.

O sacred Head of my crucified Saviour, be Thou my certain succour during my life's conflict, and my sure place of retreat in my last agony with death.

7. And lastly, I reverently approach to Thy dear Heart, O amiable Lord Jesus, opened with a cruel lance, in the sight of Thy blessed Mother and Thy beloved disciple, for the love of my soul. O my Jesus, I here implore Thy pardon for all my perverse affections and irregular appetites. Give me Thy leave, O my living

Lord, to creep into this sweet *Hole of the rock*,* this sacred *Cleft of the wall*, this unlocked Safe of heavenly treasures, this saving Ark of the New Testament, and shut Thou, O Jesu, the door from without, that free from the deluges of all wickedness and dangers of the world, flesh, and devil, I may sit solitarily, silently, and sweetly hearkening to Thy divine whispers in my elevated soul.

Purge all my iniquities, O my dear Saviour, in the precious blood streaming from Thy open side, and replenish my heart with Thy perfect love. O, drown me, wound me, burn me, and consume me in Thy divine flames of affection, that I may love Thee strongly, purely, perfectly, perseverantly.

O, grant me to leave all things with alacrity for Thee, my beloved Jesus, though never so great; to loathe all things joyfully for Thy love, though never so good; to do all things contentedly for Thy honour, though never so hard; to suffer all things patiently for Thy sake, though never so painful; and to persevere constantly in my pious practices for the sole satisfaction of Thy holy will and accomplishment of Thy blessed pleasure.

O, let me be incessantly calling and knocking at this sacred gate of mercy. Let me be still sighing and seeking after Thee, my Jesus, my Saviour, my Lord,

* The Bridegroom of the Canticles thus addresses His Beloved: '*My dove in the clefts of the rock, in the hollow places of the wall, show Me thy face, let thy voice sound in My ears: for thy voice is sweet, and thy face comely.*' Cant. ii. 14.

and my Love. Let me be always thinking, ever talking, and perpetually tending to unite my heart to Thine, to conform it unto Thine, to transform it into Thine, and Thou all mine for time and eternity.

Grant also, dear Jesus, that I may truly love all things in Thee and for Thee. O, inflame my charity, quicken my faith, rectify my intentions, strengthen my confidence in Thee, destroy all complacency in myself, establish me in all these good purposes, and let me be reminded of my now promised duty, and encouraged to proceed forwards in the path of perfection, as often as I shall eye the sacred image of Thy crucified humanity. Elevate my aspiring soul unto Thyself, O Jesus my Lord, above all chances, changes, and creatures. O, let it be so totally attentive to Thy presence, so entirely taken up in Thy contemplation, and so wholly absorbed in Thy love, that no outward objects may touch or trouble it, no inferior cares or cogitations may entangle it, nothing may impede its free intercourse with Thy heavenly friendship, nothing may stop it from the sweet influence of Thy divine graces, or any way interrupt its happy quiet and holy tranquillity.

O dear and opened Heart of my dying Lord Jesus, be Thou my sweet comfort during this life's pilgrimage, and my sure sanctuary in my last moments.

SUNDAY.

Of Perfect Union with God.

The Seventh Exercise.

1. O infinite, immense, and unmeasurable abyss of all bounty. O ever-flowing fountain of mercy. O undrainable sea of love. O my Lord, my Sovereign, my Saviour, and my Sanctifier. Behold I return unto Thee, the sweet Source of my beginning; I run unto Thee, the gracious Preserver of my being; and I desire to rest in Thee, the only Hope of my soul's happiness.

Be Thou, henceforth, O my Creator, the sole object of my thoughts and the only object of my love. Be Thou, O God of my heart, heart of my life, life of my soul, and soul of my love, my portion and my inheritance for ever. I choose Thee only, I offer up myself wholly, I consecrate myself heartily, and dedicate myself eternally to Thy love, honour, and service.

Ah, good God, where dwelleth Thou? Which is the pleasant place of Thy abode, O King of Glory and Comforter of my soul? I seek nothing but Thy lovely presence; I desire nothing but the presence of Thy love. My soul sighs to see Thee, my heart covets to have Thee, my love longs to enjoy Thee, and I can expect no perfect content until I am totally united unto Thee.

If I now beg a glimpse of Thy divine face, O my glorious Lord, then a drop of Thy heavenly grace, and afterwards a dram of Thy dear affection; yet in all this it is Thyself, O sweet God, which I demand; Thy whole self is the only satiating object of my boundless desires and unlimited affections.

2. I desire to love Thee, O only amiable Lord God, by all means and beyond all measure, until I am totally transformed into Thee by love. O, do Thou freely and fully possess my spirit, guide it, govern it, enlighten it, inflame it, elevate it, inform it, and transport it how, and when Thou pleasest. O, let all unspiritual love be quite banished, all multiplicity vanish away, and all impurity and self-seeking be swallowed up. Let Thy love be my light, my liberty, my life.

Lord, I desire but two things in this world:—To love, taste, and enjoy Thee, my best beloved; and:—To be humbled, despised, rejected, and esteemed a reprobate for Thy love.

O sweet life! O loving Jesus! What a heaven, what a happiness is it to love Thee! O, how lovely, how loving, and yet how little loved is my God!

O Source of all goodness, and Centre of all good souls! What is the greatest love of mother, friend, life, or anything else? Art not Thou, my God, all this to me, and all in all? Ah, my soul, what didst thou ever best love? And didst thou love thy Lord God as much? I blush, O my dear Lord, I sigh, and am ashamed to answer. I will henceforth do anything, suffer anything, and leave all things for Thy love. I will not live but languish, not breathe but burn, by reason of ecstasy and excess of love.

3. O fire! O flames! burn, consume, annihilate! Alas, beauty of angels! how late and how little do I love Thee! O, come into my soul; behold a poor lodging; yet such as it is, it is all Thine. I conceal nothing, I reserve nothing; heart, soul, spirit, all is Thine own; compose all, dispose of all, depose all unruly passions, impose what penance Thou pleasest. I accept it, O my Lord; only repose peaceably on my soul, and let no foul or false affection interpose itself or disturb this blessed union.

O that I could please and praise Thee purely, perfectly, perpetually. O that I could love Thee faithfully, freely, and fully in all and above all things, O my All and my only Love.

I acknowledge myself bound, O Lord, in Thy chains of charity. I am burned in Thy fire, I am wounded and won to Thy love. But what shall I say, what can I give? All I have is not worthy of Thee, and yet is Thine already. Ask, my sweet Lord, and have; choose, and take; make me such as Thou desirest, and then take me to Thy desire.

Give Thyself, O great God, to my soul, and then take my soul with Thyself in it: my life, liberty, love, and all is Thine own. My last will is already made in which I bequeath all to Thee—Thine own Death and Passion, all Thy mercies and merits, all the praises and perfections of Thy dear Mother and the blessed saints and angels, and all the goods, glories, and splendours of all Thy creatures.

All that I am, have, and can, both spirituals and temporals—kindred, friends, riches, health, honours, estates, offices, devotion—all is at Thy disposition. I am resolute, O my Lord; I am resigned and indifferent to have them increased or diminished, to use them to Thy glory, or to lose them altogether.

4. I give Thee back, O merciful Maker, my whole being, either to be what Thou wilt, or to be nothing at all; to love Thee, or not to live at all.

I offer to Thee, O pious Redeemer, my sins to pardon, my works to perfect, my will to purify. I offer Thee my wounds to cure, my soul to cleanse, and my spirit to comfort.

I offer to Thee, O holy Spirit, my intentions to rectify, my inclinations to sanctify, my affections to deify.

Finally, I offer all for One, I give all to One, and all I desire is to be all one with Thee, my All and only Lord and Love.

Thou hast given me, O my bountiful Creator, the whole world upon one small and easy condition, saying: *Child, give Me thy heart.* O Lord, let this condition never want the coöperation of Thy grace, and let me never want Thy grace to fulfil it perfectly.

O my Lord, all that I have is but two small mites! I cast them into Thy hands, and had I more I would give more. Dispose of them both, dear Lord, of my body and soul, as best pleaseth Thee, that Thy will may be perfectly performed, and Thy name purely sanctified in both.

O sweet God of my heart! Let me embrace Thee in the two arms of profound humility and perfect charity.

O, let my heart faint and melt away in the fire of Thy divine love, let me lose myself to find Thee, be out of myself to live in Thee, and be empty of myself to be full of Thee.

O Sun of Justice, dissolve with a beam of Thy brightness the frost of my heart, and resolve it into tears of affection.

5. O beautiful and best beloved of my soul! I am weary of this wretched world; and I breathe, thirst, and sigh after Thee, the sweet Fountain of life-giving and soul-saving waters. O Thou true rest and refreshment of my faint and feeble heart, out of whom there is neither comfort nor content, let me shroud myself under the shadow of Thy wings until iniquity and infirmity have an end.

Come, Lord Jesus, speak Thy sweet words of love to my languishing soul, for Thy servant hears Thee. Give me courage, alacrity, fervour, and fidelity in Thy service the few remaining moments of my wretched and wearisome pilgrimage.

O rest long expected and much sighed after, where shall I seek Thee, and when shall I find Thee? Where dwellest Thou, O dear Spouse, at the mid-day, in the desire of love? Where is Thy secret cabinet of contemplation, which Thou hidest from the wisdom of worldlings, and revealest to little ones and humble of heart? O, show me the way of divine union, wherein Thou reposest with the simple, solitary, and mortified soul. O, let my poor heart have the honour and happiness to rest in Thee, to remain with Thee, and to be united to Thee.

O God of love, wound my soul with Thy sweet wounds of love, which nothing can cure but death; wean it from the world's vanity, and wed it to Thy increated verity, that treading all creatures under me, I may be rapt into Thee, my Creator, above myself, and there, like the happy dove in the secure ark, repose my weary and faint limbs in the bosom of Thee, my sovereign Lord and Lover.

6. O divine Wisdom! Lead me into the solitude, speak unto my heart, teach me Thy holy will in all occurrences. My deep sighs and secret desires are not hidden from Thee. Thou knowest nothing can fully cure, comfort, and content me but Thyself, the *One* and only *thing necessary*. O, take myself and all, and give me that '*One Thing*' in whom are all things.

O sweet waters of divine love, which flow from the blessed bosom of the Divinity, and from the open side of my Saviour's humanity, cleanse my poor soul, and like pure oil, penetrate and possess every part of my spirit; irrigate and inebriate it, overflow and absorb it, that it may be transformed and conformed to the divine Spirit, so that all my actions, thoughts, and affections may be spiritual, divine, and deiform.

O, let my ravished soul, full of life and fire, break forth into these flames of joy and jubilation: *I found Him whom my soul loveth; I held Him: and I will not* *let Him go.** This is He Whom by reading I sought, by meditation I found, by prayer I desired, and by contemplation I enjoy.

O, how fetid is the earth! How loathsome are all creatures to me! O taste, O sweetness, O true and solid pleasure! O, how great is the difference between this spiritual delight and all fleshly delights! O, the multitude of Thy sweetnesses which Thou hast laid up, O Lord, for them that fear and love Thee. O light! O delights! O ecstasy of spirit!

Wound me, O sweet God, burn me, consume me, crucify me! Let me cry out with that lover:—'Restrain, O Lord, the floods of Thy grace, or enlarge my heart, for I can endure no longer. I thirst, Lord; give me this water. O when? How long? How much?'

7. O my soul, how good is it for us to be here! O sweet and secure home and harbour! Let us remain and rejoice here for ever. I will keep Thee, O my dearly Beloved, and never forsake Thee; I will conjure Thee to remain with me; I will rather lose myself than leave Thy presence.

My Beloved is mine; His honour is mine, His heart is mine, His heaven is mine. Behold, I am His; behold the key, the keeper, the soul, the body, the Lord—the whole, O my God, is Thine. Behold my liberty, my life, my love—all is Thine, O my Jesus, and Thine alone. Teach me to love Thee above all things and in all things; dwell like a bridegroom in my

* Cant. of Cant. iii. 4.

heart, and reign like a king in the most secret closet of my soul.

*Come, Lord Jesus, come quickly ;** take full possession of Thy own. Come and please Thyself, love Thyself, and serve Thyself in me, as Thou desirest and deservest to be pleased, loved, served.

Let Thy love, O King of love, be the life of my soul and the lease of my life, that when I cease to love I may cease to live.

In Thy love, O Jesus, I end this act of love, though my desire actually to love Thee be endless. O, let me live and die in Thy love, and for Thy love, that by love I may for ever reign and remain with Thee, in Thy kingdom of love. Amen.

---

* Apoc. xxii 20.

Third Treatise.

OF THE STEPS AND DEGREES OF PERFECTION.

They shall go from virtue to virtue: the God of gods shall be seen in Sion. Psalm lxxxiii. 8.

THE FIRST AND LOWEST DEGREE OF PERFECTION.

Upon the first step of this ladder stand beginners who are faithful Catholics.

1. THE first step and groundwork of all virtue and perfection is, to be well settled in the Catholic faith, fearful of God's severe judgments, and careful to avoid all mortal sin. This is the church-porch and entrance into God's holy Temple. But they who stand here remain cold in charity, careless and undiligent in their lesser duties, remiss in spiritual exercises, negligent in thinking of their obligation by which they stand engaged to tend towards perfection; and finally, they greedily gape upon all conveniences of their corrupted nature, and give themselves up to glut and solace their depraved sensuality.

But they have little inward light,

2. These beginners have but very little or no inward light; they know not what is the meaning of mortification, what it is to get into their interior, or what introversion signifies; but they seemingly

satisfy themselves and rest secure in this:—that they have a will to avoid the known and capital sins, and thereby hope to escape hell and avoid God's heavy judgments.

3. Surely such souls stand upon very unsafe and slippery ground, and their salvation is in a doubtful and dangerous condition, for they are so blinded and bewildered with self-love and sensuality that they cannot well distinguish, perfectly discern, nor rightly judge what sins are of mortal danger and what not; so that, conversing daily amidst such multitude of perils, and shaking hands with the world the flesh and the devil with so much freedom, and so little care and precaution, what do they else but dance, as it were, upon the very brink of hell, from whence, if they once tread awry, they infallibly tumble headlong into that bottomless dungeon of eternal perdition.

and stand on slippery ground.

4. Yet, in case they should indeed foot it so warily all their lifetime that death takes them neither tripping, nor fallen into mortal sin—a thing most rare, and not to be presumed on by any one who carries himself so carelessly—they shall nevertheless be saved, *yet so as by fire.** They must expect a most sharp and severe punishment, a long and piercing purgatory, by reason of their unmortified affections to venial sins, by reason of their giving scope to their unbridled senses, their neglect of God's love, their coldness in charity, and their tepidity in tending to perfection. And as for their good works, they are not then

Though they may be saved, yet so as by fire.

* 1 Cor. iii. 15.

likely to be of much avail, since their groundwork was servile fear, their end self-love, and their whole drift and intention altogether sinister and wanting in that purity and perfection wherewith they should have been performed.*

THE SECOND DEGREE OF PERFECTION.

On the second step stand proficients who shun venial sins and consequent sensuality,

1. They stand on the second step who, hearkening to God's holy inspirations, following His internal attractions, and obeying the sweet invitations of His Spirit, keep themselves disengaged from all vain affections to the world, yield not to the enticements of flesh and blood, resist the suggested temptations of the devil, and carefully avoid all occasions of offending their Lord and Maker, so much as venially. To help on this pious design, they put themselves into good company, seek to converse with virtuous people, are diligent in their devotions, zealous frequenters of the sacraments, and painful practisers of the corporal and spiritual works of charity.

but are slow in

2. But because they are yet slow in the pursuit of solid virtue, and slack in their tendency to

* Though we should have succeeded outwardly in life, and have won position, and have gained renown, though we should have laboured much, and have written works, and have built churches, and should have saved many souls, yet this will avail us nothing, and give us no comfort or confidence in the hour of death, if in these things we have left God out, and sought our own gratification and not His honour and glory. O, the folly of working for anything save for God alone! O, the vanity of all things which do not advance the soul in perfection and lead it to the perfect love of its divine Saviour!

perfection, they are still subject to fall into their enemies' snares and ambushes, for they are terrified at the difficulty of getting an entire conquest over their passions and imperfections, and therefore seem to satisfy and solace their minds with what they have already done and left for the love of God, presuming overmuch upon His goodness, flattering themselves with a certain self-security, and fancying that they are in a sufficiently good condition.

tending to perfection,

3. Whence, they fall into a false opinion of their own worth, and an erroneous conceit that little or nothing is wanting to them: all of which maxims manifest a secret pride and presumption, and render them by degrees careless of their further increase and progress in the path of spirituality.

and subject to conceit.

THE THIRD DEGREE OF PERFECTION.

1. Unto this step those proficients are ascended who have more perfectly vanquished all affections to the world, subdued their sensuality to the rule of reason, and changed their slothful and sluggish indisposition into a noble and generous resolution of mortifying each unruly passion, and wrestling with their evil inclinations. And to this end, they fall seriously and severely to work, applying corporal austerities, fastings, watchings, wearing of hair-cloth, long vocal prayers, and faithfully practise such painful means as may probably help them forward in their desired conquest over themselves in the

On the third step stand they who, casting off sloth, tame themselves with austerities.

acquisition of virtues, and in their tendency to perfection.

But their intentions are not pure.

2. But because their intentions in the performance of these pious practices are not pure, sincere, divested of all selfishness, and done simply for God's supreme honour alone, but have some small mixture of servile fear, which looks upon hell and punishment; or of self-love, which eyes heaven and reward rather than God's only pleasure and liking;*

Nor are they well grounded in self-denial.

3. Therefore, they are yet seduced by the devil's subtlety, and drawn into a certain secret delighting in their own supposed good deeds, relying overmuch upon these *outward exercises*, and neglecting their *inward man*, by not laying there the true groundwork of solid virtue, which is perfect *mortification* and *self-denial;* but following the track of nature in its love to these seeming sensible and satisfying practices, not duly weighing how highly these hinder the operation of God's holy Spirit in their souls.

* 'I once saw three solitaries,' says S. John Climacus, 'who at the same time had received the same injury. The first felt piqued and disturbed, but because he dreaded divine justice, held his peace. The second rejoiced at the bad treatment he had experienced, because he hoped to receive a reward for its patient endurance. Nevertheless, he was grieved on account of the person who had inflicted the outrage. The third thought only of the fault of his neighbour, whom he loved sincerely, and who had offended God, and therefore wept for him with heartfelt tears. Thus in these three servants of God we behold three different emotions; in the first, the fear of chastisement; in the second, the hope of recompense; and in the third, the disinterested and tender love of God and of our neighbour.' *The Holy Ladder of Perfection*, p. 177.

THE FOURTH DEGREE OF PERFECTION.

1. Unto this step they have climbed who, rightly considering the nobility of the inward exercise, enter into themselves, and there study diligently how they may unite their souls to their Creator with fervent desires and filial affections.

Upon the fourth step stand they who have become interior;

2. Yet these are oftentimes self-seekers, lovers of their own will, and desirers of solaces and sweetnesses in their devotions, rather than the pure pleasure of God:—*they glory in their own way of the spirit, and prefer it before that of their brethren;* and this shows that they have a touch of spiritual pride, and convicts them of immortification.

but yet look for solaces,

3. And though in time of comfort they seem well resigned to endure all dereliction, yet they are troubled when any cross comes upon them, and discouraged when the least adversity befalls them. If they are commanded to leave what they love, or do what they like not, they soon show what they are, and what *spirit leads them;* they declare their disobedience, fall into dislikes and murmurings, and make apparent the hypocrisy of their pretended resignation. Such persons, therefore, must strive seriously to restrain this wilful propriety, and give themselves up truly and totally to God's good pleasure, and the guidance of their spiritual director, without any manner of restraint or reservation,* which is the only secure and short way

and are discouraged by adversities.

* 'As he who journeys in unknown ways without a guide easily

for them to attain to the next higher degree of perfection.

THE FIFTH DEGREE OF PERFECTION.

On the fifth step stand they who are fully resigned and perfectly obedient,

1. On this step are placed those pious souls who truly renounce their own wills in all their actions, exercises, and devotions, and are fully resigned to the divine pleasure and disposition. These promptly obey, not only God's inward calls and their superiors' commands, but even the beck of all men living, in all things which appear consonant with God's honour, and conducing to their self-denial and mortification.* Their chiefest care is to preserve cleanness of heart, their daily prayer is to purchase purity of conscience, and their unwearied endeavours aim only at the perfect union of their souls to their sweet Saviour.

but fail for want of experience and courage.

2. But because they are not yet masters in this sacred art, but young and raw scholars in this track of true and total resignation, they sometimes fail for want of courage, constancy, steadiness, and solidity in it; all their affections are not absolutely rooted out and mortified by sufficient use and experience in spirituality, and this makes them still waver in their vocation, stagger in their resolution,

wanders, notwithstanding all his prudence, from the right path, so he likewise who undertakes to guide himself in a religious life may very readily lose himself, though he possesses all the wisdom and knowledge of the world.' St. John Climacus, *The Holy Ladder of Perfection*, p. 439.

* Read *Sancta Sophia*, vol. i. tr. 2, sect. 2, chap. xiv.

slip down now and then into some lower pit of self-love, and admit of some little point of propriety; yet they soon arise, return, and regain their standing by the help of *self-denial* and *resignation*.

THE SIXTH DEGREE OF PERFECTION.

1. Upon this step stand those holy contemplatives who, by much experience and long-continued diligence, have gotten a perfect habit of resignation, and a resolute perseverance and constancy in their good purposes, free from all admixture of self-will, propriety, or the least taint of contradiction against their Lord's will and pleasure, faithfully acknowledging that all things whatsoever, even the greatest adversities and most grievous temptations, turn to the spiritual advancement of such souls as truly seek God, and this is their only aim and employment.

On the sixth step stand they who have a habit of resignation,

2. Yet even into these high entertainments with God there may creep in a certain secret inclination to themselves, and an over-eager appetite towards gusts and ghostly comforts, upon pretext to be thereby enabled to endure all desolation and adversity; and this intention being not precisely pure from all propriety, and absolutely perfect in divine charity, is a great impediment to the operation of the Holy Ghost in their souls. For whatsoever gifts of nature or grace, outward or inward, temporal or spiritual, are not directly used in order to our own humiliation and our Creator's honour, are abused

but desire comfort to enable them to endure adversities.

by us to our great prejudice in spirituality, and prove hindrances and stumbling-blocks in our way to perfection.

Here also they stand who are entirely indifferent,

3. And upon this same step stand also another rank of holy persons, who have brought their inward man to an entire indifferency in all things, who are neither puffed up by prosperity nor dejected by adversity, who have their Lord's will for the sole law of their actions, and His only love for their '*All in all.*' They desire to be truly conformable to their crucified Saviour, and to keep an internal quiet, content, and constancy in all desolation and dereliction; they are well grounded and settled in a simple and sincere affection to their Lord God, which enables them, not only to do great and heroic things, but also to suffer all grievous and hard matters.*

but yet rest in God's favours with some propriety.

4. These illuminated souls receive many sweet and secret graces from the hands of the heavenly bounty, as rewards of their sincere fidelity. Their understandings are replenished with light, their memories are possessed with objects of piety, their wills are burned and consumed with perfect charity; but yet these abundances of divine favours may sometimes turn to their prejudice, when they rest in them with even the slightest spiritual gust and propriety.

5. Here, furthermore, are seated those almost per-

* See the *Fourth Degree of Love*, § i. Also *Appendix* to the following Treatise—*The Ladder of Divine Love*, p. 334.

fect souls who have really resigned themselves and all purely to God's pleasure, are fully contented with Him alone, and remain wholly satisfied with all that He either sends or suffers, looking upon Him only, and not upon any of His gifts or goods.

Here also they stand who are satisfied with God only,

6. These are yet more frequently visited from above with divine illustrations, and solaced with high and heavenly comforts; but because they are not as really resigned to leave them and to be bereft of them as they are ready and willing to have and enjoy them, they seem to have yet a little point of secret propriety left within them, and must, therefore, take yet a higher flight before they can perch upon the uppermost step of this spiritual ladder, which is the seventh and highest degree of perfection.

but are not as willing to leave divine favours as to have them.

THE SEVENTH AND HIGHEST DEGREE OF PERFECTION.

1. Whereunto those elevated and perfect souls are soared which are thoroughly inflamed, absorbed, and ecstasied in divine contemplation, wholly dead to the world, abstracted from flesh and blood, and living, as it were, only by the vivacity of God's love, and by the quickening of His holy Spirit within them.

On the seventh step stand the perfect contemplatives,

2. These are the dear darlings, blessed minions, holy favourites, and happy spouses of the Most High, though they sometimes live here below in perpetual oblivion and obscurity. They are brimful

God's faithful friends and dear favourites.

of heavenly gifts and graces, lifted up above themselves to taste the inexplicable sweetnesses and behold the unspeakable glimpses of the Divinity. Yet they rest not in these sublime prerogatives with the least pleasure or propriety, but utterly renounce all self-seeking and interest, being securely grounded in solid faith, clothed only with naked charity, and accompanied with abyssal humility, counting themselves worthy of all abjection, conceiving themselves the very worst of all creatures, and contenting themselves to be by all so taken and treated. Their whole comfort is in the *Cross of Christ:** they neither look for such plentiful showers of heavenly feelings, visitations, illuminations, and influences of the Spirit, nor ungratefully neglect them, but remain in perfect indifferency, and offer themselves up as obedient instruments to all that the Holy Ghost shall vouchsafe to operate by or in them. They receive all things from their Creator's hands into their open and disinterested souls, as if they felt them not, ever praising the divine piety, admiring His liberality, returning all to His honour, resigning all to His will, and being satisfied with His providence and disposition in all temporal and spiritual events whatsoever. Finally, their *outward man* desires no earthly consolation; their *inward man* breathes nothing but the pure love of God; and their *whole being* begs nothing but a perfect conformity to his cruci-

* Such was the sublime perfection of St. John of the Cross, who upon being asked by our Lord what he desired in reward for all the sufferings he had endured for the love of God, answered: '*Domine, pati et contemni pro Te*—O Lord, to suffer and to be despised for Thee.'

fied Lord and Master in all things, but especially in *self-denial* and *abnegation*, the only safe and secure guide of each step in this his long pilgrimage towards perfection.

Fourth Treatise.

OF THE STEPS AND DEGREES OF DIVINE SERAPHICAL LOVE.

Tell my beloved that I languish with love. Cant. v. 8.
My beloved to me, and I to him. Cant. ii. 16.

THE FIRST DEGREE OR STEP OF THE LADDER OF DIVINE LOVE.

In the first degree the soul is wounded with love,

1. UPON this first step stands the pious soul, which after a long experience in the way of the Spirit, and a serious application of herself to the practice of solid virtue, having truly entered into her own interior, and happily ascended the steep mountain of perfection, *is become deeply wounded with love*, sweetly *sick of love*, and heartily *languishing with love;* so that she cries out with that fainting spouse in the Canticles:—*O, tell my beloved that I languish with love.**

and finds no rest in creatures.

2. *This sickness is not unto death, but for the glory of God;*† for the soul in this state defies all sin, deserts whatsoever is not God, and desires Him only: she grows weary and sick of all creatures, and aspires after the embraces of her Creator. And as an infirm person loseth appetite and loathes all the wonted contents of nature, so here the soul feels no gust, takes no pleasure, finds no comfort in any earthly objects. She lies sick, and seized by this mystical fever, caused

---

* Cant. v. 8. † John xi. 4.

by the violent heat of heavenly love ;* and here she is in the degree of contemplative purgation, when she finds no support, no stay, no taste, no quiet, no content in anything whatsoever ; and therefore she soon soars up from this step to the next.

* St. Francis of Sales explains in the following passages what is meant by being 'wounded' with love:—'Love always precedes the affections, of which it is the source and origin. As it penetrates deeply into the will, which is its seat, it is said to wound the heart. St. Denis says that love has a sharp point, by which it penetrates the soul. The other affections also enter it, but it is love which opens them a passage, by piercing the heart. It is only the point of an arrow which wounds ; whatever part enters after this point only enlarges the aperture, and increases the pain. . . .

'Those who have long and faithfully exercised this sacred virtue of divine love receive a kind of wound which God Himself inflicts on those whom He designs to raise to an exalted perfection. He presses and solicits the soul, by powerfully attracting her to His sovereign goodness, and exciting feelings of ardour which she had never before experienced, and which produce great astonishment.

'The soul, thus animated, exerts all her endeavours to wing her flight towards the divine object who so strongly attracts her towards His Divine Majesty. But she soon perceives that her efforts are insufficient, that she cannot soar as high as she aspires, and that her love for God is far from having attained the perfection she desires. Who can express the extreme anguish which she experiences from this conviction? Invited on one side to fly to her Beloved, and restrained on the other by her own weakness, and the weight of the miseries of this mortal life, she longs for the wings of the dove, that she may fly away and be at rest. But these ineffectual desires only serve to torment her; they keep her suspended between efforts to bound to her God, and weakness which prevents her from doing so. The great Apostle had experienced this struggle when he said:—*Unhappy man that I am, who shall deliver me from the body of this death?* (Rom. vii. 24.) In this case it is not the desire of an absent blessing which wounds the soul; she feels that the God whom she loves is present; that He has already introduced her into the mystical cellar where He keeps His precious wine, and that He has implanted in her heart the sacred standard of His love. But God, who sees that she is wholly His, ceases not to pursue her, and from time to time He wounds her with new arrows, by imparting to her a conviction that the God of her affections is infinitely more amiable than loved.

THE SECOND DEGREE OF LOVE.

In the second she seeks her Physician,

1. Wherein she rouseth and raiseth up herself, and casts about which way she may *seek and find her loving Physician*, who alone can cure and comfort her. She gets up early, and eagerly inquires after Him, without intermission or cessation, whom she failed to find in her bed at night,* in the first degree. She faithfully follows the prints of His steps, turns over Nature's book, dives into all creatures, questions all she meets :—O, *have you seen him whom my soul loveth?*† Yet she stays nowhere, stoops not to the lure of any created object; she demands, and passes on; she

'The soul then endures inexpressible anguish, because she sees that the ardour of her love is not much increased by her redoubled exertions; that her power to love is nothing in comparison to her desire; and that the God whom she sighs to love in proportion to His infinite amiability will never be sufficiently or worthily loved. She makes new efforts, but each succeeding endeavour, rendering her more sensible of her weakness and misery, renews and augments her suffering.

'A heart thus transported with love for God allows no limits to its desire of loving Him, and yet acknowledges that, comparatively with what the Almighty merits, it can neither worthily love nor sufficiently desire to love Him. This insatiable desire is like an arrow which pierces it. The wound it inflicts occasions a sweet pain, because those who ardently desire to love take great pleasure in this desire, and would consider themselves most unfortunate if they did not incessantly sigh to love what is sovereignly amiable. Desire produces sorrow; yet the happiness which results from desire renders pain pleasing and agreeable.

'The blessed in heaven, who are aware that they do not love God as ardently as He deserves to be loved, would experience the poignant anguish occasioned by this conviction; their desire of loving more ardently would be an eternal source of suffering, if the will of God did not anticipate their wishes, prevent this desire, and establish them in the sweet and unalterable repose they enjoy.' *Treatise on the Love of God*, pp. 270-273.

* '*In my bed by night I sought him whom my soul loveth: I sought him, and found him not.*' Cant. iii. 1.

† Cant. iii. 3.

leaves all for Him whom she only loves and longs after; she holds no discourse with angels themselves, but listens only to His heavenly voice, and desires nothing but to see a glimpse of His beautifying countenance:—O, *show me thy face; let thy voice sound in my ears.**

2. Here love bears all the sway, and hath made so deep an impression in the pious soul that she is perpetually solicitous for love, ever sighing after love, and still caring, seeking, and stretching after her well-Beloved in all things. All her thoughts tend to Him, all her discourses point at Him, all her affairs end in Him. If she sleeps, she dreams of Him; if she wakes, she talks of Him. Finally, she is always, in all things, in all places, transported into this object of her love, and swayed towards this centre of her life, and, recovering new strength, ascends upwards to a further degree.

and is ever thinking of Him.

THE THIRD DEGREE OF LOVE.

1. Wherein she works with more heat and vigour, and of which the King-prophet speaks:—*Blessed is the man that feareth the Lord; he shall delight exceedingly in His commandments.*† Whence may be inferred that if fear, which is love's daughter, causes such effectual desires, how efficacious will those desires be which proceed immediately from love itself!

In the third she fears her own unworthiness and the love of her Beloved,

2. The soul in this degree *believes that her best*

* Cant. ii. 14. † Psalm cxi. 1.

works done in the behalf of her Beloved are very base and inconsiderable; she runs over her registers of accounts, sums up her numerous exploits, measures her long sufferings, and surveys her high services; and they seem at best but poor and mean performances of a greater duty, and she finds them nothing worth by reason of the excess of affection which inflames and consumes her.* If Jacob's love to Rachel had so powerful an influence upon his spirit, that his twice-seven-years' apprenticeship seemed to him *but a few days, because of the greatness of his love,*† what admirable effects will not the Creator's love produce in that soul which it hath absolutely seized upon, entirely possessed, and thoroughly penetrated in this third degree! She will be piously troubled and angry with herself that she doth so little for so great a Majesty; and if she might lawfully, she would most willingly give up herself to be minced into a thousand morsels for His love, honour, and service, and receive therein full comfort, content, joy, and satisfaction. It truly seems to her that she troubles the earth she treads upon and the air she breathes in, and that she unprofitably takes up a place in the world as a barren tree, which brings forth neither flowers nor fruit. Hence springs a further admirable effect, that she verily thinks herself the worst of all things created, considering what she owes and calculating what she pays. For *love* teacheth her

and deems her best actions worthless.

* How many and illustrious examples of this loving humility do we meet with in the lives of the saints!

† Genesis xxix. 20.

how much God deserves, and *humility* tells her how little she doth. And because she finds that all her best endeavours are full of defects and imperfections, and that her highest way of corresponding to the love of her heavenly Lord is so low and unbeseeming His Majesty, she is inwardly pained and confounded in herself. A soul in this state is far from any puff of pride, presumption, vain-glory, or censuring of others, and is therefore duly disposed to mount up to the next degree.

THE FOURTH DEGREE OF LOVE.

1. Which is, of *suffering for her Beloved*, freely and cheerfully, without the least repining or reluctancy, because true love makes the heaviest burden seem light and the greatest labours easy. In this estate was that spouse when she spake to her Beloved :—*Put me as a seal upon thy heart, as a seal upon thy arm; for love is strong as death, the lamps thereof are fire and flames.** The Spirit hath here such a vigour that it absolutely subjects and subdues the flesh, and slights all motions of sensuality as much as a well-rooted tree doth the movement of one of its little leaves. Here the soul seeks not at all her own taste or comfort either in God or in any of His gifts, nor demands any grace in order to her own solace and support; but all her care is, to cast about her which way she may render some acceptable service to the Divine Majesty, and how she may content and please

In the fourth she willingly suffers for love.

* Cant. viii. 6.

Him in anything which she can do or suffer—since He deserves it for His love and goodness towards her—though such services cost her never so dear.

Many seek their own content in God, but few seek to give God content.

2. Ah, good God! how many of Your followers seek in You their own content and comfort, sigh after Your favours, expect Your caresses, and run after Your gifts and graces! But, alas, how few are they who strive to give You content and to present You with any worthy gift at their own cost and charges without some touch of self-love or self-interest! You are ever open-handed, O bountiful Creator, and ready to shower Your heavenly benefits upon our heads; but we are always loth to employ that in Your love which we receive from Your liberality, though this is the only way to have them continued and increased.

How heroic love is rewarded by ineffable visits.

3. This degree of love is very high and heroic. For as the soul here seeks the Lord so seriously and adheres to Him so sincerely, that she is ready, willing, and desirous to suffer anything for Him, so His Divine Majesty often and ordinarily rewards this her fidelity with putting her in possession of joy, and giving her many secret, sweet, and delicious visits. For the immense love of the Word Incarnate Christ Jesus permits Him not to see His loving spouse suffer purely for His sake without hastening to her comfort and succour.* Hence she speedily gets up to

* Let us no longer live and not love! Let us seek after God with all our diligence, desire Him with all our will, love Him with all our

THE FIFTH DEGREE OF LOVE.

1. Which moves the inflamed soul to a certain *holy impatience in her desires of being joined to her Beloved.* She is seized with such a vehement ardour to overtake Him and to be united to Him, that all delay and tarrying seems to her tedious and insupportable. She thinks often to have found Him, caught Him in her arms, clasped Him in her bosom, but perceiving herself still frustrated of her desired object, faints through her eagerness of spirit; as she did who cried out:—*My soul longeth and fainteth for the courts of the Lord.**

In the fifth she is impatient in her desires of love,

2. She cannot subsist long in this condition. She must either obtain her love or cease to live. She is as eager in her desires as Rachael was to see herself a mother when she said to Jacob:—*Give me children, otherwise I shall die.*† Here the soul feeds altogether on love, as she only hungers and thirsts after love. So that she quickly raises herself up to

and must either attain it or die for it.

THE SIXTH DEGREE OF LOVE.

1. Where she *runs lightly, swiftly, and nimbly after her Beloved,* being fortified with faith, lifted up with hope, and quickened with charity. Of this

In the sixth she runs lightly, swiftly,

---

heart, and cling to Him with all our strength. Let us stand in His presence as empty vessels waiting to be filled with the riches of His plenteous mercy. And let us not ask for His gifts because of their sweetness and delight, but in order to be able to love Him the more, and thereby to be the more pleasing in His eyes.

* Psalm lxxxiii. 3. † Genesis xxx. 1.

and sweetly after love. degree the Prophet speaks when he says:—*They that hope in the Lord shall renew their strength, they shall take wings as eagles, they shall run and not be weary, they shall walk and not faint.** The reason of this lightness is the overspreading and dilatation of these three theological virtues in the soul, whereby it becomes so elevated that it wants but little of a total purification; whereupon that enlarged soul said:—*I have run the way of Thy commandments when Thou didst enlarge my heart.*†

2. Hence, she grows hardy in love, and putting on Grows bold and confident in love, a confident boldness, is piously, amorously, and strongly transported beyond the ordinary limits of reason; so that she stays not according to judgment, retreats not according to counsel, nor governs and represses her impetuosity, violence, and forwardness by the rules of modesty and bashfulness, because the peculiar favour which her best beloved shows her communicates to her a holy and heavenly audacity.‡ In this state was that hardy spouse who begged a kiss of her Beloved's mouth;§ and Moses, when he peremptorily said to God: —*Either forgive them this trespass, or if Thou do not, strike me out of the book that Thou hast written.*||

3. And then, burning sweetly in pure and perfect and becomes union with her Beloved, she cries out:—'I have

* Isaias xl. 31. † Psalm cxviii. 32.

‡ Witness St. Francis Assisi, whose ardent and exuberant love made him appear a fool in the eyes of the carnal world.

§ '*Let him kiss me with the kiss of his mouth.*' Cant. i. 1.

|| Exod. xxxii. 31, 32.

found the long-desired object of my affection; I will not let go my hold, nor permit Him to escape out of my embraces.' Here her holy hunger and thirst is satisfied, and she enjoys such inexplicable treasures of delicious love, that were whole volumes filled up with the description thereof, the greater part would still be left untold. And from this state the amorous soul passes on to the last degree, which belongs not to this mortal life.

united to her Beloved.

THE SEVENTH AND LAST DEGREE OF LOVE.

1. Which likens her totally to her well-beloved Creator, by the *clear vision of divine essence:* and this she enjoys as soon as she (having here in this world arrived at the sixth degree of this divine ladder of love) departs hence to her happy eternity.

In the seventh she enjoys her Beloved perfectly,

2. These blessed souls, which are very few in number, are sufficiently purged and purified by love, which here hath done in them that which Purgatory doth in others elsewhere; so that to them belongs that beatitude:—*Blessed are the clean of heart, for they shall see God.**

is purified by love,

3. Now, we say, this divine vision causeth a total resemblance of the soul to God, following that sentence of St. John:—*We know that when we shall appear we shall be like to Him, because we shall see Him as He is.*† So that all that which the soul is and hath shall be like God by participation. Here nothing at all can

and transformed into God.

* Matt. v. 8. † 1 John iii. 2.

be concealed from her, according to our Saviour's words: —*In that day you shall not ask Me anything*;* because she looks at the clear mirror of the Godhead, wherein herself and all things are most plainly and perfectly seen. But until that day comes, though the soul be raised never so high, yet God is always hidden from her in some manner, so that there always lacks in her something of this total resemblance to the Divinity.

The glorious fruits of this mystic ladder.

4. Thus, O amorous soul, by climbing this mystical ladder of divine love upon which God Himself leaneth, you get out of yourselves and all things, and fly up into the Divine Being; for love, like fire, tends always upwards, with a perpetual desire to be plunged and engulfed in the centre of its proper sphere. Apply yourselves, therefore, seriously to this holy and inward exercise, that you may attain to these heavenly effects. Embrace with your open heart and arms your good, great, and gracious Lord and Love; and resolve with that holy spouse:—*I held him, and I will not let him go.*† *Come ye to him*—this divine Sun—*and be enlightened.*‡ He will clear your darkness, errors, and ignorances, dissipate all your dulness in devotion, dry up the dirt of your concupiscences, encourage you in the carrying of your cross, give you a general alacrity in the performance of all your actions and undertakings, and replenish your souls with unspeakable sweetnesses, comforts, and contents.

5. Come, I say, and only bring with you these three

* John xvi. 23. † Cant. iii. 4. ‡ Psalm xxxiii. 6.

companions, Faith, Love, and Resignation; and leave all other things to the divine disposition. Represent to your thoughts a woful and bedridden creature, lying grievously tormented with a burning fever, his physician prescribing abstinence from drink as the only and assured way for his cure and recovery; his compassionate friends visiting him, seeking to divert his pains with their pleasant discourses and to charm his disease with the delight of music, &c. Ah, what unwelcome comforts are all these things to him who can fix his mind on nothing but to drink; who thinks of nothing, talks of nothing, demands nothing, desires nothing, delights in nothing, but only to refresh his ardours, quench his thirst, and assuage his tormenting heat! This is your case, O dear souls. This should be the beginning, middle, and end of your whole life and business in this world. Nothing but God, God, God. Neither science nor ignorance, neither music nor misery, neither delights nor desolations should touch, trouble, or amuse your faithful, loving, and resigned hearts. God is your only aim and end—

It can only be mounted by faith, love, and resignation.

1. To languish after God.

2. To seek God.

3. To fear the losing of God.

4. To suffer for God.

5. To be weary of delay in your love to God.

6. To run lightly, confidently, and sweetly unto God.

7. And, finally, to enjoy God, and live in God and with God eternally.

APPENDIX.*

Of the Pure Love of God, and by what Signs we may Know It.

As soon as a man hath by perfect Abnegation withdrawn his affection from all *creatures* that are without him, and also withdrawn them from *himself* by pure Resignation, he falls with his whole affection and adhesion upon the *gifts* of God. For God, out of His infinite goodness, presently rewards this Abnegation and Resignation with interior light, gust, comfort, and consolation, and to these Nature instantly converts itself, resting therein with propriety, as it did before in external creatures. And when these comforts are withdrawn, it remaineth impatient and grieveth, and is not quiet until it obtain them again. Nature recreates itself also in the

* This striking chapter is full of deep ascetical wisdom. It points out luminously in what the pure love of God consists; whilst, in setting forth the signs whereby we may know it, it dispels the thoughts of those vain and imperfect souls who imagine that they have already arrived at a pure and perfect love of God, whilst their hearts are still occupied with inordinate affections. It will, therefore, serve as an appropriate Appendix to the *Ladder of Divine Love*, will supplement what may be wanting to that golden little treatise, and will, I trust, be found of much service to many. It is taken from the thirteenth chapter of the *Kingdom of God in the Soul*, a work of the utmost rarity, written originally in Flemish by F. John Evangelist of Balduke, a Capuchin of great learning and sanctity, and edited in English, 1657, by Dom Bennet Stapleton, D.D., monk of the English Congregation O.S.B. The devout F. Faber of the Oratory used to speak of this as one of his favourite ascetical works. The old English translation, which I have before me, bears an elaborate 'License' from the Right Rev. F. President, O.S.B., of that day, which terminates thus:—'Given under our hand and seale in our Monasterie of S. Lawrence' (after the French Revolution established at Ampleforth, 1802) 'in Dieulward' Fr. Laurentius Reyner, Præses Cong. Angl. Ordinis S.P.N. Benedicti, licet indignus. By command of our V.R. Fa. President, B. Augustine Constable, Vice Secretarie.'

consideration of future rewards, and rejoiceth and exulteth in them with propriety, yea, resteth therein.

And although man in this life may well enjoy the internal gifts of God—since to that end they are given him from God—nevertheless they do greatly hinder him when he adhereth unto them and resteth in them with propriety; and he is in no whit less hindered from true spiritual *death* and annihilation, and consequently from perfect union with God through them, than through adhesion to exterior things without him. In like manner, although it be permitted, yea, though it be virtuous and good, to hope for, desire, and long after future happiness, yet inasmuch as this is done with propriety, and not simply with a perfect resignation to God—for man looks therein to his own comfort, profit, and good—it likewise doth hinder his Death, Annihilation, and Union with God. Wherefore, the third thing which is requisite for a man to find God perfectly is:—That the Abnegation of all creatures and the Resignation of himself be done purely for the love of God. For the soul, being now naked, stripped of all exterior things and freed from all internal adhesion to herself, remains within herself ready to be carried and brought still further; and this happeneth when the pure love of God is adjoined to abnegation and resignation, whereby she is lifted up above herself into God, Whom she perceiveth the more clearly in proportion as her love is pure. Thus saith St. Bernard:—When a soul does not seek or desire anything for herself with self-love, neither felicity nor honour, nor anything else, she then is carried wholly into God, and she hath but one perfect desire, viz. to be led by the King into this bedchamber, and to adhere solely unto Him and enjoy Him, and continually beholding Him face to face, to be transformed into the same image, from glory to glory, as from our Lord's spirit.

This pure love of God consists in this:—That a man deny absolutely all created things, and resign and deliver up himself wholly unto God, without intending thereby any merit, comfort, profit, or any other benefit, internal or external, temporal or spiritual, and that he doth this merely for God, Who only doth deserve his love, to Whom he belongeth, and Who hath demanded it at his hands; holding himself contented therewith, without seeking aught else, or desiring, no, not that experimental feeling of God which—as has been said—is thereby necessarily engendered in the soul. This love is pure, for it beholdeth God only in Himself.

And although a man thinketh that he hath this pure love of God, yet he must not presently believe such to be the case, since he may sooner be deceived in this than in any one of the former points. For this pure love is contrary to the present nature and inclination of man; and for this reason, that being turned from the true love of God, he is now wholly bent upon himself, having continually in all his doings and omissions an eye to his own profit, convenience, and comfort, and this self-seeking is now become so natural unto him, that he can scarcely be reclaimed from it. And therefore, it is very rare to find any one that doth not in some sort seek himself in God, at all events after the last-mentioned manner; to wit:—In converting himself to God, thereby to find God experimentally, desiring it more for himself than for God. And in this, Nature doth work very subtlely and secretly, so that it is exceedingly hard to give a certain sign whereby any one may know whether he hath the pure love of God or no; especially is it so as long as he enjoyeth within himself internal gust and comfort, since he resteth therein much more hiddenly than he did in external things. It were necessary, then—as hath been said—that man should have tasted God in Himself, above all gifts, before he can well discern whether he loveth God purely or not; for by the least self-love God becomes obscured within him, and he loseth the noble presence of God *sine medio.*

Notwithstanding, to give the beginner a sign whereby he may know whether his love be pure or no, he shall, in the exercising of the aforesaid Abnegation of all created things and the absolute Resignation of himself, turn aside his intention from all gifts which he either actually hath or could have, and behold God purely in Himself, and propose this unto himself:—That although there were no heaven to be expected hereafter, and that God would not in any way reward him in this life, nor would ever manifest Himself unto him, that nevertheless he would willingly forsake all things and resign himself wholly unto Him, purely because He is God.

pure love many a one hath, unknown to himself, although he do practise the aforesaid Abnegation and Resignation out of a good intention for God.

Such a one may be compared to a bird that is loose and free and able to flee where she lists, but remains willingly captive in the cage, because she is therein fed, and will not fly forth though the door be open to her, through a foolish fear she hath that, being forth in the air, she should not be so certain of her food. So this man, through an abnegation of all creatures, and resignation of himself to God, hath the way open to God, but he remains yet willingly captive in his senses; because therein he enjoys a sensible comfort, without which he will not live, and which he thinks he shall not find out of himself in God. Wherefore, for such a one to come to God by pure love, he must, through aridity and desolation, be forced and, as it were, be driven into a perfect conformity to God; like the aforesaid bird, who, when her meat is taken from her, is forced to leave the cage and fly into the air, and trust to her finding nourishment there.

If, however, the soul wishes to help herself to arrive yet sooner at God, she shall take into her consideration some moving reason, as the divine worthiness, of which St. Augustine saith :—'He loveth Thee, O Lord, less than is befitting Thee who loveth anything but Thee, or what is not loved for Thee. And truly, who loveth God for His gifts loveth not God, but himself.' For, as saith St. Bernard :—'all that which you seem to love for another, you really love not, but that whither the end of the love tendeth; not that through which it tendeth.' This pure love is also commanded us in the Gospel, where He will have us to love Him with all one's soul, with all one's power.* Whereupon saith St. Gregory:—'It is to be diligently noted that the divine word, when it commands God to be loved, doth not only teach us with what love, but also with what measure we must love Him, when it saith, *with one's whole heart.*' To which perfect love ought most of all to move us, the pure love through which God gave His Son unto us, of Whom it is written, *God so loved the world as to give His only-begotten Son:*† the pure and great love of God the Son, also, Who suffered so great and grievous torments, and lastly, such an ignominious and painful death for us; for *greater love than this no man hath, that a man lay down his life for his friends.*‡ And again, He testifieth His love to us to be such as His heavenly Father's is to Him:—*As the Father hath loved Me, I also have loved you.*§ And what greater purity of love can there be than that which is betwixt the heavenly Father and His Son?

* Matt. xxii. 37.
† John iii. 16.
‡ John xv. 13.
§ Ibid. 9.

Fifth Treatise.

OF THE CHOICEST MAXIMS OF MYSTICAL DIVINITY.

Whosoever shall follow this rule, peace on them and mercy. Gal. vi. 16.

MAXIMS OF MYSTICAL DIVINITY.

THE FIRST MAXIM.

That our End is Perfection and Divine Union; and that Prayer is the Way to it.

The spiritual man must aim at divine union.

1. It is not sufficient for us, who are resolved upon a spiritual course, to lead an ordinary good life, which consists in the avoiding of sin and scandal, and in the punctual performance of our external duty to God and our neighbour; but our end and aim must be to attain the perfection of God's holy love, and a happy union of our souls with their first beginning, by living in abstraction, recollection, and perpetual contemplation, so far as God's holy Spirit shall enable us and our frailty can correspond.

And for this end make use of prayer.

2. The chief means to attain this end is *prayer*, without which all religion is but a shadow without a body, or a body without a soul; and all outward observances will prove but a superficial, not a real, devotion. For it is the constant doctrine of di-

vines,* that what God in His eternal disposition hath determined to bestow upon us He gives us in time by the intervention of prayers, tying, as it were, to this instrument the conversion of sinners, the advancement of souls, the perfection of the saints, &c. So that, as His divine decree is that we must till the earth if we will reap the fruits thereof, and provide materials if we will raise up buildings and the like, so His absolute order is that we must *pray* if we will have spiritual benefits to be poured into our souls, and supernatural gifts and graces granted unto us.

3. Let us, therefore, in the first place, resolve to prosecute prayer courageously, constantly, and perseverantly, at set times, if we intend to make speedy progress in sincere virtue and lay a sure groundwork of solid spirituality; and let nothing, upon any pretext whatsoever, hinder or divert us from it, as far as obedience and discretion will give us leave.† Exhortation to pray.

* 'Considerandum est quod ex divina providentia non solum disponitur qui effectus fiant, sed etiam ex quibus causis, et quo ordine proveniant. Inter alias autem causas sunt etiam quorumdam causæ actus humani. Unde oportet homines agere aliqua, non ut per actus suos impleant quosdam effectus secundum ordinem a Deo dispositum; et idem etiam est in naturalibus causis. Et simile est etiam de oratione; non enim propter hoc oramus, ut divinam dispositionem immutemus, sed ut id impetremus quod Deus disposuit per orationes esse implendum; ut silicet:—"Homines postulando mereantur accipere quod eis Deus omnipotens ante sæcula disposuit donare," ut Gregorius dicit; *Dialogorum*, lib. i. cap. 8, à med.' (S. Thoma, 2. 2. Q. 2, q. 83, art. ii.)

† See *Fifth Maxim*, § 3.

THE SECOND MAXIM.

That Beginners may profitably make Use of this following Exercise of Mental Prayer and Introversion until they Obtain greater Light and more Experience in the Way of the Spirit.

This divine exercise consists of three parts in general, and nine points in particular, viz.

I. *Preparation of three acts, viz.*

1. An affective and lively apprehension of God's presence.
2. A cordial and profound act of humility.
3. A pure intention to please and praise God only.

II. *Consideration of three points, viz.*

1. My wounds, both internal and external.
2. My wants, which are many, in every degree.
3. My wishes and humble desires.

III. *Conclusion also of three acts, viz.*

1. Contrition for my sins.
2. Resignation in my wants.
3. Complacency in God, and confidence in His goodness.

The above scheme more fully developed:—

Part I.

THE PREPARATION OF THREE ACTS.

§ 1. A lively apprehension of God's presence, not only in all places and all creatures, by His power and essence, but in our souls, by His mercy, love, care, and providence.

O my soul, where are we? Who seeth us? What is

He that is with us, and within us, by whose light we see, by whose fire we burn, and by whose love we live? Live, my most gracious and glorious and sweetest Lord; in whose presence I kneel, in whose arms I rest, and after whose love I breathe. O that Thou wert as dear to my soul as Thou art near it! Alas, why doth it not care as much for its God as He doth for its good? Why do I not love Thy presence, O my amiable Lord, since Thou art present by love? 1. Presence of God.

Thou art my Father, my Physician, and my Food; hear me, heal me, help me. I am wounded, I am wicked, I am wretched. Out of Thee there is no rest, without Thee there is no hope; remain with me, reign within me. Let me be Thine, all Thine, ever Thine!

§ 2. Profound and cordial humility, acknowledging unfeignedly before God and His angels our wickedness, weakness, and wretchedness; what we are, and what we deserve; and so resting quiet in our centre of nothing.

O my soul, what have we been? What are we? What have we? What can we do? What do we deserve? What do we desire? What hath our loving Father and liberal Lord that He hath not given us? What have we, proud and prodigal children, that we have not received merely from His merciful hand and heart? What have we received that we have not abused by self-love or self-complacency? 2. Profound humility.

O sweet Jesus, give tears to my eyes, words to my tongue, sighs to my heart, and love to my spirit, for I need them all to deplore my misery and implore Thy mercy; to admire Thy beauty and adore Thy bounty; to sigh after Thee, and suffer for Thee. What I have been it grieves me to remember; what I am, after so many signal benefits on Thy part and serious promises on mine, I am ashamed to think; what I deserve, I am afraid to call to mind; what I desire, I am ignorant how to ask.

Lord, for Thy mercies' sake, for Thy Mother's sake; by Thy bowels of mercy and her breasts of meekness; by all that Thou hast suffered for me and she for Thee; by all that is dear to Thee in heaven and earth, forget and forgive what I have been — my past folly and wickedness; pity and protect what I am—my present frailty and weakness; be satisfied for what I deserve, supply what I desire, and be mindful of me in life and death.

How much, O my God, do I wish to leave all, and lose myself to find Thee, to humble myself to please Thee, and to hate myself to love Thee. But these hard and high matters I dare scarcely promise. How, then, and when shall I practise them? Yet without Thee, O sacred humility, there is no solid centre to rest in, no true sweetness to take delight in; therefore, O my God, I come to Thy school to learn this necessary lesson; teach me, touch me, wound me, and win me unto Thee.

§ 3. Pure intention to please and praise God only; to be all His, ever His in what manner and measure He best liketh, both in this prayer and all things whatsoever.

Behold, therefore, O my Lord, how, out of pure
3. Pure intention. obedience to Thy will and confidence in Thy

mercy, I now approach to please and praise Thee; not to receive great matters from Thee, for I am unworthy; nor to conceive great matters of Thee, for I am incapable; but to leave all for Thee, to be '*humble of heart*' beyond all, and to love Thee more than all; this is to conform both to my condition and obligation. I come to prayer, O my only Lord and Love, not to have much, but to give up all; to be Thine, all Thine, ever Thine, in life and death, for time and eternity, as Thou best pleasest.

I come, O my centre and sweetness, to seek Thee and sigh after Thee; yet I am content neither to find Thee nor feel Thee, but only to see Thee by faith, and to suffer for Thee with fidelity. I am satisfied and contented that Thou art so good, great, glorious, rich, and happy in Thyself. I am confident that Thou, in Thy good time, wilt make me rich in Thy mercy and happy in Thy love. Yea, in this pilgrimage I desire no other happiness than true humility, nor greater riches than naked charity.

Part II.

The second part is the Meditation, showing, first to ourselves, and then to our God as His poor beggars, these three things:—

§ 1. Our wounds, both internal and external; to wit, our sins, ingratitudes, daily failings, strong passions, &c.

Ah, my sick and sinful soul, how weak and wounded are we in every degree, in all parts, in each 1. Our wounds.
member of body and faculty of mind!

1. All is out of order, all is pride and self-love. How impenitent are we in sorrowing; how impatient in suffering; how inconstant in persevering; and yet how constant in sinning!

2. My understanding is blind to good, clear-sighted to evil; my will is perverse, peevish, cold, sensual; my memory is weak, full of idle images, subject to distractions.

3. My affections are vain, my passions violent, my inclinations vicious.

4. My Faith is little, my Hope less, my Charity least of all.

5. So forward to Extroversion and dissolution, so backward to Introversion and compunction, so full of imperfections and immortifications.

6. So little confidence in Thy mercy, so little patience in my misery, and almost no performance of my good purposes.

7. So curious to censure others, so careless to keep myself and curb my own senses.

Finally, all is self-love, self-will, self-conceit, self-seeking, pride, propriety, partiality, which are my daily and dangerous diseases.

O Father of Mercies and only Physician of my soul, Thou art almighty and all-bounty: these are my wounds and impurities, and if Thou wilt, Thou canst both cure and cleanse me; and if Thou wilt not, I will remain content as I am. I am willing to continue weak, so I be not wicked; to be wearied and wounded, so I be not utterly tired, overturned, defeated, and without victory. Cut, kill, crucify, O Lord; only spare me for eternity.

§ 2. Our wants, for we are not only needy, but naked; not only poor, but beggars, who neither know how to deserve an alms nor how to desire it.

O my poor soul, what do we want; nay, what do we not want? 2. Our wants.

1. True light, true liberty, true love, true life.

2. A settled attention, a simple intention, a serious introversion, a sincere conversion.

3. Humility of heart, conformity of will, purity of soul, indifferency of spirit.

4. Wisdom to know God's will, strength to execute it, patience to persevere in it.

5. Resolution to suffer for our Saviour, devotion to sigh after Him, diligence to find Him, constancy to remain with Him.

6. Courage to endure all, faith to forego all, hope to expect all, charity to give all, and confidence to gain all.

7. Finally, we want all we should have. Yet our loving Lord is ready to bestow on us all that He hath.

O my God and All, Thou art all that I want. Give me Thyself, and all my wants and wishes will be at an end. Thou art all my safety and my only security, all my refuge and my only centre. Until I can return unto Thee, or wholly turn into Thee, let Thy Cross be my Purgatory, and Thy Will be my Paradise, for other heaven upon earth I can never hope to find. Until then I must be content to sweat and sigh under the burden of this mortal life; to sit like Job upon a dunghill, forlorn and forsaken by all, full of sores and sorrows; to remain a perpetual and pitiful patient, scarcely feeling patience in myself, and finding no compassion in others.

§ 3. Our wishes and desire. What can a wounded wretch wish, but to be cared for and cured? What can a naked beggar desire, but to be clothed and comforted with some few rags and crumbs? What can a blind and cold person ask, but light and love?

This, O my Sovereign and sweet Lord, is the sum and substance of all my wishes and requests. O that I could go out of myself and get into Thee! That I were dissolved from my loathed body to the end I might dilate my heart in Thy love, contemplate Thy divine Face in perfect liberty, and please and praise Thy Majesty eternally! For, in this prison of flesh and vale of tears, I faint under the weight of my temptations, I fall under the burden of my troubles, and I continually fail in the prosecution of my pious purposes.

3. Our wishes.

O that Thy Will did so rule me and reign over me, that it were a torment to decline ever so little from it! O that Thy Love did so freely and fully possess my heart, that there were no room at all remaining for any bastard or base love of things created! Good Jesus, how truly happy and holy should I be if I could clearly behold my own *Nothing* in Thy *All;* if I could embrace crosses as crowns, and swallow down all contempts and confusions as milk and honey! O, when shall I be so elevated in spirit above myself, by ecstasy of love, as to be able and willing to humble myself under all creatures without repugnance?

Alas, shall I never be content to forsake all and be forsaken by all? Yea, having lost and left all for One, to be left by that One Who is my All, and so remain quiet in my own nothing! How long shall I lie wallowing in flesh and blood? How long shall I delay and dally in false loves? How long shall I sigh and not enjoy, seek and not find, live and not love?

Come, my Lord and Love! Lord Jesus, come quickly! Let the fire of Thy sweet love so consume in me all dross of self-love, and so transform my spirit into Thee, that I may take all from Thee indifferently, give all to Thee liberally, and rest and repose in Thee eternally.

Lord, let me be Thine, or nothing! Love, or not live!

Part III.

The third part is the Conclusion, which consists also of three acts.

§ 1. Contrition, which is an humble and hearty sorrow for our sins, ingratitudes, disloyalties, tepidities, &c.

O my God, how little did I love Thee when I so carelessly offended Thy Majesty! O that I had never sinned mortally, though it had cost me my life immediately! O that I were sure never more to swerve from Thy sacred will and commandments! Let me henceforth endure, dear Jesus, a thousand deaths of my body rather than admit one deadly sin again into

1. Contrition.

my soul. O, pity and pardon my past follies and frailties, and prevent me with Thy gracious blessings against future falls!

How great, O Lord, is my obligation to serve and please Thee, were it but for Thy favours conferred, Thy benefits bestowed, and Thy love poured out upon me! And yet, ungrateful wretch that I am, how poorly have I corresponded with them!

O that I had so deep a sense of my sins, that my heart might break with sorrow! Hide not, O Lord, Thy face from me, shut not up Thy mercy-gates against me; for though I have most grievously gone astray, yet I am resolved upon an entire amendment, correction, and reformation of my whole man. This strong resolution, which is Thy gracious gift, establishes my hope in Thy goodness, emboldens my confidence in Thy mercy, and gives me courage and comfort in Thy love.

§ 2. Resignation in all our wants, wishes, desolations, and distresses to the divine will and pleasure.

I am indifferent, O my dear Lord, to sickness and 2. Resignation. health, to light and darkness, to delight and desolation. I am Thine, sweet Jesus: put me where Thou wilt, do with me as Thou wilt, send me what Thou wilt. I am content not only to have nothing, but to be nothing, so Thou, O my Lord, be all things unto me!

I acknowledge myself unworthy to beg, and less worthy to obtain; and therefore I resign myself still to beg, and yet still to want even that which I most wish

—which is all light, all liberty, all love, all comfort, all content, yea even all virtue, peace, and perfection, so long as it shall please Thee. O Father, I am Thine, ever Thine, all Thine, body and soul, for time and eternity. Live Jesus only!

§ 3. Complacency and confidence: the first, that our God is what He is; the next, that He will heal our wounds, supply our wants, satisfy our wishes, and turn all to our good.

3. Complacency and confidence.

I am glad, O my glorious Lord God, that Thou art so worthy of all love, though I of all others am not worthy to love Thee. I am as joyful for what Thou art, O great God, as if all Thou hast were all mine, and I will love Thee in all I am and have, as being all Thine. Thy cross is my comfort; Thy will my welfare; Thy love my life: so that if I can but suffer for Thee, do Thy will, and follow Thy love, I shall do all that is necessary.

I am indeed dry, dark, and desolate; but since it is Thy will I am sure it is my good, and therefore sufficient for me and satisfactory to Thee. I hope Thou wilt one day complete Thy own heavenly design in my soul, healing my wounds, supplying my wants, fulfilling my desires, and filling my yet empty heart with Thy sweet presence and perfect love. In the mean time I will say and sing:—

'Live, Jesus!
'Live, my Lord, my Love, my Life, my All!
'Whose name be blessed by all,
'Whose will be accomplished in all,
'Whose honour be advanced above all.'

Advice respecting the preceding exercise :—

1. We must perform it daily, diligently, discreetly, and with great confidence and courage.

2. Yet without undue attachment, that it may neither hinder the operation of the Holy Ghost within, nor works of due obligation and obedience without.

3. If in the practice of this introversion we find dryness and feel little devotion, we may sometimes fitly resume—in place of the second part, or Consideration—our wonted exercises, whereto our minds are more addicted; ending the same with the Conclusion here prescribed, being ever duly disposed to follow the Holy Spirit's invitation to higher matters. If we faithfully observe these things, we shall infallibly receive comfort, and speedily perceive our own unspeakable profit and progress by the practice of this pious exercise; as being, indeed, the end of all other external devotions, and the short, sure, simple, and royal road leading to a spiritual, devout, and divine life.

THE THIRD MAXIM.

That of all internal Prayer, the Affective is most noble, necessary, and profitable.

For the end and drift of all discursive prayer is, to move, inflame, and enkindle our affections in the love of God and virtue; and therefore all discursiveness must be left by little and little, as our souls can more and more *live in faith*, and free themselves from material objects, images, and conceptions, and only bend to God by a sweet and secret *motion of the will*, and an amorous correspondence with the divine operations and inward impulses of His holy Spirit; treading down and transcending all things under God by discreetly forgetting and unknowing them.*

THE FOURTH MAXIM.

That Meditation is a seeking, Contemplation a seeing of God.

PRAYER in general, according to the well-known division, is either vocal or mental. 1. Prayer is either vocal or mental.

Mental prayer is *an Elevation of our Spirit into God.*† For as our Creator is elevated above all creatures, so our souls cannot see, talk, and treat with Him purely and perfectly, but by 2. Mental is an elevation of our spirits into God.

---

* St. Denis, the Areopagite, gives much the same exhortation to his friend Timothy in the following sublime and mystic words:—'But do thou, beloved Timothy, with thy whole energy bent upon mystical contemplation, restrain thy senses and the workings of thy intellect; and shut out every object of sense and of intellect, and everything that is or that is not; that so, in as far as may be permitted thee, thou mayest rise in an unknowable way to union with Him who is far above all that thou canst be or know; for by a generous and entire and unhesitating withdrawal of thyself from all things, thou shalt, by thus renouncing all things, and of all bereft, be drawn up into that supernatural splendour of the obscurity of God.' *De Myst. Theol.* cap. i. § 1. See also my *note* to *Maxim* 10, § 2.

† St. John Damascen, lib. i. *De Fide Orth.* cap. xiv., gives the same description:—'Oratio enim est ascensus spiritus ad Deum;' by which ascension, says St. John Chrysostom, 'we flee from the intercourse which we have with coarse and fleshy nature and are united with the angels. See Bona's most beautiful and ravishing work, *Via Compendii ad Deum*, cap. vi.

leaving creatures, and lifting themselves up above them all.

This Elevation is by means of Meditation, Contemplation, Thanksgiving, and Petition, which are the wings by which our souls fly to God, and the four essential parts of prayer; all others, as Preparation, Lecture, Examen, Points, Conclusion, and the like, being only accidents and properties of them.

3. Which may be effected in four ways.

We meditate when we seek after truths, and cast about for reasons to rouse our wills to the embracing of God's love, Christian virtues, or works of piety and perfection. For our understandings are, as it were, the steels, and our wills the flints, which no sooner touch each other but the sparks of holy affections presently fly out, inflaming and actuating our disposed souls with heavenly love.

4. The difference between meditation and

We contemplate when we steadily and immovably behold God by Faith, believing that we have Him truly with us and within us; and so leaving all other subjects, objects, reasons, and discourses to look on Him as present, love Him in silence, and feed on His only satiating sweetness.*

5. Contemplation.

* St. Bernard defines contemplation in these words:—'Contemplatio est verus, certusque intuitus animi de quacumque re; sive apprehensio veri non dubia'—A true and certain intuition of the soul regarding anything; or an indubitable apprehension of the true (S. Bern. lib. ii. *De Consid.* cap. ii.). Another writer:—'Contemplatio est perspicuæ veritatis jucunda admiratio'—Contemplation is a delightful enjoyment of the clear truth (Auctor libri *De Spiritu et Anima* apud August. c. xxxii.). St. Thomas's definition is characteristically short, clear, and pithy:—'Contemplatio est divinæ veritatis simplex intuitus'—Contemplation is the simple intuition of divine truth (*Sum. Theol.*

And this contemplation is either ordinary, perfect, or transcendent. 6. Which latter is threefold :

Ordinary Contemplation is when our souls make use of their imagination, and of such ideas as they have drawn from sensible objects, which being first purified, subtilized, and immaterialized by the understanding, conduct them safely to their Creator. a. Ordinary;

Perfect Contemplation looks directly upon the uncreated light, fixes its view upon the eternal verity, and rests immediately upon the Divine Being and perfections, without any admixture of fancy or assistance of creatures. This is called Dark Contemplation,* because our souls, disunited and freed from all inferior objects, and receiving no illumination from below, are wholly dazzled and, as it were, blinded with the bright splendour of God's incomprehensible Majesty, framing no sensible idea of Him, but beholding Him with the eyes of Faith,† by way of negation, and simple adhesion to His divine Essence. b. Perfect;

2. 2, qu. 180, art. 1 and 3). Alvarez gives a fuller definition:—'Est liber, perspicax, et certus intuitus Dei, ac rerum celestium, admirationem inferens, in amorem desinens, et ex amore procedens'—It is a free, clear, and certain intuition of God and celestial things, exciting admiration in the soul, proceeding from and terminating in love (*Alvarez*, tom. iii. lib. v. par. 2, cap. i.).

* St. John of the Cross terms it the 'obscure night of the soul.' F. Baker, O.S.B., F. John Balduke, Dame Gertrude More, O.S.B., and other ascetical writers style it the contemplation of God 'in naked faith.' Hilton calls it 'lightsome darkness and rich nothingness' (*Scale of Perfection*, p. 296).

† F. Baker describes the operations of the soul in its transition from ordinary contemplation (which he calls the prayer of 'forced immediate acts') to that of perfect or passive contemplation, in these words:—'In forced immediate acts of the will, especially at the begin-

Transcendent Contemplation mounts up yet higher

e. Transcendent. above all intelligible species,* and may truly be

ning, there is some degree of meditation, which is the thinking on the object, and thereupon internally producing the act or affection itself, and quietly continuing and resting in it till all the virtue of it be spent. There is likewise always some use of images, and in the beginning these images are more gross, but afterwards, by practice, they grow more pure, and all manner of discourse ceaseth; yea, the soul will begin to reject all distinct images, and apprehend God without any particular representation, and only by that obscure notion whereby faith informs us of His totality and incomprehensibility, and this only is truth, whereas all distinct images are but imperfect shadows of truth. How great is the security of a soul thus operating purely by the will! How free is she from those errors and dangers into which she may be led by the curious searching subtlety of the understanding! Here *God Himself is only her light*, and not any imagination of her own.' *Sancta Sophia*, vol. ii. treat. 3, sect. 3, ch. i. §§ 15, 16.

* The discoursings, operations, and speculations of the intellect chain the soul to the prison of the body, whereas divine contemplation transcends all human operations, transports the soul out of itself, and transforms it into God. St. Denis says that contemplation transcends all intelligible things—'Omnia intelligibilia transcendat.' And in this sense St. Gregory the Great describes our holy Father St. Benedict as one 'scienter nescius et sapienter indoctus' (*Dialog.* lib. ii. cap. i.). 'Contemplation, or mystical theology,' says St. Denis, 'is neither sensation, nor reasoning, nor any movement, or operation, or habit of the mind, nor anything that can be explained by what we understand. But in the perfect stillness of the mind that is illuminated by it, it is known to be something above all that the mind can comprehend. And since it contains something so mysterious and unspeakable, the words used about it will be so too; and it is called Theology, because that which is above all things must be about God.

'Do Thou, therefore, O Holy Trinity, Who rulest over perfect wisdom in the hearts of Christians, Who guidest the mind to think aright on divine things, and not to hanker after superfluous knowledge—do Thou direct us to that sublime summit, than which we can conceive nothing more sublime, nothing more supremely unknown, nothing more supremely knowable, nothing more exceeding all denial of understanding or all affirmation of intelligibility. For although such sublimity as this is totally incomprehensible, yet it is not unknown as though it did not exist at all, but as a real existing thing, albeit it surpasses all intellectual light, whether of knowledge or of ignorance; for it is, at the same time, supremely intelligible and supremely unknown.' *De Myst. Theolog.* cap. i.

termed the cousin-german of beatifical vision, and that last heaven whereunto St. Paul was rapt, where not only all use of sense is extinguished and all activity of the understanding abolished, but the spirit totally transported, absorbed, and inflamed with seraphic love, and the whole inward man drowned, annihilated, rapt in ecstasy, and ineffably united to the Divinity: so that the thus elevated soul can neither say or consider :—*God is with me*, or, *I am with God*, for such advertency or reflection is sensible, whereas this most eminent contemplation imports an absolute silence and forgetfulness of ourselves and all things whatsoever, and an entire conjunction with our Creator, as shall be hereafter further declared.*

The four essential parts of Prayer are performed in this or the like manner :—

Taking some mystery of our Saviour's life—as, for

* This same doctrine is taught by the great mystic doctor, St. Denis :—'Darkness is dispelled by light, and more perfectly by abundance of light; so ignorance is dispelled by knowledge, and more perfectly by abundance of knowledge. If, then, we take ignorance as the excess, and not as the privation, of knowledge, we may assert, with all truth, that those who have this light and knowledge with regard to things are hidden from that ignorance which regards God. For His exceeding darkness puts all light into the shade, and shrouds all cognition. And if any sees God and understands what he sees, he has not seen God at all, but some one of His creatures which have being, and are capable of being apprehended; but He Himself, transcending all being and all understanding, by this very absence of being and cognition both exists above all being and is understood above all understanding. And this most perfect ignorance, in its preëminent sense, is knowledge with regard to Him who is above all knowledge.' *Epis.* i. *Caio Monacho.*

example, His prayer in the Garden of Gethsemani—

1. The four parts of prayer exemplified:

for our subject or groundwork, we *first* examine our conscience, ask pardon for our sins, and make resolutions of amendment. *Secondly*, we give up our will irrevocably to God, seeking purely His glory, and not our own pleasure, &c. *Then* we enter upon the first essential part of prayer, which is—

a. Meditation;

Meditation; considering our dear Redeemer in His bloody sweat, sighing, weeping, praying, and His disciples sleeping. Upon this sad spectacle we make some discourses concerning the Person Who suffers, the love wherewith He suffers, the subject for whom He suffers.

b. Contemplation;

Then our affections being moved by these considerations and inflamed in God's love, we glide sweetly and insensibly into Active Contemplation, leaving all discourses, and looking, with our eyes of Faith, upon our suffering Lord.

c. Thanksgiving;

And having melted away in His loving presence for as long a time as our devotion or the Holy Spirit's invitation lasts, we heartily thank Him for having thus suffered for our salvation.

d. Petition.

And *lastly*, we implore His grace that we may faithfully follow His steps; and above all, that He will grant us His love, which we must filially, affectionately, humbly, and confidently beg at the conclusion of all our exercises.

THE FIFTH MAXIM.

That continual Recollection is the Exercise of Exercises, and the immediate Way to bring us to Perfection and divine Union.

THAT we may rightly conceive the truth of this Maxim, let us here, in the first place, take a view of the whole manner, meaning, method, and practice of this sublime exercise in these ensuing Canons.

1. That all places are proper for recollection, but the quieter the place is the more suitable is it.

Wheresoever we live we may and should send up our petitions, and breathe forth our affections to our everywhere present Lord and Lover, in public and in private, in tempests and in calms, amidst all noises of employments and in quiet corners of retreat. Job prayed well on a dunghill, and Jonas in the whale's belly; but nevertheless Judas did not so do in his apostleship and in the society of Jesus. Yet when solitude, silence, and repose may be obtained, they are the fittest instruments of contemplation,* and therefore are most highly to be prized and most diligently embraced:—*I will lead her into the wilderness*, says our Lord, *and I will speak to her heart.*†

2. That to pray on our knees is a posture most pleasing to God.

* So also St. Thomas:—'Solitudo, sicut et ipsa paupertas, non est ipsa essentia perfectionis, sed *perfectionis instrumentum*. Unde et in Collationibus Patrum, dicit Abbas Moyses, quod "pro puritate cordis solitudo sectanda est."' 2. 2, q. 188, art. 8.

† Osee ii. 14.

Let us not hunt for excuses, pretend want of strength, nor cloak our laziness and languor with that misinterpreted maxim:—That prayer must have the quietest, easiest, and least-constrained composition of body; but rather let us imitate our Lord and Saviour —since all His actions are for our instruction—Whose humanity lay often prostrate on the earth,* praying and adoring His Divinity, and let us follow the example of His Apostle, who frequently bowed his *knees to the Father of our Lord Jesus Christ.*† Let us, I say, submit willingly to this direction, unless evident weakness or infirmity hinder us; for this adoration and a far higher is due to the Divine Majesty; and therefore let us conceive the contrary to be a manifest temptation of our enemy.

3. That we must, especially at first, fix for ourselves certain and set times of recollection.

Let us not complain for want of conveniency, time, or opportunity to follow this exercise; for if our wills be ready, time cannot be wanting. If our stomachs call on us for meat, or our bodies for warmth, we can find time to feed and clothe them. Are our souls less worthy of attention? Let us rather steal time from our sleep and recreation than want it for Recollection. And since all our time is given us by God to be spent in His love

* '*And when He was gone forward a little He fell flat on the ground; and He prayed that if it might be, the hour might pass from Him.*' Mark xv. 35. '*And going a little further He fell upon His face, praying and saying: My Father, if it be possible let this chalice pass from Me.*' Matt. xxvi. 39.

† Ephes. iii. 14.

and service, let us give back unto Him at least a tithe thereof, and dedicate two hours of four-and-twenty, one in the morning and the other in the evening, to His particular honour.

4. That we must make an act of pure intention at our entrance into Recollection; as thus:—

'I intend, O my God, to employ each moment of the short time I shall remain in Thy presence in adoring Thy Majesty, admiring Thy goodness, begging Thy pardon for my offences, Thy mercy for the souls in Purgatory, Thy succour for the Church's necessities, Thy assistance in such an extremity, Thy strength against such an inclination, Thy grace for the getting such a virtue. I am here on my knees, O Lord, to perform these homages, and present these petitions.'

This intention will endure virtually throughout the whole time of prayer, and make our seeming idleness and stillness active and meritorious.

5. That we must briefly examine our consciences, and produce acts of contrition, self-confusion, humility, and resolutions of amendment, saying from the very bottom of our hearts, in this or the like manner:—

'O my Lord, my God, my All! Thou deservest all praise, honour, and service, because Thou art good, gracious, and glorious. I will henceforth rather lose all than leave Thee, O my God, without Whom all is nothing; and since Thou art so good in Thyself, and so good to me, I will, by thy grace, never more offend Thee. I will confess my sins, amend my life, perform my penance, walk carefully, humbly, obediently, resignedly in Thy presence; and unto all this am I moved principally by the infinite greatness and beauty of Thine own divine Being and perfection.'

In the particular examen of our consciences—which must never be omitted in the beginning of our Recollection—we must mark to what vices we are most inclined and wherein we are most frail, and then trample that down violently and resolutely; for this captain-imperfection* being conquered, the rest will soon yield and submit. And in the next examen, we must impartially search and censure ourselves, and see whether our falls in that kind are still as frequent as they were formerly, and so set upon our enemy again with fresh fervour, vigour, courage, and constancy until we have gained the complete victory.

6. That we must also make an act of perfect resignation before setting about this exercise, leaving ourselves entirely in God's hands. He is our Father; let Him dispose of His children and all that concerns them as He best pleaseth, saying:—

'O my Lord, my Father, my Lover, do with my life, my health, my temporals, my spirituals, my body, my soul, *all, all,* as Thou wilt. I come not hither tc seek my own will, but to conform myself to Thy will in all things, and to remain in that very state—neither more, nor less, nor otherwise—which best pleaseth Thy Divine Majesty.'

* That is, our predominant passion.

7. That we must bring with us some theme, subject, or groundwork of our Prayer and Recollection.

As some mystery of our Saviour's Life, Death, Passion; man's last end; some vice to be conquered; some virtue to be obtained; some divine perfection to be admired; or some ejaculatory sentence to be so long dwelt and pondered on till our souls feel themselves inclined to quit all discoursing and acting, and to remain quiet in an exercise of pure faith and perfect resignation.

8. That we must look on God by faith, and leave off all discoursing.

This we must do when, conceiving by means of a lively faith that our Lord is in us and in all things, we humbly beg Him to teach us the holy lesson of divine love; and so, keeping ourselves in His presence, bidding good-night to all creatures, objects, and images whatsoever, we only and immediately *eye the beloved object of our souls*, and rest quietly, contentedly, silently, and sweetly absorbed into the Divinity.*

9. That we must carry God with us from our Prayer.

Let us not leave our dear Lord in the oratory when we rise from Recollection, but bear Him along with us continually in our hearts, talking still with Him and of Him, eating and drinking in His company, sleeping with Him in our arms, working, walking, recreating, doing all things with Him, in Him, for Him, and ever

* See *notes* to *Maxim* 3 and 4.

praying to Him, and praising Him Whom we have with us and within us in the closet of our souls.

10. That we must put on Christ and imitate His example in all our actions.

Our Saviour Christ is our Master; let His life therefore be our model, and His practices the patterns which we always study to express and imitate. Let us comport ourselves in eating, drinking, sleeping, speaking, praying, and doing all things as we conceive Christ did, or would do upon the like occasions if He were now living upon earth in His humanity. Let us study to have this rule-of-three always at our fingers' ends:—1. To think as Jesus did. 2. To speak as Jesus did. 3. To do as Jesus did; so striving to become, as it were, a Jesus Christ by imitation.*

Thus briefly, we have the whole manner and method of this transcendent prayer and divine exercise of recollection: to wit, 1. to go into some retired spot; 2. and there placing ourselves on our knees; 3. twice every

* 'This fiery love is perfect, and maketh the soul that is in love to imitate her Beloved, the sorrow-stricken God-Man, which is the perfection of all perfection. And because he who perfectly loveth another striveth to be transformed into him in his manners, and to do those things that are more pleasing unto him whom he loveth, so too he who loveth Jesus, the God-Man, endeavoureth to be transformed into Him and into His habits, and to do what is pleasing unto Him, and to be made like unto Him in his manner of living. The more perfect, then, a man is in his love of God, so much the more let him endeavour to do what He did, and willeth and commandeth and counselleth to be done, and to avoid all things that might be displeasing unto Him; and he ought to continue in this his whole life long, because the God-Man, as long as He lived in this world, lived in the continual and most bitter cross of penance.' *Visions and Instructions of B. Angela of Foligno*, p. 301.

day; 4. to make an act of pure intention; 5. to examine our consciences and produce acts of contrition; 6. and resignation; 7. then to think on the subject of our prayer; 8. leave off all discourses and look on God by faith; 9. carry God with us from prayer; 10. and, lastly, put on Christ by imitation. This is the short and secure way to divine Union and Deiformity, when faithfully performed, discreetly practised, and carefully accompanied with profound humility, perfect obedience, and an absolute submission to our spiritual director, as shall be more fully shown in the subsequent Maxims.

THE SIXTH MAXIM.

That for this pure, perfect, and transcendent Prayer no certain Rules can be prescribed.

THE ground of all prayer, even the purest, is—as hath been said—some mystery, some devout sentence, some virtue, or ejaculatory dart until our affection be moved. Now, if by continual introversion and special grace our wills be drawn irresistibly by the simple view of our beloved Lord, it is needless to use this ordinary means.

When our affections are thus enkindled, they break forth into flames of love and aspiration. Then, the heat increasing, our prayer grows more inward, our sighs deeper, our love greater, our hearts more ardent in their desires of union, which is *Active Contemplation:* wherewith our souls, being overcome and drowned in their

Lover's presence, leave Him to speak, move, and act all things with us* and within us, and so we sleep in *Passive Contemplation*, freed from all objects of creatures, and sweetly united by pure love to our Creator.

The Degrees, therefore, of Prayer in general are these :—

1. Devout reading, or mixed prayer.
2. Vocal prayer.
3. Meditation or Consideration.
4. When the affection is excited to Vocal Aspirations.
5. When, the heat and light increasing, Mixed Aspirations or Affections, partly vocal, partly mental, are excited.
6. Then still more Abstract and Simple Prayer.
7. After which comes Active Contemplation.
8. And lastly Passive.

In this last state we may and must leave all rules, and help ourselves by experience and the light of faith ; but especially by following and humbly obeying the internal motion and attraction of the Holy Spirit of God, upon Whom chiefly depends the perfection of this great work. For further explanation whereof:—

* This expression, '*with* us,' implies some movement and coöperation on the part of the soul, and frees our author from all charge of Quietism.

THE SEVENTH MAXIM.

That the Contemplative must be very observant of the divine Visits, Lights, and Calls.

1. We must take heed of tying ourselves to any set form of words, points, or methods of mental prayer after we have made some progress in this practice of Recollection, for this were directly to impede the free operation of God's Holy Spirit within us.* When, therefore, we shall perceive our souls drawn from discourses to this higher exercise, we must humbly and readily relinquish our former hold, and give scope and leave to the divine invitation, busying ourselves no longer in our former fears and customs, but making use of such inward or outward expressions as fervent love will suggest and furnish us withal, conforming ourselves perfectly to God's will and coöperating with His grace, yet so as not to run before it; for this is the other extreme, which equally hinders the operation of the divine Spirit. Wherefore, a quiet, indifferent, and industrious attention and correspondency—still willingly giving way to obedience for fear of delusion—is the very best disposition to receive these heavenly visitations.

We must not tie ourselves down too rigidly to any set method,

* This chapter breathes that Benedictine liberty of spirit which gives a soul liberty to do, not what it *likes*, but what it *ought*. Listen to F. Baker on the above point:—'The general rule and advice, therefore, in the matter is, that accordingly as souls, upon experience and observation, do find themselves disposed to any kinds of acts or affections, whether of one kind only or several kinds mixed together, so they must order their exercises and recollections, preferring the savour and profit that their souls find in them before any rules, methods, or authority of examples.' *Sancta Sophia*, vol. ii. tr. 3, ch. ii. § 23.

BB

2. We must not, then, be troubled if we break our old customs to embrace God's will: He is the end of all our exercises, and the end being obtained, the means must cease. O, how many are called by God who refuse or resist Him by tying their spirits to this or that practice, and so debar Him from elevating their souls to Himself as He pleaseth. They are loth to leave God in their usual devotions for God in contemplation. If they begin not their prayers *thus,* and *thus* end them, they think they have done nothing, and remain wholly unsatisfied. Thus they become proprietors in their wills and slaves to their exercises; and because they cast not themselves absolutely into the two arms of God—*will* and *love*—they make small progress in the way of solid perfection.*

but willingly quit our old customs.

THE EIGHTH MAXIM.

That the only Way to get true Peace of Mind is to be totally Resigned to God.

1. Resignation is *a putting away of our own will, and a placing of God's will in its stead.* It is, as it were, a certain transfusion of our wills into His, and an unclothing ourselves of all desires but

What resignation is.

* 'Let her not tie herself so rigorously and superstitiously to any of the said acts; but that if without searching there should be offered to her any other kind of act or affection (be it resignation, love, or aspirations, &c.), which may be gustful to her, let her entertain it, and therein abide as long as the relish of it lasteth, and that ceasing, let her return to prosecute the acts of the present exercise.' *Sancta Sophia,* vol. ii. treat. 3, sect. 3, chap. ii. § 8.

that God's holy will be fully accomplished in heaven and earth.

2. Without this resignation we shall never find peace in God nor in ourselves; and the way to attain to it is to receive all that happens as from God's holy hands, and to be content to bear it as long and in what manner and measure He pleaseth. Let us not be troubled under a false pretence of zeal at this place, that company,* &c.; for it is not *that*, but *ourselves*, who stand in our own light.

There is no true peace without it.

3. First, then, let us seek God purely in all — see Him present in all; take as from Him all; return back unto Him all. Let us be indifferent in all; praise God in all; be quiet and content in all—in sickness and health, in light and darkness, in peace and trouble, in life and death; to be expelled out of Paradise with Adam; to lie full of sores and sorrows with Job on a dunghill; to be forsaken by all with Christ on the cross; to be poor, naked, nothing;† being ever

How to be obtained.

* It is great humility always to remain satisfied with the place and position in which we find our lot cast, and to labour therein peacefully and zealously without casting a wistful eye either to the right or the left. Men foolishly seek peace of mind and contentment from without, whereas it comes from within. For happiness is not in *place*, but in union of the soul with God; so that he whose love is centred in God is never solicitous about the future, nor troubled at whatsoever befalls him.

† This high state of perfect resignation the saintly beggar in the *Parable* had attained, who, when asked by the rich man how it was he contrived to be so happy and contented in the midst of so much poverty and misery, replied, that the cause lay in his entire resignation to the will of God in whatsoever befell him. 'The rich man, confounded and amazed at the divine wisdom of the untutored beggar, and scarcely giving credit to his words, finally put to him this one

ready to say cordially, cheerfully, and with an humble and habitual indifference:—'Yes, O Father, yes, I will; it pleaseth Thee, it shall please me; well, good, best of all; so be it, my good Lord, for time and eternity, in this and in all things.' A soul thus resigned can never be troubled with any cross or calamity, for she eyes God's will,* and embraces His providence in all occurrences; nothing troubleth her, but only that His divine pleasure is not perfectly performed in herself and in all creatures.

How to be resigned in desolations.

4. If in her prayers she be seized with dryness, dulness, she gratefully confesseth that state to be best for the protecting of her spirit; she neither complains of nor considers her inproficiency in her pious exercises, for she comes not to prayer for spiritual sweetness or for graces, but to do God's will, to receive

more question:—"But if your will be so wholly resigned up to God and transfused into His will that you can be content to be disposed of by Him in everything without reserve, pray what would you do should it seem good to Him, for the manifestation of His omnipotent Majesty, to cast you down into the abyss of hell? What would you then do? Could you be content, think you, with His will and pleasure? Speak out plainly." "He cast me into the abyss of hell!" said the beggar with a cheerful smile, his countenance here beginning to shine like an angel. "But even let this be supposed, seeing that we may suppose as well what cannot as what can be. Why, certainly, if He should, I have two arms whereby I would embrace Him still and not let Him go. The one is true *humility*, and that I lay under Him, and by it am united to His most sacred Humanity. The other is divine *charity*, which is the right arm, and that I cast about Him, and by it am united to His Divinity. And by this arm I would hold Him so fast, and so clasp it about Him, that He would be forced to descend into hell with me. And I cannot but think that it is much more desirable to be in hell with God than to be in heaven without God. Heaven without Him would be a hell to me, and hell with Him a heaven; for wherever He is, there must heaven be also."' *The Beggar and No Beggar*, § 2, p. 10.

* 'O Lord, all our evils come from our not fixing our eyes upon Thee!' St. Teresa, *Way of Perfection*, p. 77.

what He pleaseth, to suffer what He permitteth. And because this resignation is the key to her true progress, she makes frequent and fervent acts of resignation in this or the like manner :—

5. *Take my will totally to Thee, O my God; govern it absolutely, and submit it perfectly to Thine own. And because I cannot deliver it up, O my dear Lord, as Thou desirest, take it from me by violence, cut off all impediments, break all my fetters for me, bring me forcibly and bend me absolutely to a blessed conformity to Thy will and pleasure.* Acts of resignation.

Let my whole employment in this life be the practice of this point. Let me neither think of pain nor look upon recompense, but resignedly behold Thee, because Thou art in Thyself so good, so great, so glorious, so amiable, so admirable.

I give up my will, O divine Artist, to be plunged, purified, polished, hammered, filed, and fired in the furnace of Thy love. O, do with it and with me as Thou best knowest and pleasest! It is for this that I now come to prayer, and for this only, that I may be taught this happy lesson of denying my own and doing Thy will.

Or thus briefly :—

Lord, I put my will and all that concerns me, inwardly, outwardly, temporally, eternally, into Thy holy hands; dispose of all as Thou pleasest, and direct me in all to do Thy divine will.

6. Having made this act and oblation, let us reflect seriously upon what we have said and done, When an act of resig-

nation has been once made, it should never be recalled.

and that in giving away our will we have put the best pledge we have into God's hands, and out of our own power. Let us, then, beware of so infamous and ignoble an action as to recall the gift so solemnly delivered, or to do again our own will in anything whatsoever.

THE NINTH MAXIM.

That a Contemplative Soul must lay a solid Groundwork, to serve her in Time of Desolation.

No soul can always be absorbed in God;

1. For no soul can in this life be always elevated to the Divinity, and therefore will sometimes need a stay to rest upon till she can take breath and repair her forces, in order to her higher soarings in contemplation.

but needs a resting-place, as the Humanity of Christ.

2. This resting-place may most fitly be the Humanity of Christ,* which is the very way and door to the Divinity, and upon which, when she returns to herself after she has been absorbed into the divine light, she may confidently rely

* When a soul finds herself growing weary of pure introversion, and that she can no longer keep her powers free of all images and fixed on the pure Divinity, 'in such cases,' says F. Baker, 'it not only may be permitted, but ought to be enjoined, unto a soul to give ease unto herself by quitting for a time such painful introversions and addresses to the pure Divinity, and instead thereof, exercise herself in producing other acts less painful, because less introverting, as acts or affections to the Humanity of our Lord, to angels, saints, &c. Yea, she may sometimes address her internal speech to her own soul, or to some persons or creatures absent, yet all with reference to God, for otherwise it would not be an act of religion, nor profitable to the soul.' *Sancta Sophia*, vol. ii. treat. 3, sect. 3, chap. ii. § 17.

and repose. And without this prop, the higher she ascends, the lower will be her fall back again.

THE TENTH MAXIM.

That in this high Exercise of Recollection, the three Theological Virtues, Faith, Hope, and Charity, must perfect and possess the three Powers of our Souls, Understanding, Memory, and Will.

That a soul cannot here be united immediately to God, save by means of faith, hope, and charity,

1. It is, in the first place, to be observed as an undoubted truth, that a soul cannot in this life be united to God immediately by her understanding, memory, will, imagination, or any other sense, power, or faculty whatsoever, but only by means of Faith in her Understanding, by Hope in her Memory, by Love in her Will.

which must possess respectively our understanding, memory, and will,

2. These three virtues must therefore be introduced, by our coöperating with the divine grace, into the three powers of our souls, in the purest and perfectest manner that is possible, if we will arrive at the height of divine union. 1. *Faith* must so possess our understanding as to deprive it for the time of all other knowledge than that of God alone.* 2. *Hope* must blot out of our memory all

* This takes place when the soul is so transported and ravished into God, that she forgets all human things, and is illuminated from above by the pure Divinity in such a manner that the brightness of its light darkens and eclipses in her soul all gross and earthly knowledge. To this supernal state our author refers when he speaks of 'treading down and transcending all things under God, by discreetly forgetting and *unknowing* them' (*Maxim* 3). This 'unknowing' is that 'darkness'—*caligo*—of Exodus xix. into which Moses is said to have ascended, as St. Maximus testifies (*Schol. S. Maximi et Paraphr.*

images and thoughts of possessing anything but God alone. 3. *Charity* must unclothe our wills of all affections, joys, contents, satisfactions in anything that is not God only. For Faith tells us of things which cannot be understood by natural light and reason; Hope looks upon such things as we have not, hold not, possess not; and Charity removes our love from all creatures to employ it all on our Creator.

and thereby perfect the three powers of our soul,

3. The three powers, therefore, of our soul must be perfected by these three virtues: our understandings must be informed with this pure Faith; our memories freed from all distracting images by this pure Hope; and our wills filled with divine affections by this pure Charity; thus refusing, denying, and emptying our whole souls of all that is not this perfect Faith, Hope, and Charity.

and render it inviolable against the snares of the devil and of self-love.

4. In this divine practice is found an absolute assurance against all the subtle snares of the devil and self-love. For a soul which is thus entirely stripped and bared of all *active knowledge, proprietorship, and love of things created* must needs remain in God in a certain tranquillity, passiveness, cessation, sleep, annihilation, absorption; so that out of God there can be found nothing for Satan, sin, or sensuality to assail.

But to facilitate the understanding and practice of

Pachym. in Epistola i. tom. 2). And of it St. Denis writes:—'Illa perfectissime in bonam partem *ignorationem*, *notitia* est ejus qui est supra omnia quæ in cognitionem cadunt' (*Epist.* i. *Caio*).

this high matter, upon which the whole edifice of this holy Recollection and divine Union stands as on a foundation, let us particularly explain and exemplify how the understanding is to be placed in pure Faith, the memory in pure Hope, and the will in pure Charity

---

THE ELEVENTH MAXIM.

That our Understanding must be settled in pure Faith.

1. THE practice of this point is thus:—Having conceived some mystery of our Saviour's Passion, or the like, for the subject of our prayer, we ponder a while upon it, not so much to admire our Lord Jesus as to imitate Him; and we desire to know His virtues, that we may practise them in our own persons by His perfect example. **How the understanding may be established in pure faith.**

2. Then we make an act of Faith, saying:—*I firmly believe that this my suffering Saviour is not only a man, but also my Sovereign Lord God. I believe that He, being Almighty, submitted Himself to Pilate, being the Creator became a creature, being immortal became mortal; and that inasmuch as He is God, He is with me, within me, without me, about me, above me, beneath me, and so in all creatures which have a being.* **Make an act of Faith.**

3. Afterwards we speak further to our Saviour:—*O my dearest Lord and Love, teach me now my* **Beg Christ's assistance.**

lesson that, in requital of what Thou hast done for me, I may keep Thee company in Thy sufferings.

Leave off all discursive prayer,

4. And then we quit all discourses, thinking we have no understanding at all left, and looking on our sweet Saviour by Faith, which hath this property, as St. Thomas testifies, to elevate the soul to God, and free it from all creatures. For so long as there are discourses going on in our understanding, images and phantasies in our memories, joys or tenderness in our will, these powers have not purely God, but sensible things for their object; because God, being above all sensibility, must be found void of all creatures; and consequently, if we can be totally abstracted from all things created, we shall infallibly lay hold of our Creator.

and all exercises that savour of the senses.

5. It is therefore impossible, says the divine St. Denis,* to be truly united to God, unless we leave all material operations, both in sense and in spirit; that is, unless we lay aside all sensible emotions, all discursiveness, all imaginations, and all ways of human wisdom. Till we can do this, let us not think to become perfect contemplatives.†

* *De Mystica Theol.* cap. i.—Quænam est divina caligo. See *note* to *Maxims* 3 and 4.

† 'Wherefore St. Bonaventure saith very well that all images are impediments to the soul which is to be united to God, and he terms them spots and blemishes; and therefore he admonisheth the soul that the eye of her understanding must be wholly blinded, and that she must content herself with naked faith, which takes God divinely, as He is in Himself. Note, there is nothing more excellent and profitable than that the soul accustom herself to walk in this true faith, continually moving and stirring herself to God through the same.

THE TWELFTH MAXIM.

That our Memory must be settled in pure Hope.

1. Which is done by forgetting all things created, heaven, earth, ourselves, all; and being wholly taken up with God, and absorbed in the Divinity; so that by a simple remembrance that we are with God, and without looking back to reiterate the same reflection, we repose and slumber sweetly in Him, staying upon no image whatsoever, even of our Saviour Himself. For as He, inasmuch as concerns His Humanity, called Himself *The Way*,* so He thereby insinuated that we were not to remain in the way, but to march on to our Way's *end*, which is His Divinity.

How this pure Hope is to be brought about.

2. No marvel, then, if we find in the canons of mystical divines this doctrine:—*That to arrive at the height of Contemplation, we must leave off all sort of meditation, though it be on the life and death of our Lord and Saviour.*† The reason of

The doctrine of mystic divines explained.

For *unless she come to this, she will never attain to any sublime exercise.* Hence St. Chrysostom saith:—Without faith none can receive any knowledge of high matters. And it is like unto him that hath undertaken without a ship to pass over the sea; his arms and legs after a while being tired with swimming, he is presently swallowed up by the waves. In like manner, those who lean upon their own judgment and reason suffer shipwreck before they come to know the Truth.' *Kingdom of God within the Soul*, p. 174.

* John xiv. 6.

† 'The truth is, that for the attaining to contemplation it is not *necessary* (speaking of precise and absolute necessity) that the acts whereof the exercises consist should immediately be directed to the *pure Divinity*, though it cannot be denied but that such are the most perfect and most efficacious, because the most introverting. And,

it is plain: because in all meditation there is ever something which is sensible, to which nature, applying itself, hinders our souls from soaring up to the highest point and quintessence of contemplation, which is, and can be only, a pure, spiritual, and insensible thing. It is true that the consideration of the life and death of our loving Saviour is a most powerful means to mount up to this contemplation of His Divinity, but let us not make that the end which is but the means and way to it.

THE THIRTEENTH MAXIM.

That our Wills must be settled in pure Charity.

That the will must be weaned from the desire of all joy.

1. THIS is done by withdrawing it from all sort of joy proceeding from any natural, supernatural, or moral good. Joy is a certain content which our wills take in something we prize, and this joy is either *active*, when we may leave it, or *passive*, when it is not in our power to quit it. Now, to take joy and content in natural goods, as health, wealth, friends, &c., or in wit, sagacity, prudence, &c., is a plain vanity. To joy in moral goods, as in the exercise of virtue, &c., is to imitate the pagan philosophers, who loved virtue for virtue's sake, and made that their end which is only the means to it. Supernatural

---

therefore, a soul must give over all other addresses, either to the Humanity of our Lord or to any angel or saint, whensoever she is interiorly moved or enabled to actuate immediately towards God Himself, Who is likewise the end and ultimate object of all other speakings and actuations.' *Sancta Sophia*, vol. ii. treat. 3, sect. 3, chap. ii. § 18.

goods are either the gratuitous gifts of God, as the working of miracles; and we must free our wills from any joy proceeding from these prerogatives, since they may be conferred upon reprobates; or they are such goods as have relation to sanctifying grace, as Faith, Hope, &c., and which, if they be not accompanied with perfect Charity and final Perseverance, are nothing worth.

2. We may here take notice how little reason some persons have to be troubled because they have not these extraordinary gifts, since they may be impediments, if ill-used or overmuch adhered to, rather than helps to divine union.* For, says St. Denis, all these things are not God, but only some

None need be troubled at not having extraordinary gifts.

* 'Let it not be supposed that a sister who has great favours is better than the others. Our Lord guides every one as He sees necessary. If she makes good use of these, they will prepare and dispose her for becoming a great servant of God; but sometimes God leads the weakest this way, and so there is nothing herein to approve or condemn; we must look to virtues only, and esteem her the most who serves our Lord with the greatest mortification, humility, and purity of conscience, since she is the most holy, although we can know little for certain here below, until the true Judge shall reward every one according to his merits. Then we shall wonder at seeing how different *His* judgment is from what we are able to understand here below' (St. Teresa, *Interior Castle*, p. 184). And in her *Way of Perfection*, the same saint says:—'It is very important to understand that God does not conduct *all* in the same way; and perhaps she who thinks herself the lowest is the highest in the eyes of God. Because all in this house give themselves to prayer, it does not follow that all must be contemplatives; this is impossible, and it will be a great consolation for her who is not a "contemplative" to know this truth, for God only gives this gift; and since it is not necessary for salvation, nor required for our future reward, let her not think that it is here demanded of her, because without this she is sure to become very perfect, if she does what has been said. It may even be that she has more merit, because it costs her more pains; and our Lord treats her as a valiant person, and keeps in reserve for her all that which she does not enjoy here' (p. 79. See also p. 83).

effects of His favour, ordered by His providence to attract us to His love.

Thus the three powers of our souls, understanding, memory, and will, are to follow these three objects—Faith, Hope, and Charity. Now, our Lord is our loving Master, to Whom we must have continual recourse, and Who, seeing our loving desires and diligent endeavours, will infallibly instruct us in the particular and inexplicable ways of this divine and perfect contemplation.

THE FOURTEENTH MAXIM.

That this Exercise of Recollection and Annihilation is the short and secure Way to divine Union.

Why annihilation is the securest and shortest way to divine Union.

1. For a soul that is truly humbled and annihilated hinders not at all God's holy operation within her, but leaves herself in His hands—not at all relying upon any discursive arguments or ideas, which she has coined in her own mint—as a child in his mother's arms, who corrects it, cherishes it, washes it, and orders it as she pleases. And must not this needs be the shortest, nearest, surest, and most proportionate way to divine Union? For, before God created us, we were either nothing at all, or we were in God's ideal being; and so were God Himself, because *all that is in God is God.* Now, His Divine Majesty gave us our present *being,* and we losing ourselves, because we abused this our being, have no better way to regain ourselves than by *not-being,* that so we may come to *be* that which we are not, by deny-

ing that *being* which we are. O secure annihilation! What can hurt thee who is nothing ?*

* By the following sublime passage, taken from one of the greatest ascetical writers of the seventeenth century, the reader will be possessed of what is meant by total Abnegation, perfect Resignation, spiritual Death, spiritual Nothingness, and Annihilation :—

'Many men know of mortification and abnegation, but few come to the knowledge of their nothingness. And therefore God, as He is our blessed end, and hath His kingdom in our souls, is known by very few. To declare this, it is to be noted that after man had by prevarication lost the happy state and true life wherein God had first placed him, he manifoldly, through inordinate affections, fell upon creatures: first upon his own self, and afterwards upon inferior things without, also upon the gusts of God, yea upon God Himself, in all which he liveth and resteth inordinately, *seeking his own ease and interest*, whereas he ought only to seek God's honour and greater pleasure. Now, all these inordinate assumed lives must thoroughly be mortified and utterly destroyed before we can truly obtain God.

'The first inordinate life is the love which man hath to creatures, which is the grossest, and maketh the soul furthest from God. The second, which he hath to himself, is less gross. The third, which he hath to the gifts of God, is still less; and the fourth is the least gross of all. For by how much the more the adhesion is grosser and the object unseemlier, by so much the more is the soul of necessity estranged from God. The soul cannot rest in creatures that are without her, without she also resteth in herself; and yet she may rest in herself, and not rest in creatures without her. Likewise she cannot rest in herself without she also interiorly resteth in the gusts of God; nor in the gifts of God, without she resteth also in herself, since she desires them for herself and her own use. When she resteth not in the gifts of God (which is seldom), she seeks to rest in God through a natural and experimental certainty. All these lives and restings hinder the spiritual Death and Annihilation, and consequently the true enjoying of God, wholly and totally, as hath been said.

'It is easier to the devout soul to mortify and take away the grosser adhesion than the lesser; for Nature, having nothing else left her, holds herself with all her forces thereunto—like as in the corporal death, where the last separation of the soul from the body is the most difficult and painful, life depending thereon. Hence, when we have mortified and separated the soul from all external creatures, she much more subtilely rests in herself and the gifts of God, and still more subtilely, secretly, closely and lastly in God. Hence, it is necessary to propose unto the soul seeking God certain parts or points whereby she may deliver or free herself from all those lives or loves, and obtain in place

In this annihilation God Himself becomes our

2. If we thus leave ourselves will-less, self-less, being-less, we suddenly become plunged into the unerected Being of God, and living in Him only by Faith, Hope, and Love, our enemy—as

of them this happy Death and Nothing above mentioned. I say, therefore, in brief, that the right way to this Death or Nothing, and consequently to God (which in divers books, after several methods, and in sublime words and senses, are described), consists in an utter and absolute Abnegation of all created things, and a perfect Resignation of oneself out of pure love to God through a naked and an habitual faith. What we understand by these words we will presently declare, and it shall appear by what follows, that the soul is perfectly separated from all creatures, as also from herself, and is consequently wholly *dead* and *annihilated*, as touching affection, to all creatures.

'Through an utter Abnegation, she dieth to all external creatures; through perfect Resignation, to herself; by pure Love, to all the gifts of God; and by naked Faith, to God Himself, as far as seeking herself with any kind of propriety in Him. And so by this perfect Nothing and Death she is recollected, with all her powers to herself, in herself, and at length made fit to be carried above and out of herself into God. By this utter Abnegation of all external created things she becomes recollected to herself: by that perfect Resignation she is yet more simple and uniformly recollected in herself, as also unloosed and unwrought from herself. The pure Love opens to her a way above herself, and converts her right to God, and the naked Faith fasteneth and fixeth her there; and, taking leave of all her senses, the knowledge which therewith she hath that God is in her doth assuage and quiet in her all desires and longings, and holds also the will recollected in herself in a high peace in her hidden interior and innermost spirit, when God is truly present. And when the soul remains there, having in this manner all her forces and powers united and recollected, she obtains all the parts in her (as we will hereafter speak of), and thus at last she is happily elevated to that noble contemplation of God for having then fully freed herself from all impediments mediating or interposing between God and her; and she remains with all her capacities naked and bare, converted to God, Who through His infinite mercy the very same instant doth infuse into her His divine light, endowing and irradiating with the same the clean and pure soul who simply for His love hath put herself into such a poverty and emptiness of all things. And so the spirit, with great simplicity and freedom, is elevated to the happy enjoying of the secret presence of God, to which by her own strength she can in no wise attain.' *The Kingdom of God in the Soul*, pp. 120-125.

has been already said*—finds nothing to lay hold on, because our annihilated souls are nowhere but in God, where they are securely covered and protected under His wings, and Who is obliged, if we may say so, to be our bulwark of defence against all assaults of our enemies.† bulwark of defence.

THE FIFTEENTH MAXIM.

That all sorts of People may safely addict themselves to this holy Exercise of Recollection.

1. It is true that this way of prayer is delicate and slippery for beginners to tread in. Yet, if they will faithfully and strictly observe these few necessary precautions here prescribed, they will find, to their unspeakable comfort, that to be most true in themselves which experience hath proved to be true in others; who, though deeply engaged in worldly vanities and affections, falling seriously, resolutely, courageously, and humbly to divine Contemplation and Recollection, became—after being some time employed in purging their souls from sin, and settling themselves in virtue according to counsel and obedience—quickly, truly, and totally changed, and were conducted, as it were by a nearer cut, without pains and tediousness, to higher perfection than they could have attained in a long time by the ordinary ways of discursive meditation. That the prayer of Recollection infallibly leads souls to high perfection.

* See *Maxim* 10, § 4.

† This state corresponds to St. Teresa's *Seventh Mansion*. See *Interior Castle*, p. 220.

2. For this is most certain, that God denies not His grace to those who do what lies in their own power. Now any one of us, being assisted with God's grace and a good will, may do this:—1. We may purge our souls from sin, by confession, contrition, satisfaction, the means ordained by God and His Church. 2. Resign and give up ourselves, and all that we have, are, and can, to God's Divine Majesty. 3. Adore Him in spirit and truth, and present ourselves before Him as His poor, needy, naked creatures. 4. Abstract our understandings, memories, and wills from all objects and images of creatures, though never so good, high, and holy. 5. Enter into the obscurity of Faith, Hope, and Love, and leave our souls, as it were, sleeping and swallowed up in the abyss of the Divinity. 6. And finally, all we have to do is briefly this:—*We must leave our houses empty, that our Lord and Lover may take full possession;* and then we may assure ourselves that at the very instant in which our dear Lord shall find our hearts vacant, He will enter presently into them, inhabit them, instruct them, and show them how sweet He is to those souls who truly seek Him.*

If we do what lies in our power, God always gives us His grace.

3. Let us but persevere constantly and courageously in this pious practice, and we shall soon perceive our unspeakable profit and progress; and though it seems to ourselves that we perform

Only persevere, and we shall attain divine Union.

* '*The Lord is good to them that hope in Him, to the soul that seeketh Him.*' Lam. iii. 25.

it with much impurity and imperfection, yet our continued endeavours, assisted by God's concurring grace, will speedily raise us up to divine Union.

THE SIXTEENTH MAXIM.

That outward Observances are Helps in the Practice of this Exercise.

1. All external practices, duties, and mortifications, as fastings, disciplines, retirements, vocal devotions, &c. must be directed to further our internal conversation with God, and to help us in the acquisition of solid virtue and divine Union; for else they will but puff us up, and make us proud of nothing, profiting little with much labour.*

All external observances should minister to interior devotion, otherwise are worse than useless.

2. Yet we must be wary of offending against the least ordinance of the Church, order of the House, or disposition of our Superiors; we must be conscientious, careful, and punctual in each ceremony and constitution, omitting nothing on pretence that it is no great matter, nor commanded under sin, or not much conducing to our spiritual advancement; for this is a token of an ignorant, unfaithful, or indiscreet spirit. God's will is as well in little as in great things; and whoso is careless in small matters will soon fail in higher.

We must not offend against the least ordinance or rule.

* 'Quid prodest solitudo corporis, si solitudo defuerit cordis.' S. Gregorii Magni, *Moralium*, lib. xxx. cap. 12.

THE SEVENTEENTH MAXIM.

That Prayer for others is best practised by a general Intention.

We must not lightly promise;

1. We are not lightly to promise the performance of particular prayers for others, either living or dead. This sort of charity hinders, diverts, and dissipates our souls, breeding multiplicity, whereas *one thing only is necessary.*

nor oblige ourselves to pray for particular persons;

2. We must therefore omit all such obligations as may renew old affections, and labour to forget and forsake all, that we may more purely adhere to *One* Who is our *All in all.*

but for all in general,

Wherefore, let this general, virtual, and cordial intention suffice for all cases of this nature. First, that we desire to be partakers of all prayers, sacrifices, and merits of the whole Church Militant and Triumphant, as far as God shall please and we need. Next, that we intend to pray for all—and especially for those who have desired it or to whom we stand in any way indebted—as we do for ourselves.*

unless there be some

3. And this, without any personal reflection, is more profitable to our friends and less prejudicial to

* There lies much deep spiritual wisdom in this counsel. For as the end of prayer is to detach and abstract the soul from all vain thoughts and affections towards creatures, elevate it above itself, and unite it so closely and intimately to the Divinity as to render it totally lost and absorbed therein, and dead and insensible to all things earthly; so it follows that whatsoever creates in the soul multiplicity, excites its fancy, rouses its old affections, or distracts and takes it off from the simple thought and vision of God alone, should be avoided and rejected by those who are aiming at the still, secret, blissful, and naked possession and enjoyment of God found in perfect contemplation.

ourselves: all of which, however, is to be understood only so long as no peculiar promise, occasion, or circumstance induceth a special *obligation* and performance. special reason to the contrary.

THE EIGHTEENTH MAXIM.

That all Virtues are best practised by addicting ourselves to Contemplation, or this internal Exercise of Recollection.

1. THE chief way to practise virtue and prevent temptations, is not by directly and formally reflecting upon them, which imprints images upon the soul and hinders her from attending purely to God in her interior, but by a virtuous and vigorous binding of her will to God; for being thus seriously and sweetly attentive unto Him only, she can by a happy disdain forget and pass through all occurring trials and difficulties with ease, and conduct herself with so much regularity and so discreetly as to content both God and man. All virtues are practised in contemplation;

2. Now, all virtues, as we have said, are practised in a most excellent manner in this holy exercise, and this appears first in Faith, of which we are taught to make a lively act at the very outset of this exercise. And in what way can this virtue be more heroically put into practice than by having our souls lifted up above all sensible objects, all discursive reasonings, all human wisdom? viz. Faith,

3. Hope is here practised; for we lie at God's feet as poor beggars, hoping to obtain His grace in Hope,

order to the performance of His will, and expecting all good from His meet mercy.

4. Here also our love is exercised, because our will Charity, covets nothing but to content our Creator, and rests separated from all that is not Himself for the sole love of Him.

5. Here is the practice of perfect resignation; for Resignation, we wish neither quiet nor disquiet, glory nor infamy, pleasure nor pain, but only the fulfilling of God's will, and a desire to be left in what state He best pleases.

6. Patience must be here necessarily practised with Patience, respect to the crosses and contradictions suggested by sensuality in this afflicting exercise.

7. All sin is here destroyed, which is an aversion Destruction of sin, from our Creator and a conversion to creatures. Here, however, by means of perfect Faith, we remain, as it were, adhering* closely to God, and governed by His inward grace, which fills all outward motions, stifles all concupiscences, and makes us unconscious and forgetful of ourselves and all things created.

8. As for mortification, it is here practised in a Mortification, high degree; for he that tastes the sweets of the spirit soon grows disgusted with all carnal delights. Here the flesh is totally supplanted and the senses quieted; for the eyes see no outward object, the ears attend to no noise, the tongue remains silent, the under-

* A soul is said to 'adhere' to God when it cannot be drawn away from the contemplation of Him without a certain violence.

standing contemns all curiosities, the memory draws a veil over all images, the will is disengaged from willing or not willing anything; finally, here is an entire destruction of all sensuality.

9. Obedience is perfectly practised, because the wings of discourse are clipped and the understanding captivated by Faith. Obedience,

10. Humility can nowhere more appear than when a soul is so annihilated as to trust neither little nor much to herself. O rich nothing! What spiritual mines, what masses of treasure doth a soul find that hath thus happily lost herself in her loving Lord! Humility,

11. Adoration, sacrifice, devotion, and all acts of Religion are here effectually practised. In a word, if we will be perfect, says Thaulerus, we must learn this abstraction, that is, this suspension of discourse, and silencing all the workings of fancy, understanding, memory, will, leave our souls to the absolute guidance of our loving Lord, according to the doctrine here delivered. This is the short and secure way to make all our actions divine and celestial. Adoration and all acts of religion.

§ 1. Some Examples for the Practice of this Divine Way of Prayer.

1. Receiving the Blessed Sacrament, I say to my heavenly guest:—*My God, make me partaker of these sacred mysteries, that my soul may enjoy the effects for which they were by You instituted.* Then being secured by an act of Faith that I have received His body, blood, soul, and divinity, I settle myself in How to communicate;

that holy idleness and abstraction before described, and remain silent and recollected, hearkening what my dear Lord will speak within me.

2. So, when I have taken some point of my Saviour's
how to pray; Passion for the subject of my prayer, I say:—*O my Lord, communicate to my soul what You endured in this mystery, to the end that she may enjoy those effects for which You suffered it.*

3. In like manner, when I go to take my rest, I say:
how to take our rest; —*Silence, my soul, for our God is here present with us and within us;* and in this verity, recollecting myself in Him, I rest all night in prayer,* or at least my Lord takes it as if I did, because my soul covets to continue in the same happy abstraction, recollection, and annihilation during the whole time of sleep.

4. Thus a virtuous, introverted, and recollected soul
and do all things for God's glory. doing what lies in her to rest always in her centre, which is God, may follow and fulfil the counsel of the Apostle, which is, to *pray without ceasing,** and to do all things, even her natural and

* To pray, it is not necessary that the soul should have an actual and conscious attention. The attention due to prayer is either habitual, virtual, or actual. St. Thomas defines these three different degrees of attention thus:—'Habitualis est quædam animi propensio ad attendendum, *qualis etiam in dormientibus referiri potest;* actualis est quando quis actu elicito vult attente orare; virtualis, vero, est qua quis ex virtute prioris attentionis nimirum actualis orationem continuat.' *Summa Theo.* 2. 2, quæst. lxxxiii. art. 13.

It is good for religious to go to bed with an inclination and desire to be early up; for such a desire will cause their sleep to be mixed with some little spiritual solicitude, which will dispose them to wake sooner, rise less unwillingly, and repair to choir more devoutly.

† 1 Thess. v. 17.

necessary actions of eating, drinking, sleeping, &c., for God's glory; and these pure desires and intentions render all of them meritorious.*

§ 2. Some further Advice for the Practice of this pure Prayer.

1. Before we thus recollect ourselves in God, we may make what acts we please; but when once we have entered into it, we are to remain still, quiet, silent, insensible, immovable, as a stock to be fashioned, or as a stone to be carved, according to the heavenly Workman's design. We must leave ourselves entirely to be moved and managed as best pleaseth our divine

The first advice.

* Nothing sets the heart so much at liberty, or so easily enables the soul, after it has been distracted by external occupations, to return again to interior recollection, as to be led in our outward actions by no self-seeking, no disquieting desire, no covetous grasping, and to be swayed by no particular love or bias towards anything; but in all things to consult diligently, deliberately, and calmly what is for the greater glory of God and the common good, peace, and happiness of those committed to our care; and after having prudently and maturely decided what is the best course, then to carry it through with all possible strength and firmness, irrespective of any labour or pain which it may cost. This pure intention, aiming only at God, leads a man to seek nothing, and lifts him up above all things, in such a manner that he is able to see, consider, and weigh whatsoever is said or done against himself or others, or, on the other hand, whatsoever tends to his or their honour and commendation, without it affecting or agitating him. Men will wonder at his unalterable wisdom, meekness, calmness, and strength. He remains peaceful and unruffled in the midst of slander and abuse. He is silent under injuries, neither does he pour himself out upon creatures; for being informed and transformed by divine love, he does not permit such things to trouble him, but passes above them to the contemplation of God, in Whom he rests and rejoices, with Whom he lovingly converses, in Whose light he sees, judges, and acts sweetly and mightily, freed from the slightest tinge of human passion, and exceedingly comforted and fortified against all tribulation.

Master, Who both knows what are our necessities, and how and when to supply them.

The second advice. 2. We must take special notice, that as all arts have their proper terms, so this sacred science of Mystical Divinity hath its peculiar phrases and expressions. Divine matters may not be handled according to the manner and method of school subtleties, but are to be represented only with simplicity, piety, and a holy liberty of words, which Contemplatives make use of without metaphysical questions and arguments.

In what sense mystical writers are to be understood. 3. When, therefore, we find in S. Bonaventure, Eschius, Thaulerus, Rusbrochius, Blosius, and others :—That a soul divinely and intimately united to God doth clearly see and experience what she obscurely believed by Faith; we are not to infer that she therefore loseth her faith in this life; for this mystical experience takes not away our faith, but fortifies, comforts, and clears it.

So, when it is usually said by these spiritual writers: —That such a degree of contemplation, of virtue, or of pure love is the very summit of perfection; it is not meant that a soul which is ascended thither can climb no higher in this her exile; for that highest degree of perfection hath a latitude of many degrees of grace, whereby a soul may still increase in sanctity, and ascend each moment to a nearer vicinity with her Creator.

When, likewise, we meet with this doctrine :—A soul arrived at Union and Transformation carries herself passively, she acts not, but suffers; God doth all within her; we are to understand that such a soul doth very little or nothing in comparison to what she did in her former discursive exercises, because she here, in this state, finds all done in an instant, and therefore leaves those painful employments to repose sweetly in a kind of holy idleness of Contemplation and Union with God, which pacifies all her senses, silences all discursiveness, and lulls all her powers asleep with His charming love and ravishing presence. Nevertheless, she remains still here, actually loving and looking on her Lord, and consequently is not totally idle, but is coöperating with His grace. In this sense, St. Denis* said: —The soul of blessed Hierotheus was raised to such a union with God, that it suffered more than it acted, because in this passive contemplation the soul follows not her accustomed operations. Thus we see our understanding works not so much when it receives its nourishment from a higher knowledge as when it gets it by constrained and laborious application; nor our will in like manner, which commonly follows the motives proposed by the understanding, to which it is united.

4. That which is most important in this exercise of Recollection is the practice of Faith, Hope, and Charity. For, by the act of Faith all our knowledge is annihilated;† by the act of Hope all thought of our

The third advice.

* *De Divinis Nominibus*, cap. iii.

† That is, the soul is lifted up so high into the Divinity by transcendent contemplation, and the eye of faith is illuminated so brightly by the divine rays which shine in upon it, that all knowledge acquired

worth is cast out by denying our own strength, and relying merely on God's assistance; by the act of Charity all our wills and affections, which are not God, in God, and for God, are abandoned: so that by these three acts the whole man is drowned, suppressed, stifled; and consequently our enemy the Devil finds nothing at all to lay hold on, nor any way open for his entrance into our annihilated hearts, but is constrained to remain always foiled and ashamed of his ineffectual efforts.

The fourth advice—for beginners.

5. Beginners in this exercise must vigorously apply themselves unto it for some time, till by use and experience they acquire a habit of Recollection. They must therefore, in the first place, carefully cleanse their interior from all objects whatsoever, and then lock themselves up with God in this inward retreat. For as in vain we shut our doors and windows, if the thief be already hid in our house, so the closing of our senses from exterior objects helps us little or nothing, if in our interior there lurks anything which is not God.

The fifth advice—of

6. In all our vocal and mental devotions our chief aim must be Attention to God. There are three

by human art and industry appears to the illuminated understanding of the soul darkness and ignorance, becoming lost and as it were 'annihilated' in the ineffable brilliancy of this divine illumination. Into such a state St. Paul was rapt when he was caught up into Paradise, and heard secret words, which it is not granted to man to utter (2 Cor. xii. 14): as also our most glorious Father St. Benedict, who, being lifted up out of himself in prayer, beheld, as St. Gregory testifies (2 *Dialog.* c. xlv.), the whole world under one ray of the sun.

forms of Attention. 1. To the words, which is good. 2. To the sense, which is better. 3. To God, Who is the only end of all our actions—which is best of all.* Let our thoughts, therefore, be taken off from all created objects, though never so good, and fixed steadfastly upon the uncreated and essential goodness. This is the main thing which we must aspire to during the whole course of our life, not only in our prayers, but in all our practices:—To be more attentive to our Lord and Love than to the action we have in hand. This is the philosophy of perfect lovers, to live more truly where they love than where they breathe.

attention to God.

7. It is not here meant by the preceding doctrine that a soul should not meditate at all upon the subject or theme of her prayer, nor first master it well by attentively considering it. No; this is not discouraged, but counselled. Only, we add, that as soon as affections are sufficiently kindled, and that our inflamed souls are in a fit state, and disposed to put themselves into the aforesaid Abstraction, Recollection, and Contemplation, they straightway embrace it, and leave off all those methods and discourses† which are fit for schools and sermons, but not for Prayer and Contemplation.

The sixth advice—that from Meditation we must rise to Contemplation.

It sufficeth us, therefore, to remember the mystery,

* 'Triplex est attentio, quæ orationi vocali potest adhiberi; una quidem, qua attenditur ad verba, ne aliquis in eis erret; secunda, qua attenditur ad sensum verborum; tertia, qua attenditur ad finem orationis, scilicet ad Deum, et ad rem pro qua oratur.' *Sum. Theolog.* 2. 2, q. lxxxviii. art. 13.

† See *Maxim* 7.

apprehend it thoroughly, imprint it deeply in our hearts, and then observe the prescribed order. For, when one hath sufficiently heard and understood what can be said for his good, he needs neither hear nor speak more of it, but presently fall to the practice. In this case, to hearken after new things seems more tending to satisfy curiosity than to the increase of inward virtue; as he that eats before he hath digested his former meals nourisheth bad humours, but nothing betters his own bodily strength.

The seventh advice—that we must harbour no objects or images.

8. When, therefore, distinct notions, forms, or images intrude themselves into our memories, let us not harbour or entertain them, but return amorously to our Lord present within us, and think no more of such particulars than is absolutely necessary for the knowledge and performance of our duties. The best way, then, to increase our inward strength of spirit is to work courageously, and suffer patiently in silence and solitude, forgetting all creatures, unknowing all objects, transcending all human events and accidents. What if the whole world perished, and the frame of heaven and earth be dissolved? *What is it to thee?** Follow thou thy Lord and Love. For, indeed, he that hath his mind diverted and distracted with such fancies in prayer is little attentive to God's presence.

The eighth ad-

9. As concerning our Understanding and Will, we are to take notice that when the Understanding

* John xxi. 22.

proposeth God to the Will as just, wise, powerful, or under any particular attribute, the Will is elevated by that sight alone, and so that act of love is limited, transcribed, and less perfect than if God were proposed in a more eminent way, as the Supreme Being, surpassing infinitely all that can fall within the range of human conceptions in this life. Though, therefore, the Understanding may and can propose some actual and particular conception of God to the Will, yet it is far better and of higher perfection to do it in general, confusedly, and in a negative manner; for, as St. Gregory the Great says:—'Our truest knowledge of God is to know that we can fully know nothing of Him.'* This is to know by *ignorance*, and it is signified by Elias covering his eyes with his cloak when God passed before him, because all our knowledge is disproportionate to God, and therefore we must shut our eyes totally, if we will contemplate Him perfectly.

vice—how God is to be proposed to our understanding in an eminent and negative way.

O holy ignorance! What peasant is so simple, what soul endowed with ordinary capacity is so senseless, as not to conceive and comprehend the easy art of this excellent manner of prayer? for, having been admitted to faith, and adorned with the gifts of the Holy Ghost in baptism, she hath all that is required to make her capable of this Contemplation. We deny not that she

* 'Tunc ergo verum est quod de Deo cognoscimus, cum plene nos aliquid de illo cognoscere non posse sentimus.' S. Gregorii Magni, *Moralium*, lib. v. cap. 36.

stands in need of God's special assistance to elevate her to this height; for this maxim is always presupposed:—That God concurs with human acts as the First Cause, and to supernatural acts as the Author of grace. As for Passive or Infused Contemplation, as it is altogether supernatural, so is it totally God's work; and this we possess when we cannot at all meditate, and yet persevere in this holy, amorous, and *negotiative idleness.**

The ninth advice—that we take and make use of what is most conducive to our spiritual advancement.

10. If what is here set down for the practice of this prayer seems intricate or tedious to any one, let such a soul make choice of what she conceives most expedient for her comfort, and leave the rest. For it is not intended that she should be tied to this or that way, but only that she should be convinced and confirmed in this truth:—That to behold God with a simple understanding (which is nothing else than *Active* Contemplation) is more pleasing to Him and profitable to herself than to seek after Him by the sublimest discourses.

* In this sublime Contemplation 'there remains no middle thing or impediment betwixt Jesus and the soul, save bodily life alone. And then is the soul said to enjoy spiritual rest. . . . This restful labour is very far from carnal idleness and from blind security. It is full of spiritual work; and it is merely called rest, because grace freeth the soul from the heavy yoke of carnal love, and maketh it strong, and free through the gift of spiritual love to work gladly, softly, and delectably in all things to which grace moveth it to work in. And on this account it is called a *holy idleness* and a most *busy rest;* for it is indeed a rest, by reason of the stillness of the cries of fleshly desires and unclean thoughts. This stillness is made by the inspiration of the Holy Ghost through the sight of Jesus.' Hilton's *Scale of Perfection*, p. 297.

11. Retire, therefore, O contemplative souls, from all sensible and intelligible objects, and recollect, abstract, annihilate, and lose yourself in God; for *there*, even in the most refined conceptions, your enemy may find ground to lay his snares; but *here*, you are in sanctuary and safety, where he can never reach or touch you. Here, and here only — in this silence from all discourses, in this solitude from all creatures, in this idleness from all action, in this retreat into the Divine Bosom, in this resignation and conformity to God's will—you may taste His sweetness in its proper source; here, and here only, are full and overflowing measures of delight. Created pleasures scarcely reach the soul before they are consumed in the senses, and therefore can never quench our inward thirst after God.* He alone is able to content and quiet us, Who is our first beginning and our last end.† And whosoever dives into this truth will make higher account of one crumb of this contemplation than of all earthly crowns and kingdoms.

An exhortation to Contemplation.

THE NINETEENTH MAXIM.

That corporal Austerities must always be subject to Obedience.

1. Austerities are sometimes *necessary*, sometimes *obligatory*, and sometimes *dangerous*.

Austerities are threefold: either,

---

* 'Quicquid homini offeratur, non potest ejus desiderium satiare? cum ille capax sit infiniti boni, et res omnes creatæ certis terminis circumscribantur.' Bellarmini, *de Ascensione Mentis in Deum*, grad. quart. cap. iii.

† Apocalypse i. 8.

By necessary austerities are meant the restraint of 1. Necessary; our senses, tongues, conversation, self-will; and in this sort of mortification there is no danger of excess.

Those austerities which are commanded, must be 2. Obligatory; preferred before those which are voluntary.

Corporal austerities are the most dangerous and 3. Or dangerous. least profitable when performed by order of our own will, without entire submission to our superiors' direction; for these are more worthy of reprehension than of praise.*

2. But the chief austerity of life consists in the The chief austerity is continual interior Recollection. continual application of ourselves to interior Recollection, Introversion, and Contemplation. For here we perpetually chain up our thoughts, yoke all our senses, reform our appetites, correct the disorders of our passions, regulate our actions, shackle our wills, and admit nothing into our souls which may trouble or retard them from totally tending to their Lord and Lover; so that, in the opinion of all spiritual men, this is the most meritorious way of doing penance. For what is this continual prayer but an absolute bondage of the whole inward and outward man, since we may not taste, touch, will, or do anything we have a mind

* Hence this saying of the ancient Fathers of the desert:—'Si videris juvenem voluntate sua ascendentem in cœlum, tene pedem ejus, et projice in terram; quia non ita expediet ei,'—If you should see a young man going up to heaven by his own will, seize him by the leg, and pull him down to the earth again; because this is not expedient for him. *Verba Seniorum*, lib. v. cap. x. no. 3.

to? And though this blessed slavery may bring us in time to a heavenly tranquillity of life, yet the due and daily practice of this denial and death of the will doth so emaciate our truly mortified bodies, that they rather need sometimes to be nursed than to be any further punished.

THE TWENTIETH MAXIM.

That Contemplatives must always have the Seven Truths which concern the Divine Nature, and whereon all Contemplation is grounded, either habitually or formally, in their memories.

1. THAT God is an Eternal Being: He hath ever been, and ever will be, and it is impossible for Him to be otherwise. 1. God is an Eternal;

2. That God is an Immense Being: He so fills and penetrate all things and all places, that His Being bears them, and not they Him, Who is an Infinite Fulness. 2. Immense;

3. That God is a Simple Being: He is All in all creatures, All without them, and All in each part of them; because having in Himself no parts by reason of His infinite simplicity, He must necessarily be with all His perfection wheresoever He is. 3. Simple;

4. That God is an Unchangeable Being: He can neither change in respect of place, because He is everywhere; nor in respect of time, for He is Eternal; nor in what concerns Himself, because He is infinitely Perfect; and therefore there is in Him nothing superfluous to reject, nor defective to amend. 4. Unchangeable;

5. Independent;

5. That God is an Independent Being: all things depend on Him, live in Him, are preserved by Him; and all being is ordained to the glory of His bounty, whence they had their beginning.

6. All sufficient;

6. That God is an All-sufficient Being: He remedies all that is amiss, supplies all that is wanting, communicates all that is good, satisfies all desires, without the least diminution of His own infinite perfections.

7. Incomprehensible Being.

7. That God is an Incomprehensible Being: no created understanding can comprehend what God is; all our knowledge is too shallow and limited to reach His heights, yet our spirits are dilated by the light of Faith; and though our Creator may not be comprehended by the creature, yet He may be known by whom He pleaseth, when He pleaseth, and as much as He pleaseth.

These truths, and other infinite perfections of God, give light to our dark and weak understandings, in order to the knowledge of His Sovereign Essence.

THE TWENTY-FIRST MAXIM.

That ejaculatory Prayers best dispose the Soul for Contemplation.

Distracted souls should especially make use of ejaculations;

1. If a soul finds great difficulty in disengaging herself from worldly imaginations, and to apply herself to God by Recollection, let her content herself in breathing forth heartily these or the like short words:—'O my God, when shall I love You?

when shall I embrace You?' Let her repeat them affectionately and perseverantly, and she shall sooner be inflamed with divine love than by the subtle consideration of the greatest secrets of heaven; for it is the will which unites us to God, not the understanding.

2. These acts of the will* are the spiritual wings of the soul to lift her up and unite her to her Beloved: they are short, sharp, and swift darts and desires, shot by our burning hearts, and reaching heaven in an instant.† Our forefathers, the saints, frequently used them, and most highly prized them;‡ for being short, they troubled not the memory; being fervent, they rouse our dulness and dryness to

which are the spiritual wings of the soul,

* Acts differ from aspirations. Acts are affections of the will, produced without any distinct motive represented to the understanding, and only flowing after some effort of the soul. Aspirations are affections of the will, occasioned by a divinely-illuminated understanding, and flowing freely and purely from an internal impulse of the Holy Spirit. All contemplative prayer may be reduced to these two above-mentioned exercises. The former is called imperfect contemplation; the latter, perfect contemplation: and in proportion as the purity and promptitude of these aspirations are great, so the contemplation is said to be more or less perfect and sublime.

† 'These short prayers are called *Aspirations*, because by them we breathe unto God, and through them God animates our efforts; for whilst we aspire to God we breathe nothing but God, and the heat of charity is sustained through these aspirations no less truly than the life of the body is by the air we breathe. They are also called *anagogical*, that is, uplifting motions, because by them we are drawn from earthly things and raised up to supernal things, and brought at length to a blessed union with God. They are also sometimes called *ejaculations*, because, like swiftly-flying darts (jacula) and arrows, they are aimed at the Sacred Heart as at their mark, and from It draw forth heavenly favours. Finally, they are called *affective prayers*, because they are the affections of the heart and the desires and purposes of the will; for an Aspiration is nothing else, as Gelenius explains, than a swift affection towards God as the Suprems Good.' Bona, *Via Compend. ad Deum*, cap. vi.

‡ See following *note*.

affection and devotion; being frequent, they still renew our attention to God's presence, and put us perpetually in mind of our duties.

and may be elicited on all occasions.

3. The method of putting into practice this exercise is, to take occasion from all objects, actions, and accidents to pray and praise God. Do we eat; let us give God thanks. Do we walk abroad; let us praise Him Who produced all things which we behold from the abyss of nothing. Do we look up into the beauty of the heavens; let us admire the Creator in His creatures. Have we sinned, or are we tempted; let us lift up our hearts to God, and say:—'O Lord, permit me not to fall and offend Thee. To die, alas! I am content, when Thou disposest; but to sin, O preserve me from this disaster!' Other times let us burst forth into aspirations of love, as:—'My Beloved for me, and I for Him.' Of resignation, as:—'Not my will, O Lord, but Thine be done. What do I desire in heaven or on earth but Thee, O my God?' Of pure intention, as:—'It is for You, O my God, that I fast; it is for Your sake that I obey my superior; it is to please You that I study, work, pray, &c. Your will, O Lord, is mine; Your content is mine; I have no other Ay or No but as You will, or will not; all my pleasure is only to please You.'

Those ejaculations are the best which our own hearts

4. This rule is to be observed:—That, though all ejaculatory prayers are good, yet those are best, most profitable, and powerful, which our hearts, moved by God, conceive of themselves; though

they be expressed in words never so plain and simple. Nor is there any need of much variety of aspirations; for one only word, being often and amorously repeated, may serve for many days, when our souls find therein sweetness and profit, and speak unto Him Whom they look upon as present with their eyes of faith.* have conceived.

* St. Francis of Assisi used to spend whole nights in repeating only these words:—*Deus meus et omnia!*—My God and my all! Blessed Didacus Martinez, the Apostle of Peru, used sometimes to say six hundred times during the day this single prayer:—*Deo gratias!* and he used to exhort others to do the same, declaring that there was no shorter prayer, nor one more pleasing to God. Cassian was continually repeating these words:—*Deus in adjutorium meum intende;* and St. Marcillo, that verse of the Psalmist:—*In corde meo absconde eloquia tua, ut non peccem tibi.* Judith, when about to cut off the head of Holofernes, gathered up her soul in these words:—*Confirma me, Domine Deus, in hac hora.*' St. Mary Magdalen, on recognising her Lord after the resurrection, poured forth her burning soul in one word: —*Rabboni!* (John xx. 16.)

The author of the *Divine Cloud* makes the following quaint and striking remarks on the prayers of Aspiration:—'A man or woman being made afraid of some sudden chance of fire, or of the killing of a man, or of any other vehement accident, such as is wont forthwith and suddenly to be in the height of the spirit, is driven, by reason of the suddenness of the thing, and of his necessity, to cry or to pray for help. And how doth he cry? Forsooth, not in many words, nor yet in one word of two syllables. And why? Because he thinketh it overlong to tarry about the declaration of his necessity and of the agony of his spirit; and therefore he bursteth out vehemently with a great screech, and crieth out with some one word, and that of one syllable, as is this word "Fire!" or else this word "Help!" or such-like. Now, like as this little word "Fire!" pierceth the ears of the hearers sooner, and stirreth their affection more effectually, than a longer discourse doth, even so doth a short word of one syllable sound in the ears of the Almighty God, not only when it is spoken, but also when it is inwardly meant in the deepness of the spirit; which depth also is called the height of the spirit; for in spiritual matters all is one, height and depth, length and breadth. Such a short word, I say, so meant, doth sooner enter, and pierceth further in the ears of Almighty God, than doth a long Psalter unmindfully mumbled in the teeth. And therefore it is written, that a short prayer pierceth the Heavens' (*The Cloud of Knowing and Unknowing*, pp. 121-122). Hence

This exercise is most easy and efficacious.

5. This exercise is most easy and most efficacious; and they who shall piously persevere in it shall soon find their hearts inflamed with the love of God, and changed from all worldly affections.

THE TWENTY-SECOND MAXIM.

That the Presence of God is the great Exercise of Contemplatives, and the shortest Way to Divine Union.

Why it is called the great Exercise;

1. THIS exercise is called great, because God Himself taught it in the infancy of the world to His faithful servant Abraham:—I am thy God, saith He, and thy protector; walk in My presence, and thou shalt be perfect.*

and the shortest way to Union.

2. It is called the shortest way to divine Union, because it is a summary of all the exercises of prayer, which alone will conduct our souls to the hidden treasure of perfection, and replenish them with those celestial riches which our loving Lord is wont to communicate to His dearest friends in this life.

Father Baker declares that the simpler and plainer the acts of the will are, the more profitable and efficacious are they in uniting the soul to God. And for this reason he recommends that such *Soliloquies* as those of St. Augustine, or such ejaculations as are found in St. Bernard and St. Teresa, should be confined to times of spiritual reading, and not made use of in hours of Recollection, 'because the pleasingness and exquisiteness of the expression gives too much exercise, and contentment to the fancy, and by that means distracts and enfeebles the actuation of the will.' But then he adds, with true Benedictine liberty of spirit, 'yet if souls do find their profit more by the use of them, let them in God's name make choice of such.' *Sancta Sophia*, vol. ii. treat. 3, § 3, chap. i.

* '*I am the Almighty God: walk before Me, and be perfect.*' Gen. xvii. 1.

3. God is present in several manners, according to our understanding:— The various ways in which God is present in His creatures.

a. He is everywhere present by His essence; which being infinite, cannot be contained within the limits of any place.

b. He is everywhere present by His power; He moves the heavenly orbs, fixes the earth, governs all His creatures, &c.

c. He is particularly present in heaven, by the manifestation of His glory.

d. He is specially present in holy places, by grace, benediction, and readiness to hear their petitions, bless their persons, and accept their sacrifices of praise, who shall there meet together to present them.

e. He is especially present in the hearts of His holy people, by the inhabitation of His Holy Spirit.

f. He is especially present in the consciences of all men, where He sits as witness and judge of all their actions, good and bad.

4. For the practice of this exercise of God's presence we may help our thoughts with these seven similitudes, stirring up in our souls an ardent desire to feel the like effects of His all-present Majesty. Seven similes for the practice of the presence of God.

I. How the soul is in the body; all in the whole, and all in every part of it, moving, animating, informing all; giving it life, beauty, &c.

II. How the meat we eat is digested and changed into our substance.

III. How a little worm lying in the warm sunshine is environed about with its beams, made bright, hot, and as it were burned and inflamed.

IV. How a black coal amidst a great fire is ignited, all on fire, and well-nigh all fire.

V. How a little piece of paper is saturated through with oil falling on it, which by degrees spreads itself out all over, that the whole seems rather oil than paper.

VI. How a small quantity of water in a vessel of wine is swallowed up, lost, changed, annihilated, and turned into wine.

VII. How a sponge in the midst of the ocean is all compassed within and without, absorbed, imbued, possessed, and as it were inebriated with water.

The effects that the presence of God works in our lives.

5. O that we could always have this actual faith and thought, that God stands a visible witness and judge of all our doings; that if we go forth, He spies us; if we go in, He sees us; if we light the candle, He observes us; and when we put it out, He also marks us. Should we not, then, behave ourselves as becomes so holy a presence? Should we not be very impious and impudent to give up our reins to sin and sensuality?

O that we would always remember and weigh this stirring truth!—That God is the great Eye of the world, watching over our actions; an ever-open Ear, to hear all our words; and an unwearied Arm, to crush sinners into ruin. How speedily would sin then cease amongst us! How soon should we obtain an habitual fear and reverence of God! What greater inducement can we have to walk without blame than to consider that we act before that Judge Who is infallible in His sentence, all-knowing in His information, severe in His wrath, and powerful to inflict punishment?

This perpetual eyeing of God is properly a building to Him a chapel in our hearts, into which we may securely and sweetly retire in the midst of all worldly varieties.* This is to walk with God, as Enoch did,† and to be in continual conversation with the Divinity.

A higher way to practise the presence of God.

6. A more sublime way to practise the presence of God is to look always upon Him without any discourse, by a simple act of lively faith; not to question how or in what manner He is present, nor to fix our eyes upon His inaccessible splendours, because as yet they are only nigh unto us; we are but travellers, and we must expect until the bright day of eternity shine upon us and show Him unto us as He is in Himself. We must not think here to *behold* Him, but be content to *believe* Him present with us and within us, and that we live, move, and have our being in and by Him.

---

* It was the practice of St. Catherine of Sienna, as blessed Raymond, her biographer, records, to build as it were a little chamber within her own heart, into which she could retire and dwell with God. O happy chamber, in which the soul, freed from the noise and tumult of creatures, listens to the whisperings of the Creator, and enjoys in tranquillity His sweet communings! Enter thou, my soul, into the joy of this rest!

† '*And all the days of Henoch were three hundred and sixty-five years. And he walked with God, and was seen no more, because God took him.*' Gen. v. 23, 24.

In this manner of practising God's presence, it is not needful to form any conception or representation of God; as that He is here by us, or in any special place, or in such a form or figure: for we speak here of the presence of God *as He is*, which excludes all these imaginations; and therefore it sufficeth to behold Him by faith, simply believing that He is here and in all places, that He fills the whole universe, and each corner and creature therein contained, and that He is more intimately within us than we are with ourselves.*

THE TWENTY-THIRD MAXIM.

That Humiliation is a Token of God's Love

In what spirit humiliation is to be received.

1. When any occasion is offered us of humiliation, abjection, or mortification, let us not examine how, whence, or from whom it comes, but joyfully accept it, embrace it, and kiss it, as a rich

---

* So also St. Augustine:—'Tu autem eras interior intimo meo, et superior summo meo.' *Confes.* lib. iii. cap. vi. And Cardinal Bona teaches the same thing:—'Si Deus est in omnibus rebus, ut fides docet, proculdubio etiam in nobis est, *magis intimus nobis quam anima corpori*, qua de causa a Platonicis *Anima mundi* dicitur; non quasi pars et forma ipsius, sed tanquam perfectissima causa, tribuens omnibus esse et operari.' Then continuing, he warns the reader that it is always safer to seek and behold God within himself than in creatures outside of himself, since the grace and beauty of external things often so occupy and ravish the soul, that it gets detained and satisfied in these things instead of pushing forward and resting in the Creator Who dwells within them. Of this St. Augustine complained when he said that he had sought God outside of himself, when he should have looked for Him within himself—'Mecum eras, et tecum non eram' (See *Via Compendii ad Deum*, cap. vii.). He that will enjoy God *within* must first forsake and forget all such things as are *without*.

relic and royal token of God's great love and favour towards us. Let us force our sensuality to swallow it down and digest it; for though it be bitter, it will purge and perfect our spirits.

THE TWENTY-FOURTH MAXIM.

That Humility is the solid Groundwork of all Spirituality.

Christ's lesson is humility.

1. WE are to engrave this necessary lesson, not only upon our oratory and in all our books, but upon the very doors of our hearts and in the depth of our souls:—*Learn of Me, because I am meek and humble of heart, and you shall find rest to your souls.** O sweet Saviour, O meek and merciful Lamb of God, teach me this lesson, which I stand in such need of. O that I could perfectly practise it! How purely and peaceably then should I both live and die!† Meek and humble spirits converse together like mourning turtles, like innocent lambs, and like cor-

---

* Matt. xi. 29.

† 'Be well assured that he who hath in his desire and in his endeavour no care for any other thing save humility and charity, and who is always crying to God that he may possess these virtues, shall, through such desire and consequent labour, profit and increase not only with respect to these two virtues, but to all other whatsoever together with them, such as chastity, temperance, and the rest, although he pays little attention to these in comparison with the others, namely, humility and charity. Yea, he will profit more in one year than he would without this desire and labour in seven years, though he should strive against gluttony, lust, and other such bodily vices continually, and beat himself with scourges every day from morning even until evening. Set thyself, therefore, about humility and charity, and though thou usest all thy diligence and industry to come by them, yet wilt thou have enough to do to get them. And if thou canst but get them, they will direct thee quietly and secretly.' Hilton's *Scale of Perfection*, p. 127.

poreal angels, turning the blessed family where they live into an earthly paradise.

Three degrees to be observed in the external practice of humility;

2. In the external practice of this virtue we are to observe chiefly these three degrees :—*Firstly*, to forbear, forego, deny, and submit our own judgments heartily, humbly, and really, not only to our superiors, but also to all others, casting ourselves at their feet, to be trodden on as dust and dirt ; and this as near as may be for God's sake.

Seeondly, not to care what others say or think of us, which point, with that other of not meddling with what concerns us not, will soon bring us unspeakable peace and purity, thinking always with ourselves : 'What is that to thee? Follow thou thy Saviour.'

Thirdly, to get a habit of patience, condescension, yielding, and being silent in all occurrences and contradictions.

and three in its internal practice.

2. In the internal practice of humility we are also to observe these three degrees :

Firstly, to confess and acknowledge ourselves more wretched and wicked, impure and imperfect, ungrateful and unworthy of all grace and favour, than any soul created.*

* This we may do sincerely and easily by weighing the following considerations, presented us by the blessed Abbot Blosius :—'If you consider that those who to-day are so bad, to-morrow may be more perfect than yourself, and that if they had received the gifts that are granted you from above, they could lead a more holy life than yourself, and that you would sin more grievously than they, if you were not prevented by a more abundant grace ; I say, if you consider these things, you will easily observe how fit it were that you should prefer every sinner to yourself.' *Mirror for Monks.*

Secondly, to be glad that others treat us for such as we really take ourselves to be, and repute us forlorn and forsaken creatures, unworthy of all company and comfort.

Thirdly, to die utterly to ourselves, and be totally mortified in our appetites and desires, renouncing absolutely all dominion and self-seeking. These short words contain infinite perfection. And to move us powerfully to the prosecution of this virtue we may thus question ourselves.

3. *First*. Do not all things humble themselves to serve me, both in heaven and earth—the Saints to pity me, the Angels to protect me, the Mother of God to remember me, the Son of God to redeem me, and God Himself to remain with me, reign within me, comfort me in my prayers, feed me in communion, relieve me in tribulation?

Motives to humility.

Second. O strange humility of my Saviour! Not only to descend unto, but into, a wicked worm; not only to eat with a sinner, but to be eaten by a sinner. O strange pride in me, to see the Lord of heaven and earth so humbled in His Incarnation, Passion, Communion, and yet to see a beggar so proud, a sinner so lofty-minded, and dust and ashes, have such difficulty to stoop!

Third. Upon earth, do not all things serve me for body or soul; some to nourish me, some to clothe me, others to cure me, others to correct me, others to comfort and instruct me? Even my betters, superiors, and confessors must humble themselves to me, because my pride will not bend to them. All creatures must be subject to me, and I will not be subject to my Creator. Alas, what mean I? When shall I begin? O secure and sweet humility, when shall I practise thee?

Fourth. Doth not all the world, all that I am and have—my body, my soul, my actions, my sufferings, my sins—furnish me with sufficient arguments of humility? What was I from eternity? What am I? What shall I be? What have I that I have not received? What have I received that I have not abused?

Fifth. Upon whom doth the Holy Ghost promise to rest but on humble and quiet souls?* Stoop, O dust and ashes! O amiable humility, how necessary art thou for me, how pleasing to God and man! With what comfort and quiet dost thou enrich thy possessor! O heaven upon earth! What do I not get by humility! What do I lose by pride and presumption!

THE TWENTY-FIFTH MAXIM.

That Silence and Solitude are our Heaven upon Earth.

How these two

1. THESE are the proper instruments of Contemplation,† whereby our souls sit silently and soli-

* '*To whom shall I have respect, but to him that is poor and little and of a contrite spirit, and that trembleth at my words?*' Isaias lxvi. Also: —'Quies est apud Te valde, et vita imperturbabilis.' *S. August. Confessiones*, lib. i. cap. x.

† Such also is the teaching of St. Thomas, who speaks of solitude as an instrument of perfection—'solitudo est instrumentum perfectionis'—

tarily* lifted up above themselves, by transcending all things created and uniting themselves to their Creator. instruments of contemplation are to be observed.

We must observe them diligently, discreetly, and devoutly; not out of a sullen or melancholy humour, nor in a disdainful and offensive manner, nor out of pride and singularity, nor to avoid an occasion of mortification, nor to escape the company of such as we brook not and have an aversion to; but with an internal cheerfulness, and in order to converse with God in spiritual joy and fervour. And the ordinary method of practising them may be reduced to these four ways:—

First. To retire and observe strictly, at certain fixed times every day, that silence which, in proportion as our calling allows of it, we have resolved upon.

Secondly. To avoid various unnecessary and im-

and as belonging to the Contemplative life rather than to the Active—solitudo non est instrumentum congruum actioni sed contemplationi, nisi fortè ad tempus. He who leads it should stand in need of no external solace, but find sufficient support in himself alone—solitarium debet esse sibi per se sufficiens—for the eremitical life is not the life of an ordinary contemplative, but of a perfect one—solitudo competit contemplanti qui jam ad perfectum pervenit. Hence it would be the height of presumption in a religious to attempt to lead a life of this kind without having first attained to a signal degree of perfection or received a special call from God. This St. Benedict indicates in his holy rule (cap. i.). And St. Athanasius tells us in his Life of St. Anthony that this saint, on hearing the words:—*If thou wilt be perfect, go sell all that thou hast, and give to the poor*, immediately obeyed the call; but that it was only after he had made great advancement in perfection that he left the society of men and became a hermit. So far beyond the natural powers of man is the eremitical life, that he who leads it must either be sunk on a level with the brute, or lifted above the heavens into God—'Ille qui aliis non communicat, est bestia aut Deus.' Vide *Sum. Theol.* 2. 2, q. 188, art. 8.

* '*He shall sit solitary and hold his peace.*' Lam. iii. 28. Jod.

proper occasions and times for speaking, extroversions, negotiations, companies, curiosities.

Thirdly. To speak modestly and moderately in time of speaking.

Fourthly. To yield easily to others, and not contest in words, for all consists in denying and humbling ourselves.

In Contemplation there is a threefold silence.

2. Now, in Contemplation there are three sorts of silence :—

I. When all fancies, imaginations, and images cease in the soul, so that she is silent as to any created object, desiring no worldly thing, but driving from her all that is not entirely God, to Whom only she is silently, joyfully, and quietly attentive.

II. When in this great calm she sits with *Mary* at her Lord's feet, in a certain spiritual idleness, as if saying :—*I will hear what the Lord God will speak in me ;** to whom He answers :—*Hearken, O daughter, and see, and incline thy ear, and forget thy people and thy Father's house.*†

III. When she transforms herself all into God, her will tasting His sweetness, and she slumbering in His bosom in absolute silence, desiring nothing more, because fully satisfied.

So that there is a threefold silence :—1. When no creature talks to us, as having no such objects in our understandings and memories. 2. When we talk not to ourselves, as totally forgetting ourselves, and con-

---

* Ps. lxxxiv. 9. † Ps. xliv. 11.

verting our inward man to God alone with a submissive subjection, climbing above ourselves by that act of faith, whereby our understanding is united immediately to God. 3. When God talks not to us, but leaves us in the enjoyment of this divine sweetness and elevation of ourselves above ourselves. O heavenly silence! This hath been experienced by some, but by none can be adequately explained.

THE TWENTY-SIXTH MAXIM.

That the perfect Love of God and Hatred of Ourselves must be our constant and continual Employment.

1. We cannot love God unless we hate ourselves; and if we would truly know how far we are advanced in this love and hatred, we must weigh first how willingly we can and do submit our judgment in things contrary to our natural inclination; secondly, how quietly we can and do suffer such things as are opposite to our sensuality, as hard usage, pains, confusions, &c.

How to know whether we love God and hate ourselves.

We must not imagine that we have any degree of pure and perfect love until our affections are so totally *transformed* into God* that He freely and fully pos-

* 'There is a threefold transformation by which the soul is transformed into God. For sometimes the soul is transformed into the will of God, at another time along with God, at other times within God and God within her. The first transformation taketh place when the soul striveth to imitate the life of the sorrow-stricken God-Man; because in this is manifested the will of God Himself. The second transformation taketh place when the soul goeth farther and is united with God, and loveth God, not by the will alone, but together with this hath

sesses our spirit, guides it, enlightens it, inflames it, elevates it, how and when He pleaseth; His love being our only light and life, and we desiring only two things in the world—first, to love, see, taste, and enjoy God only; secondly, to be humbled, despised, reviled, rejected, reputed reprobates for His love. O sweet life! O loving Lord Jesus! What heaven, what happiness is this! We may stir up our souls to an ardent love of God by these and the like motives:—

Motives to love God.

2. *First.* What is the object of our love, and Who is the author of all our good? Is it not God only? What have we—nay, what hath He—that He hath not given us merely of love and for love, thereby to woo, to win, to wed our loves, our souls, our spirits to Himself?

Second. Who has created, redeemed, converted, called, and conserved us until this present? What hath He not done and endured to purchase our love?

Third. What is the greatest love in the world of mother, wife, friend, life, soul, &c.? Is not God more than all this to us; yea, all in all? What did we ever best love? Did we love God as much? O, let us blush, sigh, and be ashamed at our gross ingratitude! Live henceforth, O my Jesus, my only Lord and Love!

Fourth. Whose image do we bear? Whose bitter

great feelings and delight in regard to God. Yet these can be expressed in words and conceived. The third transformation taketh place when the soul is so transformed within God and God within her, that she feeleth and tasteth the deep things of God to so great an extent that what she feeleth can in no ways be expressed in words nor conceived, save by him alone who feeleth it.' *Visions and Instructions of Blessed Angela of Foligno*, p. 296.

death was our ransom? Whose body and blood is our daily bread and drink? Who suffered so much for us and from us, expected us so patiently, invited us so sweetly, received us so mercifully? O Lord, what shall we do or say? We are bound in Thy chains of charity. We love Thee. We are all Thine.

Fifth. Upon Whom do we depend each moment for our whole being, both of nature and of grace? Our bodies depend not so much on our souls, nor our life upon the air, as all things—body, life, soul—depend upon Thee. O powerful Lord God! O that I had whole worlds to offer Thee, infinite bodies to suffer for Thee, and innumerable souls to love Thee!

Sixth. Have we not an inclination to love? For what were we created? Can we better employ our love than upon God? Doth any creature better deserve it or more desire it than our amiable Creator?

Seventh. Can anything else fully quiet us in this life, or totally content us in the next? O no, sweet Saviour! Thou art my only safety, security, sanctity. O, what did I ever love in the world which did not in the end bring me remorse and repentance? Is not all mixed with many occasions of sin and misery; all vain, inconstant, fading, foolish, deceitful? Our souls, O Lord, are created to and for Thee, and until they turn and return unto Thee, they will never find perfect peace, quiet, nor content.* What quiet had the prodigal

* 'Fecisti nos ad te, et inquietum est cor nostrum, donec requiescat in te.' *S. August. Confes.* lib. i. cap. i.

child till he returned to his loving father? *Jerusalem, Jerusalem, be converted to the Lord thy God.** Why wilt thou seek after puddle water, whereas thou mayest purely quench thy thirst at the fountain-head? I thirst, O my Lord; *give me this water.*†

Eighth. To Whom must we have recourse amidst all the distresses of this miserable life? Who will or can comfort us in the pains and pangs of death? Who must be our judge after death? Who must be our eternal bliss and beatitude? Thou only, O our Lord and Love, art all this, and all things else to our souls. And shall we please a creature to displease Thee, our Creator? No, Lord, we will die to all creatures that we may live to Thee eternally.

Ninth. O my soul, upon what canst thou employ thy whole stock of love more reasonably than upon Him Who for thy love freely forfeited His own life?

Tenth. To Whom canst thou give up thyself more profitably than to Him Who promiseth eternal life for thy love, and that He will be all thine if thou wilt be all His?

Eleventh. To Whom canst thou turn thy heart and wed thy affections more necessarily than to Him Who threatens eternal death if thou love Him not? O King of Glory, why menacest Thou us with hell if we love not? Can there be a heaven without Thy love, or a hell with it? Or is there any heavier hell or death than

* Osee xiv. 2. † John iv. 15.

not to love Thee? Had we not better cease to live than cease to love? O, what shall I answer if I love not!

Twelfth. What can make a soul more truly honourable and happy than to love God as He commandeth? What privilege to be admitted into privacy with God, to enjoy His company and conversation, enter into His secret chamber, eat at His table, repose on His breast, be His favourite,* become all one with Him! O honour most admirable! O holiness most amiable! O happiness most angelical! O Life! O Love!

THE TWENTY-SEVENTH MAXIM.

That Confidence in God's Goodness is the main Support of our Spiritual Edifice.

1. We must be confident that our loving Lord will, first, pardon our sins; secondly, strengthen us in all our necessities; thirdly, bring us finally to eternal happiness. And to strengthen this confidence, we must deeply engrave these two following maxims in our souls, and then we shall easily be content to leave ourselves in the arms of His paternal providence and lose ourselves in the abyss of His piety:—First. That whatever befalls us comes immediately either from His will or His permission. Secondly. That He will turn all, even our frailties and failings, to our spiritual good. We may further

Three points respecting which we must have confidence, and the two maxims that will insure it.

* Original text 'minion.'

weigh what wonderful cause we have for confidence and comfort.

Motives to place our confidence in God. First, in heaven;

2. First, in heaven, where we have :—I. *Bowels of mercy* in God the Father, to Whom we cry daily as His Son taught us :—*Our Father Who art in heaven.** Will not a good father forgive the fault and forget the folly of his returning and repentant child?

II. *Wounds of mercy* in God the Son, the least of which was sufficient to redeem a thousand worlds; whereby, we being reconciled and made His friends, will He deny us anything that is necessary?† Is not each drop of His dear blood a motive of loving confidence, and able to melt us into a filial dependency on Him?‡

III. *Promises of mercy* in God the Holy Ghost, Who hath assured us of His continued comforts till the consummation of the world.

IV. *Words of mercy* when He said:—*As I live, I desire not the death of the wicked, but that the wicked turn from his way and live. Turn ye, turn ye from your evil ways; and why will you die, O house of Israel?*§ What hard heart would not be touched with

---

* Matt. vi. 9.

† '*He that spared not even His own Son, but delivered Him up for us all, how hath He not also, with Him, given us all things?*' Rom. viii. 32.

‡ 'O Tu bone Omnipotens, qui sic curas unumquemque nostrum tanquam solum cures, et sic omnes tanquam singulos.' *S. August. Confessiones*, lib. iii. cap. xi.

§ Ezech. xxxiii. 11.

tenderness, and say reciprocally:—'As I live, O my Lord God, I detest all sin, and convert myself totally to Thee, that I may live with Thee, and love Thee eternally. O holy conversion! O happy contract!'

v. *Breasts of mercy* in the Mother of Jesus. O Jesus, be to us a Jesus! O Mother of Jesus, be to us a Mother of mercies! Let the care of thy honour be ever in our hearts, and the care of our welfare always in thine.

vi. *Castles of mercy* in the Angels, who are before and behind us, to watch over and protect us.*

vii. *Oracles of mercy*, the prayers and sufferings of all the Saints, pitying our misery, and purchasing pardon for us. If we put all this together, we shall find all heaven for us. What matter, then, if all hell be against us? *Why are ye fearful, O ye of little faith?* †

3. Secondly, on earth in the Church Militant, what is not for us? Sacraments, Scriptures, Examples, Prayers. If we go not to heaven, in whom lies the fault? What could God do that He hath not done? And what could we have more than we have for our consolation and salvation? Who can but take courage, comfort, and confidence?

secondly, on earth;

4. Thirdly, look upon Christ Jesus. 1. Why

thirdly, in Christ;

* St. Thomas (*Summa*, 1. 2, qu. 50, art. 3), St. Denis (*De Cœlesti Hierarchia*, cap. iv.), and Card. Bellarmine (*De Ascensione Mentis in Deum*, grad. 2, cap. ii.) teach that the angelic choir is so great and multitudinous as to exceed in number all things created. What, then, is there to fear, since we have so invincible an army to intercede and fight for us?

† Matt. viii. 26.

came He into this world? 2. How did He carry Himself in it towards sinners both in His life and death? 3. Why was He *called Jesus,** and termed *a friend of publicans and sinners?*† 4. Why did He say that He came to call sinners, and not the just,‡ and to do mercy, and not justice? 5. What access and comfort gave He to all sinners? 6. What was His last will and testament? 7. What His last words?—*Father, forgive them, for they know not what they do.*§

fourthly, look on God's perfections;

5. Fourthly, ponder God's perfections. 1. He is our Maker, we the work of His hands. Doth not every artist love his own handiwork? Hath not every one a natural proneness to protect, improve, profit, and perfect his own? Even so our loving Lord takes care of us. He hides and harbours us, *as the hen doth gather her chickens under her wings;*‖ He defends us *as the apple of His eye.*¶ *Can a woman forget her infant, so as not to have pity on the son of her womb? And if she should forget,* says our Lord, *yet will not I forget thee,* because *I have graven thee in My hands.*** 2. He is all-might, all-wisdom, all-goodness. Put these together:—'I have a Father and Maker that loves me exceedingly; He knows my necessities, and what is

* '*His name was called Jesus, which was called by the angel before He was conceived in the womb.*' Luke ii. 21.

† '*The Son of Man came eating and drinking, and they say: Behold a man that is a glutton and a wine-drinker, a friend of publicans and sinners.*' Matt. xi. 19.

‡ '*I will have mercy and not sacrifice. For I am not come to call the just, but sinners.*' Matt. ix. 13.

§ Luke xxiii. 34

‖ Matt. xxiii. 37.

¶ Deut. xxxii. 10.

** Isaias xlix. 15-16.

best for me; He is rich enough to provide for me. Will He let me perish? Will He reject me?' Then reason further with yourself thus:—'In whom shall I confide if not in God? In myself, or in others?' We are all inconstant, all ignorant of what is best, all impotent, and require means to help us. *It is good to confide in the Lord, rather than to have confidence in man.**

6. Fifthly, reflect upon our own experience. 1. Whom did God ever deceive in His promises? 2. Who ever heartily called upon Him and was refused? 3. Hath He not hitherto marvellously protected and preserved you, and disposed all for your good?† Why, then, should you doubt or distrust His providence for the time to come? No:—*Blessed be the man that trusteth in the Lord.*‡ *Heaven and earth shall pass away,*§ but no tittle of my hope in Thee, my dear and only Saviour. This shall be my anchor and stay:—*Although He should kill me, I will trust in Him.*‖ I will rest secure in His divine providence, and endeavour to get an habitual and stable trust in His paternal protection,¶ without any care or fear, as doth

fifthly, our own experience.

* Psalm cxvii. 8.

† 'O my Lord, when we see that Thou dost frequently deliver us from dangers into which we rush, even so as to offend Thee, how can any one believe that Thou wilt not deliver us when our only aim is to please Thee and in Thee to find our joy. I can never believe it. God in His secret judgments may permit certain things to have diverse issues, but what is good never ended in evil.' St. Teresa's *Foundation*, p. 26.

‡ Jerem. xvii. 7. § Mark xiii. 31. ‖ Job xiii. 15.

¶ 'The Providence of God differs from His grace, His protection, His mercy, and His consolation. His Providence is His general superintendence and preservation of the universe. His grace is a superna-

a child in his father's bosom. This is the ready way to become immovable and immutable, quiet and contented.

Is He God? Is He good? Is He my God, my Father, my Jesus, Jesus crucified? Is His goodness infinite? Doth He want power, wisdom, or will to pardon, protect, and perfect me? I must surely have little faith, less hope, and no love, if I will not take Thy words, O Lord, Thy works, Thy wounds, Thy life, and Thy love as secure pledges of Thy care towards me, and as sufficient motives to place my whole confidence in Thee.

THE TWENTY-EIGHTH MAXIM.

That the Measure of our Progress in Perfection is the Conformity of our Will with the Divine Will.

The conformity of our will to the Divine is the measure of our perfection.

1. For our perfection consists in love,* and the greatest sign of love is to have one and the same will with the beloved, so that the more we have of our own will, so much the less have we of God's will and love, and, consequently,

---

tural gift of light and strength which He imparts to His creatures. His protection, which may be termed His special Providence, is an effective care or interest thrown around the members of His Church. His mercy is bestowed upon those who return and devote themselves to His service. His consolations are the heavenly dews which He showers upon those who sincerely love Him.' St. John Climacus, *The Holy Ladder of Perfection*, deg. xxvi. § 24.

* 'Let us remember, daughters, that true perfection consists in the love of God and our neighbour; the more perfectly we observe these two precepts, the more perfect we shall be. Our whole rule and constitutions serve for nothing else, but are so many means for enabling us to do this with more perfection.' *The Interior Castle*, p. 48.

so much the further are we from the union of our spirit with Him.

2. O what holiness and happiness, what a privilege and prerogative it is to have one will and spirit with God! Is not this to be a Saint, an Angel, another Christ, a little God? Did not Christ say:—*Whosoever shall do the will of My Father that is in heaven, he is My brother, and sister, and mother.** O, who would not change wills with God?

Yea, in this conformity consists all perfection.

3. What can befall me—sin only excepted, which is the fruit of my own perverse will—but what comes from Thee, my most sweet Lord and loving Father? Good and bad, comfort and distress, life and death, all are from Thee. And what can happen to me from Thee but that which is for my good? If my Father be my Physician, shall I not drink the chalice He tempers for me? What better sacrifice can I offer up to Thee than my will? In all other oblations I give but a part of myself, or something belonging to myself; but in this I give the principal, leaving no right to myself; nay, I am no longer myself, but Thy servant and Thy slave.

Motives to encourage us in its practice.

Why were we placed in this world, O my soul, but to perform the will of God? Why entered we into the school of perfection, but to learn to practise it purely and perfectly. To what end are all our prayers, communions, exercises, &c., but to know God's holy will, and to follow it? What profit have we reaped hitherto

* Matt. xii. 50.

in following our own will? What will become of us if we continue in it? What means are there to amend for the future but humble obedience, and absolute submission of our will in all and to all, leaving all to God, doing all for God, and receiving all from God, that He only may be all in all. What can endanger me but my will? What will? Why, my will past, present, and to come. But my past I detest; my present is that God's will be done; and for the time to come I desire that this my present will may stand irrevocable for ever. How often have I done the will of others for my own ends, in order to please them or else to please myself? And shall I not do now as much to please my Lord God? Yes, Lord, I will what Thou wilt—neither more nor less—and without exception, without reservation, without delay.

The fruits of this exercise.

4. What fruits shall I reap by this conformity of my will? 1. Having no will, I can neither sin, err, nor be deluded. 2. There is neither judgment nor hell for me. 3. I shall find peace and rest, and remain constant and contented amidst all accidents and changes, and so begin my paradise of delights in this 'vale of tears.' 4. I shall be freed, both in prayer and in the practice of virtue, from all troublesome fears, scruples, disquietudes, indiscretions, and illusions, all of which are derived from the disorder of my will, and from want of this true conformity and indifference. 5. This gives everything I do, renounce, or suffer a double grace, merit, and crown. O only sweet, short, and sure way! who

would not leave, yea loathe, his own will for so many advantages and pleasures?

5. What do heaven and earth, Angels and Saints, but God's will? What do the souls in hell but suffer for having done their own will? What did Christ Jesus and our Blessed Lady upon earth? The one said:—*I came down from heaven, not to do My own will, but the will of Him that sent Me.** The other said:—*Behold the handmaid of the Lord; be it done unto me according to Thy word.*† I say also with heart and mouth:—'O my Lord, I am entirely Thine; put me where Thou wilt, give me what Thou wilt, use me how Thou wilt, so Thou wilt go with me, and give me leave to bear and embrace Thee with the two arms of perfect conformity and of lively confidence.'

All creatures do the will of God.

6. What made the Apostles, Martyrs, Virgins, so constant and contented amidst their torments and trials? What made those Saints so courageously defy the devils, flocking about them like so many lions and monsters:—'If God have given you power and permission over us, take us, devour us, hurry us headlong into hell, we will not contradict His will; but if not, why do you labour in vain?' What made Job so patient on his dunghill; Abraham so resolute to sacrifice his son? And finally, what made Christ in His bloody sweat cry out:—*Yet not My will, but Thine be done?*‡ All this was caused by the will of God, which they desired to follow and fulfil to the last gasp and

Examples of this conformity.

* John vi. 38. † Luke i. 38. ‡ Luke xxii. 42.

last drop of their blood. O holy and happy souls, when shall I imitate you? O my sweet God, that Thou couldst say of me as Thou didst of that Thy servant:—*I have found David, the son of Jesse, a man according to My own heart, who shall do all My wills.** Or that I could say as heartily as he did:—*My heart is ready, O God, my heart is ready*† to accept and execute Thy holy will in all things whatsoever! O my God, let all self-will and self-love henceforth die in me, and let Thy only will and love remain and reign in my spirit; for I am most sure till I faithfully follow this rule I shall never find real peace or contentment.

THE TWENTY-NINTH MAXIM.

That Restlessness of Mind is the Bane of Devotion and the Curse of Contemplation.

1. For it is not a single and simple temptation, but a source whence many spring—a monster with many heads, and the greatest evil, sin only excepted, that seizes on the soul. Let us, therefore, shun it with all possible speed and diligence, and refuse to give it the least entrance into our hearts upon what pretence soever.

Restlessness is not a single evil.

2. If we perceive ourselves inclined to be easily troubled, let us duly practise these two points:—*First*, carefully forearm and fortify our interiors against all future misfortunes, crosses, and contingen-

How to prevent it.

* Acts xiii. 22. † Psalm cvii. 2.

cies, by devoutly performing our morning prayers and exercises of recollection. *Secondly*, prudently shun company and occasions of extroversion; bridle our tongues till the tempest be blown over;* hide ourselves in a corner; turn our souls to our Saviour; read something of devotion; and in matters of moment impart our mind to some virtuous friend.

3. It we will always keep internal peace, we must observe these three rules:—*First*, we must not do anything with the simple view of edifying others, but we must always propose the further end of God's honour; nor anything which may justly displease, distaste, disedify, or contristate them. *Secondly*, we must not be eager, curious, or solicitous to please or satisfy ourselves; yea, nor to perform our duty towards God with stereotyped scrupulosity. *Thirdly*, all our pleasure must be to please God; yea, we must not please ourselves in the pleasure we find in serving and pleasing Him; for generally it sufficeth that we are heartily willing and quietly careful to serve our Creator, please Him in all things, and displease neither Him nor any one in anything; and so go on in our introversion with perfect freedom and liberty, simplicity and purity, without further fears or reflections.

A means to keep inward peace.

4. Let us, I say, keep on quietly and steadily, according to order and obedience, in our exercises of humility, recollection, and inward conversa-

We must curb importunate desires.

* 'When you are superioress, never blame any one in anger, but only when it is blown over, and thus your rebuke will do good.' *Admonitions* of St. Teresa, No. 59.

tion with God, checking and curbing all importunate pretensions, desires, and resolutions of doing strange matters; and resting content in what God sends and our poverty affords, neither running beyond His grace nor beyond our own strength.

Of little meddling comes great peace.

5. Let us leave all intermeddling with others' doings and affairs, looking only to our own care and charge, thinking all others more perfect than ourselves, and being truly glad that our dear Lord is purely loved and perfectly served by them. This is a sure way to avoid many stumbling-blocks of our enemies, to begin to taste the joys of heaven in this life, to live without solicitude, and die without fear or trouble.*

* 'Son, be not curious, and give not way to useless cares. What is this or that to thee? Do thou follow Me. For what is it to thee whether this man be such or such, or that man do or say this or the other? Thou art not to answer for others, but must give an account for thyself: why therefore dost thou meddle with them? . . . All things therefore are to be committed to Me; but as for thy part, keep thyself in good peace, and let the busybody be as busy as he will. . . . Be not solicitous for the shadow of a great name; neither seek to be familiarly acquainted with many, nor to be particularly loved by men. For these things beget great distractions and great darkness in the heart.' *The Following of Christ*, b. iii. chap. 24.

'Whenever a man is beset, disquieted, or taken up with external things which are done by others, then, so to speak, he is out of doors, not within; below, not above. For extroversion into sensual conversation and considerations is an impediment to interior fruition. Never therefore is contemplation joined with commotion; never with troubles, grievances, disturbances, the discussion of other things, scrupulosity, disquietude, from whatever source they may arise. While these last, the union of the Word is never added, that is to say, the most chaste and untransformable embrace of the Bridegroom. But if any man love the Word, the Bridegroom, truly and effectively, so naked, free, strong, and unincumbered by all things must he be as hardly to have any choice in the least or in the greatest; and just as

6. For further practice on this important point, and to obtain this happy peace and content of mind:—

Further means to obtain this peace of mind.

First. We must carefully avoid and contemn all curiosity to see, hear, know, or have a hand in what concerns us not.

Secondly. We must labour to be, as it were, blind, deaf, dumb, insensible, passing by all things or letting them pass by us. Our motto must be such as that of Solomon:—*Vanity of vanities, and all is vanity;** or that of St. Giles:—*One to One;* or that of St. Francis: —*My God and my All;* or that of St. Teresa:—*Whatsoever hath an end is nothing;* or that of our Lord Jesus Christ:—*What is it to thee? Follow thou Me.*†

Thirdly. What is it we shall see, hear, or know? Novelty, vanity, a transitory toy, a foolish fable, an impertinent object, a flying shadow, a false deceit.

Fourthly. To what end? Either it will defile our souls, or disquiet our minds, or distract our spirits, or divert our intentions, or imprint idle images, or excite our passions, or renew our vicious affections — all of which are great hindrances in a spiritual and contem-

---

Eternal Providence shall dispose, so to be wholly content with God, nor to allow his peace of heart to depend in anything on the estimation of men or on accidents. . . . And he ought in a certain manner to grow hard, like flint, in the various things that happen unto him, so that they may hurt him in nothing, but frequently and powerfully be beaten back and recoil. For how can that hurt him which is a gain to him in all things that happen? Of all things, therefore, that come upon him or meet him let him ever think:—Our Lord hath sent this or that, in order that I may be more perfect and acceptable to Him.' *The Fiery Soliloquy with God*, ch. xxxv.

* Eccles. i. 2. † John xxi. 22.

plative course. Ah, poor souls, what amiable and admirable light and love do we leave and lose for a vain curiosity!

THE THIRTIETH MAXIM.

That Crosses are to be suffered, not sought; to be taken, not made; to be concealed, not complained of.

The reasons of this advice are set forth.

It is far better to take crosses, when, where, and how we find them, than to make them ourselves; for this is loss of time and nourishes self-love. Let us not therefore cast ourselves indirectly upon difficulties, or seek out occasions of humility and patience, but be ready to receive and accept with indifference such as befall us, and we shall find enough to do. Let us make as little outward show as may be of our inward sufferings, but keep them to ourselves,* till obedience and just reason induce us to reveal them, and then let us do it simply, sincerely, and resignedly. O, what peace, what profit, what pleasure shall we find in this practice? Complaints are commonly accompanied with self-seeking, and small troubles are sooner cured by quiet suffering than by much showing or speaking of them. Doth this cross come from men, or is it not rather permitted and provided by our beloved Lord from all eternity, to purify us from pride, to purge us from the love of creatures, and to dispose us for heaven and happiness?

* 'O, learn to endure a little for the love of God, without letting every one know it!' *The Way of Perfection*, p. 54.

THE THIRTY-FIRST MAXIM.

That Temptations cannot hurt us, if we cast our whole Care upon God.

WHEN temptations, passions, repugnances, or repinings rage in the inferior part of our souls, we are presently to reflect:— Four rules in time of temptation.

1. That we have made choice of God's love for our end, and resolve to stand by it till death.

2. That we must willingly submit to the trouble as long as it shall please God to permit it.

3. That we must continue in our practices of piety and recollection, as if we felt no afflictions; neither thinking of them nor fearing them, but assuring ourselves that nothing can injure us so long as we rely upon God and acknowledge our own weakness.

4. That prayer must be our chief refuge and support against all their surprises; and therefore we may say briefly and heartily:—'Perfect Thy strength, O powerful Lord, in my weakness; let Thy mercy triumph on the throne of my misery. I detest from my heart whatsoever is contrary to Thy holy will in this point, N. . . . and in all things. I resign myself to suffer it as long and in what manner Thou pleasest, though ever so repugnant to my crooked nature. Sweet Saviour, remain with me, and let Thy love reign in me, and then I shall neither want other company nor desire further comfort.'

THE THIRTY-SECOND MAXIM.

That we must rise above all Desolations, Derelictions, Afflictions, and Distractions, by means of generous Resolutions.

1. In time of desolation, &c., we are not to dispute with ourselves, nor examine the causes or circumstances of our sufferings, for we are then neither competent nor unbiassed judges, but we must defer this until the time of prayer. Talk not now with your passionate, distressed, and biassed heart, but speak to God about some other thing, transcending and dissembling your trouble in some such manner as the following :—'Good God, when shall this pilgrimage have an end? My life is a continual warfare upon earth, wherein all is vanity, all is affliction of spirit, all is full of frailty, misery, instability. O Lord, what is man that Thou shouldst be mindful of him? A weak reed, shaken by every wind and stricken by every little cross and contrariety, burdensome to himself and troublesome to others. It is more profit and less danger to suffer desolation than to abound with consolation; to desire sensible love and contrition than to feel it; to resist temptations, distractions, passions, with patience and resignation than to have none at all.

How we should conduct ourselves in such times.

2. This is a sign of high and heroic virtue :—

Four signs of heroic virtue.

I. To be resigned when it seems we neither are nor can be resigned.

II. To be patient when we are brimful of motions to anger.

III. To be humble, meek, and quiet in time of sickness, serious business, multiplicity of employments.

IV. To be constant and invariable in all the diversities and varieties of our own changeable humours, dispositions, inclinations, internal invitations, external instigations.

The prayer of aridity is good and profitable.

3. Let us not think we lose our time when we are involuntarily distracted in prayer, but rather comfort ourselves in being deprived of all comfort, because we then remain in that state in which God would have us.* Let us conceive ourselves as within the walls of a strong castle, without which are great noises, outcries, tumults, alarms, but we, safe and secure within, slighting their vain attempts. If

* 'Surely a matter of great comfort it is to a soul, and ought so to be esteemed, that in her will (which is her principal faculty and, indeed, all in all) she may be united to God in the midst of all distractions, temptations, and desolations; and that being so united, she will be so far from receiving any harm by them that she will, by their means, increase in grace, so that although she do not receive any extraordinary illuminations, nor any satisfaction to her natural will by such distracted prayer, yet doth she get that for which such illuminations and gusts are given, to wit, a privy but effectual grace to adhere unto God and to resign herself to Him in all His providence and permissions concerning her; and grace gotten by such an afflicting way of abnegation is far more secure, and merits more at God's hands, than if it had come by lightsome and pleasing consolations; since this is a way by which corrupt nature is transcended, self-love contradicted and subdued, even when it assaults the soul most subtly and dangerously, to wit, by pretending that all solicitudes and anxious discouragements caused by distractions do flow from divine love, and from a care of the soul's progress in spirituality. Lastly, this is a way by which charity and all divine virtues are deeply rooted in the spirit, being produced and established there by the same means that the devil uses to hinder the production of them in negligent and tepid souls, or to destroy them when they have been in some measure produced.' *Sancta Sophia*, vol. ii. treat. 3, sect. 1, ch. vi. § 8.

our desires be to love God, and our intentions to be with Him, and we hold no discourse with other allurements, we have made a good and profitable prayer.

THE THIRTY-THIRD MAXIM.

That Perfection consists in putting off all Propriety, and putting on pure and naked Charity.

THIS will make us love God above all things, and all things in and for Him only, uniting our spirits to God and in Him to our neighbours.

A method for exercising this spiritual unclothing of our souls:—

Behold, O my Lord and Love, I totally and in general renounce all things but Thee, casting myself into the arms of Thy most holy disposition and protection. O my soul, return sweetly to thy seat of rest, repose quietly and confidently in the bosom of Divine Bounty, remain here without diverting or distracting thyself to other objects, rely securely upon His mercy and providence, cutting off all superfluous cares and solicitudes, and protesting that thou desirest nothing but the advancing of His honour, and the accomplishing of His will; His love, and Himself!

Take courage, my poor soul; for if thou art left lonely sometimes and deprived of thy Lover's sweetness, of the feelings of His comforts, and of the pleasures of His presence, it is only that He Himself alone may possess thee. O my Lord and Lover, look upon this soul, which I have endeavoured to strip entirely of all sensual affection. To this end I have not only abandoned but hated Father, Mother, Brethren, Sisters, Lands, Living, Liberty, yea my own Life, that I might become Thy disciple; and were it yet to be done over again, I would cast off my Mother and run past my Father to come to Thee, my loving Jesus. Confirm, O Lord, my courage. Live, O rich abnegation! Live my Beloved to me, and I to Him! Let me see no one but only Jesus. Leave alone His other gifts, however excellent and holy they be—yea, rather am I resigned either to leave them or to keep them in the manner and measure He pleaseth: it is my own Saviour that I alone seek and sigh after. Disengage me, then, my Lord, 1. of all sin, great and small; 2. of all affection to it, even to the least venial; 3. of all curiosity; 4. of all sensuality; 5, of all inordinate passion; 6. of all vanity; 7. of all self-love and self-will. Let me be reduced to nothing. Divest me of myself, and put on me Thy crucified Self. Deprive me of all that is distasteful to Thee, that Thou mayest say of me:—*This is My beloved son, in whom I am well pleased;** this is My disciple whom I, Jesus, love; *this is My rest for ever and ever: here will I dwell, for I have chosen it;†* in this heart is My harbour, there you shall infallibly find Me.

* Matt. iii. 17. † Ps. cxxxi. 14.

THE THIRTY-FOURTH MAXIM.

That Zeal and Eagerness must be tempered with Moderation and Discretion.

Cautions against indiscreet zeal.

1. We must moderate our natural vivacity, activity, and agility of spirit by shunning all precipitation and indiscreet forwardness and fervour.* Slow and sure, let us look before we leap; let us carry our eyes in our hands; for that which is well done is twice done, and a thing warily begun is well-nigh half done. Let us lend our hands, but not give our hearts, to any work. Let us endeavour to perform all our actions with a free and disinterested mind, without which all is drudgery and slavery.

Against over-eagerness.

2. Let us not be over-eager. Perfection consists, not in multiplicity of action, but in simplicity of intention; not in variety of exercises and devotions, but in peace of mind and purity of heart; not in saying or doing much, but in suffering and loving much. Let us sometimes check our importunate spirit, as Jesus did Martha:—*Martha, Martha, thou art careful and art troubled about many things. But one*

* 'All acts of impetuosity and violence are so far but effects of self-love, and proceed not from the divine Spirit, which is altogether stillness, serenity, and tranquillity. And let us not suspect that such a calm performance of our duty argues a tepidity and want of fervour. On the contrary, such actions so done are of more virtue and efficacious solidity. For the fervour which is indeed to be desired is not a hasty motion and heat in the inferior nature, but a firm and strong resolution in the will, courageously—yet without violence that is outwardly sensible—breaking through all difficulties and contradictions.' *Sancta Sophia*, vol. i. treat. 2, sect. 1, ch. viii. § 8.

*thing is necessary,** which is, a real, cordial, and total abnegation of thyself in all things. Let not indiscreet zeal serve for a cloak to cover our passionate hearts and inward hatred of others. True zeal is full of compassion and free from indignation; and perfect charity either will not see what is amiss in others, or seeks out the best interpretation of it, excusing the fault and pitying the offender.

THE THIRTY-FIFTH MAXIM.

That we must never rely upon our natural Judgment, Experience, and Knowledge.

1. THIS hath deceived many, and cast them headlong into confusion and despair. Hence so many apostasies, rebellions, dissensions, divisions, and scandals in religion. O, how pleasant, beautiful, and edifying a thing is it to see persons of great perfection, glorious endowments, venerable for age, honourable for learning, renowned in dignity, to be truly humble, supple, simple, soft like wax, capable of any impression, and condescending to others' reason and command! *Blessed are the meek,*† humble, and obedient spirits; for God will not permit them to go astray or be deceived.‡

This has been the ruin of many.

---

* Luke x. 41. † Matt. v. 4.

‡ God is better pleased by obedience than by sacrifice, and this is the surest way to the will of God and the shortest cut to perfection. Never let the devil deceive us into imagining, under any pretext, that we shall be the losers by giving up our own will and following that of another for the love of Christ. Listen to the counsel of the great St.

THE THIRTY-SIXTH MAXIM.

That we must seek no Comfort in any Creature.

How this holy maxim is to be put into practice.

1. In order to put this maxim into practice, we must cheerfully forsake all, and be content to be forsaken by all, resting only in God by prayer, patience, and confidence. Adieu, friends,

---

Teresa:—'Our Lord will not suffer Satan to have so much power as to deceive us at all to the hurt of our souls, so long as we live under obedience with a pure conscience' (*Foundations*, p. 25). And elsewhere:—'God never allows any one who is truly mortified to sustain any loss, except it be for his greater gain' (*Way of Perfection*, p. 83). Speaking of a soul that is determined to love God and has resigned itself into His hands, the same saint says:—'Thou, O Lord, hast taken upon Thyself to guide it in the way the most profitable to it. And even if the superior be not mindful of the soul's profit, but only of the duties to be discharged in the community, Thou, O my God, art mindful of it; Thou preparest its ways, and orderest those things we have to do, so that we find ourselves, without our knowing how, by faithfully observing for the love of God the commands that are laid upon us, spiritually growing and making great progress, which afterwards fills us with wonder. So it was with one whom I conversed with not many days since. He had been for fifteen years under obedience, charged with laborious offices and the government of others—so much so that he could not call to mind one day that he had had to himself; nevertheless he contrived to find, the best way he could, some time every day for prayer, and to have a conscience without offence. He is one whose soul is the most given to obedience that I ever saw, and he impresses that virtue on every one he has to do with. Our Lord has amply rewarded him; for he finds himself, he knows not how, in possession of that liberty of spirit, so prized and so desired, which the perfect have, and wherein lies all the happiness that can be wished for in this life; for, seeking nothing, he possesses all things. Such souls fear nothing, and desire nothing upon earth; no troubles disturb them, no pleasures touch them; in a word, nobody can rob them of their peace, for it rests on God alone, and, as nobody can rob them of Him, nothing but the fear of losing Him can give them any pain; for everything else in this world is, in their opinion, as if it were not, because it can neither make nor mar their happiness.

'O blessed obedience, and blessed the distractions caused thereby, by which we gain so much! That person is not the only one, for I

familiars, confessors, counsellors, angels, books, exercises. Welcome, solitude, crosses, eclipses, flames, wounds, moans, darkness, desolation, deaths:—*Yea, Father, for so it seemeth good in Thy sight.** Is the creature in which I delight more loving, lovely, or beautiful than God my Creator? Hath it been more bountiful or beneficent to me? Can it more justly require or more liberally requite my love? Can it make me holy or happy, quiet or content? Shall I leave light for darkness, life for death, substance for shadows, all for nothing? Answer impartially, and resolve effectually.

A still more perfect way of practising it.

2. The higher practice of this maxim in order to contemplation is, to estimate things according to their real value, and then, alas, what comfort can a devout soul, who hath tasted the sweetness of her Beloved in contemplation, find in the best of creatures!† How far are they from affording her any solid and substantial satisfaction in her sorrows, sadness, or desolation! Therefore she wisely and care-

have known others like him, of whom, not having seen them for very many years, I asked how they had been spending the time that had gone by; all of it had been spent in the labours of obedience and of charity; on the other hand, I observed such spiritual prosperity as made me marvel. Well, then, my children, be not discouraged; for if obedience employs you in outward things, know that even if you are in the kitchen our Lord moves amidst the pots and pans, helping us both within and without. . . . I believe myself that when Satan sees there is no road that leads more quickly to the highest perfection than this of obedience, he suggests many difficulties under the colour of some good, and makes it distasteful. Let people look well into it, and they will see plainly that I am telling the truth.' *The Foundations*, pp. 32, 33.

* Matt. xi. 26.

† 'Qui bibere incipit aquam celestem, in qua sunt omnia, nihil expetit, nihil requirit amplius.' *De Ascens. Mentis in Deum*, gr. 4, cap. iii

fully keeps herself to recollection, resigns herself absolutely to the divine pleasure, continues steadfastly in the presence of her Creator, seeks to treat with Him privately and alone, and leaves worldlings to follow their appetites, *like the horse and the mule, who have no understanding.** O, what far greater happiness is it to suffer in the sweet company of God than to enjoy all such false and fantastical pleasures as all creatures can confer in the company of men! My soul refuseth this comfort; I remember my God, and in Him I am alone delighted.†

True Contemplatives are never sad or solicitous.

3. And, indeed, they who faithfully and fervently addict themselves to spiritual recollection are never either sad or solicitous, except in appearance. For what can they want who are with God? In Him they find gardens to walk in, fountains to bathe in, palaces to dwell in, dainties to feed on, and all pleasures to delight in with such infinite advantages, that they cry out, enravished :—'My God and my All!' These Contemplatives need not your compassion, O worldlings! They are not so drowned in

* Ps. xxxi. 9.

† Such is the sentiment of a soul pierced with a vehement and impetuous yearning to possess God. 'She seems,' St. Teresa says: 'to feel herself to be in a strange solitude; all those who live on earth are no company for her; no, nor would (I believe) those in heaven be, if her Beloved One were not there present; everything torments her, and she sees herself like some one hanging in the air, neither able to rest on anything belonging to earth, nor able to ascend into heaven. She is burnt up with this thirst and cannot obtain water. O my God and my Lord, to what a state dost Thou bring those who love Thee! Yet all is little in comparison with that which Thou afterwards givest them in return.' *Interior Castle*, mans. 7, p. 200.

melancholy, so plunged in sorrow, so little enjoying themselves as you imagine. No, your own poor souls are seriously to be pitied, which are so wide of wisdom, and so wedded to sensuality, as to relinquish true life and liberty, sincere comfort and contentment, for the shadows and smokes of the world. For this is most certain:—That whosoever leaves recollection to look after earthly consolation enjoys neither God nor the world; whereas a soul that retires herself from the world to possess God enjoys truly both God and the world together.*

THE THIRTY-SEVENTH MAXIM.

That we must walk and persevere in these our spiritual Exercises with the two Feet of Faith and Obedience.

To perform this, we must put into practice the following arduous, lofty, and divine exercise:—

We must	1. Leave all for One, *i.e.* all others for God.	By Recollection.
	2. Leave one for All, *i.e.* ourselves for God.	By Abnegation.
	3. Leave One and All, *i.e.* God Himself, when He withdraws Himself.	By Resignation.

* 'What is more comforting here below than for a soul to be drawn off by divine grace from the noise of worldly business and the turmoil of carnal desires, and from all vain affection towards creatures, into rest and the calm of spiritual joy, secretly perceiving the gracious presence of Jesus, and wondrously fed with the joy of His invisible blessed face? Verily, I think that nothing can make the soul of a lover of Jesus full of gladness but His gracious presence, as He shows it to a pure soul. Such a one is never oppressed, never sad, but when he is with himself in his own sensuality. He is never completely happy but when he is out of himself as being with Jesus in spirit.' Hilton's *Scale of Perfection*, p. 309.

The best and only means to accomplish this divine work in our poor and weak souls is to observe diligently these five cardinal points :—

First point. To have an ardent desire, affection, and intention to love, see, please, and enjoy God.

Second point. To curb our senses in all curiosity, vanity, fears, apprehensions, &c., which may either defile our souls, or disturb our minds, or distract our spirits; either seduce us from the right way or affright us when we are in it.

Third point. Then we must take *Jesus* by the right hand by faith and confidence, abandoning ourselves totally to His mercy, and resting in His providence with a filial indifference.

Fourth point. We must take our *Spiritual Guide* by the left hand by punctual obedience.

Fifth point. In our way we must have these or the like thoughts, recollections, and devotions :—Well, I am going to heaven, to my Father and Creator, to my eternal rest and centre, to see, love, and praise my God for evermore. There only is true life, true love, true light, and true liberty. O Jesus, how long! O Jerusalem, when!

Jesus is with me and for me; Him I will follow, after Him I will sigh, and for Him I will suffer, come what may. If I err, let my guide look to it, for I am obedient; if I stumble, Jesus will not let me fall, for I am faithful.

If I cannot have the fruit of penance, I will keep that of obedience; what I cannot get by recollection I will procure by resignation; what I want by languor and indifferency, I will supply by confidence; though my deserts fail, my desires shall prevail. What hath an end is nothing; live eternity!

Sometimes let us hearken to Jesus speaking:—'O My child, My servant, My spouse, what are all things to thee? *Follow thou Me.** Let all pass; I am here. All is One, and One is all; trouble not thyself with multiplicity. Be silent, and I will answer for thee; be content, I am thy sufficiency; be indifferent, all is My will; be confident, all is well. I will never desert thee, nor withdraw My eyes, hand, and heart from thee; therefore go on quietly, courageously, confidently.'

Other times let us answer Him meekly and faithfully:—'O good Jesus, save me, for I am Thine! O sweet Saviour, support me, for I am weak! O loving Guide, direct me, for I am blind!'

Thus boldly let us keep on our way:—1. Passing all, by insensibility. 2. Surpassing all, by fervour. 3. Passing under all, by humility. 4. Passing over all, by generosity and elevation of spirit.

Under this maxim are solved many grave doubts which arise in our daily progress to perfection. They are chiefly these:—

THE FIRST DOUBT.

If we fear that God will forsake us by reason of our ingratitude and disloyalty.

1. It is true we have been, are still, and ever shall

* John xxi. 22.

We must confide in the merits of Jesus.

be ungrateful, tepid, and defective in our correspondence to the divine love and light; and God may in justice forsake us, and yet be a good God; but we must be confident in His mercy that He will not do it in fury and rigour for the sake of Jesus, though He may sometimes withdraw the feelings of His presence to try our loyalty. His holy will be done! Let us never say:—God will forsake us; but say:—We will never forsake God. Let us first say:—Doth God love us? Who can doubt it! And do we love Him? If we desire to do so, we do.* Let us never say:—We shall never amend, all is lost;† but let us often say:—We are sinners, wicked, wretched, weak, and no one more so than we; but it truly grieves us to be so; we will endeavour to remedy all; and of this we are confident, since our God is all-mighty, all-mercy, all-meekness. Him we will serve, and in Him we will trust, in spite of nature and of the devil; and for Him all desolation and death itself is most welcome unto us.

* Because to love God is to adhere to Him by the will.

† Neither let us ever put it forth as an excuse, when we have done amiss:—'We are not angels; we are not saints.' Though we be not angels or saints, it is a great happiness to consider that we may become such with God's grace and assistance. We shall have to be saints some day or other, if we hope ever to enter into heaven. Why should we not endeavour to become so at once, and purge our souls now thoroughly of the old Adam, instead of leaving it to be done by the searching and piercing flames of purgatory. Fear not that God will fail to crown our efforts in the task. He will not be wanting, if only we, on our part, do what lies in us. But, alas, in the things of God we are such cowards. We should pray daily, then, for more grace and courage.

The Second Doubt.

If our sins trouble us with respect to confession and satisfaction.

Let us cast off servile fear, and be confident that what is past is pardoned by God's mercy and our humble confession; and what is to come may be prevented by God's grace and our own diligence and endeavours.

We must trust in God's mercy for the past, and for the future to His grace.

The Third Doubt.

If we can neither pray with fervour, nor suffer with patience; neither feel God present, nor be content in His absence.

Let us have recourse to these four things, which will supply our defects and satisfy for our faults:—1. Obedience. 2. Resignation. 3. Confidence. 4. Good desires. Therefore, in all our fears, crosses, and troubles, let us make use of these four points in this or the like manner:—'O my Lord God, Who deservest from me all love and honour, and Whom I desire to serve with all my soul, behold, I come out of confidence in Thy mercy, having no other end but only to please and praise Thee; wherefore, I resign myself to Thy will, beseeching Thee to turn all to Thy glory and my good.'

We must have recourse to four remedies.

The Fourth Doubt.

If we fear that God is angry with us, that we want grace, that we only seek ourselves, that we yield to all temptations.

Let us build upon these three foundations:—1. Humility in acknowledging our own deformity. 2. Sincerity in confessing it. 3. And confi-

We must build upon three foundations

dence of pardon for it. And so persevering constantly and courageously in a course of prayer, according to direction and obedience, we shall soon find ease, rest, and peace.

The Fifth Doubt.

If our consciences are unquiet and our souls fearful by reason of our proneness to sin.

We must apply eight salves to our troubled conscience.

Let us apply these following salves, and put this lint into our spiritual wounds, as deep as we can, every day for a time, till the cure be perfected:—

1. Let us be assured that we are now at this present moment in a state of grace, supposing we have already or are now resolved to do what is necessary for the expiation of our past sins, and the avoiding all sins for the future.

2. That having a will to please God and perform our duties, our prayers are profitable to us, and acceptable to God; and we may without presumption take courage and comfort, though we are yet full of passions and imperfections.

3. That the feeling of troubles, fears, temptations, are neither sins in us nor signs of God's anger against us.*

* 'It does not follow, when the inferior faculties are in disorder, that the same disorder should be communicated to the superior also. It does not always lie in our power wholly to suppress the instability and obstinacy of the imagination, nor the unruliness of sensuality, which ofttimes do resist our superior reason. But we are always enabled by the ordinary grace of God to keep in repose our superior soul, that is, to hinder it from attending to the suggestions of the

4. That we are not bound to reflect continually whether we have consented to sin or not, nor to judge whether this or that consent be mortal or venial, nor to meddle with the sins of our past life, having endea-

imagination (which we may reject), or to deny consent or approbation to the motions of sensuality; and this, at least, it must be our great care to do. Neither ought a well-minded soul to be discouraged or dejected at the contradictions that she finds in sensuality; but resisting it the best she can, she must be resigned and patient with herself, as she would be at the refractory humours of another, till, by God's blessing, a longer exercise of prayer and mortification do produce a greater subjection of sensual nature to reason and grace. In the mean time, she may comfort herself with this assurance, that all merit and *demerit lies in the superior will*, and not at all in sensuality considered in itself, and as divided from the will. During the conflict between reason and sense or appetite, there may be a real tranquillity in the superior region of the soul, although the person be not able to discern that there is any such quietness; yea, on the contrary, to fearful natures it will seem that whensoever the sensitive part is disturbed, the spiritual portion doth also partake of its disorders; and this uncertainty, mistake, and fear that a fault has been committed is the ground of much scrupulosity, and by means thereof, of great unquietness indeed, even in the superior soul, to persons that are not well instructed in the nature and subordination of the faculties and operations of the soul.

'However, a well-minded soul may conclude that there is a calmness in the reason, and in the will a refusal to consent to the suggestions of sensuality, even in the midst of the greatest disorder thereof, *whilst the combat does not cease*, and as long as the outward members, directed by reason, and moved by the superior will, do behave themselves otherwise than the unruly appetite would move them. For example, when a person being moved to anger, though he find an unquiet representation in the imagination, and a violent heat and motions about the heart, as likewise an aversion in sensitive nature against the person that hath given the provocation; yet, if notwithstanding *he refrains* himself from breaking forth into words of impatience to which his passion would urge him, and withal contradicts designs of revenge suggested by passion, such a one practising internal prayer and mortification is to esteem himself *not to have consented to the motions of corrupt nature*, although, beside the inward motion of the appetite, he could not hinder marks of his passion from appearing in his eyes and the colour of his countenance.' *Sancta Sophia*, vol. i. treat. 2, sect. 1, chap. viii. § 3, 4, 5, 6.

voured to discharge our consciences once of them in confession.

5. That we may and must convert our hearts to God humbly and confidently at all times, in what state soever we be, without hesitation or apprehension, preferring His will before our own quiet.

6. That in saying our office or prayers it sufficeth that we have a good intention to praise and please God and satisfy our obligation, using moral diligence in driving out bad thoughts, and so we need trouble ourselves no further.

7. That so long as we make choice of God for our God, and of His will for our only end, and can say cordially :—'I love God, I desire no sin,' we need fear nothing.

8. That we are not *bound* to do that which our conscience dictates or what we fancy it tells us is a divine call, for this is the way never to have true peace and to be ever subject to illusions.* Therefore let us follow the old, simple, and secure rule :—1. trust; 2. obey; 3. let pass; 4. and pray. These will prove our safest haven in the sea of this world, and our heaven upon earth; thus may we enjoy the peace of God, and lodge in our hearts the God of peace—be blind, and yet see God.

N.B. These aforesaid salves are to be used accord-

* To bind oneself by vow always to do the most perfect thing would be the climax of presumption, unless, like St. Teresa, one had received a special call from God to do so.

ing to discretion, and with the approbation of our spiritual director.

Sixth Doubt.

If we are full of fears and apprehensions of our state, because of experiencing in our souls such slender effects of God's grace and love, and have little devotion, no inward peace.

1. Such souls can never be cured till they submit their judgments, look with more confidence upon God's mercy, and seek less their own satisfaction and assurance. For this is an infallible truth:—That in this life (without revelation) we can have no certainty of our state, but must still live in ignorance as to that knowledge.* To hold the contrary is *heresy*,† and to seek it inordinately is *self-love* and *curiosity*. We must, therefore, work out our salvation betwixt fear and hope; and if we should see or feel anything in ourselves which should make us secure, it were very suspicious and dangerous.

We must rely more upon God, and seek self less.

2. Let us humbly observe these three points:—1. Resolve still to serve and please God in the best manner we can. 2. Resign ourselves to His will and divine ordinance for time and eternity, without further reflections. Build upon the word and warrant of our director, and rest quiet and confident. They who seek more knowledge and satisfaction by feel-

And observe these three rules.

* '*Man knoweth not whether he be worthy of love or hatred*' (Eccles. ix. 1). And St. Bonaventure: 'Scire se habere charitatem, non est necessarium ad salutem, sed solum habere.' Cited by Dr. Sweeney, O.S.B., in his *Life and Spirit of F. Augustine Baker, O.S.B.*, p. 172.

† Calvinism.

ings and reasons, seek but their own trouble and ruin; and if we find not here peace and comfort, we must thank ourselves, since it is our *disobedience* and *self-seeking* that causeth it.

The Seventh Doubt.

If some extreme cross, calamity, or affliction hath seized our hearts, &c.

A method of practising perfect resignation.

Let us hasten to our Lord God with an humble and confident affection, and kneeling before Him,

1. Kiss the crucifix, saying:—'O my dear Lord! O my sweet Jesus! O my All and only Good!'

2. Then tell Him you are troubled, as you would tell your spiritual director, and that you know not what to say or do.

3. Acknowledge heartily that you deserve no comfort, but to have heaven shut against you, and hell let loose to torment you.

4. And that if you would seek comfort you desire not to seek it out of Him, or in anything contrary to His divine will and liking.

5. Then say:—'O Lord, I have no other Physician for my soul but Thee; behold my wounds! Thou art my Father; behold my wants! Thou art my only Friend; behold my wishes and desires!' Then expose them unto Him, and hearken what counsel and comfort He will give you.

6. Take again the cross, kiss it, embrace it, resign yourself to suffer.

7. And with an internal act of indifferency, being confident that this cross and trouble is His will and will be for your good, desire to bear it, and whatsoever else He shall lay upon you, knowing He will enable you to suffer all things.

8. Have no recourse to creatures for your solace, but drink purely and plentifully at the fountain-head; and be not weary—you suffer for eternity!

The Eighth Doubt.

If we desire to conquer the devil and overcome all temptations whatsoever.

General remedies against temptations: 1. A strong resolution to gain the victory.

1. Let us often read, observe, and practise these general remedies. The first is a strong courage and firm resolution to fight and get the victory, and not to yield even at our last gasp. *Resist the devil, and he will fly from you.** If we fear him, he will follow us and exult over us; if we play the cubs, he will play the lion; but let us be lions, and he will soon show himself a coward. Let us, then, fight as befits soldiers of Christ manfully, so as to give honour to Him and to the dev[illegible]ear, who is chained to our hands, and may bark, but cannot bite, unless by blindness and madness we come within his reach.

We fight in the presence of God.

2. Let us remember in our combats that *we are made a spectacle to the world, and to angels, and to men.*† Who would not fight valiantly and confidently before such spectators? God beholds

* James iv. 7. † 1 Cor. iv. 9.

us as our Judge to reward and crown us if we overcome. Christ, as our Captain, helps us to overcome. All the rest of the heavenly Court pray for us, that we may bear off the palm. Fear not, my soul; there are more with us than against us.* God and His angels are on our side; who can withstand us? *If God be for us, who is against us?*†

3. Let us further reflect that we plead, not only our own cause, but God's, Whom in our persons the devil seeks to injure and dishonour. Let us, then, rather die than suffer our good Master's honour to be stained by our cowardice; our dearest blood will be well spilt for such a king and country. O, what a privilege to suffer for the sake of Jesus! *Let God arise, and let His enemies be scattered.*‡ *Arise, O God; judge Thy own cause.*§ Thine is the battle; we are Thy champions.

We fight for God's honour,

4. Let us also ponder well what St. Paul tells us on God's part:—*And God is faithful, Who will not suffer you to be tempted above that which you are able,*|| but will draw our good out of our temptations. He knows what clay we are made of, what force we have; and (which is above all) He loves us as the apple of His eye. If He seems sometimes to sleep a while, yet He both sees and succours us. Courage, therefore. If we be already at hell's gates, He can and will bring us back again; if we *should walk in the midst of the shadows of death,* let us *fear no evils.*¶

and are never tempted above our strength.

* See 2 Paral. xxxii. 7. † Rom. viii. 31.
‡ Ps. lxvii. 2. § Ib. lxxiii. 22. || 1 Cor. x. 13. ¶ Ps. xxii. 4.

5. The second remedy is a distrust in our own strength and trust in God's help. *He is the protector of all that trust in Him ;** and the general reason given in Scripture why God helps His servants is, because they hope and trust in Him ; so that His honour becomes compromised if we rely upon His succour ; whereas, if we trust to our own strength, we have little to do with God, and thinking much of ourselves we quickly fall into blindness of heart, unless God brings us to the acknowledgment of our own nothingness by some strong affliction, and makes us cry out with Job :—*Behold, there is no help for me in myself.*†

2. Distrust in self and trust in God.

6. The third remedy is prayer. *Watch ye and pray, that ye enter not into temptation.*‡ Let us turn our hearts to converse with God, which is better than to reflect upon our temptations and troubles. Let us be so attentive to Him, that we have neither leave nor leisure to give ear to satanic suggestions, but transcend them by a generous resolution rather to die than admit anything contrary to our Lord's love and pleasure.

3. Prayer.

7. The fourth remedy is to observe the root, groundwork, and occasion of the temptation, and to pull it up, cut it off, and destroy it.

4. Avoid the occasion.

8. The fifth remedy is to cure one contrary by another. If we be tempted to pride, let humility be our aim. Let us never cease from speaking, writing, reading, meditating, praying for and

5. To destroy one vice by aiming at its opposite virtue.

* Ps. xvii. 31. † Job vi. 13. ‡ Matt. xxvi. 41.

practising it, till we get an habitual loathing of pride.

9. The sixth remedy is to resist it at the beginning, when it is yet weak. Let us kill the cockatrice in the shell, lest, being hatched, it poison us. Let us be wise, and not save a penny and have to lose a pound, nay, to lose all we are worth eternally.

6. Resist the beginnings.

10. The seventh remedy is to reveal it to him who is encharged with our souls.* This diminishes our grief, lessens our trouble, is an act of humility meriting grace and comfort, and confounding our enemy, who cannot brook to have his deceits discovered.

7. Reveal it.

11. The eighth remedy is to avoid idleness. Let the devil always find us well employed, and we shall easily avoid his temptations. He that is idle hath ten devils to attack him; he that is well busied hath but one. Let us, therefore, distribute our exercises over certain hours, that we may be sure to avoid this mother of all sin and mischief, and the greatest bane of our souls—idleness.†

8. Avoid idleness.

The Ninth Doubt.

If we want comfort in long and dangerous temptations and troubles.

1. Let us consider what experience and the Scrip-

* 'If you conceal yourselves from your confessor or superior, or if they command you something and you do not obey, this is evidently a temptation.' *Way of Perfection*, p. 199.

† 'Abhor idleness, the parent of all evils, and the certain ruin of the soul; sedulously expel indolence from thy mind. Though thy body may sometimes languish, yet thy reason must never yield to sloth; but thou must be prompt in spirit and in will.' Blosius, O.S.B., *Canon Vitæ Spiritualis*, cap. xxx.

tures teach us:—*The life of man upon earth is a warfare;** that wars and commotions are within us, from our concupiscences and original corruption;† that there is a law in our members rebelling against the law of our minds;‡ that when we are resolved to give ourselves to the service of God, we must prepare our hearts for temptation.§ The great Apostle and Vessel of Election was sorely tempted;|| and shall we poor worms and sensual creatures wonder at feeling contradiction and combats in our nature? Let us not deceive ourselves, thinking to find quiet as soon as we convert ourselves to God by prayer, for it is then rather that the devil will storm, the flesh rebel, the world murmur, when they most fear to lose their possession. And if it were not so, what need of such continual mortification?¶ Why did our heavenly Master teach us to pray that we might not be led into temptation?**

Experience and the Scriptures prepare us for temptation.

2. Christ Himself was tempted, and why should we be dismayed?†† Are we less pleasing to God

The example of

---

* Job vii. 1.

† '*From whence are wars and contentions among you? Are they not hence, from your concupiscences, which war in your members.*' James iv. 1.

‡ '*I see another law in my members fighting against the law of my mind.*' Rom. vii. 23.

§ '*Son, when thou comest to the service of God, stand in justice and in fear, and prepare thy soul for temptation.*' Ecclus. ii. 1.

|| 2 Cor. xii. 7.

¶ St. Paul, in his epistle to the Colossians, considers man's body as made up of sin and sinful inclinations, and says:—'*Mortify, therefore, your members, which are upon the earth; fornication, uncleanness, lust, evil concupiscence, and covetousness, which is the service of idols.*' iii. 5.

** Luke xi. 4.

†† I never found any one so religious and devout as not to have

Christ. because we are tempted, and not rather more acceptable for suffering for His sake? Thou errest, brother, says St. Jerome,* if thou thinkest a Christian can be ever free from persecution; then art thou the most dangerously assailed when thou knowest not that thou art attacked. For *all that will live godly in Christ Jesus shall suffer persecution;*† whereas, others who live sensually may seem to feel no rebellion, because, having nothing of God's spirit in them, their enemies find nothing to war against.‡

A hopeful sign. 3. Let us not then be troubled that we are tried with temptations, for it is a most assured sign that we fight not under the devil's banner, but have revolted against him, who persecutes, not his friends, but his enemies.§

---

sometimes a subtraction of grace, or feel a diminution of fervour: no saint was ever so highly raptured and illuminated as not to be tempted at first or last.' *Following of Christ*, b. ii. chap. ix.

* 'Erras, frater, erras, si putas unquam Christianum persecutionem non pati: tunc maxime oppugnaris, si te oppugnari nescis.' *Epis. ad Heliodorum.*

† 2 Tim. iii. 12.

‡ Read *Following of Christ*, b. i. chap. xiii., b. ii. chap. ix.

§ 'There are two temptations, the outward and the inward, which give birth to all the others, four sorts; thus distinguished: light and secret temptation, light and manifest temptation, powerful and secret temptation, powerful and manifest temptation. . . . The first and the third of these four temptations are, for the most part, under the inward class. The second and the fourth fall under the outward, and are almost always fleshly, and therefore easily felt. The other two are spiritual, concerning spiritual faults, and are often hidden and secret when they are most hurtful, and are therefore much more to be feared. Many a one who doth not suspect it nourisheth in her breast some lion's whelp, or some viper's brood, that gnaws the soul. Of such Solomon saith: Traxerunt me, et ego non dolui; vulneraverunt me, et ego nescivi.' *The Ancren Riwle*, p. 222.

The Tenth Doubt.

If we wonder at God having us to suffer temptation, since our frailty is subject to yield, and so we offend His Divine Majesty.

He hath good reason :—

1. Lest we should become careless in our duties. Therefore He tells us :—*For a small moment have I forsaken thee, but with great mercies will I gather thee.** What is a moment of time in proportion to eternity, wherein He means to overflow us with delights in His own kingdom?

The reasons why God permits us to be tempted.

2. Lest we should take this place of banishment for our country, this pilgrimage for our paradise.

3. To purge us of our past follies, sins, ingratitudes ;† to satisfy for future purgatory ;‡ and to prepare and perfect us for a crown of glory.§

4. To make us truly wise, truly humble, truly virtuous.

5. To keep us at our pious exercises ; for many would otherwise neglect prayer, slight obedience, and shun mortification, whereas now they stand carefully upon their guards.

---

* Isaias liv. 7.

† '*As silver is tried by fire, and gold in the furnace, so the Lord trieth the hearts.*' Prov. xvii. 3.

‡ '*If we suffer, we shall also reign with Him.*' 2 Tim. ii. 12.

§ '*To him that overcometh I will give the hidden manna, and will give him a white counter*' [an allusion to the custom of giving a white stone, or counter, to those that were tried and acquitted, and also to persons promoted to a dignity], '*and in the counter a new name written*' [this 'new name' is the eternal recompense], '*which no man knoweth but he that receiveth it.*' Apoc. ii. 17.

6. To teach us how to help our neighbours by our own trials, for *he that hath not been tried, what manner of things doth he know** either for himself or others?

The Eleventh Doubt.

If we are solicited by our enemy to unchasteness.

1. Know that God hath called us to serve Him with purity and integrity of body and soul. This is the end of our vocation. See, then, that you walk worthy of it, lest that terrible sentence of the Holy Ghost be pronounced against us:—*In the land of the saints he hath done wicked things, and he shall not see the glory of the Lord,*† which none can see but the clean of heart.

None but the clean heart shall see God.

2. Let us comfort ourselves in this: that as it is not sinful but natural to feel rebellio us motions, so it is not only possible but easy to overcome them, not in ourselves, but in God, the gracious Giver of strength and comfort.

'My grace is sufficient for thee,' 2 Cor. xii. 9.

3. Let us have an ardent desire to live chastely, and make firm and frequent resolutions to continue so, whatever it costs us. How many thousand chaste spouses of God, made of the same mould as we are, keep perpetual virginity!

Desire to live chastely.

4. Let us seek diligently and practise seriously such remedies as are proper for the preservation of this jewel; amongst which the chief is mortification of our rebellious flesh by austeri-

Use the necessary remedies, i.e. mortification.

* Ecclus. xxxiv. 11. † Isaias xxvi. 10.

ties. Hence St. Thomas derives the word chastity from chastising.* It is better that our stomachs pain us than our consciences, and that we lose health of body than purity of soul, and the salvation of both. This remedy of mortification is absolutely necessary when carnal motions arise first in the body, and then react upon the imagination; but if from the fancy they descend to the body, we are to apply these following remedies:—

1. Let us avoid idleness.

2. Let us change our employments. If we are assaulted in company, let us seek solitude; if in solitude, let us hasten into company.

3. Silence, temperance, and custody of the senses are also three powerful preservers of chastity.

4. Let us make great account of the slightest provocation or pleasurable feeling, and shake off the first motions as we would a burning coal from off a new garment.

5. Let us humbly, yet modestly and discreetly, lay open their nature and manner to our spiritual guide.

6. Let us carefully avoid all suspected company, familiarity, and meetings, though our intention be ever so spiritual.

7. Let us strive rather to slight, scorn, and neglect these temptations than formally to resist them.

8. In vehement temptation:—*First.* Make the sign of the cross upon your heart. The remedies

* 'Nomen castitatis a castigatione sumitur.' Sum. Theo. 2. 2, qu. 151, art. 2.

against vehement temptations.

Second. Use some brief and burning aspirations, as :—'Lord, deliver me. I suffer violence; O my God, answer for me. I am Thine, O Jesus, body and soul; help me.'

Third. Defy the devil with St. Anthony :—'Fie, beast! Thou wert an angel. I who am now a beast will aim to be an angel, and get thy lost place. Begone! this dwelling is already occupied; Jesus is here, Who is my Lord and Love. I am engaged with my first and purer affection.'

Keep prepared a place of refuge for spiritual shelter.

9. Let us prepare beforehand certain places of refuge for our shelter and succour till the storm be passed over, as :—*The Presence of God* and His angels; saying: 'How is it possible? God sees me, and shall I sin in His sight?' *Death and eternity :*—'The delight is momentary, the punishment eternal; death is at my door, and shall I venture?' *Christ's sacred wounds :*—Let us there hide and save ourselves, and say: 'My God hangs on the cross, and shall I think of yielding to pleasure?' *The love of God :*—'O Jesus, my love and my life, I will either love Thee or love nothing at all. Let me rather lose my life than Thy love.' *Humility :*—'Thou art just, O my Lord God. Thy will be done. My pride is the cause of this villany, which I feel.' . . . And take this for an infallible truth: —We must be humble, or we shall not be long chaste. Let us be obedient to our superiors, or let us not look to have our flesh obedient to our spirits. *Devotion to saints :*—Excelling in this virtue, especially to the most

chaste Virgin Mary. And the last remedy is to make use of these antidotes in good time, orderly and discreetly, without which no rules or directions will aught avail us.

The Twelfth Doubt.

If we are in extraordinary desolation and darkness.

We must live by Faith in this case, and know that a sensible love of God and of virtue is not now necessary, but to cling to Him and to serve Him upon principle and the dictates of reason suffices. Our fidelity to God is shown in the performance of our duties now as at other times, without losing either our confidence in Him or seeking comfort in our sufferings, but aspiring, if not sweetly, yet sincerely unto Him, in this or in the like manner:—'Lord, I choose Thee and accept of Thy divine pleasure and providence in all things. I reject whatsoever may possess that place and dominion in my soul which is due to Thee alone. Dispose of me and mine as shall be most for Thy honour and glory. Let me be either all Thine, or nothing at all.

A sensible love of God is not necessary.

The Thirteenth Doubt.

If we are tempted to despair of God's mercy by reason of our frequent falls and relapses into sin.

This grievous malady springs from three causes or errors; for they who are troubled in this point do not truly weigh:—1. What God is. 2. What sin is. 3. What contrition and sorrow of heart is.

The three causes of despair.

2. Almighty God is a boundless and bottomless sea of mercy. He is natural bounty itself. He is ever ready to receive, revive, and relieve a penitent soul, though she alone had committed a thousand times a day the sins of the whole world. He considers not what she hath been, but what she desires and resolves now to be; and whosoever denies His power of will to pardon sinners as often as there are moments in time, goes about to deprive Him of His honour and divinity itself; for He could not be God if He were not good and faithful in His promises. O loving Lord God, Who art not only ready to receive a penitent's petition, but even wooest him to present it, who can truly consider what Thou art and despair of Thy mercy?

What God is.

3. Sin is a voluntary and deliberate aversion from God and conversion to creatures. Contrition is of that efficacy that it delivers from all sin, giving confidence of pardon for the past and courage to avoid it for the future. Let us apply this for our comfort.

What sin and contrition.

THE FOURTEENTH DOUBT.

If we are perplexed with great sadness.

1. This passion is a great hindrance to devotion and perfection; it is the bait of the devil, the bane of our spirits, the root, mother, and misery of infinite miseries and mischiefs.

Sadness a great evil.

2. The chief causes of sadness are these:—

The causes of it: 1. Nature;

Nature. When melancholy oversways the sanguine humour, this can neither merit nor demerit; but the devil takes occasion thereby to fill our spirits with unquietness: these have need of physical as well as of spiritual physic.

3. A tenderness of heart and a compassionate love of ourselves. We cannot brook the least con- 2. Self-love;
tradiction; but we sigh and sob as if all the world were interested in our misfortunes, and should bear a part in our doleful duty. The remedy were to bid such weep on for their penance, or use some corporal austerities.

4. An immortification of our passions, which, when we seek in good earnest to root them out, as- 3 Passions;
sault us so strongly, that it seems impossible to cure them; and hence we grow sad. The remedy is to conquer this bad nature by counsel, courage, and diligence. Let us pray heartily, suffer willingly, stoop humbly: it is for heaven we fight and suffer!

5. A secret root of pride, vain esteem, and false opinion we have of ourselves; so that when 4. Secret pride;
things fall not out according to our liking, expectation, or importunate desire, we grow sad and troubled. Surely the proud have no true rest:—*There is no peace to the wicked.** Let us remedy it, therefore, by learning of Christ true humility and meekness, out of which there is no hope of quiet.

6. An indiscreet zeal and over-greediness of perfection, which makes us eat more than we can 5. Indiscreet zeal;
digest, and so cast it up again with great pain; undertaking austerities, exercises, introversions, &c., beyond

* Isaias xlviii. 22.

our capacities without counsel, and so we remain afflicted, being unable to go forward, and ashamed to go backward. Let us remedy this by humble obedience to a discreet guide.

6. Instability of heart;

7. Want of fervour in our vocation, instability of heart, and inconstancy in our exercises, leaving, changing, interrupting them, through laziness or levity. This leaves a worm gnawing at our conscience, with continual disquiet and sadness. Let us remedy this with St. Bernard's counsel:—'Wilt thou never be sad? Live well. A devout man is always cheerful; and a good conscience is a continual feast.'

8. Disordinate love and affection to creatures.* Let

* Blessed Angela of Foligno traces the growth and evil effects of inordinate love in the following wonderfully discriminating subtle passage:—'There are others who love some devout man or woman with a *spiritual and perfect love*, because they love them wholly according unto God. But this love at times groweth too great and becometh *bad*, except it be subjected by the weapons of great discretion; and at times it becometh *carnal*, or *useless and hurtful*, by too much conversation one with the other, and useless waste of time, because their hearts have become indiscreetly bound up together. For this love groweth, and from this growth there ariseth a desire of enjoying the presence of the person loved, which, if it be not enjoyed, maketh the love weak, and if it be, maketh it grow too much, and to be wholly transformed into the person loved; so that all that pleaseth the other pleaseth him that loveth, and all that displeaseth the other displeaseth him. And because the soul hath not weapons sufficient to subjugate this fervour of love, which continually increaseth, and is without perfect regulation or discretion, it must needs in the end turn into inordinate love. And if the person loved so inordinately be without the weapons aforesaid, and be wounded with a like sword of love, then is there great cause for fear, because then they begin to manifest one to the other the secret of their love, and amongst other things, they manifest one to the other how they mutually love one another, saying to each other:—"There is none in the world whom I love so much, or whom I so carry in my heart." And these things

us love all only for God, and we shall be content and quiet in the loss of the most lovely and beloved creature in the world. God alone will supply all other loves and losses. 7. Love of creatures;

9. A jealous and envious eye. This is a dangerous and lamentable cross; for all the perfections of others are ours when we love them in others, but when 8. An envious eye;

they say because they must needs speak of what they feel; and thus they desire to love each other, even for the sake of devotion and the spiritual usefulness which they believe to be in this love; and the temptations which occur with regard to anything forbidden, which may arise out of this love, are at first resisted by the reason, because as yet it is not wholly choked by love. But afterwards, when love hath grown stronger, the reason beginneth to be clouded over, and the spirit beginneth to be weakened, and to believe that the touch of the person loved, and other such things, are not sin, nor hurtful to the soul, and therefore it permitteth this to be done, and so beginneth to grow faint, and to fall away from the state of perfection little by little. Moreover, after that the reason hath given way a little, being choked by love, it beginneth to make no account of anything that is dangerous, and to say:—"This can be done, for I intend no evil, and it is not a great sin." And little by little such things are accounted lawful, and thus by the growth of love each one is transformed and transposed into the other's will, so that he doeth everything that the other wisheth, for there is no other reason to say him nay; so that the person loving followeth the person loved in everything he wisheth; and by reason of this inordinate affection, if he be invited to do evil, he cannot say him nay; and if he be not invited, he himself inviteth the other, feeling that this is pleasing to him whom he loveth; and then he withdraweth himself from prayer and abstinence and solitude, and all virtues in which he had been wont to exercise himself, and all his divine love is changed into this miserable love. And sometimes this love increaseth to such an extent, that even the words of the person loved and his presence no longer satisfy as before. But loving more, he desireth to know whether the person loved be also wounded by the arrow of love, like himself; and if he is able to know this, then there is danger for both; for then, trusting and secure of one another, when neither words nor presence satisfy, both are inclined unto the performance of every idle and evil work. And therefore I say, that I suspect love above all things, and in it all evil is included; wherefore, beware of the serpent.' *Visions and Instruction of B. Ang. Foligno*, pp. 292-295.

we hate them, they are nails in our eyes and thorns in our hearts, which do extremely torment us. O madness! Have we not sufficient miseries at home in ourselves, but we must suck poison, like spiders, out of others' honey; and what is their crown must be our cross. What greater wickedness than to pine away with grief at others' good? The remedy of this is by endeavouring to get true charity, the property of which is to weep with the weepers, rejoice with the joyful; to love others' good as our own. Let us avoid *curiosity,* if we would eschew envy; for a curious eye is the fuel of an envious heart. Let us remain like bees in our hive of introversion, and there make provision for the winter of Death and Eternity.

10. Frequent failing in good purposes, and relapses
9. Frequent relapses. into sin. We question whether our past sins are pardoned, and are uncertain whether our present confessions are good. This is of one evil to make two; for we have done amiss, and now, by losing courage and confidence, we make ourselves unfit to do better. Let us remedy it by acknowledging our fault, using violence to ourselves, and following spiritual direction.

OTHER REMEDIES AGAINST SADNESS.

1. Prayer is a sovereign remedy. *Is any of you*
1. Prayer; *sad? Let him pray.** God is our only joy and comfort. Let us, then, lift up our hearts to Him, and lay open our wants and desires before Him with resig-

* James v. 13.

nation, Who both can and will abundantly comfort us:—Ah, my poor soul, why art thou sad, and whence comes it that thou art troubled? Is not our God good and gracious, Who hears thy sighs and sees thy sorrows? What wantest thou which He cannot or will not give thee, when He sees it most expedient for thee?

2. Sometimes let us sing spiritual songs, which greatly confound the devil. 2. Singing;

3. Other times we may fitly divert our thoughts by some external recreations or employments. 3. Recreation;

4. Let us endeavour to make external and internal acts with fervour, though perhaps without re- 4. Fervent acts; lish; as embracing and kissing a crucifix, and speaking reverently and lovingly to it.

5. A discreet taking of the discipline obtains wonderful comfort; for the soul is called from the 5. A discipline; inward troublesome pensiveness to the outward pain, and the devil flies away, seeing his companion the flesh so roughly handled.

6. Frequent communion is an excellent cordial, strengthening our hearts and rejoicing our spi- 6. Communion; rits.

7. Let us discover the effects and manner of our sadness to our spiritual guide, and take his 7. Discovery of it; advice, simply and humbly: this is the remedy of remedies.

8. Let us take heed of making use of these remedies only that we may be at ease, and avoid 8. Indifference; affliction; but let us use them for the prevention of the

danger which may ensue; and for the rest remain perfectly indifferent and resigned.

9. Few desires;

9. If we will be free from sadness, we must labour to keep far from us unquietness of mind; and if we will have our minds quiet, we must have few desires, and those few only to love and please God.

10. Honesty and straightforwardness.

10. Finally, let us beware of three things:—1. Of following our sensuality in meat, drink, talk, ease, &c. 2. Of vain-complacency and self-opinionness. 3. And, above all, of hypochondria, hypocrisy, double-dealing, and cunning with our director; for no marvel if he starves and pines away who lies to the Holy Ghost. If we are simple as children, our loving Father will give us sweets and comforts. Woe to hypocrites, for it will go ill with them in the latter day!

OTHER ANTIDOTES AGAINST MELANCHOLY AND PUSILLANIMITY.

1. Faith;

The reason of our being so often troubled and shaken is because our spiritual edifice is not supported by these three solid props:—1. Faith; for if we captivate our understandings to believe what God Himself hath told us, what His Church hath taught us, and what our ghostly guides still preach unto us, how can we choose but be comforted and satisfied?

2. Abnegation;

2. Abnegation; for if we have made good confessions, have endeavoured to satisfy God and our guide, and have a will to obey him in all things, we

may rest secure. Let us not say:—'What shall become of us? Shall we persevere?'* for the desire to know this convicts our hearts of secret pride and self-love. Let us, therefore, deny ourselves, saying:—'God's holy will be done in and with us for all time and eternity; and whatever becomes of us, we will serve Him till death, because His love deserves it.' What need we seek a further security of God's friendship towards us in this life than to find in our souls these two things: first, that for the time past we have done penance, consisting in confession, contrition, and satisfaction. Secondly, that for the time to come we give ourselves totally to God, to serve and please Him the rest of our life in the best manner possible. Let us put our souls in this disposition, and go on with courage, and never more trouble ourselves.

3. Solid confidence; for if we know God is merciful, and that Jesus hath suffered enough for all sinners, whereof we are the chief, how can we but hope that He will be our Jesus? Let us think thus:—God loves us, and we desire with all our hearts to love Him,

3. Confidence.

* 'A certain person, who oftentimes doubted whether he were in a state of grace or not, on a time fell prostrate in the church, and said thus:—"O that I might know whether I should persevere in virtue to the end of my life!" And anon he heard inwardly in his soul the answer of our Lord, saying:—"What wouldst thou do if thou knewest thou shouldst persevere? Do now as thou wouldst do then, and thou shalt be safe." And anon he was comforted, and committed himself wholly to the will of God, and all his doubtfulness ceased, and never after would he curiously search to know what should become of him; but rather he studied to know what was the will of God, and how he might begin and end all his deeds to the pleasure of God and His honour.' *Following of Christ*, b. i. ch. xxv.

and we trust in His love, and for it we will both sigh and suffer, pray and obey, deny ourselves, and die to all creatures. This sauce will digest all our bitterness.

THE FIFTEENTH DOUBT.

If we suspect that our sadness and temptations proceed from our own fault or negligence, or some secret sin, or our want of correspondence to God's grace.

1. If it be so, must we therefore complain, and not rather the more conform ourselves to God's will. We have often deserved hell; our past sins and present negligences merit eternal punishments; and is it not a special favour to be punished in this life with temporal troubles and temptations? This is not hell, nor an eternity of discomfort, nor what we deserve; why, then, are we not both content and grateful?

Our sufferings are less than we deserve;

2. In this fatherly chastisement there is both Mercy and Justice. *Justice*, because we have often shut the doors of our hearts against God, giving a deaf ear to His calls, and therefore it is just that we should now call and knock at the gate of His mercy, and not be heard. *Mercy*, because our sufferings are small in comparison to our deserts. If this be most true, why lament we our misfortune? Is there any proportion between time and eternity, betwixt this desolation and the never-ending lamentations of the damned in hell?

2. Tokens of God's mercy and justice;

3. Let us, then, receive and kiss His paternal rod with a filial reverence, crying out with St. Au-

3. Therefore kiss

gustine :—'O Lord, spare us not here, so Thou spare us hereafter. We have merited hell, and dare we ask sweetness in prayer? O pride and presumption! It is sufficient, Lord, that Thou admittest us into Thy presence, and permittest us to open our unworthy mouths unto Thee, and lament our misery before Thy Divine Majesty; and shall we have hearts to murmur or tongues to complain of any usage?'

and embrace them.

The Sixteenth Doubt.

If we doubt that God is displeased with our prayers, that our afflictions befall us through our own fault, and cannot satisfy ourselves to think we have done what God requireth.

1. We must firmly believe that, besides our own fault, which deserves it, our chastisement is a disposition of the most high and holy Providence of God, Whose wisdom imparts His blessings as He knows best for His servants. If all receive not spiritual refreshment and joy in prayer, let them say with St. Bernard :—'Give me, O Lord, simplicity, humility, and charity; but for higher favours, as I am unworthy of them, so I am incapable of making use of them; I leave them, therefore, for Thy special friends and favourites.'

Chastisements are also sent by God

2. Let us, therefore, conceive these afflictions to be sent us from God. *First*, to humble us; for should He visit us with great lights, and elevate us in contemplation, we should presently take complacency in our imaginary devotion, and prefer ourselves before others. *Secondly*, to try our fidelity and

to humble us and to try our fidelity,

perseverance in His love; for the chief end of prayer is to obey and please God, and offer Him all that we are and have; but to receive relief and comfort is only the secondary end.

3. Let us further consider that this very internal trouble and anguish may and ought to comfort us, as being a token of God's love; for love is the first wheel of our natural and spiritual clock, setting all the other passion awork. If, therefore, we grieve that we serve God so tepidly, this grief proceeds from love, and is an evident sign of a good will to serve Him.

and are pledges of Hi, love.

4. Let us ground ourselves in that often-repeated maxim:—That all things do not only befall us by God's permission, but also that He sends them for our good. And, therefore, let us say with the confident and courageous Judith:—*Let us believe that these scourges of the Lord, with which like servants we are chastised, have happened for our amendment, and not for our destruction.**

An inspiriting maxim.

The Seventeenth Doubt.

If Nature hath shown herself a stepmother unto us in giving us a hard and harsh disposition, whence proceeds a reluctancy to works of virtue and mortification of vice, so that we despair of ever overcoming ourselves.

1. Let us take courage:—*The kingdom of heaven suffereth violence, and the violent bear it away.*† And let us lay hold of these two truths:—*First,*

Take courage,

* Judith viii. 27. † Matt. xi. 12.

2. That God's will is that all should be saved, and therefore He gives every one sufficient grace and means to that end. If, then, we have the worst nature in the world, and do but correspond diligently with that grace which God gives us, we have no reason at all to fear. Let us fight valiantly under Christ, our good Captain, with the armour of prayer and mortification, and not cease to be His soldiers so long as any blood and breath remain in our bodies. Let us learn to discover, and then—as others do—to detest our own peevish and perverse disposition. Let us not flatter ourselves, but lay the axe to the root, not to the branches; to wit:—Resolve to humble our proud hearts on all occasions with courage, constancy, and confidence for one year, and we shall find more peace and quiet than we can imagine. If we sweat drops of blood, it is for eternity, where not one drop shall be lost, nor one wound uncounted, nor one soldier uncrowned!

and bear in mind: 1. God wills all men to be saved;

3. *Second.* That to have bad natures and to feel motions against grace, reason, &c., is neither sinful, nor is it an imperfection, so long as we yield not our consent to their dictates.

2. That to have a bad nature is not sinful.

The Eighteenth Doubt.

If, on the contrary, our nature is so facile and flexible that we scarcely find difficulty in anything; we wonder on hearing of rebellions, contradictions, desolations, &c., from all of which we are secure and free; and therefore we fear that our actions are founded rather upon nature than upon the supernatural.

It is true that devotion and perfection consist

not in this external peace and ease, but in the victory over ourselves, in habits of solid virtue, in pure charity and indifference. We are therefore, in this case, to humble ourselves, and to conceive we know not what mortification and abnegation mean. What marvel if a soul which is seldom introverted is rarely distracted; if they who have no care of their senses nor custody of their hearts are not troubled with their wanderings; if where there is no sap of solid devotion, there is no sense of dryness and desolation! O dangerous and unquiet peace!

Beware of a false peace.

THE NINETEENTH DOUBT.

If we so addict ourselves to recollection, that we look upon works of obedience and charity, and the external practice of our duty, as impediments to perfection.

Of such it may be said:—*You know not of what spirit you are.** Let us not vainly adhere to our imaginary devotions, so as to neglect the least work of obedience.† Without charity and obedience all our prayers are abominable in His sight, Who said:—*Not every one that saith to Me, Lord, Lord, shall enter into the kingdom of heaven; but he that doth the will of My Father Who is in heaven, he shall enter into the kingdom of heaven.*‡

Devotion must never be preferred before duty.

* Luke ix. 55.

† 'Oratio impediens obligationem est illusio, et oratio quæ nescit relinquere Deum propter Deum, nec subvenire fraternæ charitati obligatoriæ, et pœnitentiam præfert obedientiæ, vel amentia est, vel manifesta illusio.' Schram, *Theolog. Mystic.* § 472.

‡ Matt. vii. 21.

THE TWENTIETH DOUBT.

If we find such a calm in our passions, imperfections, and temptations that we hope the worst is past.

Let us never flatter ourselves with such fancies, or admit the least conceit that we have entirely conquered any one passion or imperfection;* but, humbly, vigorously, and constantly keeping on in our track of Mortification, Recollection, Introversion, think that these calms, comforts, and cessations are sent us as honey-sops and milk for children, because we are yet weak, and want courage to encounter such stronger temptations wherewith others are tried, and that our loving Lord communicates these favours and friendships unto us, not as best meriting them, but as most needing them.

Never harbour such a delusion.

THE TWENTY-FIRST DOUBT.

If scrupulosity overwhelms us.

1. As *Carelessness* is a dangerous impediment to perfection; for instance, when one shall say:— 'This is not mortal; this is but a counsel, not a precept; this of perfection, not of obligation' (for whosoever will obtain the true spirit of devotion and recol-

The evils of scrupulosity.

* 'Think not therefore that thou hast found true peace when thou feelest no grief; nor that all is well with thee when thou hast no adversity; nor that all is perfect for that everything cometh after thy mind. Nor yet that thou art great in God's sight, or specially beloved of Him, because thou hast great fervour in devotion and great sweetness in contemplation; for a true lover of virtue is not known by all these things, nor doth the true perfection of man stand in them.' *Following of Christ*, b. iii. ch. xxv.

lection must be far from this opinion); so also *scrupulosity* is another extreme, equally hindering our spiritual progress, and more damaging than sin itself. For this trouble of spirit takes away all internal strength, comfort, and courage of well-doing, and makes us slide insensibly into despairing of doing better, till at length we give up all hope, and either pine away in these melancholy and desperate thoughts, or else yield ourselves to pleasures and sensuality, and sometimes to the devil himself, so as to find some means of solace and satisfaction. Believe it, inordinate Fear, Sadness, and Scrupulosity will soon bring a soul into a labyrinth of miseries and a hell of mischiefs; and therefore she must speedily get *confidence in God's mercy* and *alacrity of mind*, or she will never be able to overcome her difficulties, nor persevere long in spirit.

A short and certain remedy.

2. The way for a soul to get this confidence and joy is briefly this: 1. To trust and obey her discreet guide, who is to assign her a set form of confession for once a week. 2. He must be resolute and rigorous, taking all upon his own conscience, if she promises faithfully to obey him. 3. He must assure her that she more offends in want of Confidence and Obedience than in all her other sins put together; and that if she will not believe this, her disease is incurable. This is the short and safe cure of this dangerous disease. But that we may better understand the nature of our malady, let us note seven sorts of conscience:—

3. *A false, corrupted, large, and libertine conscience,*

making scruple of nothing, but swallowing down all things.

Seven sorts of conscience.

A lax conscience, stretching to all and caring for nothing, but to avoid great and grievous sins.

A presumptuous conscience, yet not good, because it takes occasion to sin out of a confidence in God's goodness and hope of His mercy.

A troubled conscience, but not good for want of confidence.

A troubled and also a good conscience, yet weak; of those who being newly converted to God lament their past life with bitter tears, and yet are full of rebellious passions, &c.

A good, quiet, and confident conscience; of those who are careful to please God, to avoid all sin, to be serviceable to all, burdensome to none; making use of friends by preference, foes by patience, and all men by good will.

An erroneous, timorous, and scrupulous conscience, making doubts and difficulties of all things.

4. From what has been said we may say there are, generally speaking, two sorts of bad conscience: the one too lax, calling good evil and evil good; the other too rigorous, finding sin where there is none, and taking imaginations for offences, and shadows for substances.

Two sorts of bad conscience.

5. The first of these consciences, which is over lax, must be cured by removing the causes, which are generally four:—

The remedy for an over-lax conscience.

I. Negligence in learning what belongs to our religion, vocation, profession, obligation, and salvation; for whoso knows not what he is bound to know shall not be known by God.*

II. Pride and shame in asking and informing ourselves.

III. Obstinacy and presumption when we will trust to our own judgments and abilities, and not submit to our betters.

IV. Bad affections and perverse wills, led by passion and blinded by self-love from seeing the truth. These having one foot already in hell, must pluck it out by violence, using the contrary remedies.

A cure for the over-rigorous conscience.

6. The second conscience, which is over rigorous and scrupulous, may also be cured by the removal of the causes, which may be reduced to these:—

I. A timid and nervous nature, arising from a want of caloric: here is need of a twofold physician, one for the body, to prescribe it good diet; the other for the soul, to confirm it in Hope, by the consideration of God's mercy, Christ's merits, Scripture promises, and superiors' warrants.

II. Some infirmity or sickness, as *mania*, which hurts the forepart of the head, and diminishes the imagination; melancholy, which affects the middle part, and diminishes reason; frenzy, which seizes

* '*If any seem to be a prophet or spiritual, let him know the things I write to you, that they are the commandments of the Lord. But if any man know not, he shall not be known.*' 1 Cor. xiv. 37, 38.

on the purses or nets of the brain, which are the cells of judgment. This cause hath need of the like cure.

III. The devil, by God's permission for various causes. This is cured by not caring what humour we are in, but by endeavouring with courage and confidence to please God whether we are sad or merry, fervent or desolate; making use of prayer and counsel.

IV. An indiscreet and foolish treatment of our bodies. The way to cure this is to follow the rules of discretion, and to find out our own strength and disposition; yet still taking heed of the opposite extreme of flattering our sensuality under pretence of spirituality.

V. The keeping company with scrupulous persons, or misunderstanding some spiritual books. Remedy this by shunning such company, laying aside such books, and obtaining from your director a rule to rely upon, and believing nothing against it.

VI. A secret and subtle self-love and pride, under the mask of fear and care of our souls. Against this we must submit our judgment to obedience, for we are all blind in our own cause; and this is not only the best, but even the necessary remedy for such as are particularly bound to obedience.

VII. Ignorance of the mysteries of our faith, and of God's mercy, which makes us think our obligation greater than indeed it is, God more severe than He is, and His yoke heavier than it is. To remedy this we must see and consider wherein we judge amiss, and upon what we ground our particular fears; for that is the easiest way to remove them.

VIII. Let us weigh the virtue of the physic which must cure our disease; to wit: *First,* the infinite goodness of God and the merits of Christ; and what soul can then fear, having so gracious a God and so great a ransom? *Secondly,* the credit and compassion of the Blessed Virgin and the prayers and patronage of saints and angels, who being themselves secure are solicitous for for us. *Thirdly,* the testimony and sweet promises of holy Scripture; for how often hath God told us:—'I am prone to pity; I am ready to receive sinners; I will help those who strive manfully?' If, therefore, He denies not His mercy to them that seek it, and if they seek it who do what lies in them, O, let us be confident that He will not deny us His mercy. He also frequently calls upon us:—*Turn ye to Me, and I will turn to you.** Now, He cannot but speak the truth and fulfil His promise; and doth not that soul convert herself to God who doth her best to get His grace and be reconciled unto Him? Who, then, can choose but be of good comfort if he be of good will?

A summary of the foregoing doctrine.

7. By this doctrine and these prescribed remedies, it appears that the only way to overcome scruples is:—

I. To obey our spiritual director.

II. To make every exertion on our part.

* Zach. i. 3.

But here arise two difficulties in this easy lesson.

8. The first is:—If our director's knowledge be slight, his experience less, and his conscience not very good, how dare we trust our souls to his dictum? First difficulty.

To this Gerson answers:—'Thou wise judge, I say thou errest and art deceived, for thou hast not committed thyself and thy soul to a man because of his discretion and learning, but to God Himself; and for His love thou obeyest man because he is by Him ordained thy prelate and superior. Therefore our obedience will be oftentimes so much the more pleasing to God and profitable to our souls by how much the more infirm and unworthy he is whom we refuse not to obey for God's sake.'* Answer.

* 'When we have commenced the career of piety and obedience, let us no longer judge the actions of the virtuous director who has been the object of our choice, although we may occasionally see in him the slight faults incident to every mortal and wayfaring man; for we shall certainly derive no fruit from our obedience if we continually sit in judgment upon his actions.

'It is absolutely necessary for those who desire to preserve an entire and unshaken confidence in their directors to engrave so indelibly on their hearts the good deeds which they see them perform, that nothing may be able to efface them from their memory; so that when the wicked spirits would inspire us with mistrust in these our spiritual guides, we may at once arrest their accusations by recollecting the virtues which we have witnessed in these servants of God. For the more prompt and active the body is in its exercises, the more is confidence strengthened and increased in the heart. But if any one loses this confidence he will fall, because that which has not faith for its foundation is not solid, is not worthy of a supernatural reward. If the thought of judging your director in some particular circumstance arise in your mind, reject it as you would the sin of impurity, and never give the least encouragement, the least admittance, the least opening to this baneful serpent. Say boldly to this monster, that you

9. The other difficulty is:—If we cannot satisfy ourselves that we do our uttermost, and know not whether we have performed our duty.

Second difficulty.

St. Thomas answers:—'We must first remove that which hinders grace, to wit, sin. Secondly, we must convert our hearts from creatures to our Creator. In a word, we must detest sin and choose God, and follow the ordinary means which He has appointed in His Church for our direction; and this is the summary of our duty.'

Answer.

The Twenty-second Doubt.

If we fear we detest not sin sufficiently, because we feel not as great a sorrow for an offence against God as we do sometimes for a temporal loss.

Let us assure ourselves: *First*, we can never have as much sorrow for our sins as God's justice in rigour requires. *Secondly*, God doth not exact it of us, because it is not in our power. *Thirdly*, true sorrow consists not in feeling, but in reason and free will. *Fourthly*, it is better sometimes to have sorrow only in desire than in feeling. *Fifthly*, it is not necessary this corporal or sensible grief be as great for a spiritual as for a temporal loss; but it sufficeth to use human and moral diligence, with a firm purpose of avoiding sin. *Sixthly*, it is dangerous for weak and

Six most salutary directions.

have received no authority to judge the actions of your spiritual father; on the contrary, he has been appointed to sit in judgment upon yours. I am not commissioned to be his judge; but he is deputed to be mine.' St. John Climacus, *Ladder of Perfection*, deg. iv. § 6, 7.

timid consciences to make such comparisons and reflections as these:—'If such a thing should happen, what should I do? Should I rather choose death than such a sin?' And the like. I say there is no obligation to make such acts.*

The Twenty-third Doubt.

If we cannot ground ourselves in a firm hope of mercy, because we are so frail and inconstant; sin daily and amend not our lives; receive God's blessings and repay ill for good; promise, protest, and vow fidelity, and practise little or nothing.

Tell me, afflicted soul, should you see Christ die daily for your daily sins, would you despair of His mercy? Even so efficacious is His former death. If you fall hourly, rise courageously, and purpose to stand more constantly, and fear nothing; but draw humility out of your frailty, saying:—'What am I proud of now? Where are my strong resolutions? Why do I judge others? Who is so feeble, fickle, frail as I am? O Lord, this is the worm that is so proud!' Then cast all into Christ's sacred wounds, and leaving all there, go on with as much quiet and confidence as if you had not sinned.

We must be courageous and draw humility out of our frailty.

* Yea, it is rash and foolish to do so. For strength to resist temptation does not depend upon man's endeavours, but upon God's grace; and since grace is a pure gift of God, which He sometimes is sparing of, and at other times mercifully bestows in an extraordinary and superabundant measure, it follows that it is impossible to tell the issue of a temptation or trial until it be over and past. Therefore timid souls, instead of troubling their minds and wasting their time upon these vain speculations, should rather study to know and perform God's will in their actual duties of the present, and confidently rely on His mercy and goodness to surmount the dangers which lie concealed in the dim and uncertain future.

THE TWENTY-FOURTH DOUBT.

If we go not on with alacrity, because we know not that our sins are forgiven, that our confessions are good, and that we are in the state of grace.

1. We must take notice that in seeking these assurances we may oftentimes directly lose them. *First,* in seeking them too eagerly and unquietly. *Secondly,* in being self-lovers, and unwilling to be troubled. *Thirdly,* in being ignorant of what we are bound to know; for it seems that we conceive those works nothing worth which are performed without relish, content, satisfaction to ourselves, and quiet.

How peace is sometimes lost in the very search after it.

2. The way, then, is briefly this, To seek true peace: *First,* in God. *Secondly,* from His mercy, not our own industry. *Thirdly,* to be resigned to want peace if He so please. *Fourthly,* to omit nothing we would or should do, because of the trouble we feel.

Means to acquire true peace.

THE TWENTY-FIFTH DOUBT.

Though we cannot in this life be infallibly certain that we are in a state of grace, yet if we could comfort ourselves with most probable tokens of grace whereby we might feel the pulses of our hearts, and somewhat ease our anguish.

Four signs of a good conscience.

1. St. Thomas and St. Bernard give these four signs of a good conscience:—

I. To feel a ready willingness in our hearts to hear God's word, and to learn the means to love and serve Him.

II. To feel a forwardness to do good works.

III. To feel a hearty sorrow for offence against God.

IV. To feel a firm purpose to avoid all sin.

2. Gerson adds a fifth :—' Whosoever can pronounce heartily and sincerely these three Verities, though he have committed all sins and should be visited with sudden death, let him assure himself he is in the state of grace. A fifth sign.

'*The first Verity*, O Lord, if in this or that I have sinned against Thy goodness, it truly displeases and grieves me, and I am ready to do penance for it, because I have offended Thee Who art worthy of all honour, and have transgressed Thy law and will, which is most holy, just, and reasonable.

'*The second Verity*, O Lord, I have a good purpose and desire by Thy grace to take heed I fall not into sin again, and to avoid to the best of my power the occasions thereof, and to mortify my passions and bad inclinations.

'*The third Verity*, O Lord, I have a good will and purpose to confess my sins entirely in the time and place according to Thy ordinance, and that of Thy holy Church.'

3. We may add to these :—The devout frequentation of the Sacraments, which give life and sanctifying grace; the warrant of a skilful director; and a lively confidence in the divine bounty. Three other signs.

THE TWENTY-SIXTH DOUBT.

If we are troubled because we know not well whether we have given consent to sinful thoughts.

Rules to know when we consent to sin.

1. If when the thought is represented we presently fly to the crucifix, expel it, disdain it, dislike it, it is not sin, but *merit*.*

2. But if we carelessly linger on it when well perceived, it is venial.

3. And if we consent to the thought and desire the action, our sin is the same as if the act had been committed.

4. But if we intend not the act, but linger delightfully in the thought, and the thing itself be mortal, and deliberately entertained, this sin is also mortal.

THE TWENTY-SEVENTH DOUBT.

If we cannot well distinguish between venial and mortal sin.

Three warnings.

1. What need we determine? Let us confess it as it is committed.

2. Mortal sin, says Richard of St. Victor, cannot be committed without great corruption of him who commits it, or great hurt to his neighbour, or great contempt and neglect of God. And St. Thomas says:—'He sins mortally whose total intention of mind is withdrawn from God, Who is our last end.'

---

* 1. Non datur peccatum nisi voluntarium.

2. Nihil volitum nisi præcognitum.

3. On the other side, we have the words of St. Augustine:—'Nemo invitus bene facit, etiamsi bonum est, quod facit.' *Conf.* lib. i. cap. xii.

See also *note* to *Fifth Doubt*, § 3.

3. Let us conclude with St. Augustine and Gerson:—That it is dangerous, even in prelates and confessors, to define what is mortal sin, or give rules therein.

THE TWENTY-EIGHTH DOUBT.

If that saying of divines terrifies us: 'He that acts in a state of doubt sins;' and 'In things which are doubtful the securer part is to be chosen.'

We may, in things which are doubtful, safely follow a probable opinion. Now scruples are not doubts, but *false apprehensions;* and therefore on all sides we may, and sometimes must, go against our own erroneous consciences, especially when obedience commands it.* Let us therefore, with St. Augustine, lay hold of that which is certain, and let go the uncertain;† and what way is more sure and secure than obedience?

Scruples are not to be treated as doubts.

THE TWENTY-NINTH DOUBT.

If, finally, we are apprehensive and fearful lest we should grow weary in the way of virtue, and not persevere constantly in our spiritual exercises.

1. Let us excite our tepidity by the frequent perusal of this following discourse, and act accordingly:—

A method for inflaming the soul with courage to persevere.

2. The Patriarch Jacob, in hope of obtaining the beautiful Rachel, served Laban seven years with diligence and patience; but being cozened by that disloyal

* To follow our own will in preference to the command of our superiors is clear pride and a manifest sin. The scrupulosity which thus obstinately adheres to its own opinion is of the devil, and should be confessed along with other sins of pride, vanity, and conceit.

† 'Tene certum, dimitte incertum.' See *note* to *Maxim* 35.

worldling with ill-favoured Lia, what doth he? He neither loseth courage nor confidence, but with new constancy begins his other seven years' service, with such admirable alacrity, and a heart so fixed upon his desired reward, that *they seemed but a few days, because of the greatness of his love.**

Serve God with hope of beatific vision.

3. O my soul, thou seekest and sighest after eternal beatitude, consisting essentially in the blessed vision and fruition of God, signified by Rachel, according to St. Bernard. For this thou hast bound thyself to serve God. But, alas, the world, the flesh, and the devil do so often beguile and blind thee that thou takest blear-eyed Lia for beautiful Rachel,† the world for heaven, the flesh for the spirit, and diabolical illusions for divine inspirations.

Labour constantly so as to be crowned.

4. But what? Lose not courage nor confidence; renew thy protestation of loyal service; serve one other seven years, suffer another slavery, in order to obtain heaven, to die in final grace, and to be eternally joined to that blessed Bounty thou lovest. Follow Jesus to Mount Calvary—to *Consummatum est*‡—to thy last gasp. If thou stumblest, fall not; if thou fallest, up again and march; stand not, but go forward; for *He that perseveres unto the end, he shall be saved.*§ Let neither frequent temptations, nor fearful imaginations, nor strong passions, nor bad inclinations, nor repeated

* Gen. xxix. 20.

† '*But Lia was blear-eyed: Rachel was well-favoured, and of a beautiful countenance.*' Gen. xxix. 17.

‡ John xix. 30.

§ Matt. x. 22.

falls, nor ordinary frailty, daunt or dismay thee. God is good and gracious, meek and merciful. Thy reward is infinite and eternal, and thy friends are more in heaven than on earth. Persevere, then, and go forward. If thou canst not run, at least go steadily, surely, and securely after Christ thy Captain, crying :—'*Draw me after Thee,** O most dear Lord, for I desire to follow Thee and no other; but I am weak and lame, and therefore I make use of two crutches—a strong resolution never to forsake Thy love, and a lively confidence in Thy grace, goodness, and mercy.'

Heaven is worth suffering for.

5. O holy and happy, O precious and highly-to-be-prized perseverance! O final grace, the patrimony only of the elect and portion of the predestinate! Fight manfully, O my soul; get good habits timely, resist valiantly; fast, watch, pray, sigh, and suffer perseverantly; heaven is worth thy pains. Persevere, O my soul; persevere, persevere; that done, all is done; that wanting, all is undone. This, O Satan, thou knowest full well, and therefore little carest thou to see me zealous for a Lent, for a year, for a time, so in the *end* thou mayest make me tired, tepid, and careless of my progress and perseverance. It is my perseverance which thou only enviest, because that only conquers thee, and crowns me eternally. I discover thy two main snares, O subtle enemy, into which thou wouldst allure my unwary soul; and thy first design failing, which was to delay my conversion to God's service, thou pursuest my

* Cant. i. 3.

second, which is to weary me in my well-begun enterprise.

6. To put off my conversion thou urgest youth, long life, time enough—thy daily and dangerous deceit, by which more Christians perish than by any other of thy guiles and stratagems. Thou knowest the peril of delay in a matter so important as is our conversion, perfection, salvation. Thou art not ignorant how one sin draws on another; how he that is to-day unfit will be less so to-morrow; how custom grows into nature, breeds blindness, hardness of heart, and insensibility; how old diseases are hardly and rarely cured; how God withdraws His grace when it is abused, refused, neglected; how much His justice by delay is exasperated, and that we heap coals on our own heads by our negligence. Thou art well-skilled in the uncertainty of our frail life, knowest the dangers, chances, changes, and accidents which may speedily overwhelm us; therefore thou whisperest:—'Stay a little, defer yet for a time'—till God, in Whose hands are the moments of all time, takes all time from us who have so long abused the opportunity of time, and sends us into pain eternal without time.

There is peril in delay.

7. But seeing me resolutely and violently breaking all thy chains, running, and crying with St. Augustine:*—'Why shall I longer say to-mor-

Time is short, eternity long.

* 'Jactabam voces miserabiles. Quam diu? quam diu? Cras et cras? Quare non modo? quare non hac hora finis turpitudinis meæ? Dicebam hæc, et flebam amarissima contritione cordis mei.' *Confessionum*, lib. viii. cap. xii.

row? Why not now, even this very moment?—thou now strivest to undermine my perseverance. But take courage, O my soul; thy time of enduring will soon end, and thy crowning joy will be without end. Hearken not to thy sworn enemy's enchantments; sit not, stand not, sleep not, but pray, watch, and *walk whilst thou hast light* and life, *that the darkness* of eternal night and death *overtake you not.*'*

Christ is always ready to aid us.

8. And since thy loving Lord is both able and willing to succour and support thee, and to turn everything to thy advantage, even thy imperfections, frailties, and failings—for thou art assured that as sure as God is God, so sure is it that He will permit nothing to befall us but for our greater good and His own glory, and that it is most grateful unto Him when we so judge of Him—doubt not of His providence and protection, nor fear to permit Him to deal with thee as He best pleaseth, and to remain perfectly indifferent to all His divine ordinances and dispositions,† saying:—'Since it

* John xii. 25.

† 'Art thou fallen into the snares of adversity? Ah, look not upon this mishap, nor upon the trap wherein thou art caught; look upon God, and leave all to Him. He will have a care of Thee. Throw thy thoughts upon Him, and He will nourish thee. Why dost thou trouble thyself with willing or diswilling the events and accidents of this world, since thou art ignorant what were best for thee to will, and that God will will for thee, without thy trouble, all that thou art to will for thyself? Await therefore in peace of mind the result and working of the divine pleasure; and let His willing suffice thee, since He can never cease to be good. For so He commanded His well-beloved St. Catherine of Sienna. "Think on Me," quoth He to her, "and I will think for thee."' St. Francis of Sales, *Treatise of the Love of God*, b. ix. ch. 15; Douai, 1630.

is Thy will, O Lord, it is certain to be for my good; be it so. I am as sure Thou lovest me as that Thou livest with me. Away, then, all diffidence, disloyalty, inconstancy! How many saints have you perverted; how many souls have you damned? Without thee, O holy perseverance, all is lost; with thee, all is secure—grace to the end, glory without end! Welcome, holy confidence! the main support of my life, and the life of my perseverance. I am content, O my Lord, to be conducted by Thee for time and eternity, as Thou best pleaseth. Lead me by land or by water, by desolation or devotion, by darkness or day, by sickness or health, I will adhere to Thee constantly.

Desire to advance no faster than Christ wishes.

9. 'If it be Thy blessed will, O loving Lord, that I creep as a snail towards perfection, I will neither be troubled nor dismayed; I desire not to fly faster than Thou enablest me, which I acknowledge to be not only beyond my deserts, but better for me than my own desires. Finally, I here make a general resolution, and a generous resignation of my whole self into Thy holy hands, hoping that it will give worth and value to all my actions and sufferings.

A form of general resolution and resignation.

10. 'O my Sovereign and sweet Master, my whole will and desire—according to my great obligation, former profession, and present protest—is to serve and love Thee, and to fulfil Thy blessed will in all things, and to be wholly Thine at all times, and in all things whatsoever. It is Thy honour I only aim at, Thy glory I only intend, and Thy

will I only seek to accomplish. To Thee alone I render and wish all benediction and eternal praise, and with cordial joy I say *Amen* to all that is possessed by Thy most amiable and perfect goodness; and joining my humble desires and devotions with all those that love Thee, I implore that we may be all Thine, and that Thou wilt be All in all.'

Conclusion.

11. And now, O my soul, since thou hast in some sort happily begun a course of Prayer, Recollection, Abnegation, and Humility, according to obedience and supported by confidence, let the devil storm, let flesh and blood rebel, let the world murmur; answer them all:—'*Quod scripsi, scripsi**—my vows and promises must and shall stand, and I am content to sign it with my blood. I will sooner die than swerve from my well-settled resolutions, or cancel the free deed and gift of myself to my Saviour's service: darkness, desolation, death, and devil shall never make me change. Live my good purposes to love my dear Lord, unchangeably, irrevocably, eternally!'

My Beloved to me and I to Him.†

I have fought a good fight, I have finished my course, I have kept the faith.

As to the rest, there is laid up for me a crown of justice, which the Lord the just Judge will render to me in that day: and not only to me, but to them also that love His coming.‡

* John xix. 22. † Cant. of Cant. ii. 16. ‡ 2 Tim. iv. 7, 8.

*Blessed is the man that endureth temptation: for when he hath been proved he shall receive the crown of life which God hath promised to them that love Him.**

Be thou faithful unto death; and I will give thee the crown of life.†

* James i. 12. † Apoc. ii. 10.

WOULD THAT

	You knew the Past. I.	You understood the Present. II.	You provided for the Future. III.
I. With sorrow for	1. The evil done, against	(1) God, (2) Your neighbour, (3) Yourself.	
	2. The good left undone		(1) By not rooting out vice, (2) By not engrafting virtue, (3) By not striving after perfection.
	3. The time lost, than which is	(1) Nothing more precious, (2) Nothing more fleeting, (3) Nothing more desirable.	
	4. Christ slain		(1) Cruelly by His enemies, (2) Wickedly by His friends, (3) Willingly for both.
II. With shame for	1. The many blessings received	(1) In soul, (2) In body, (3) In temporal affairs.	
	2. The vanity of the world, by which		(1) The covetous are duped, (2) The sensual allured, (3) The proud ensnared.
	3. Your proneness to sin, through	(1) The slothfulness of the flesh, (2) The enmity of the devil, (3) The enticement of the world.	
	4. The shortness of life, which is		(1) More fragile than glass, (2) More fading than smoke, (3) Swifter than the wind.
III. In fear of	1. Approaching death, which is	(1) Most certain, (2) Most uncertain, (3) Most bitter.	
	2. The anger of the Judge, who is		(1) Infallible because of His Wisdom, (2) Inflexible because of His Justice, (3) Irresistible because of His Might.
	3. The fire of Hell and Satan's rage, than which is	(1) Nothing more cruel, (2) Nothing more horrible, (3) Nothing more miserable.	
	4. The loss of the everlasting and unfailing reward, in which is		(1) The absence of all evil, (2) The presence of all good, (3) The fulfilment of all desires.

INDEX.

www.ingramcontent.com/pod-product-compliance
Lightning Source LLC
La Vergne TN
LVHW050909080826
845145LV00001B/26

* 9 7 8 0 9 8 1 9 9 0 1 9 4 *